D1551175

Canadian
Industrial Relations

CANADIAN INDUSTRIAL RELATIONS

Sixth Edition

FRANK KEHOE, B.A., M.B.A.

MAURICE ARCHER, B.Sc. (Econ.), M.A.

TWENTIETH CENTURY LABOUR PUBLICATIONS
P.O. Box 244, Oakville, Ontario L6J 5A2
Tel: (416) 845-3100   Fax: (416) 845-3704

SIXTH EDITION

Copyright © 1991 Frank Kehoe and Maurice Archer

Canadian Cataloguing in Publication Data

Kehoe, Frank, date
    Canadian Industrial Relations

6th ed.
Includes index
ISBN 0-9690739-1-7

1. Industrial Relations — Canada

2. Labour Relations — Canada

3. Labour — Law and Legislation

4. Trade unions — Canada

5. Archer, Maurice, Date, II.   Title

HD8106.5.K4 1991   331'.0971   C91-093905-5

Printed and bound in Canada for
Twentieth Century Labour Publications

First Edition, 1980

ISBN 0-9690739-1-7

About the Book . . .

Canadian Industrial Relations is an up-to-date Canadian textbook that describes clearly and succinctly the various components of the Canadian industrial relations scene, notably the framework used, the parties involved, the laws that apply, and the negotiation and administration of collective agreements in both the private and public sectors.

As well as descriptive and analytical material, the book contains twenty case studies, an actual collective agreement, and three collective bargaining simulations; two short ones for introductory purposes and a longer one for in-depth analysis. Based on realistic situations, with current bargaining statistics and other relevant information included, the simulations are suitable for resolution by students who are called upon to act as company and union negotiating teams engaged in a series of collective bargaining sessions. The book also contains an example of an actual arbitration award and a glossary of industrial relations terms.

About the Authors . . .

Frank Kehoe obtained both a B.A. and a Master's Degree in Business Administration from the University of Toronto. His business career has centred on the Industrial Relations area including senior management positions with several major Canadian companies and consulting activities with numerous other organizations including smaller companies. This experience includes extensive activity in the negotiation of collective agreements and arbitration of disputes under collective agreements. He lectured at McMaster University Business School before joining Ryerson Polytechnic Institute where he is Professor of Labour Relations.

Maurice Archer received his B.Sc. (Econ.) from the London School of Economics and his M.A. in Economics from Yale University. He is a well-known author of Canadian business and economics texts, and worked in banking and real estate before joining the Ryerson Business Faculty as Professor of Business Management.

Figure 1.1 — *A Schematic Presentation of the Canadian Industrial Relations System*

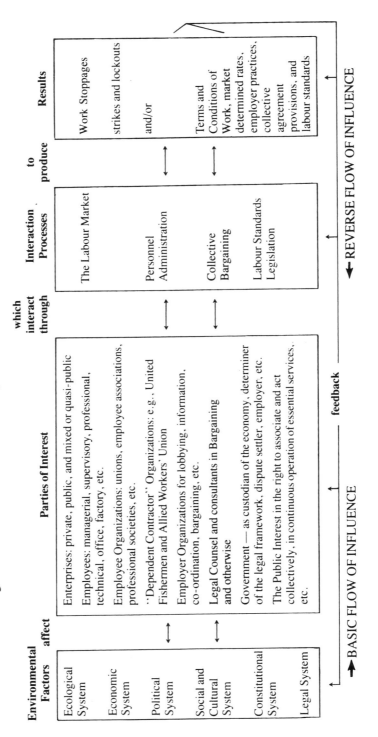

Source: *Canadian Industrial Relations*, The Report of the Task Force on Labour Relations, Ottawa: Queen's Printer, 1969, p.10.

PREFACE

The material in this book is organized in accordance with the model of Canada's industrial relations system shown in Figure 1.1. Thus, in Part A, we look at the basic framework for industrial relations, or, put in another way, the setting for the collective bargaining process, with its occasional labour-management battles and other dramas. It involves an examination of many factors: the economic, social and political circumstances that underlie our North American type of employer-employee interaction; the constitution that divides legislative power in labour matters between our federal and provincial governments; the statutes that govern our labour relations and the history of their development in Canada; and the concept of ''protection of the public interest''.

In Part B, we look at the parties involved in industrial relations: the labour unions and other employee representatives, their nature, history and philosophy; the employers and their associations, policies and practices; and the so-called third parties such as (a) our governments which get involved in conciliation and other attempts to promote harmonious employer-employee relations and (b) the public which often bears the inconvenience and even hardship that prolonged strikes or lockouts often cause, particularly by public sector employees such as teachers, fire-fighters, postal workers, and air traffic controllers.

In Part C, we describe how a trade union recruits new members and how it becomes certified as the bargaining agent for a firm's employees. We also examine the certification procedure itself and give an example of an actual certification application. We then consider how, although unusual, a union may lose its bargaining rights. Finally, we consider the ''unfair practices'', forbidden by law, that a union or employer may engage in at various stages of the collective bargaining process.

In Part D, we consider how a collective agreement (the basic document that governs employer-employee relations in a unionized business firm or other organization) is negotiated and what it contains, including the provisions of union security. We also consider what can happen if negotiations fail and how an outside conciliator is often brought in to help the parties reach agreement. Finally, we discuss the different types of strikes and other labour action that can occur and the action of an employer in locking out its employees.

In Part E, we examine the nature and purpose of a grievance procedure and how an outside arbitrator is used to resolve disputes arising out of the collective agreement. We then discuss the key issues of discipline and seniority that are often the subject of labour-management dispute in the day-to-day interpretation of a collective agreement.

In Part F, we look at industrial relations in the public sector and the changes that have been made in recent years— notably, the extension of the right to strike to many public service employees.

In Part G, we describe some of the attempts that have been made to improve industrial relations in Canada, notably employee stock ownership plans and participative management.

In Part H, entitled Collective Bargaining Simulations, we provide three simulations and a collective agreement. The first simulation, a short one, is contained in Chapter 22. The second, a short one, is also found in Chapter 22. Students can be formed into management and union teams and asked to resolve the differences between them as the basis for a new Collective Agreement. The third simulation, Consolidated Electrical Products, contained in Chapter 23, is more sophisticated, requiring greater effort on the part of union and management negotiating teams to reach a new agreement. With these simulations, handled as suggested, students should get the feel of actual contract negotiations. The agreement that is being renegotiated, in the case of Consolidated Electrical Products, is set out in Chapter 24.

In Part I, we include a selection of case studies covering different aspects of the industrial relations process.

In Part J, there is an example of an actual arbitration award.

Finally, in Part K, we provide a glossary of industrial relations terms.

Each chapter begins with a summary of objectives and an outline of the topics covered. Most chapters end with Key Concepts and Review Questions.

Summary of Contents

Table of Contents

PART C: UNION ORGANIZATION AND CERTIFICATION

PART E: ADMINISTERING THE COLLECTIVE AGREEMENT

PART F: THE PUBLIC SECTOR

PART G: THE WAY AHEAD

PART H: COLLECTIVE BARGAINING SIMULATIONS

PART I: CASE STUDIES

PART J: EXAMPLE OF AN ARBITRATION AWARD

PART K: INDUSTRIAL RELATIONS GLOSSARY 435

PART A

The Framework for Industrial Relations

CHAPTER 1: CANADA'S SYSTEM OF INDUSTRIAL RELATIONS

Chapter Objectives

- *To examine the meaning of the term "industrial relations"*
- *To describe the basic model used by academics and others to explain Canada's industrial relations system*
- *To distinguish between the terms "labour relations" and "union-management relations"*
- *To explain the term "collective bargaining" and identify the key factors involved in the collective bargaining process*
- *To explain what labour economics, personnel management, and organizational behaviour are and how they relate to industrial relations*

Chapter Outline

1.1 Industrial Relations Defined

1.2 Framework for Analysis

1.3 Labour Relations Defined

1.4 Collective Bargaining

1.5 Labour Economics

1.6 Personnel Management

1.7 Organizational Behaviour

This book is about the theory and practice of industrial relations in Canada. Our first step therefore is to define exactly what we mean by the term "industrial relations" and its relationship to other related terms such as labour relations, union-management relations, collective bargaining, and labour economics.

1.1 INDUSTRIAL RELATIONS DEFINED

According to most writers and practitioners, *industrial relations* is a broad term that covers all forms of interaction between employers and employees. Therefore all the other terms mentioned above describe specific aspects of this whole system of employer-employee interaction. They are in effect subsystems of the industrial relations system. Also, logically, personnel management (or administration) and organizational behaviour, although usually treated as separate areas of study, can be considered as an integral part of industrial relations.

The term "industrial relations system" refers to the institutional framework within which employer-employee interaction takes place. Thus, according to the Woods Task Force on Labour Relations in Canada, the industrial relations system is:

> "the complex of market and institutional arrangements, private and public, which society permits, encourages or establishes to handle superior-subordinate relationships growing out of employment and related activities."[1]

1.2 FRAMEWORK FOR ANALYSIS

A great deal of effort has already been expended by various people in setting out in conceptual form a basic framework for the analysis of industrial relations.

Dunlop Model

In the United States, John Dunlop presented in the 1950s what is now considered to be a classic model involving four basic elements.[2] These four elements, according to Dunlop, are as follows:

1. *The actors* — These are the three key parties which Dunlop called the "actors", involved in industrial relations:

    a) employees, their organizations, and their spokespersons;

    b) employers, their organizations, and their spokespersons; and

    c) government agencies and specialized private agencies concerned with employer-employee relationships.

---

[1] *Canadian Industrial Relations*. The Report of the Task Force on Labour Relations. Queen's Printer, Ottawa, 1969, p. 9.

[2] John T. Dunlop, *Industrial Relations Systems*, Rinehart and Winston, New York, 1958.

2. *The environment* — These are environmental factors such as production technology, size of the market, and the relative prestige and power of the employers and labour unions.

3. *Ideology held* — This is the ideology held by each of the "actors". Unless these ideologies are compatible between the partners and between each party and the general public, no industrial relations stability is possible.

4. *The Web of Rules* — These are the rules and regulations that govern the economy and the workplace and the parties within them.

Craig Model

Later, in Canada, Professor Alton Craig developed a schematic model of the Canadian industrial relations system that was subsequently used, in adapted form, by the Woods Task Force.[3] This schematic model is set out in Figure 1.1. It states, in its simplest version, that environmental factors (such as the legal system) affect the various interested parties (such as employers and labour unions) who then interact (through, for example, collective bargaining) to produce results (such as a strike or a collective agreement). The model also shows that there is a basic flow of influence in one direction and a reverse flow in the other. For example, labour unions are affected by existing laws but also help determine new legislation and repeal of the old.

Four Basic Elements

The four basic elements that can be identified in this industrial relations model are as follows:

1. The ENVIRONMENT

a) *Ecological System*
— What is the physical environment, including technology used in the workplace?

b) *Economic System*
— How is work organized? What is the factory population? What is the level of unemployment? How is income distributed? Are employees' real earnings substantial? Are workers becoming worse off in time of inflation?

---

[3] Alton W. J. Craig, *A Model for the Analysis of Industrial Relations Systems*, a paper presented at the annual meeting of the Canadian Political Science Associations on June 7, 1967.

c) *Political System*
   — Are workers permitted to form unions? Are unions recognized as bargaining agents for workers? Are employers required by law to bargain in good faith with the unions? On whose side is the government?

d) *Social System*
   — Is there deep-rooted animosity between labour and management? Does class warfare exist on the factory floor? Do employees willingly accept orders? Do they resent authority?

e) *Cultural System*
   — Are unions part of the tradition of the people? Are workers willing to join unions? Are workers naturally loyal and disciplined?

f) *Constitutional System*
   — Who has legislative jurisdiction over labour matters? What is the jurisdiction of the federal and provincial governments?

g) *Legal System*
   — What rights and duties does the Common Law place upon employer and employee? What statutory laws govern labour-management relations, working conditions, wage rates, holidays, occupational health and safety, etc.?

2. The PARTICIPANTS

a) *Employees and their organizations*
   — labour unions
   — staff associations
   — Labour Councils
   — Labour Federations
   — Canadian Labour Congress and CNTU
   — Professional Societies

b) *Employers and their organizations*
   — domestic and multinational corporations
   — industry associations
   — government enterprises, departments

c) *The Federal and Provincial Governments*
   — Labour Relations Boards
   — Arbitration Commissions
   — Conciliators and mediators
   — Ministers of Labour
   — Departments of Labour

   d) *The Public*
- — Consumers' Association of Canada
- — newspapers
- — irate citizens

3. The INTERACTION PROCESS

   a) *Demand for different types of labour*
- — rates of industry growth
- — rates of mechanization and automation
- — capital per worker
- — foreign product competition

   b) *Supply of labour*
- — age, size, and rate of growth of population
- — education, skills, experience
- — female participation rate
- — immigration
- — restrictions on entry into a trade or profession
- — unemployment benefits

   c) *Wage rates*
- — supply and demand
- — minimum wage rates
- — fringe benefits

   d) *Collective bargaining*
- — union vs. employer
- — Labour Relations Act

   e) *Personnel management*
- — management's policy towards the employees
- — Theory X and Theory Y
- — Theory Z

   f) *Labour legislation*
- — Employment Standards Act
- — Occupational Health and Safety Act
- — Other statutes

4. The RESULTS

   a) *Collective agreement*
- — terms of employment
- — better wages, etc.

b) *Strikes and lockouts*

c) *Sabotage, go-slow, etc.*

d) *Closing down of plants*

e) *Government intervention.*

1.3 LABOUR RELATIONS DEFINED

This is the term most commonly used to describe the interaction that takes place between employee organizations (notably labour unions) on the one hand and employer organizations on the other. The main focus is on the relationship between the employer and its employees within a particular firm or establishment. The term covers negotiations for a collective agreement to govern the terms of employment of the labour force and the application and interpretation of the agreement on a day-to-day basis once it has come into force. Many small problems that arise in the work place are quickly settled at the foreperson or supervisor level. Others, as explained later, may require the use of the grievance procedure as set out in the collective agreement and even the use of an outside arbitrator to settle the dispute. The term, Labour Relations, is also often used as the name for the department in a large firm that has specialist responsibility for the firm's labour-management relations.

The term ''union-management relations'' is sometimes used instead of labour relations to describe basically the same thing. However, not all employees are represented by unions. Some employee associations are not certified as collective bargaining agents under the federal or provincial Labour Relations Act concerned and, in other cases, no employee association exists. So, strictly speaking, the term ''union-management relations'' has a narrower scope than the term ''labour relations''.

1.4 COLLECTIVE BARGAINING

This is the process whereby employees together, rather than singly, negotiate the terms of their employment with their employer. An employee, acting alone, has very little power to secure better terms of employment. However, all or most employees in a firm, acting together or ''collectively'', have tremendous power to do so. This collective power has been exerted through trade unions (or labour unions) that have emerged as the official representatives, or ''bargaining agents'' for the workers in various trades and industries. It has been strengthened by labour legislation that requires an employer to recognize and negotiate ''in good faith'' with the union certified as the bargaining agent for its employees. And it has been reinforced by practices such as the requirement of union membership as a prerequisite for employment.

Another ingredient of the collective bargaining process is the signing, by the company and the trade union, of a collective agreement that sets out in writing the terms of employment for a specified period (usually one, two, or three years) for the union's members. Both parties are required by law to adhere faithfully to the agreement, which includes a provision for settlement of any disputes by arbitration rather than by resort to strikes, lockouts, or other means.

In summary, the collective bargaining process involves:

1. collective rather than individual negotiations by employees with an employer;

2. compulsory recognition by the employer of the union certified as the bargaining agent for the employees;

3. the statutory requirement of ''bargaining in good faith'' by employer and union;

4. signing by both parties of a written collective agreement setting out the terms of employment of the employees for a stipulated period of time;

5. prohibition of strikes and lockouts during the life of the collective agreement, and

6. compulsory inclusion in the agreement of a requirement for arbitration of outstanding grievances.

1.5 LABOUR ECONOMICS

This is the study of the demand for, and supply of, different types of workers and the resulting wage and employment levels. On the demand side, it involves a consideration of the sales prospects of a firm and industry and the resulting need for employees, the productivity of various types of employees, the type of production technology used, and the relative costs of capital and labour. On the supply side, it involves consideration of the size and nature of the labour force, education, skills, and experience, immigration, hours of work, minimum wage levels, participation of women in the labour force, restrictions on entry into a trade or profession, and so on.

In this book (Chapter 2), we discuss only briefly the economic factors involved in labour-management relations. Nevertheless, we should recognize that the whole topic of labour economics is very important—as it deals with the economic background behind all employer-employee interaction. And this economic background is something that participants in the industrial relations process cannot afford to ignore. If an industry is dying in the face of foreign competition, no amount of labour union action can raise wages and/or increase employment for its members. At many Canadian universities, labour economics is taught as a separate course.

1.6 PERSONNEL MANAGEMENT

This term refers to the way in which a firm's managers, at all the various levels, treat the firm's personnel, or "human resources". It involves the following main areas: recruitment and placement; induction, training, and follow-up; motivation; merit rating and employee evaluation; labour relations; employee services; employee health and safety; and employee records and statistics.

The labour relations area covers such activities as: improving employee morale; the handling, on behalf of management, of collective agreement negotiations; the handling of employee complaints and grievances; the formation and administration of joint management-labour committees; and the development and enforcement of personnel policies involving discipline, discharges, layoffs, promotions, transfers, etc.

Personnel management, it should be emphasized, involves all employees in a firm—not just blue-collar, or plant employees and not just union members. Basically, it is a line function rather than a staff one although there may well be, in the larger firm, a personnel department to assist in this function. In other words, every line manager is involved in managing people. It is not just the concern of a few personnel specialists.

In terms of the industrial relations framework, personnel management is the practical translation of the point of view of one key party (the employer) towards another key party (the employee) in terms of the workplace and what the employee is supposed to be doing in it.

1.7 ORGANIZATIONAL BEHAVIOUR

This is the term used to describe the systematic study of a person's behaviour when he or she is employed in a business firm, government department, or other organization. It involves a study of the roles played by individuals in the organization and the relationship of individuals to each other. It attempts to explain how and why people in business firms and other organizations, private or public, act as they do—singly and in groups. It looks at the needs of both managers and non-managers. It enables a person to understand better the problems actually encountered in managing and working with people and the alternative solutions available when confronted by a human relations problem within an organization.

The scope of organizational behaviour includes such topics as: the needs people seek to achieve in their work; the formal and informal organization of the workplace; motivation and job satisfaction; styles of leadership; group dynamics; the work environment; delegation of authority; the overcoming of resistance to change; the creation of a harmonious climate for employer-employee relations; principles of good supervision; overcoming communications barriers; job enrichment; and discrimination in the workplace.

From the above description, it can be seen that the study of organizational behaviour can shed considerable light on the problems that occur in the workplace: why some firms have a much more harmonious employer-employee relationship than others; and how a more harmonious relationship can be developed, often with an improvement in labour productivity. Although a specialized area of study, organizational behaviour is an important part of Canada's industrial relations framework. In many cases, it is the key to better industrial relations.

KEY CONCEPTS

Industrial relations	*Labour relations*
Industrial relations system	*Union-management relations*
Industrial relations model	*Collective bargaining*
Environment	*Collective agreement*
Participants	*Labour economics*
Interaction process	*Personnel management*
Results	*Organizational behaviour*

REVIEW QUESTIONS

1. What is meant by the term "industrial relations"?

2. Explain and discuss the Dunlop model of an industrial relations system.

3. What elements are included in the Craig model of the industrial relations system in Canada? What elements, if any, are omitted?

4. Distinguish between labour relations and union-management relations.

5. What are the basic ingredients of collective bargaining? Why do most employees favour such a system? What are the arguments against it?

6. What factors determine the demand for and supply of the following types of labour in Canada: (a) auto workers; (b) medical doctors; (c) accountants; and (d) computer programmers?

7. Explain, with examples, how changes in the demand for and supply of particular types of labour, affect wage and salary rates.

8. What, typically, is the job of the labour relations, or industrial relations department of a large manufacturing firm?

9. "The study of organizational behaviour is the key to better industrial relations in most large firms." Explain and discuss with reference to a particular private firm or public organization.

CHAPTER 2: THE POLITICAL, ECONOMIC, AND SOCIAL SETTING

Chapter Objectives

- *To explain how political factors affect industrial relations*

- *To emphasize that economic factors involving the demand for and supply of labour will affect workers' employment and wages*

- *To indicate how social factors, including cultural differences among workers, have affected the Canadian labour movement.*

Chapter Outline

There are many different factors — political, economic, and social — that affect industrial relations in Canada. In this chapter, we look at each broad group in turn.

2.1 POLITICAL FACTORS

Collective Bargaining Rights

In some countries, trade unions are illegal and a person trying to organize or become a member of one is likely to be arrested and put in jail. In other countries, trade unions operate under government control and do not represent the real interests of their members. In the Western democracies, trade unions now enjoy an established place and workers are free to bargain collectively with employers within a legal framework carefully designed to protect the interests of both employer and employee. Of course, the right of employees to establish a trade union and bargain collectively with their employer has not always existed, even in the so-called liberal Western democracies. Only in this century has it come about. In nineteenth-century England, for example, the "Tolpuddle Martyrs", the agricultural labourers who tried to band their fellow workers together to fight for better wages, were charged with criminal conspiracy and, on conviction, were deported to Australia.

Personal Freedoms

Today, in Canada, and in other Western democracies, a variety of personal freedoms have come to be recognized as fundamental human rights. These include freedom of the person, freedom of speech, freedom of religion, freedom of assembly, freedom from discrimination, freedom of the press, freedom of political action, freedom from economic exploitation, the right to own property, freedom to enter into contracts, and the right to receive a minimum standard of living. These fundamental human rights have sometimes been set down on paper, often in a constitutional document or other Act of Parliament. In Canada, this is the Charter of Rights and Freedoms passed by the Federal Parliament in 1980. Of course, the maintenance of these freedoms requires a system of courts and judges that operates independently of government. It also requires the right to vote at periodic elections to change peacefully a government that might start to restrict these fundamental human rights or that proves otherwise undesirable.

Market Freedoms

One of the fundamental rights that we have mentioned is that of owning property. Without it, we would not have private firms acting as employers. As in many communist or socialist countries, the sole employer would be the state. In some countries, as in Canada, state-owned enterprises operate side by side with private ones and their employees are still allowed to bargain collectively. However, in a country in which little or no private enterprise is permitted, the temptation is for the state (which owns all or most property on behalf of its citizens) to deny to its employees the right to bargain collectively — even though they may be dissatisfied with their pay, fringe benefits, or conditions of work.

Although, in Canada, private firms are the rule rather than the exception, they are of course restricted by Parliament in many ways. "Market freedoms'' are not usually permitted priority over ''social freedoms''. Thus there are, for example, minimum wage laws, pollution control legislation, and human rights codes.

The CLC and the NDP

The trade union movement in Canada has looked upon both the conservative and the liberal parties as right-wing forces, dedicated to preserving the ''status quo''. That is why the Canadian Labour Congress (CLC) has supported the NDP, a party that offers a more radical and nationalist solution to Canada's social and economic problems. However, unlike the situation in some countries, the CLC does not advocate the overthrow of the present political, economic and social system. It merely wishes to reform it.

Quebec Labour Separatism

In Quebec, some leaders of the trade union movement have adopted a much more radical approach, advocating the reform of the present political system and its replacement by a more left-wing one. This difference in political objective between trade union leaders in Quebec and those in other provinces has made co-operation difficult. Even more of an obstacle to co-operation between Quebec trade unionists and those from the rest of Canada is the more deep-seated language difference, and the ethnic and political differences between French Canadians (''maitres chez nous'') and other Canadians. This labour ''separatism'' has already led to Quebec breakaways from national and international unions. One of the most publicized examples of conflict caused by language differences was in the Canadian Air Traffic Control Association (CATCA), as a result of the attempt to introduce bilingual air traffic service in Quebec. Quebec trade unions have also joined their own provincial labour association, called in English the Confederation of National Trade Unions (CNTU), rather than the Canadian Labour Congress to which most other unions belong.

2.2 ECONOMIC FACTORS

There are many different economic factors, involving the demand for and supply of different types of labour, that affect industrial relations.

Demand for Labour

On the demand side, we look first at the individual firm, the individual industry, and then at industry in general. In the public sector, the demand for labour also has an impact on labour relations. But this varies between different types of public employees, federal, provincial, or municipal, and with their location within Canada.

The Individual Firm

The more successful a firm is in the market-place, the better it will be able to provide good economic benefits to its employees. Of course, economic success for a firm is a combination of circumstances: favourable external factors (such as new markets), management expertise (for example, ability to take advantage of such markets and to take advantage of new production technology), and worker effort (for example, ability and willingness to produce a good-quality product at reasonable cost). Nevertheless, even in an industry that is enjoying mixed market success, individual firms can prosper depending on the managers and workers involved. And the greater the degree of management-labour harmony, the more likely it is, that this will come about.

The Individual Industry

Is it a growing or declining industry in Canada? Word-processing equipment is an example of the former; textiles an example of the latter. But again, as pointed out in the previous section, there are individual firms that can run against the tide. For example, firms which cannot succeed in producing and marketing word-processing equipment; and textile firms that are succeeding in specialty lines when much of the industry is able to stay alive thanks only to quota restrictions on foreign imports. But, obviously, it is much easier to succeed (and for workers to share in the benefits) in a thriving industry than in a dying one.

Elasticity of Demand. What is the demand for the product of the industry as a whole? Is it price-elastic? In other words, can a difference in price compared with competitive products (often foreign imports) cause consumers to switch rapidly to the cheaper product? Or is there a loyal market for the Canadian product? Do consumers prefer to buy, for example, North American cars rather than Japanese ones whatever the difference in cost? What would happen if there were an interruption in the Canadian supply as the result of a strike? Would consumers switch permanently to other sources of supply? If so, employers may be less willing to risk a strike. Does the industry enjoy a monopoly in the supply of the product? In other words, is it the only supplier — as, for example, the telephone service?

Seasonal Variations in Demand. Another factor affecting labour relations is whether demand for the product is relatively stable or whether it fluctuates from month to month or from year to year. In the first case, seasonal factors may affect demand — for example, an increased demand for TV sets in the Fall and an increased demand for sports clothing in the Summer. Most firms try to ensure steady production by stockpiling finished goods in the slow season to the extent that financing costs allow or by selecting a product-mix that dovetails products with different seasonal demands. However, this can be done only to a limited extent. From the labour relations point of view, management is particularly vulnerable to union demands at the time of year when demand for the product is high and management needs extra output to fill sales orders. Similarly, in the case of industries such as agriculture, where production is concentrated at a particular time of year, management is less able during this critical period to withstand union demands.

Cyclical Variations in Demand. It is a well-known fact that the North American economy is subject to cyclical variations in the overall level of demand for goods and services. Also, the governments of the United States and Canada, despite all their Keynesian ''pump-priming'' activities, have not been very successful in evening out such variations. It is also a well-known economic fact that industries producing capital goods and raw materials for them (for example, machine tools and the steel for their production) are subject to even more acute cyclical variations. This is because of the ''accelerator'' effect of changes in demand for consumer goods that cause even greater changes in the demand for the equipment that produces them. This means that labour relations in such industries operate in a much more uncertain economic climate than industries with a relatively stable demand — for example, medical services and pharmaceutical products. This uncertainty means much greater emphasis in contract negotiations on job security, lay-off pay, supplementary unemployment benefits, early retirement, pensions, and so on.

Foreign Competition. In North America, to make matters worse, the economic insecurity just mentioned has been heightened in recent years by the emergence of Japan, Hong Kong, Taiwan, South Korea, Singapore, Malaysia and other South-east Asian countries as low-cost suppliers of good-quality consumer goods such as cameras, watches and cars, of capital goods such as ships, and of basic manufactured raw materials such as steel and chemicals. Already, for many years, the Canadian consumer goods manufacturing sector has been wilting from the effect of cheaper and often better-made foreign goods. South-east Asian manufacturers now have not only the benefit of lower-wage costs but also of advanced technology, heavy capital investment, and apparently better labour-management relations.

Labour Cost. How important is the labour cost as a percentage of the total cost of making and marketing the product? The smaller the percentage, the easier it is for labour to obtain pay increases — as the final cost of the product will be affected less. Alternatively, the greater the labour cost as a percentage of the total cost, the larger will be the impact of a pay raise on the final cost of the product and, therefore, on its marketability. Also, of course, the greater will be management resistance to union demands for extra pay. An example of a low-percentage labour cost industry is electricity generation and supply. An example of a high-percentage labour cost industry, at least for the present, is textiles.

New Technology. Another important economic factor affecting labour relations within an industry is the state of technology used and the pace at which it is changing. In particular, there is the question: how easy is it for management to substitute machines for workers? If labour is a unique input in the manufacturing process, then it is in a much stronger position to improve its share of the firm's revenue than if it can be replaced by machines. In the nineteenth century, there were many instances of workers rebelling against the introduction of machines. One notable example was the Luddite riots in England when workers smashed textile machinery. However, examples also exist today — for example, the fight against the introduction of computerized type-setting equipment in many newspaper plants in the nineteen-seventies.

In principle, labour unions in Canada favour the introduction of new technology. Without it, Canadian manufacturers and other industries will inevitably become less and less competitive, particularly against foreign goods both at home and abroad. And if an industry cannot sell its goods, it cannot afford to provide employment for Canadians, let alone pay higher wages. In practice, unions try to negotiate safeguards for their members, including job termination allowances and retraining grants for workers who are displaced.

With the advent of relatively cheap electronic micro-processors, which allow machines to be re-instructed quickly and cheaply as to what to do, many jobs in both plant and office will disappear in the coming years. Only if industries are growing rapidly will they be able to retrain and reassign the displaced workers. As the new machines fall in relative price compared with the workers whose jobs they can replace (for example, the spot-welding robots in the automobile plants or the word-processing machines in the business office) the pace of substitution will rapidly increase. Also in industries where labour unions are not yet active or only just becoming so, unionization with resultant improvements in workers' pay and working conditions can mean that mechanization and automation will rapidly become more attractive to employers. As a result, not only may jobs be eliminated but the degree of service to the public may also be curtailed. A prime example in the public sector is the post office, where automated processing of mail has already been introduced. One of the most critical aspects of labour relations in many industries in the coming years will be the introduction of computer technology, as the microprocessor promises (or threatens, depending on the point of view) a new industrial revolution comparable in economic and social impact to that of the nineteenth century.

Given the state of the technology in a particular industry, another consideration from the viewpoint of labour relations is the ability of management to keep the plants operating in the event of a union strike. The easier it is to do so, the less potent is the strike weapon.

The type of technology employed in an industry will also affect bargaining issues — for example, wash-up time in the mining industry. It will also affect management's ability to introduce piece-work or other motivational systems.

Industry in General

If the economy is in a state of recession or depression, labour unions cannot be so ambitious in their aspirations. If management cannot afford to pay higher wages because it cannot sell the goods produced, the union will only be putting some of its members out of work by insisting on receiving more. Conversely, in time of economic boom, employers can afford to be generous and unions, aware of this, can negotiate from strength — knowing that employers, with full order books, will hesitate to risk a prolonged strike.

Regional Differences. The difference in wage rates and living standards from one part of the country to another also affects industrial relations in Canada. These differences are the inevitable result of the fact that different areas have different endowments of natural resources, labour, and public and private capital. Moreover, many regions are too isolated and small in themselves to provide a substantial local market, and, for one reason or another, are unable to sell effectively abroad or to other parts of Canada. Nevertheless, union members in, for example, the Maritime provinces naturally resent being paid less for the same work than, say, workers in Alberta.

U.S. Ownership. Many manufacturing, mining, oil and other resource firms in Canada are foreign-owned, mainly by U.S. multi-national corporations. Consequently, the head office of the parent company, usually in the United States, may have a great deal to say when its Canadian employees are being unionized or when a collective agreement is being negotiated. The resultant settlement sometimes resembles strongly in its content and character, agreements made south of the border.

International Unions. Many union members in Canada belong to international unions with their head office in the United States. Not only are the head office personnel and the total union membership predominantly American, so also is the union organization structure. These unions bargain with employers for improved pay and fringe benefits for their members in both U.S. and Canadian plants. One important result of this has been a gradual movement towards wage parity among employees both north and south of the border. This has meant higher wages for Canadian members to catch up with their American counterparts. At the same time, it has reduced the incentive for the U.S. multinational corporations to place work north of the border and has helped prevent ''unfair competition'' by lower-paid Canadian workers.

Economic Dependence on the U.S. Economically, Canada is heavily dependent on the United States. In terms of dollar value, about 75 per cent of our exports are sold to that country and about 70 per cent of our imports are purchased from it. Particularly important in trade with the United States are motor vehicles and parts, the production of which has rapidly increased since the Canada-U.S. Automotive Products Agreement, providing for limited free trade, came into force in 1965. This means that the labour movement cannot afford to push wages and fringe benefits of its members much higher than those of their American counterparts. Also, the labour movement cannot afford to be too hostile to the many U.S. multinationals operating in this country or to the United States itself. Any blockade on Canadian exports to the United States would have a disastrous effect on Canadian income and employment. This economic dependence also means that the economic welfare of Canadian union members depends as much on U.S. economic policy as it does on Canadian. Any economic recession in the United States is quickly felt in Canada. As part of the same mixed free enterprise system, industries in this country are subject to the same cyclical fluctuations in demand for their products and union members to the same economic insecurity as their U.S. counterparts. In the Communist world, by contrast, steady work is usually guaranteed but at much lower real wages and not always in the career of one's choice.

The Public Sector

Economic factors also have an important impact on public sector employees.

Federal Employees. One of the benefits of employment in the federal public service or in the many crown corporations and commissions that abound has long been job security. Today, however, pay and fringe benefits, particularly pensions that are adjusted with the rise in the cost of living, make the economic benefits of working for the federal government perhaps more attractive for many public employees, particularly in the lower levels, than working for the private sector. Economically, the right to strike that was given to many types of federal civil servants in the nineteen-sixties enabled the various public employee unions to catch up if not surpass the wages that could be earned in private employment.

The demand for the services of public sector employees shows little signs of abating. Although at election time, promises are made of cutbacks in public sector employment, the political party that is elected seems to change its mind quite quickly. Over the years, public sector employment has grown by leaps and bounds as new government departments and so on have been established. Unlike the private sector, there is little or no competition to be faced and cyclical changes in demand for government services are non-existent. Also, because many of the services provided (for example, mail delivery and medical care) are essential to the public, the effect of a strike is soon felt. As a result, there is considerable pressure exerted on the government of the day to bring such a strike to a rapid halt, even at the expense of a hefty increase in the governmental payroll. Unlike the private employer who, if driven too far, must inevitably go bankrupt, the federal government is blessed (from the viewpoint of the public employee unions) with a seemingly bottomless purse. If there is not enough money currently available, all the government needs to do is to increase its taxes or borrow some more. And to avoid the loss of voter support, particularly near election time, the government is prone to do just that. If it refuses to grant the increases demanded, it loses the sympathy of the union members. And if its "intransigence" brings about a strike, with all its inconvenience to the public, it loses their support as well. So in reality the government is in a "no-win" situation. But of course expensive wage settlements in the public sector (for example, the seaway workers settlement in the late nineteen sixties) are soon imitated by expensive wage settlements in the private sector. And before long the inflationary fires are burning again. But to the public, the relationship between public sector settlements and the rise in the general cost of living is usually obscure. Certainly one that tends to be ignored at election time.

In 1991, the federal government, as part of its budget restraint program, took steps to limit annual salary increases over the next three years for Canada's 215,000 federal public servants. It also froze departmental budgets, eliminated 10% of senior management, and froze the salaries of the Prime Minister and cabinet ministers.

Provincial Employees. Employment in the provincial public sector, particularly of publicly-subsidized employees in such institutions as hospitals and educational establishments rapidly expanded in the nineteen-seventies. This was caused partly by the federal government which, to implement its goals of a nationwide system of free medical care and universal access to post-secondary education, offered to match provincial spending in these areas. Also, the provincial governments have undertaken a number of projects, which although worthwhile in themselves, have increased the demand for qualified people.

In recent years, many provincial governments have found themselves faced with large operating deficits and have attempted to cut back on provincial spending. This new "penny-pinching" attitude has meant that many provincial sector employees have in recent years been given wage increases that have not even matched the rise in the cost of living. And this has meant increasing friction between the rank-and-file employees and the managements of these public sector institutions — for example, between nurses and hospitals.

In many cases, the public sector employees are denied the right to strike because of the essential nature of their services. However, this can lead to illegal walkouts and growing dissatisfaction and poorer service on the job. If the provincial governments continue to be faced with tight budgets, partly the result of a general economic recession and falling tax revenue, this source of conflict will remain. The situation of public sector employees is discussed more fully in Chapter 18.

Municipal Employees. At the local level, the provision of basic community services such as education, bus transit, parks and recreation, police, fire protection, electricity, water supply, sewage disposal and garbage pickup, is the responsibility of the municipal government. To provide these services, most municipalities employ large numbers of people, most of whom are represented by unions. Unless prevented by statute, these unions do not hesitate to call a strike if they believe their members are being treated unfairly. Prominent in the public eye are the elementary and secondary school teachers. Although much of the money to pay these public employees comes from the provincial government, a sizeable portion comes from local home and business owners. And any substantial increase in rates of pay and associated benefits is widely publicized and often adversely received. As a result, most of the public employees have to take a militant attitude merely to ensure that rates of pay keep up with inflation. Certainly, the days of the underpaid, under-privileged local school teacher, police officer, or firefighter are now but a distant memory, due in a large part to the emergence of the public sector employee unions.

Supply of Labour

Statistics of Canada's population growth, labour force, participation rates, employment and unemployment, and unemployment rates are contained in Appendix 2A (Canadian Labour Statistics) at the end of this chapter.

From the labour relations point of view, there has been a steady growth in the Canadian population as a whole. Thus there has been no undue pressure on the labour supply side (as, for example, from unrestricted immigration) that would impair labour's bargaining position. There has, however, been a continuing movement of the population from the East of Canada to the West. Also there have, at various times, been surpluses of certain types of labour such as teachers and nurses; and shortages of others, particularly the skilled trades such as tool and diemakers. Government licensing programs have also slowed down the increase in the supply of certain types of skilled and semi-professional persons.

One factor, not so far mentioned, affecting the supply of labour in Canada, is what is called the "labour force participation rate". This is the percentage of the civilian population, excluding members of the Armed Forces, who are members of the civilian labour force. This percentage has been steadily rising as more and more women, for economic and career reasons, enter and re-enter the work force than was traditionally the case.

When unemployment is high, the larger numbers of persons looking for work makes it more difficult for labour unions to succeed in negotiating better pay and improved conditions of work for their members. In recent years, Canada has experienced relatively high annual rates of unemployment (the number of unemployed as a percentage of the civilian labour force). The reasons for this have been touched upon previously, and include foreign competition, particularly in manufactured goods; labour-saving technology; a higher labour force participation rate; and lack of the required skills.

Of course, the rates of unemployment vary geographically. The highest rates have been in the Atlantic provinces and Quebec and the lowest in the prairie provinces. Hence the Westward flow of the population, seeking jobs. For various reasons, unemployment rates were highest among the young.

Of those employed, the vast majority is in the non-agricultural sector of the economy. Of the persons employed in non-agricultural establishments, most were in the various service industries.

2.3 SOCIAL FACTORS
Many Different Cultures

Canada, like the United States, acts as a melting pot of many different cultures. However, rather than succumb to the Canadian culture that so closely resembles that of the U.S., the French Canadians in Quebec have been making a determined effort to preserve their culture, including the use of the French language. Because their number is so large compared with other minority groups such as the Ukrainians, Poles, Germans, Italians, Hungarians, Chinese, and so on, and because they were, like the British, one of Canada's two founding races, they have been relatively successful in standing apart from the rest of Canada. This attitude, reflected politically, has inevitably carried over into the industrial relations scene, with Quebec labour officials taking a different, usually more radical stand, on many labour issues.

Immigration

Since World War II, the entry into Canada of many immigrants from Southern and Eastern Europe, often fiercely independent and extremely anxious for work, has made it more difficult for many unions to gain higher pay and other improvements for their members. In some industries (for example, house building), non-union labour is still the order of the day.

Emigration to the U.S.

Another factor working against unionization is the fact that the more discontented workers, rather than staying in Canada to secure, through union action, better employment terms, will often emigrate to the United States in search of greener pastures. Emigration to the United States acts, in other words, as a safety valve.

Canadian Employees More Law-Abiding?

Some observers consider Canadian union members to be less aggressive than their U.S. counterparts. It is remarked that Canadian union members seem more law-abiding due, perhaps, to the longer experience of being a British colony in which law and order were strictly enforced. However, this is a matter of opinion.

KEY CONCEPTS

Collective bargaining rights	*Public sector*
Personal freedoms	*Supply of labour*
Charter of Rights	*Population growth*
Market freedoms	*Participation rate*
Social freedoms	*Unemployment*
Political support	*Social factors*
Labour separatism	*Immigration*
Economic factors	*Emigration*
Demand for labour	

REVIEW QUESTIONS

1. What fundamental human rights do we take for granted in Canada?

2. In accordance with the democratic spirit, should every union have the right to strike?

3. "Trade unions are unnecessary in a communist state". Discuss.

4. In Canada, market freedoms are not usually permitted priority over social freedoms. Explain and discuss.

5. What political role do trade unions play in Canada?

6. To what extent do ethnic differences affect the trade union movement in Canada?

7. "The welfare of the employee depends ultimately on the economic success of his or her employer." What factors determine such economic success? How can the employee help ensure such success? How can he or she be sure to benefit from it?

8. "Unions prosper in both growing and declining industries." Which industries in Canada are growing? Which are declining? Discuss the statement.

9. How can "elasticity of demand" for an industry's product affect the action of (a) employers, and (b) unions?

10. How can seasonal variations in demand for a product affect collective bargaining?

11. How do cyclical variations in demand for a product affect industrial relations in any particular industry?

12. What has been the effect of foreign competition in manufactured goods on the welfare of Canadian workers?

13. How does labour cost as a percentage of the final cost of a product affect collective bargaining? What are examples of low labour cost and high labour cost industries in Canada?

14. How can technological innovation affect union members? What should be the attitude towards it of (a) management, and (b) the union?

15. How is the advent of the cheap electronic microprocessor affecting industry? Will it really mean a "new industrial revolution"? If so, what are the long-term implications?

16. How does the state of the economy in general affect collective bargaining.

17. How do regional differences affect industrial relations in Canada?

18. How does the high degree of American ownership of Canadian industry affect Canadian trade union members?

19. "International unions make good sense for Canadian workers." Discuss.

20. Canada's economic dependence on the U.S. places severe restrictions on the Canadian labour movement. Explain.

21. "The economic factors that apply to employment in private industry do not apply to employment in the public sector." Explain and discuss.

22. What policy should the federal government adopt when negotiating for pay, etc. with the public service unions?

23. Should public sector employees have the right to strike?

24. How is Canada's population growing? What has been happening to births, deaths, and immigration?

25. What is the size of Canada's labour force? How fast is it growing? What factors will affect its future growth?

26. Explain the term: "labour force participation rate". Why has the rate increased in recent years? What problem can this create?

27. How is Canada's population distributed among the various regions? How has the distribution pattern been changing? What are the reasons for such change?

28. What is meant by the "unemployment rate"? How has the rate changed in recent years? Why?

29. How does the unemployment rate vary in Canada from region to region? Why? What changes are occurring?

30. What can be done to reduce unemployment rates in Canada? Do unions share any of the blame for high rates of unemployment?

31. How is the labour force in Canada distributed among different kinds of industries?

32. How do the participation and unemployment rates vary between different age groups? Why is this? What significance does it have?

33. How has immigration affected the Canadian labour movement since World War II?

34. "Canadian union members seem less aggressive than their U.S. counterparts." Discuss.

APPENDIX 2A: CANADIAN LABOUR STATISTICS

Table 2.1 — *Canada's Population Growth, in thousands*

Year	Net natural increase (births minus deaths)	Immigration	Residual (including emigration)	Total increase	Population at start of year
1969	215	162	− 83	294	20 888
1970	216	148	− 81	283	21 182
1971	205	122	− 82	245	21 465
1972	185	122	− 74	233	21 710
1973	179	184	− 71	293	21 942
1974	179	218	− 64	333	22 235
1975	191	188	− 64	315	22 569
1976	192	146	− 64	275	22 884
1977	195	115	− 51	259	23 158
1978	191	86	− 50	227	23 417
1979	197	112	− 42	267	23 645
1980	199	143	− 33	309	23 912
1981	200	129	− 67	262	24 221
1982	198	121	− 97	222	24 483
1983	199	89	− 98	190	24 706
1984	201	88	− 95	195	24 896
1985	201	84	− 102	184	25 090
1986	192	99	− 72	219	25 274
1987	187	152	− 46	293	25 493
1988	189	162	− 39	312	25 786
1989	190	191	− 38	343	26 097
1990					26 440

Source: Statistics Canada

Table 2.2 — *Canada's Population by Region, in thousands*

Start of Year	Atlantic provinces	Quebec	Ontario	Prairie provinces	British Columbia
1969	2 020	5 961	7 388	3 480	2 042
1970	2 030	6 002	7 488	3 506	2 107
1971	2 045	6 017	7 656	3 527	2 168
1972	2 070	6 040	7 769	3 551	2 224
1973	2 093	6 064	7 870	3 576	2 280
1974	2 115	6 103	7 996	3 611	2 350
1975	2 140	6 156	8 125	3 668	2 418
1976	2 173	6 212	8 229	3 749	2 457
1977	2 192	6 263	8 315	3 839	2 486
1978	2 205	6 286	8 408	3 927	2 527
1979	2 215	6 316	8 475	3 999	2 572
1980	2 225	6 360	8 540	4 084	2 636
1981	2 232	6 413	8 600	4 191	2 718
1982	2 233	6 450	8 664	4 292	2 774
1983	2 248	6 465	8 761	4 357	2 803
1984	2 264	6 481	8 860	4 385	2 834
1985	2 275	6 503	8 969	4 406	2 863
1986	2 278	6 528	9 072	4 437	2 883
1987	2 281	6 568	9 201	4 458	2 909
1988	2 288	6 619	9 371	4 472	2 959
1989	2 299	6 672	9 523	4 500	3 026
1990	2 314	6 736	9 668	4 537	3 106

Source: Statistics Canada

Table 2.3 — *Canada's Labour Force, in thousands*

Annual average	Armed forces	Civilian non-institutional population (age 15 and over)	Civilian labour force	Labour force participation rate %	Employed	Employment rate %
1976	80	16 701	10 203	61.1	9 477	92.9
1977	81	17 051	10 500	61.6	9 651	91.9
1978	81	17 377	10 895	62.7	9 987	91.7
1979	80	17 702	11 231	63.4	10 395	92.6
1980	80	18 053	11 573	64.1	10 708	92.5
1981	81	18 368	11 899	64.8	11 001	92.5
1982	83	18 608	11 926	64.1	10 618	89.0
1983	83	18 805	12 109	64.4	10 675	88.2
1984	83	18 996	12 316	64.8	10 932	88.8
1985	84	19 190	12 532	65.3	11 221	89.5
1986	85	19 397	12 746	65.7	11 531	90.5
1987	87	19 642	13 011	66.2	11 861	91.2
1988	87	19 890	13 275	66.7	12 245	92.2
1989	88	20 141	13 503	67.0	12 486	92.5
1990	88	20 430	13 681	67.0	12 572	82.9

Source: Statistics Canada

Table 2.4 — *Canada's Labour Force, by Region, in thousands*

Annual Average	Atlantic provinces	Quebec	Ontario	Prairie provinces	British Columbia
1976	803	2 689	3 882	1 712	1 117
1977	821	2 760	3 986	1 785	1 148
1978	850	2 839	4 133	1 871	1 202
1979	871	2 897	4 271	1 952	1 239
1980	894	2 988	4 350	2 041	1 301
1981	906	3 037	4 463	2 133	1 361
1982	901	2 985	4 502	2 170	1 367
1983	923	3 038	4 561	2 208	1 380
1984	949	3 088	4 655	2 228	1 396
1985	963	3 140	4 758	2 252	1 420
1986	978	3 174	4 862	2 281	1 451
1987	994	3 253	4 992	2 288	1 482
1988	1 019	3 311	5 118	2 313	1 514
1989	1 040	3 343	5 214	2 328	1 578
1990	1 061	3 399	5 268	2 351	1 601

Source: Statistics Canada

Table 2.5 — *Labour Force Participation Rates in Canada*

Annual average	Males and Females 15 - 24	Men 25 and over	Women 25 and over	Males and Females 15 and over
1976	62.4	81.1	41.1	61.1
1977	63.2	80.9	42.1	61.6
1978	64.4	81.1	44.1	62.7
1979	66.2	81.0	45.0	63.4
1980	67.2	80.7	46.4	64.1
1981	67.8	80.5	48.1	64.8
1982	65.8	79.5	48.5	64.1
1983	66.1	79.1	49.6	64.4
1984	66.8	78.6	50.8	64.8
1985	67.4	78.5	51.8	65.3
1986	68.4	78.2	52.7	65.7
1987	69.1	77.9	53.9	66.2
1988	69.6	77.7	55.2	66.7
1989	70.2	77.6	55.8	67.0
1990	68.9	77.1	56.7	67.0

Source: Statistics Canada

Note: The *participation rate* is the number of persons actively seeking work out of the eligible population, expressed as a percentage.

Table 2.6 — *Employment in Canada, by Age and Sex, in thousands*

Annual average	MEN		WOMEN		Total
	Age 15 - 24	Age 25 and over	Age 15 - 24	Age 25 and over	
1976	1 298	4 666	1 093	2 420	9 477
1977	1 312	4 720	1 101	2 519	9 651
1978	1 340	4 816	1 141	2 689	9 987
1979	1 410	4 952	1 202	2 831	10 395
1980	1 418	5 041	1 239	3 011	10 708
1981	1 416	5 140	1 251	3 194	11 001
1982	1 226	5 010	1 160	3 222	10 618
1983	1 180	5 023	1 133	3 339	10 675
1984	1 207	5 100	1 134	3 490	10 932
1985	1 199	5 229	1 149	3 645	11 221
1986	1 218	5 340	1 148	3 815	11 531
1987	1 232	5 477	1 151	4 002	11 861
1988	1 241	5 636	1 147	4 221	12 245
1989	1 234	5 743	1 138	4 371	12 486
1990	1 165	5 783	1 089	4 535	12 572

Source: Statistics Canada

Table 2.7 — *Industrial Employment in Canada, in thousands*

	April, 1990	Per cent of total
Goods producing industries		
Forestry	40	0.4
Mining, including milling	143	1.4
Manufacturing	1 819	17.9
Construction	463	4.6
Total	2 465	24.3
Services producing industries		
Transportation, communication and other utilities	851	8.4
Trade	1 856	18.3
Finance, insurance and real estate	643	6.3
Community, business and personal services	3 635	35.8
Public administration	698	6.9
Total	7 683	75.7
Goods and Services Producing industries	10 148	100.0

Source: Statistics Canada

Table 2.8 — *Employment in Canada, by Region, in thousands*

Annual Average	Atlantic provinces	Quebec	Ontario	Prairie provinces	British Columbia
1976	717	2 456	3 643	1 641	1 021
1977	718	2 476	3 708	1 698	1 050
1978	744	2 530	3 835	1 774	1 103
1979	770	2 619	3 993	1 868	1 144
1980	795	2 694	4 053	1 953	1 213
1981	801	2 723	4 171	2 037	1 270
1982	773	2 574	4 063	2 007	1 202
1983	784	2 616	4 089	1 995	1 190
1984	805	2 692	4 235	2 020	1 191
1985	812	2 768	4 377	2 045	1 220
1986	833	2 825	4 524	2 080	1 270
1987	857	2 918	4 689	2 092	1 306
1988	893	3 001	4 862	2 132	1 358
1989	912	3 031	4 949	2 158	1 435
1990	926	3 055	4 937	2 185	1 469

Source: Statistics Canada

Table 2.9 — *Unemployment and Unemployment Rates in Canada*

Annual average	Persons Unemployed (000s)	Unemployment rates %			
		Age Group 15-24	Age group 25 and over		All ages
			Men	Women	
1976	726	12.7	4.2	6.6	7.1
1977	849	14.4	4.9	7.4	8.1
1978	908	14.5	5.2	7.7	8.3
1979	836	12.9	4.5	7.0	7.4
1980	865	13.2	4.8	6.5	7.5
1981	898	13.2	4.8	6.7	7.5
1982	1 308	18.7	8.2	8.8	11.0
1983	1 434	19.8	9.2	9.6	11.8
1984	1 384	17.8	9.0	9.7	11.2
1985	1 311	16.4	8.3	9.4	10.5
1986	1 215	15.1	7.6	8.6	9.5
1987	1 150	13.7	7.0	8.3	8.8
1988	1 031	12.0	6.0	7.5	7.8
1989	1 018	11.3	6.1	7.3	7.5
1990	1 109	12.8	6.8	7.3	8.1

Source: Statistics Canada

Note: The unemployment rate is the number of unemployed as a percentage of the labour force.

Table 2.10 — *Regional Unemployment Rates, in per cent*

Annual Average	Atlantic provinces	Quebec	Ontario	Prairie provinces	British Columbia	Canada
1976	10.7	8.7	6.2	4.1	8.6	7.1
1977	12.5	10.3	7.0	4.9	8.5	8.1
1978	12.5	10.9	7.2	5.2	8.3	8.3
1979	11.6	9.6	6.5	4.3	7.6	7.4
1980	11.1	9.8	6.8	4.3	6.8	7.5
1981	11.6	10.3	6.6	4.5	6.7	7.5
1982	14.2	13.8	9.7	7.5	12.1	11.0
1983	15.1	13.9	10.3	9.6	13.8	11.8
1984	15.2	12.8	9.0	9.8	14.7	11.2
1985	15.7	11.8	8.0	9.2	14.1	10.5
1986	14.8	11.0	7.0	8.8	12.5	9.5
1987	13.8	10.3	6.1	8.6	11.9	8.8
1988	12.4	9.4	5.0	7.8	10.3	7.8
1989	12.3	9.3	5.1	7.3	9.1	7.5
1990	12.8	10.1	6.3	7.1	8.2	8.1

Source: Statistics Canada

CHAPTER 3: THE CONSTITUTIONAL AND LEGAL ENVIRONMENT

Chapter Objectives

- *To stress that only in the recent past have workers acquired the right to bargain collectively*

- *To indicate how and when the principle of compulsory conciliation in labour-management disputes was introduced in Canada*

- *To show how unfair practices by management and then labour were outlawed in the U.S. and then Canada*

- *To trace the war-time and post-war development in labour relations policy, including compulsory union recognition and bargaining*

- *To indicate the restrictions on public sector employees*

- *To discuss how the concept of the "protection of the public interest" has been used and perhaps misused*

Chapter Outline

3.1 LABOUR JURISDICTION IN CANADA

Canada's political constitution is set out mainly in the Constitution Act, 1867. This Act, passed by the British Parliament in that year, created the Dominion of Canada and divided the legislative powers in the new state between the federal Parliament on the one hand and the provincial legislatures on the other.

Amongst the powers assigned to the provinces was the right to pass laws concerning "property and civil rights". This has been interpreted to give the provinces jurisdiction over labour matters such as hours of work, minimum wages, and minimum age of employment. However, the federal government is empowered to pass labour laws with regard to industries specifically under its jurisdiction. These include: navigation, shipping, interprovincial railways, canals, telegraphs, steamship lines and ferries, airports, air transportation, radio stations, and works declared by Parliament to be for the general advantage of Canada or of two or more provinces. It also has jurisdiction over workers employed under federal government work contracts and on works partly financed by federal government funds. The federal Parliament can also pass laws concerning matters surrendered to it by the Provincial legislatures such as unemployment assistance and old age pensions.

3.2 THE CONSPIRACY DOCTRINE

The system of English Common Law which Canada inherited from Britain had been fashioned partly to protect the interests of the English land-owning, employer class. Consequently, any attempt by workers in agriculture or in the various skilled trades to join together to negotiate with an employer was considered to be "in restraint of trade" and a criminal act, falling under the doctrine of criminal conspiracy. Thus, anyone attempting to form a trade union could be imprisoned, fined, or both. This situation continued to exist in Britain until 1871 when the British Parliament, after continued worker pressure, passed legislation which no longer made the mere combining of workers to increase wages or to reduce working hours a conspiracy in violation of the common law. However, in Canada in 1872, a Toronto printers' strike for a 54-hour work week was followed by the arrest and conviction on criminal charges of the strike leaders. Soon thereafter, the federal government, responding to great public indignation, passed the Trade Union Act of 1872 that, like the British Act of the previous year, made combinations of workers no longer a criminal offence. At the same time, another statute, the Criminal Law Amendment Act, was passed, imposing penalties for violence or intimidation during organizing campaigns and strikes. To placate employers, the Act stated that a union-management contract was not legally enforceable.

3.3 INDUSTRIAL DISPUTES LEGISLATION

By the end of the nineteenth century, several provinces had passed legislation designed to help resolve disputes between employers and employees. In 1900 the Federal Parliament followed suit, passing a Conciliation Act which gave to the Minister of Labour the authority to appoint conciliation officers or conciliation boards to help settle industrial disputes.

In 1903, after a long strike by C.P.R. trackmen, the Federal Parliament passed a Railway Labour Disputes Act which authorized the appointment of a three-man conciliation board to handle disputes. The employer and the union would each choose one nominee, and the two nominees would then choose a chairperson. The board would then investigate the dispute and try to bring about an agreement between the two parties. If this failed, resort could be made to an arbitration board. However, since such a board could make only non-binding recommendations, its influence was limited. Also, the Act did nothing to forbid strikes and lockouts.

In 1906, the Federal Parliament passed a Conciliation and Labour Act that included the best features of both the 1900 Conciliation Act and the 1903 Railway Labour Disputes Act. However, the legislation was still unsatisfactory and, following a rash of strikes, was replaced in 1907 by the Industrial Disputes Investigation Act. This Act was considered a great improvement over its predecessors and served as the model for similar Provincial Acts.

Industrial Disputes Investigation Act (IDI)

This Act, which applied to disputes involving employers of ten or more persons engaged in mining, transportation, communication, and public utility operations, made provision for a three-person Board of Conciliation and Investigation with powers similar to those in the 1903 Railway Labour Disputes Act. However, extremely important, it also required that any strike or lockout be postponed and that wages and other conditions of work remain unchanged while the dispute was being investigated. Should the Board fail to bring the parties to a voluntary agreement, the Board was required to make recommendations as to what should or should not be done by them. The Act provided for voluntary extension of its scope to any industrial dispute not coming within the groups subject to compulsion. Unfortunately, the Act gave no protection to employees who wished to join a union nor did it require an employer to bargain with the union that its employees may have formed or joined. As a result, organized labour became increasingly critical of the Act.

Toronto Electric Commissioners v. Snider

The Industrial Disputes Investigation Act, although passed by the Federal Parliament rather than by the Provincial legislatures, provided for its application to any industrial dispute. However, in 1925 the legality of the Act was challenged in court in the case of Toronto Electric Commissioners v. Snider. The Judicial Committee of the Privy Council of England, to whom the appeal went, agreed that the Federal Parliament had exceeded its jurisdictional rights. This was because Section 92 of the Constitution Act specifically assigns the matter of civil rights of employers and employees to the provinces. Consequently, the Judicial Committee declared the Act unconstitutional. Thereupon, Canada's Federal Parliament quickly amended the Industrial Disputes Investigation Act so that it would apply only to disputes within its own jurisdiction — for example, Crown corporations, railways, and longshoring.

Provincial Acts

The amendment to the Federal IDI Act also provided for the Act's applicability to employees normally outside federal jurisdiction so long as the provincial legislature gave its approval. Subsequently, between 1925 and 1932, all the provinces except Prince Edward Island passed enabling Acts. Later, Alberta and British Columbia replaced such enabling legislation with their own provincial Acts similar to the Federal one. As a result, despite the Snider decision, a new national labour relations policy emerged in Canada.

3.4 THE WAGNER ACT

In the United States, the severe economic depression that began in 1929 eventually led to the election of a Democratic President, Franklin D. Roosevelt, whose much more sympathetic attitude towards organized labour was summed up in the phrase, the New Deal. This attitude resulted in the passage through Congress in 1935 of a new National Labour Relations Act, known for short as the Wagner Act, that affirmed workers' rights to organize unions of their choice and to be free from employer interference or control in doing so. Also, under the Act, employers were required to negotiate conditions of work with the appropriate unions. The act listed five management practices considered to be unfair to labour:

a) interference with an employee's right to join a union,

b) domination of a labour union,

c) discrimination against an employee for engaging in union activities,

d) dismissal or otherwise penalizing an employee for filing charges under the Act, and

e) refusal to bargain with the union representing the employees.

A National Labour Relations Board, established under the Act, was required to investigate any complaints of unfair labour practices by management, to prosecute the companies and persons involved, and to hold and supervise elections to determine which union it should certify as the official bargaining agent of the employees in each particular bargaining unit. The Act also provided for a Federal Mediation and Conciliation Service (FMCS) which would supply mediation services on request. There was no mention in the Act of possible unfair labour practices by unions. As a result the unions had very much a free hand in recruiting new members. In 1947, however, the Act was amended to permit unions also to be prosecuted for unfair labour practices.

In the United States, in the nineteen-thirties, the American Federation of Labour and the new, but rapidly growing Congress of Industrial Organizations found the Wagner Act, with its principle of compulsory recognition of unions and compulsory bargaining with them, to be of tremendous help in their efforts to increase union membership. This was particularly so after the Act was upheld by the U.S. Supreme Court in 1937. Not surprisingly, therefore, the many trade unions in Canada affiliated with these organizations soon started to press for similar legislation in this country. One result was the preparation by the Trades and Labour Congress of a draft bill for such an Act that the provincial governments were then urged to adopt. This pressure by organized labour eventually resulted in the enactment by many provincial legislatures in the second half of the nineteen-thirties of Wagner-type labour relations statutes, some of which were based on the TLC's draft bill. However, the lack of any machinery of enforcement effectively removed the teeth from these statutes.

3.5 WAR-TIME DEVELOPMENTS

With the outbreak of World War II, the federal government, armed with its powers under the War Measures Act of 1914, temporarily re-established its supremacy in labour relations matters. Thus in 1939, just after the war began, the federal government, by means of an Order in Council, extended the coverage of the federal Industrial Disputes Investigation Act to all industries involved with the war effort. This included all the basic industries such as fishing, farming, lumber, mining, and most of the manufacturing ones as well. Later, in 1940, the federal government began to reveal its intentions for a new, comprehensive Canadian labour relations policy which in some ways closely resembled the Wagner Act. However, a novel feature, not in the Wagner Act, was settlement machinery to which disputes arising during a collective agreement or at renewal could be referred.

During the war, stronger provincial labour relations legislation began to appear on the statute books. Especially important was the Ontario Collective Bargaining Act of 1943. While purporting to deal with the problems of rights of association and negotiation, this Act went beyond the pre-war laws of other provinces by providing machinery for administration and enforcement. With its passage, Ontario labour legislation was brought more or less into line with that of the United States. However, many workers in Ontario were still subject to the federal IDI Act, as extended in wartime.

In 1944, Ottawa suspended the IDI Act, replacing it with new labour relations regulations (Order in Council PC 1003). This whole new policy, talked about since 1940, combined the IDI Act disputes-investigation principle, including the delay on strikes and lockouts, with the Wagner Act principles of compulsory recognition and bargaining. Ontario, in agreement with the new policy, repealed its statute, thereby letting industrial disputes in Ontario come under the jurisdiction of the new federal regulations. Because of the national emergency, the coverage of the new Canadian labour relations policy was very broad, extending well beyond the normal scope of federal labour relations jurisdiction. It included: (a) industries of a national or inter-provincial character ordinarily within federal jurisdiction, including Crown corporations handling or manufacturing war supplies; (b) war industries as described in the regulations, or later added by Order in Council; and (c) all other industries within a province where such province by appropriate legislation brought such industries within the scope of the regulations. The regulations themselves contained the following main features:

a) the right of employees to form and join unions;

b) protection against unfair labour practices which, if allowed to continue, would result in discouraging the exercise of the previous rights;

c) a system of defining bargaining units and certifying bargaining representatives;

d) compulsory collective bargaining;

e) compulsory postponement of strikes and lockouts, coupled with compulsory two-stage conciliation;

f) the right to resort to strikes and lockouts after compulsory conciliation procedures had been completed.

During World War II, wage increases were severely restricted. Initially, by a 1940 Order-in-Council, wage increases were permitted up to 5 per cent a year over a base wage related to the years 1926 to 1939. Also cost-of-living bonuses were allowed. However, in 1941, another Order-in-Council was issued that prohibited wages increases except as authorized by a specially established National War Labour Board that was empowered to investigate wages and working conditions in whichever industries it saw fit and to make recommendations for any changes. In 1943, another Order-in-Council was issued that authorized a wage increase only in exceptional circumstances — namely, where the present wage level was grossly inadequate. Also, during the war, labour unions and workers in general were asked, in the name of the war effort specifically, and the public interest generally, to refrain from strike action. As a result, strikes were few and far between.

3.6 THE POST-WAR PERIOD

With the end of the war, all the pent-up employee dissatisfactions burst forth. After all the war-time sacrifices, workers now wanted better pay and improved working conditions. During the war, they had seen most employers benefit greatly from the war-time demand for vehicles, ships, aircraft, ammunition, food, clothing, and so on. And this economic prosperity, to the surprise of some leading economists who predicted the same severe economic depression that followed World War I, showed no signs of abating in the post-war period — thanks to heavy consumer demand in North America and the various U.S. and Canadian foreign aid programs, particularly for Western Europe. As a result, the unions confronted employers with large catch-up pay demands and, in the face of employer resistance, called their members out on strike in many different parts of Canada.

Gradually, following this period of industrial turmoil, employers and employees made their peace. However, the labour unrest forced the federal and provincial governments to look again at the legal framework for settling such disputes. Already, towards the end of the war, the federal authorities had, at the suggestion of the provinces, prepared the draft of a federal labour relations bill. This draft was then discussed with the provinces and, after amendments, was passed by the federal Parliament in 1948. The new Act, the Industrial Relations and Disputes Act, replaced the previous war-time regulations. Like the war-time regulations, the new Act included the Wagner Act's basic principles of compulsory union recognition and bargaining and the IDI Act's principle of compulsory conciliation. Unlike the war-time regulations, the coverage of the new federal Act was restricted to industries normally within federal jurisdiction.

At about the same time, most of the provinces in Canada passed new labour relations statutes of their own, incorporating in varying degree the system of industrial relations that had developed during the war-time period.

3.7 PROVINCIAL LABOUR RELATIONS ACTS

All provinces now have Labour Relations Acts designed to promote harmonious relations between employers and employees and to facilitate the settlement of industrial disputes. One basic provision of these statutes is the requirement that an employer must bargain in good faith with the labour union that has been certified by the provincial Labour Relations Board as the bargaining agent for its employees. Another basic provision in most provinces is the requirement of compulsory conciliation in negotiations for a collective agreement. This means that before a strike or lockout may legally take place, the conciliation procedure set out in the particular provincial statute must be followed.

The provincial Labour Relations statutes also require the compulsory arbitration of any alleged violation of the collective agreement between the employer and the union, if the matter cannot be resolved by the grievance procedure set out in the Agreement. A strike or lockout is illegal while the collective agreement is in force. However, illegal or "wildcat" strikes do sometimes occur, with or without the tacit support of the union.

3.8 PROVINCIAL PUBLIC SECTOR EMPLOYEES

In most provinces, provincial government employees are denied the right to strike because of the harm that could be caused to the general public. Instead, differences between the employer and the union involved must be settled by arbitration. In Ontario, for example, labour relations between the Ontario government and its employees are governed by the terms of the Crown Employees Collective Bargaining Act. If negotiations between the government and the Ontario Public Service Employees union, representing the employees, for a new collective agreement break down, either party may ask the Ontario Public Service Labour Relations Tribunal to appoint an arbitrator.

Other types of public sector employees such as hospital workers, teachers, police officers, and firefighters, are governed by special Acts. Again, because of the essential nature of their work, they are not usually given the right to strike — only the right to arbitration.

3.9 CANADA LABOUR CODE

At the federal level, labour relations have been governed, since 1970, by Part 5 of the Canada Labour Code.

The Labour Code applies to all employees in:

a) air transport, aircraft and airports;

b) radio and television broadcasting;

c) banks;

d) Federal Crown Corporations (e.g., the St. Lawrence Seaway Authority);

e) all extra-provincial shipping and services connected thereto (such as longshoring and stevedoring);

f) works or undertakings connecting one province with another or with another country, such as rail, bus, or truck services, ferries, tunnels, bridges, canals, pipelines, telegraph, telephone and cable systems; and

g) defined operations or specific works that have been declared to be for the general advantage of Canada or of two or more provinces, such as flour, feed and seed cleaning mills, feed warehouses, grain elevators and uranium mining and processing.

The Code recognizes the right of employees to organize and bargain collectively through trade unions. However, both employers and employees are required to bargain in good faith and to include in their collective agreement a provision for the arbitration of disputes. The Code prohibits unfair labour practices (such as discrimination and coercion) by employers and employees, and provides for government conciliation officers or boards to help mediate differences between the two parties in negotiations. The administration of Part Five of the Code is the responsibility of the Federal Minister of Labour. Part of his authority — for example, the provisions covering the certification of bargaining agents — has been delegated to the Canada Labour Relations Board.

3.10 PUBLIC SERVICE STAFF RELATIONS ACT

This Act, passed in 1967, gave to federal government employees the right
to bargain collectively with the government as represented by the Treasury
Board, about wages, hours of work, and other conditions of employment.
The certified bargaining agent for each particular group of employees is
given a choice, early in negotiations for a new collective agreement, as to
how any outstanding issues should be resolved. One alternative is to use
the services of a conciliation board which, if unsuccessful, could be
followed after a specified time period by the right to strike. The other
alternative is to use compulsory arbitration, legally binding on both
parties, without the right to strike. More details are provided in Chapter
20.

3.11 PROTECTION OF THE PUBLIC INTEREST

Perhaps the most important factor that has helped shape the legal system
governing labour relations in Canada has been the desire, on the part of the
government of the day, to "protect the public interest". Ostensibly, this
concept means protecting the general public from the hardships that arise
when essential public services such as the supply of water or electricity are
cut off. In itself, this is a justifiable political and social concern. That is
why many jurisdictions deny the right to strike to various types of public
employees such as police officers and firefighters. Over the years,
however, the right to strike has been extended to more and more public
employees — not because the services provided are less essential than they
were previously but because of the relentless pressure of the unions and
employees concerned to improve their bargaining powers and the desire
for political popularity of the legislators involved.

Public or semi-public employees denied the right to strike are usually
permitted to resolve their differences with their employers (e.g. hospital
boards) by resort to arbitration. However, this has often meant awards that
are unsatisfactory to the employees concerned. As a result, the concept of
protection of the public interest is seen by many public employees today as
a government stratagem for holding down pay raises in the public sector
rather than a genuine concern for the public at large.

The concept of protection of the public interest is also occasionally used
by the government as a justification for intervening in a protracted labour-
mangement dispute in the private sector that, because of the effect of a
strike or lockout, is causing public hardship. Sometimes, the employer or
union involved may even call upon the government to step in and impose a
settlement, again ostensibly on grounds of protecting the public interest.

In fact, the real reason may be that the party concerned has got itself into a corner from which there is no escape other than by outright acceptance of the other party's terms.

The various provincial Labour Relations statutes reflect government concern to protect the public from hardships caused by management-labour disputes in the private sector. Thus these statutes forbid strikes or lockouts during the life of a collective agreement and require the use of a government conciliation officer after the expiry of a contract before a strike or lockout may take place.

KEY CONCEPTS

Labour jurisdiction

Conspiracy doctrine

Industrial disputes legislation

Compulsory conciliation

U.S. legislation

Compulsory recognition and bargaining

Unfair management practices

Labour Relations Acts

Provincial employees

Canada Labour Code

Public Service Staff Relations Act

The Public Interest

REVIEW QUESTIONS

1. Who has the right, under Canada's constitution, to pass laws governing labour relations?

2. Explain what is meant by the "conspiracy doctrine". What was its effect? Is it still applicable?

3. How, at the beginning of this century, did the Canadian government try to help resolve disputes between employers and employees?

4. Explain the significance of the case of Toronto Electric Commissioners vs. Snider.

5. What are the key principles of the Wagner Act? How did the Act affect unions in the U.S.? What was its significance for Canada?

6. What was so different about Ontario's Collective Bargaining Act of 1943 compared with previous labour relations statutes?

7. What basic labour relations principles were embodied in the federal labour relations regulations (Order in Council PC 1003) proclaimed in 1944?

8. What happened in the labour relations field in the early post World War II years? Why?

9. What are some of the key features of the provincial Labour Relations Acts?

10. How are labour disputes settled in the provincial public sector? What statutes apply?

11. What are the basic provisions of Part 5 of the Canada Labour Code? To whom do they apply?

12. What collective bargaining rights, if any, do federal government employees have? Are they permitted to strike?

13. What is the Public Service Staff Relations Act? What is one of its key features?

14. "The desire to protect the public interest has been the most important factor affecting federal labour relations policy in the nineteen seventies and eighties." Discuss.

15. "Compulsory arbitration for public service employees has been a convenient device for holding down the wages of these workers." Discuss.

PART B

Labour, Employers, Government, and the Public

CHAPTER 4: LABOUR ORGANIZATIONS IN CANADA

Chapter Objectives

- *To explain what is meant by a labour or trade union*
- *To review the reasons why workers join unions*
- *To distinguish between different types of labour unions*
- *To examine the extent of union membership in Canada and indicate the largest unions*
- *To explain how a typical labour union is organized and what are its functions*
- *To indicate the role of the union local in collective bargaining*
- *To explain how union locals are linked together by labour councils, labour federations, and central labour organizations*
- *To review the political role and economic goals of labour unions in Canada*

Chapter Outline

4.1   Labour Union Defined

4.2   Why Workers Join Unions

4.3   Types of Labour Unions

4.4   Union Membership in Canada

4.5   Labour Union Organization

4.6   Collective Bargaining

4.7   Labour Councils

4.8   Labour Federations

4.9   Canadian Labour Congress

4.10 The CLC and Canadianization of International Unions in Canada

4.11 Political Role of Labour Unions

4.12 Economic Goals of Labour Unions

4.1 LABOUR UNION DEFINED

The term *labour organization* is a broad term that includes not only various types of labour unions and other employee associations, but also various regional and central labour bodies. In this chapter, we look first at the labour unions and then at the various central labour bodies such as the CLC.

A *labour union* (also called a *trade union*) is an association of workers, practising a similar trade or employed in the same company or industry. Its basic purpose is to improve the economic welfare, including pay and job security, of its members through collective, rather than individual, bargaining of wage rates, hours of work, and so on, with employers.

In Ontario's Labour Relations Act, as one provincial example, a *trade union* is defined as "an organization of employees formed for purposes that include the regulation of relations between employees and employers and includes a provincial, national, or international trade union, a certified council of trade unions and a designated or certified employee bargaining agency".

Many labour unions use the term "union" in their official title, but many others use terms such as association, brotherhood, federation, or alliance, and in two instances (the American Guild of Variety Artists and the Newspaper Guild) the term "guild".

In the various Labour Relations Acts or Labour Codes, depending on the province, the term "trade union" is used. In fact, the terms "trade union" and "labour union" are often used interchangeably. However, the term *trade union* is more commonly used with reference to a group of workers possessing a certain type of industrial skill or "trade", whereas the term "labour union" is more commonly used with reference to a group of unskilled and/or semi-skilled workers employed in a particular industry. Throughout this book, we mainly use the term labour union.

There are, in addition to the labour unions referred to above, many *employee associations*. These are associations of employees in a particular firm or industry that have not been certified, under the terms of a Labour Relations Act or Labour Code, as the bargaining agent for those employees. Although without legal status, these unofficial or "quasi labour unions" are nevertheless recognized by the employer as the spokesperson for its employees — bargaining on their behalf or at least presenting their complaints to the employer. However, the legal status of collective bargaining outside any provincial or federal labour legislation tends to be uncertain.

In its broadest sense, a *labour union* may be considered to be any type of labour organization, whether formally or informally recognized by the employer, that represents the interests of the employees in that particular plant, store, office, or industry.

4.2 WHY WORKERS JOIN UNIONS

Each employee has his or her own personal reasons for joining a labour union. Some employees flock to join, many others need to be cajoled, and some resolutely oppose union membership.

Reasons for Joining a Labour Union

For many employees, one good reason for joining a union is that a group of employees, acting collectively, can usually negotiate much better terms of employment than if each employee negotiated alone. Thus membership in a union offers the very real chance of better pay and fringe benefits and working conditions. Also, the most effective method of enforcing the employees' viewpoint, the use of the strike weapon, demands common action by all or most employees. Otherwise the strike is ineffective in halting the employer's operations.

A second reason for union membership is that in many business firms and other organizations in which a union has been officially certified as the bargaining agent for the employees and in which a collective agreement is in force, membership in the union is compulsory for most employees, usually after a probationary employment period. Unofficially, there is also pressure to join from fellow-workers who already belong to the union.

A third reason for joining is that membership in a union increases an employee's sense of economic security. Employees no longer feel weak and alone in their dealings with management. They can no longer be dismissed at the employer's whim. There is a grievance procedure set out in the collective agreement to handle disputes and there are union officials to help ensure that the union member gets fair treatment. Also, the employee now belongs to an organization whose representatives are not only very well informed but can also talk and bargain as competently as management. The inclusion in the collective agreement, at union instigation, of seniority (or length of service with the firm) as the major criterion in lay-offs, when work shortages arise, also helps increase an employee's sense of economic security.

A fourth reason for joining a union is that human beings, as social animals, enjoy membership in a group. They feel the need to belong. And the union offers the rank and file worker the companionship of people of similar background and outlook, and similar economic and social goals. This membership bond exists not only in the workplace and on the picket line but also in the union hall where social activities are organized for members and their families.

Reasons for Not Joining a Labour Union

As the statistics show, not every worker belongs to a union, even if the option is available. Some plants are "non-union". One reason is that the employees believe they are economically better off without a union. Management may currently offer wages and fringe benefits that are equal or better than those in comparable unionized plants. Also, management may have a more progressive or enlightened approach in its treatment of rank and file employees (e.g. as in some of the new auto plants in North America). Another reason may be a negative one — management uses various forms of economic and psychological pressure on its employees to keep them from voting for a union. Instead, the employer may encourage a "token" form of employee association that represents the view of the employer more than those of the employees.

4.3 TYPES OF LABOUR UNIONS

Labour unions can be divided into various types according to (a) type of worker, (b) geographical scope, and (c) Congress affiliation.

Type of Worker

Historically, unions have been divided into two basic types according to type of worker eligible for membership.

Craft Union. This is a labour organization representing workers practising the same craft or "trade". Examples are the International Association of Firefighters, the Canadian Air Pilots' Association, and the Brotherhood of Railroad Signalmen. Today, however, some craft unions represent all the workers in a plant, not just those with a particular skill or "craft".

Industrial Union. This is a labour organization whose members usually, but not always, include most of the workers eligible for union membership in a particular company or industry, irrespective of the type of work performed. Examples are the International Chemical Workers' Union and the Canadian Union of United Brewery, Flour, Cereal, Soft Drink and Distillery Workers.

General Union. Although the traditional distinction is between craft unions and industrial unions, some unions might be more accurately described as *general unions*. This is because their membership is not

Table 4.1 — *Union Membership, by Type of Labour Union, 1990, 1989 and 1980*

Type of Union	1990		1989		1980	
	Number	%	Number	%	Number	%
National	234	23.0	228	24.9	128	17.4
International	61	6.0	63	6.9	80	10.9
Other	721	71.0	626	68.2	526	71.7
Total	1 016	100.0	917	100.0	734	100.0
			Membership (000s)			
National	2 563	63.6	2 500	63.4	1 703	50.1
International	1 283	31.8	1 278	32.4	1 571	46.2
Other	184	4.6	166	4.2	123	3.7
Total	4 030	100.0	3 944	100.0	3 397	100.0

Source: Labour Canada, *Directory of Labour Organizations in Canada*

Note: ''Other'' includes directly chartered unions and independent local organizations.

confined to one type of skilled occupation or to one type of industry. The International Teamsters' Union is considered by some to be an example of this type of labour union.

Geographical Scope. Unions can also be distinguished from each other (see Table 4.1) according to their geographical scope: international, national, or local.

International Unions. These are labour unions which charter ''locals'', or branches, in both the United States and Canada. However, because of their predominantly U.S. membership, such unions have their head office in the U.S. In recent years, Canadian memberships in such unions has been declining. This is because Canadian branches of international unions have been breaking away from the parent unions and forming their own Canadian unions — for example, the Automotive, Aerospace and Agricultural Implement Workers Union of Canada formed from breakaway locals of the International Auto Workers' Union. An example of a prominent international union is the United Mine Workers of America, with head office in Washington, D.C.

National Unions. These are labour unions which charter branches in Canada only and have their head office in this country. Examples of national unions are the Canadian Union of Public Employees, the Canadian Paperworkers Union, and the Canadian Union of Operating Engineers and General Workers. Many of the unions included under the heading of national are really provincial in scope — for example, the Alberta Union of Provincial Employees and the Ontario Secondary School Teachers' Federation.

There are two types of labour organizations that are purely local in geographical scope. First, there are *directly chartered local unions*. These are local labour unions which have been organized by and have received their *charter* (or official document of establishment) directly from the Canadian Labour Congress, the major central organization for national trade unions in Canada. Such local unions are not part of a national or international union. Membership in directly chartered local unions is usually relatively small. The second type of local labour organization is the *independent local organization*. This is a local not formally connected or affiliated with any other labour organization. Membership in such unions is also usually quite small.

Congress Affiliation

A third way of distinguishing between labour unions is according to affiliation with one or other central labour organization (see Table 4.2). These central organizations are:

CLC — Canadian Labour Congress

CSN — Confédération des Syndicats Nationaux (In English, Confédération of National Trade Unions, or CNTU)

CSD — Centrale des syndicats démocratiques

CCU — Confederation of Canadian Unions

AFL-CIO — American Federation of Labour and Congress of Industrial Organizations.

The CLC, described later in this chapter, is the central labour organization in Canada with the largest number of affiliated union members. The next largest is the CSN, prominent in Quebec. Union membership by congress affiliation is shown in Table 4.3.

Table 4.2 — *Union Membership, by Type of Union and Affiliation, 1990*

Type and Affiliation	Number of unions	Number of locals	Union Membership	
			Number	Percent
International Unions	61	3 295	1 283 867	31.9
AFL — CIO/CLC	39	2 659	876 626	21.7
AFL — CIO/CFL	10	392	203 304	5.0
CLC only	3	30	10 772	0.3
AFL — CIO only	4	111	177 568	4.4
Unaffiliated unions	5	103	15 597	0.4
National Unions	234	13 515	2 563 216	63.6
CLC	48	6 442	1 468 458	36.4
CSN (CNTU)	8	2 063	211 735	5.3
CEQ	12	441	103 141	2.6
CCU	14	90	32 394	0.8
CSD	3	176	17 695	0.4
CFL	4	41	8 010	0.2
CNFIU	9	8	2 173	0.1
Unaffiliated unions	136	4 254	719 610	17.9
Directly Chartered Unions	341		47 776	1.2
CSD	301		42 901	1.1
CLC	38		4 800	0.1
CSN (CNTU)	2		75	0.0
Independent Local Organizations	380		135 900	3.4
Total	1 016	16 810	4 030 759	100.0

Source: Labour Canada, *Directory of Labour Organizations in Canada*

Table 4.3 — *Union Membership, by Congress Affiliation, 1990*

Congress Affiliation	Union Membership	
	Number	Percent
CLC	2 360 656	58.6
AFL — CIO/CLC	876 626	21.7
CLC only	1 484 030	36.8
CSN (CNTU)	211 810	5.3
CFL	211 314	5.2
AFL — CIO/CFL	203 304	5.0
CFL only	8 010	0.2
AFL — CIO only	177 568	4.4
CEQ	103 141	2.6
CSD	60 596	1.5
CCU	32 394	0.8
CNFIU	2 173	0.1
Unaffiliated International Unions	15 597	0.4
Unaffiliated National Unions	719 610	17.9
Independent Local Organizations	135 900	3.4
Total	4 030 759	100.0

Source: Labour Canada, *Directory of Labour Organizations in Canada*

4.4 UNION MEMBERSHIP IN CANADA

Membership in labour unions has been gradually increasing in Canada and totalled 4 030 759 persons at the beginning of 1990 as shown in Table 4.4. However, as a percentage of the civilian labour force and of total non-agricultural paid workers, union membership has declined slightly in recent years.

Table 4.4 — *Union Membership in Canada, 1971-1990*

Year	Union membership in thousands	Civilian labour force in thousands	Union Membership/ civilian labour force (%)	Total non-agricultural paid Workers	Union membership/ non-agricultural paid workers (%)
1971	2 231	8 395	26.6	6 880	32.4
1972	2 388	8 639	27.6	7 052	33.9
1973	2 591	8 897	29.1	7 327	35.4
1974	2 732	9 276	29.5	7 769	35.2
1975	2 884	9 639	29.9	8 102	35.6
1976	3 042	9 974	30.5	8 238	36.9
1977	3 149	10 203	30.9	8 400	37.5
1978	3 278	10 500	31.2	8 538	38.4
1980	3 397	10 895	31.2	8 816	38.5
1981	3 487	11 573	30.1	9 495	36.7
1982	3 617	11 899	30.4	9 775	37.0
1983	3 563	11 926	29.9	9 402	37.9
1984	3 651	12 109	30.2	9 408	37.9
1985	3 666	12 316	29.8	9 626	38.1
1986	3 730	12 532	29.8	9 888	37.7
1987	3 782	12 746	29.7	10 219	37.0
1988	3 841	13 011	29.5	10 519	36.5
1989	3 944	13 275	29.7	10 891	36.2
1990	4 031	13 503	29.9	11 147	36.2

Source: Labour Canada, *Directory of Labour Organizations in Canada*

Note: The method of reporting was changed in 1980. Thus statistics for 1971 through 1978 are for December 31 of each year. But statistics for 1980 are for January 1 (i.e. — equivalent to December 31, 1979). This explains the absence of 1979 figures.

Canadianization of Union Membership

Nowadays (as shown in Tables 4.1 and 4.2) about 68 per cent of union members belong to Canadian labour unions and only 32 per cent belong to international unions. This is a significant shift from the situation in 1980 when only 50 per cent of union members belonged to Canadian unions and a complete reversal of the situation of about thirty years ago, when only 30 per cent of union members belonged to Canadian labour unions.

Canadian nationalists have long objected to the high degree of U.S. investment in Canada and to the great amount of U.S. influence in the Canadian labour movement. They claim that policies developed in the U.S.-based international unions are sometimes more concerned with problems peculiar to the United States than to Canada. Some also believe that Canadian members of international unions pay substantially more in union dues to U.S. head offices of such unions than they get back in expertise and other services and in financial benefits. However, others have argued that Canadian workers benefit more, in job security, strike support, etc. by belonging to a large international union, with larger combined financial assets, better labour expertise, and political influence. Thus Canadian costs may be increased because of the reduction in access to union know-how and experience previously available in the U.S. Autonomy may also reduce access to the financial resources of the U.S. union.

In response, some international unions have set up separate Canadian units to take better account of the political, economic and social differences of Canadian life. Nevertheless, as the statistics attest, there has been a steady erosion over the last thirty years of Canadian membership in the international unions. Greater attention by the international unions to Canadian concerns has failed to prevent some Canadian branches of international unions from breaking away to set up their own Canadian unions. The most notable example of this secession from international unions was the breakaway of the Canadian locals of the United Auto Workers (UAW) to form the Canadian Auto Workers (CAW).

Women in Unions

The proportion of women in the unionized work force in Canada has increased drastically in recent years. This increase is due largely to the unionization of the public and quasi-public sectors. This growth in the proportion of women means that the concerns of women will demand greater support and attention in the labour union movement. Women who have in many instances become the prime wage earner for their families are concerned with their ability to manage their households, maintain relationships with their children, and cope with the stresses of their dual careers, one inside and one outside the home.

An immediate concern is the length of the work week and the scheduling of those hours of work. Maternity leave and maternity financial benefits have already become a major bargaining issue and concern with the problem of day care for the children of working mothers is bound to increase.

Women are taking on more leadership roles in the work force, although still proportionately less than the ratio of women to men in the labour movement. Nevertheless, central and provincial labour organizations have increased the number of women vice-presidents and in 1986 Shirley Carr became the first female president of the CLC, after a long union career in the public sector, as a member of the Canadian Union of Public Employees. Also, the CLC now has a Women's Bureau. As women come to occupy more and more leadership positions, their influence in the labour union movement will inevitably increase.

Largest Unions

The twenty-five largest labour unions, in terms of Canadian membership are shown in Table 4.5.

One interesting point to note is that the two largest labour unions in Canada are made up of government employees. Another labour union of government employees, the Public Service Alliance, is fifth. The United Steelworkers, which was, for many years, the largest union in Canada, has now dropped to sixth.

Degree of Union Membership

Not all industries have the same degree of union membership. Thus, there is very little unionization so far among workers in agriculture, trade, finance, insurance, real estate, and service industries generally. However, this picture has been changing in recent years with nurses, teachers, and bank clerks joining the ranks of organized labour. In some industries — for example, railways, transportation equipment, leather, and paper and allied industries — the degree of unionization is extremely high.

Persons Excluded from Membership

Certain persons may be excluded from membership under the federal and provincial labour relations acts. This means that the employer has no legal

Table 4.5 — *Twenty-five Largest Unions in Canada, 1990*

Labour union	Membership (000)
1. Canadian Union of Public Employees	376.9
2. National Union of Provincial Government Employees	301.2
3. United Food and Commercial Workers International Union	170.0
4. National Automobile Aerospace and Agricultural Implement Workers Union of Canada	167.4
5. Public Service Alliance of Canada	162.7
6. United Steelworkers of America	160.0
7. International Brotherhood of Teamsters, Chauffeurs, Warehousemen and Helpers' of America	100.0
8. Federation des affaires sociales inc. (CSN)	94.6
9. Federation des enseignantes et enseignants des commissions scolaires	75.0
10. Service Employees International Union	75.0
11. Canadian Paperworkers Union	69.0
12. International Brotherhood of Electrical Workers	64.5
13. United Brotherhood of Carpenters and Joiners of America	62.0
14. International Association of Machinists and Aerospace Workers	59.6
15. Labourers' International Union of North America	57.2
16. Ontario Nurses' Association	52.1
17. IWA — Canada	50.0
18. Canadian Union of Postal Workers	46.0
19. Ontario Secondary School Teachers Federation	43.3
20. Alberta Teachers' Association	42.5
21. Federation des infirmieres et infirmiers du Quebec	41.5
22. United Association of Journeymen and Apprentices of the Plumbing and Pipe Fitting Industry of the United States and Canada	40.0
23. Communications and Electrical Workers of Canada	40.0
24. Quebec Government Employees' Union Inc.	40.0
25. Canadian Brotherhood of Railway, Transport and General Workers	39.9

Source: Labour Canada, *Directory of Labour Organizations in Canada*

obligation to recognize or bargain collectively with unions representing such persons. In Ontario, for example, persons excluded from coverage under the Labour Relations Act include domestic workers employed in private homes; persons employed in agriculture, hunting, or trapping; workers engaged in landscaping and the growing of plants; and members of the architectural, dental, land surveying, legal or medical professions employed in a professional capacity. Members of the police force, full-time firefighters, teachers, and provincial government employees, are groups covered by their own collective bargaining legislation.

4.5 LABOUR UNION ORGANIZATION

A labour union has a central (or "national") office, with various departments, and a number of branches, geographically dispersed, called union locals.

Union Central Office

The central office of a labour union has a variety of responsibilities. First, it must decide policy for the union as a whole in such matters as collective bargaining, jurisdictional disputes, new branches, enrolment of new members, union dues, etc. Second, it must operate the union harmoniously as well as efficiently, maintaining contact with branches and assisting the union locals as the need arises. Third, it must administer the union's finances in an orderly and responsible fashion. And fourth, it must maintain contact with outside bodies such as the CLC, NDP, Labour Federations, etc., participating in various conferences and other meetings to decide on a common labour movement policy on matters of social, economic and political concern.

The union central office and its staff should have considerable knowledge and experience which should be of assistance to the group that is organizing, in a variety of ways. It can help them to organize and, if it is appropriate, set up a union local. When the time is appropriate, it can assist them to apply for certification and guide them through the certification process. After the union becomes certified, the "national" can provide assistance to them in regard to the negotiation of an agreement with the employer.

As desired and as appropriate, the central office can assist in subsequent negotiations.

Very often, during the life of the agreement, the central office will provide assistance in the processing of grievances with the employer. Also, because of its knowledge and experience, it will almost certainly assist in the presentation of arbitration cases.

Again, during the life of the labour agreement, problems will probably arise between the union local and the employer. Where resolution of the matter can be assisted by central office representatives, due to their greater experience and the credibility that this experience gives them with the employer, their assistance can be called upon.

The national, because of its size and its financial resources, can provide services, as required, to its various locals in regard to such specialized areas as legal assistance, financial analysis for purpose of negotiations, and perhaps public relations, etc.

Also, the "national" can and often does provide and coordinate assistance to the local during a strike.

The Union Local

The basic unit of a labour union, formed in a particular plant or locality, is known as the *local*. In the case of an industrial union, a local may consist of either the employees of several small firms in a given area or the employees of one large firm. In the case of a craft union, the membership usually consists of persons practising a common skill — for example, bricklaying — in a given area.

The *internal organization* of a typical local will vary considerably from one union to another. One example is shown in Figure 4.1.

Figure 4.1   *Example of the Organization of a Union Local*

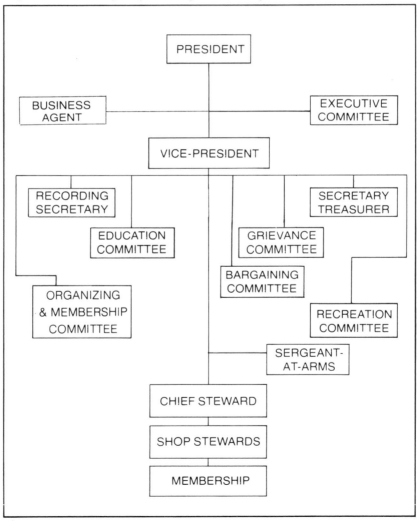

The union local has its own constitution, draws up its own bylaws governing the conduct of its officers and members, and has authority for such matters as: obtaining new members, handling grievances, collective bargaining, and recreational activities. Power is usually exercised by an executive committee, comprising the president, vice-president, and business agent. Part of this authority is delegated to the various other committees: the organizing and membership committee (which is responsible for recruiting new members); the bargaining committee that looks after negotiations for a new collective agreement: the grievance committee (which is concerned with the processing of grievances with the employer); the recreation committee (which looks after dances, parties, excursions, and so on); and the education committee (which provides information about union aims and activities to members and others). Having a constitution is a necessary step for a union local since in Ontario, for example, the Labour Relations Act requires a union to have a constitution before the provincial Labour Relations Board will consider the union's application for certification as bargaining agent.

In the plant itself, other union officials, called shop stewards, zone representatives, etc., look after the grievances submitted to them by union members. The senior steward for a particular area or division is known as the chief steward.

In the smaller locals, all the various positions are held on a voluntary part-time basis by union members working at their regular jobs. These persons are elected by the members of the local, for periods ranging from several months to several years. Only in the larger locals is there a full-time business agent whose salary is paid either by the local itself or by the national or international office. The part-time officials are reimbursed by the local for time taken from work for union business. If there is a business agent, he or she will handle much of the work of the union, helping in the enrollment of new members and in the representation of the union in grievance matters and in contract negotiations.

The powers of the local can vary considerably according to the labour union of which it is a part.

Decentralized Character of Unions

Unlike their counterparts in other parts of the world, most labour unions in Canada and the U.S. are highly decentralized. In other words, most of the action takes place at the local level rather than at the national level. It is the union local, close to the place of employment, where the new members are enlisted, where the employers send the union dues that are deducted from the worker's pay, where meetings are held to discuss the problems encountered by members at their work, where social activities are organized, where grievances are discussed, where the strike committees are formed, and where the president and other local officers as well as shop stewards are elected. Of course, the degree of autonomy that a union local enjoys will vary greatly from union to union. Nevertheless, compared with those in other countries, unions in North America are highly decentralized — with the local unions, to say nothing of the independently chartered local unions, enjoying a great deal of autonomy. Only in certain circumstances has the national or international union the right to interfere in local affairs. This high degree of local autonomy or decentralization is sometimes described as "grass- roots unionism". In some other countries, by contrast, the unions may not even have plant-level local organizations. All union matters are administered from the central office.

4.6 COLLECTIVE BARGAINING

Collective bargaining is the term used to describe the negotiations that take place between a labour union, collectively representing the employees of a plant or industry, and the employer or employers' association in drawing up a mutually acceptable labour-management agreement.

In line with the decentralized nature of Canadian and U.S. labour unions, most of the collective bargaining takes place at the local level. In the case of some large companies, the various locals will use a company-wide bargaining committee to negotiate certain company-wide issues, leaving local issues to be bargained on a local basis. Such a settlement might result in what is commonly called a company-wide "master agreement" with local supplements. In other words, each local union usually negotiates with the company that employs its members. In other countries such as West Germany and Sweden, collective bargaining is conducted at the national level by representatives of all the unions and employers in a particular industry and the agreement is binding nation-wide.

4.7 LABOUR COUNCILS

In Canada, the locals of many labour unions are affiliated with a Labour Council established by charter of the Canadian Labour Congress for their particular city or district — for example, the Toronto and District Labour Council (C.L.C.). The delegates from the various locals elect the Council's officers, who are responsible for furthering the interests of the labour union movement at the community level — for example, by lobbying municipal governments or by organizing strike aid. These district councils are sometimes called *joint boards* or *conference boards*.

In industries organized along craft lines (such as painting and decorating), unions or union locals in a particular area may form a special council to co-ordinate members' activities and resolve jurisdictional problems. Such a council is sometimes called an *Allied Trades Federation*.

4.8 LABOUR FEDERATIONS

Most provinces have a Federation of Labour, chartered by the Canadian Labour Congress, which acts as the central organization for the labour union movement in the province. The Federation holds annual conventions where delegates from the affiliated locals vote on policy matters and elect officers. The purpose of the Federation is to represent labour's interest at the provincial level, particularly in the establishment or amendment of labour legislation by the provincial government — for example, lobbying for guaranteed severance pay for workers whose employers declare bankruptcy.

4.9 CANADIAN LABOUR CONGRESS

The major central organization for labour unions in Canada is the *Canadian Labour Congress*, with headquarters in Ottawa and regional offices in most of the provinces. Most international, national and local unions, and all labour councils and federations are directly affiliated with the C.L.C. and send delegates to its biennial conventions.

Purpose

The purpose of the C.L.C. is primarily a political one: to act as the common spokesperson, particularly in Ottawa, for organized labour throughout Canada. It is also active in helping to settle *jurisdictional disputes* among the affiliated unions. These are disputes in which two or more unions claim the right to be certified as the bargaining agent for the same group of employees — employees who may or may not already be represented by a union. It also endeavours to ensure the observance of its Code of Ethical Practices. Another important function is to represent Canadian organized labour in international labour organizations such as the International Confederation of Free Trade Unions and the Commonwealth Trade Union. It also represents Canadian labour at international labour conferences.

The CLC also has a political role — it tries to influence federal and provincial government policies and the administration of existing labour and other relevant legislation by an ongoing program of communication. When new government or administration practices are being considered, the CLC tries to influence the outcome by such means as general and informal communication, formal presentations to government bodies or groups whose function it is to investigate a particular matter and make recommendations for action.

The CLC also tries to provide information and communicate its point of view through press releases and other representations to the written media, as well as to radio and television stations.

In Canada, labour relations is primarily within the jurisdiction of the provinces, so the CLC has provincial federations in order to exert political influence at the provincial level.

Jurisdictional Matters

The CLC consists of a number of different unions each with its own labour jurisdiction. This jurisdiction is as it was when the CLC was founded on May 1, 1956 or as subsequently granted or amended by the CLC. However, circumstances change — for example, companies merge, technological methods change, and new areas of union activity or interest emerge. Also, different labour unions may have different viewpoints and opinions as to their duty, opportunity and ability (a) to provide appropriate representation and support to employees in process of unionization and (b) to undertake activities to support and maintain the welfare of existing union members. The CLC attempts to resolve such interjurisdictional disputes.

Ethics

The CLC is also responsible for enforcing the Code of Ethical Practices contained in its constitution. The Code provides for, amongst other things, the right of union members to have honest elections, to run for office, and to receive fair treatment in the application of union rules. The CLC is also responsible for prohibiting corrupt practices.

If one of its member unions breaks the rules, the CLC must try to persuade the offending union to change its behaviour. If the offending union persists, the CLC may vote, at its regular convention, to expel the union from its organization.

4.10 THE CLC AND THE CANADIANIZATION OF INTERNATIONAL UNIONS IN CANADA

The CLC has long been concerned with the Canadianization of the Canadian branches of international unions. Thus, at its 1974 Convention, the CLC reaffirmed and expanded the standards of self-government that it had previously established for the affiliated Canadian divisions of international unions.

These standards provide for the election of Canadian officers by Canadian union members, the determination of policies dealing with national matters by elected Canadian officers and members, and the requirement that only Canadian elected representatives have the authority to speak for the union concerned in Canada. As regards affiliation to an international union organization, the Canadian division should be affiliated separately to ensure proper Canadian representation. Also, the international union must take the necessary action to ensure that the Canadian union membership is not prevented by constitutional requirements or policy decisions from taking part in the social, cultural, economic and political life of Canada.

4.11 POLITICAL ROLE OF LABOUR UNIONS

Labour unions through their various provincial and national labour organizations, can exert pressure in municipal, provincial, and federal politics by offering support to political parties willing to help promote union aims. Labour unions also make direct representations to the provincial and federal governments on matters of urgent importance such as a high rate of unemployment or the need for price or profit controls. The labour movement, as a whole, usually through the CLC, provides financial and other support to the New Democratic Party, or NDP.

Political Conservatism

A characteristic of Canadian and U.S. labour unions is their basic acceptance of the political and economic systems of their countries. Their emphasis, therefore, is not on radical political and economic change but on the economic welfare of their members. Only in recent years have Canadian labour unions become more active politically, with increased financial and other support to the New Democratic Party. And this party, although occupying the left-wing of the political spectrum in Canada, is not a radical political movement of the Marxist-Leninist type. It is certainly not dedicated to the overthrow of the Canadian political system and the predominantly private enterprise system that exists in this country.

The increasing number of Canadian labour unions has had its effect on the political scene. Canadian unions tend to be more politically oriented than U.S. unions and Canadian autonomy for many former Canadian branches of U.S.-based international unions has given the new Canadian unions more opportunity to debate particularly Canadian social issues such as health insurance plans, pensions, unemployment insurance, and political support for the New Democratic Party (NDP). However, Canadian autonomy has, conversely, lessened the ability of Canadian union members to influence government policy in the United States which could ultimately have an adverse effect on job opportunities in Canada.

4.12 ECONOMIC GOALS OF LABOUR UNIONS

The primary goal of the labour unions active in Canada is to secure from employers greater economic benefits for their members. This includes better pay and fringe benefits as well as greater job security and improvements in working conditions, including occupational health and safety. This union philosophy, with its emphasis on economic rather than political goals, is sometimes called "business unionism". However, so far as most Canadian and American union leaders are concerned, North American style democracy and the private enterprise system, despite their faults, have provided union members in this continent with one of the highest material standards of living in the world.

KEY CONCEPTS

Labour organization	*CLC*
Labour union	*CSN*
Trade union	*CSD*
Employee association	*CCU*
Craft union	*AFL*
Industrial union	*CIO*
General union	*Union membership*
Non-union plants	*Union central (or "national") office*
International union	*Union local*
National Union	*Decentralization*
Directly chartered local unions	*Labour Council*
	Labour Federation
Independent local organization	*Canadian Labour Congress*
Congress affiliation	*Political goals*
	Economic goals

REVIEW QUESTIONS

1. How would you define a labour union or trade union? Is there any difference between the meaning of these terms?

2. Distinguish between a trade union and an employee association.

3. Why do people join labour unions? Why do they sometimes refuse to join?

4. Distinguish between craft unions and industrial unions.

5. Distinguish between international and national unions.

6. What are the two basic types of local labour organizations?

7. Explain the following abbreviations: CLC, CSN, CSD, CCU, AFL-CIO.

8. How substantial is union membership in Canada? Is membership increasing as a percentage of the labour force?

9. To what extent is union membership Canadianized?

10. What proportion of union members are female? What effect can increasing female participation have on the Canadian labour movement?

11. Which are the largest trade unions, by membership, in Canada? What type of unions are they?

12. Why are some industries more heavily unionized than others?

13. In which industries has union membership been rapidly growing in recent times? Why?

14. Which persons are excluded from coverage under the federal and provincial labour relations acts?

15. Explain the possible role of a union central office, or "national".

16. How is the union local typically organized? What is the local's role?

17. What is the role of the shop steward? How is he or she selected? What qualifications does he or she need?

18. What is a union "business agent"? What does he or she do?

19. Explain the nature and purpose of (a) labour councils, (b) labour federations and (c) the Canadian Labour Congress. How are they linked together?

20. One of the functions of the CLC is to help settle "jurisdictional disputes" among affiliated unions. Explain.

21. Why are North American labour unions said to be highly decentralized? What are the possible reasons for this? What are its benefits for union members?

22. Compare the local collective bargaining that takes place in North America with the system in West Germany and Sweden.

23. What is the CLC's attitude towards Canadianization of the labour movement in Canada?

24. North American labour unions are said to be guided by a philosophy of "business unionism". Explain and discuss.

CHAPTER 5: THE CANADIAN LABOUR MOVEMENT — HISTORY AND PHILOSOPHY

Chapter Objectives

- *To review the nineteenth century origins of Canada's labour movement*

- *To explain how many Canadian unions gradually became "internationalized"*

- *To describe the Winnipeg general strike, its causes and effects*

- *To chronicle the sufferings of labour in Canada and the U.S. during the Great Depression and the resultant changes in labour legislation*

- *To explain the enmity that arose between craft unions and industrial unions*

- *To indicate how the Second World War affected the Canadian labour movement*

- *To detail the post-war strife between labour and management and the reasons for it*

- *To describe the growth of the Quebec labour movement*

Chapter Outline

5.1 Nineteenth Century Origins

5.2 National versus International Unions

5.3 The Winnipeg General Strike

5.4 The Depression Years

5.5 Craft Unions versus Industrial Unions

5.6 The Second World War and its Aftermath

5.7 Labour Unions in Quebec

5.1 NINETEENTH CENTURY ORIGINS

Historically, the Canadian labour movement can trace its origins to the early nineteenth century when several small local unions were formed among skilled workers to fight particular issues. Thus, for example, printers were organized in Quebec City in 1827 and in Montreal and Hamilton in 1833. In Toronto the York Printers were organized in 1832. However, most of the early efforts to form unions were of relatively short duration. One exception was the Toronto Typographical Union which was established in 1844 and has existed ever since. An unsympathetic government, employer opposition, worker apathy, and a still predominantly rural society all helped check the growth of unions in Canada. Also, extremely important, under the common law inherited from Britain and based on precedent (or prior court decisions), persons organizing a union or calling a strike might well be charged with the criminal offence of "conspiracy to restrain trade" and, on being found guilty, subject to imprisonment and heavy fines. Only towards the end of the nineteenth century was legislation passed by the Canadian Parliament to help prevent this. And only towards the end of the century did government leaders, federal and provincial, start to give mild approval to the concept of trade unions and the collective bargaining process.

Unfortunately, during this long period of union growth, there was a great deal of dissension among the various unions based largely on two basic ideological conflicts: the first between craft unions and industrial unions on grounds of membership eligibility; and the second between national and international unions on grounds of nationalism. Nevertheless, with growing economic prosperity, linked in part to the introduction of tariff protection in 1879 and the building of the Canadian Pacific Railway in the years 1881 to 1885, more and more workers joined labour unions. In fact railway unions just followed the railroad westward. In Nova Scotia in 1879, the coal miners formed the first coal miners' union in North America. This union, the Provincial Workmen's Association, was later broadened to include many different types of workers as well as coal miners — for example, iron workers, steel workers, railway men, tramway men, glass blowers, boot and shoe workers, and retail clerks — a classic example of a "general union".

External Influences

Immigrants to Canada during the nineteenth century included many persons who had been active in labour unions in the British Isles. As a result, several British unions established locals or branches in Canada.

Thus, for example, the Amalgamated Society of Engineers set up its first local in Canada in 1850 and three more in 1851. Also, a number of immigrants already familiar with the concept of trade unions, helped establish Canadian unions without any official assistance. Examples of the establishment of such purely Canadian local unions were the shipbuilders at Quebec City and Victoria in 1862, and a variety of trades in Quebec in 1865, including bakers, tailors, bricklayers, stonecutters, wharf-porters, longshoremen, and bookbinders.

Although British immigrants were and still are very active in the Canadian labour movement, the closeness of the United States has made the American unions the predominant external influence on organized labour in Canada. The first union to come to Canada was the Iron Moulders in 1861 followed by, for example, the Locomotive Engineers in 1864; the National Typographical Society, and the Cigarmakers in 1865; the Knights of St. Crispin (shoemakers) in 1867; the Railway Conductors in 1868; and the Coopers in 1869.

Trades Councils

Initially, the various trade unions were solely preoccupied with their own affairs. However, in 1871, five craft unions joined to form the Toronto Trades Assembly. And by 1873, Trades Councils, uniting various local unions, were active in Ottawa and Hamilton. In that same year, on the initiative of the Toronto Trades Assembly, a convention of trade unions was held in Toronto, attended by delegates from 31 locals of 14 unions located in Ontario. Letters of approval were also received from Typographical unions in Quebec City and Montreal. At this convention, it was decided to establish a central national labour organization, to be called the Canadian Labour Union. Meetings of the C.L.U. were then held in each of the years from 1874 to 1877. However, the serious economic depression that afflicted Canada beginning in 1878 caused the meetings to come to a halt.

In 1881, after the depression, the Toronto Trades Assembly was replaced by the Toronto Trades and Labour Council. Other labour councils were formed in London, Montreal, Ottawa, Brantford, Hamilton, Vancouver, and Victoria during the 1880s. Nationally, a convention of labour unions, organized by the Toronto Council in 1883, established a new central labour organization, which later came to be known as The Trades and Labour Congress.

5.2 NATIONAL VERSUS INTERNATIONAL UNIONS

Initially, the unions formed in Canada were purely Canadian ones with no outside links. However, in the 1860s, some of the craft unions such as printers and moulders, began to establish fraternal, and later formal, links with similar U.S. unions. The incentives to do so were several: the greater opportunity for a Canadian union member with a union card to find work in the U.S., should he decide to move South; the greater psychological strength derived from membership in a larger organization of similar craftsmen; and greater financial strength. The American union that ''took in'' a Canadian branch came to be called an International Union. These international unions, exclusively of the craft type, were joined together in the U.S. in a central organization called the American Federation of Labour, or AFL for short.

The international unions gradually became stronger in Canada so that in 1902, for example, under pressure from the AFL, the Trades and Labour Congress, Canada's central labour body, even amended its constitution to the effect that it would not recognize a national union if an international union existed in that same jurisdiction. Furthermore, at this same convention, the TLC elected John Flett, a paid officer of an international union, as its new president. It also refused to seat delegates from the Montreal Federated Trades Council, a purely Canadian body.

In Quebec, unions of French-speaking workers, completely independent from the international unions, were formed with the active encouragement of the Catholic Church.

5.3 THE WINNIPEG GENERAL STRIKE

On May 15, 1919, a variety of unions went on strike in Winnipeg because of the refusal of Winnipeg employers to negotiate with a newly established metal trades council. The metal trades workers, who earned from $12 to $15 a week, were incensed by the fact that, because of inflation, the purchasing power of their wages had fallen drastically while employers had benefitted from high profits throughout the war. The strikers' demands included: (a) recognition of the metal trades council, (b) an 8-hour day and a maximum 44-hour week, (c) double rate of pay for overtime work and 1-hour premium pay for night-shift work, and (d) a pay rate of 85 cents per hour for skilled workers and 25 cents per hour for apprentices.

Sympathy with the metal workers was widespread, fuelled in large part by general dissatisfaction with Canada's social and economic system, particularly the high rates of inflation and unemployment, the latter being aggravated by soldiers returning from the first World War. Workers who went on strike to support the metal workers' demands were from both the private and public sectors, including postal workers and the police. The strikers effectively halted all production, construction, transportation, and communications in Winnipeg and the surrounding areas and succeeded in closing the hotels, banks, and other main buildings. A Central Strike Committee comprising 287 delegates (three from each of 94 union locals and five from the TLC) administered the strike.

The Canadian Prime Minister, Robert Borden, arguing that public servants had no right to strike, sent the RCMP to Winnipeg, followed by a battalion of soldiers and two Lewis machine guns. The federal government then ordered all postal workers back. Likewise, the provincial government ordered back all telephone workers, and the municipal government all police and firemen. However, the postal workers and police refused to return and most were dismissed.

The principal leaders of the strike were then arrested on June 17 and held in jail for 72 hours. That same day, in front of the Winnipeg Town Hall, a large crowd assembled only to have the Riot Act read to them by the mayor and to become involved in a confrontation with 50 mounted RCMP and "special" police, that ended with two persons being killed and 30 injured. The Canadian government then placed the city under military rule and many arrests were made. On June 26, the strike effectively broken, people returned to work. Many were locked out, blacklisted, dismissed or otherwise discriminated against.

5.4 THE DEPRESSION YEARS

In the fall of 1929, the stock market collapsed, to be followed by the worst economic depression in history. By 1932, at the bottom of the "Great Depression", about one-third of the labour force in Canada and the United States was unemployed. Even for those fortunate enough to have jobs, conditions were bad. Hours of work were long, wages were low, and wage cutting was rampant.

Workers Unity League

The increasing mass misery gave impetus to a new group — the *Workers Unity League*, founded in 1930. Included in it were unions like the Amalgamated Mine Workers of Nova Scotia, the Mine Workers Industrial Union, and a number of Textile, Furniture and Rubber locals in Ontario.

The WUL never became a major force in Canadian trade union life but it was important. In 1932, its membership was reported to be 40,000. It was active in organizing the non-union workers and in helping to conduct strikes. In fact, in 1934 it claimed leadership in 90% of the strikes that had been fought. Its constituent unions were all national and industrial, in line with its support of the principle of Canadian as compared with international (or U.S. dominated) industrial unions. When its membership is combined with that of the Canadian and Catholic Confederation of Labour and all Canadian Congress of Labour, it shows that by the middle 1930s about half the total trade union membership in Canada was grouped in national unions.

Major Strikes

Bitter strikes were fought in those early depression years. For example, in September 1931, at Estevan, Saskatchewan, 500 coal miners, members of the Mine Workers Union of Canada (WUL) went on strike when the mine owners refused to negotiate. The miners demanded an eight-hour day, a minimum of $5.40 per day for underground work, and union recognition. Present in Estevan were 47 RCMP constables armed with rifles, revolvers, and machine guns. As the strikers passed by the town hall, the RCMP and local police opened fire. Three miners were killed, between 12 and 18 wounded, and almost 50 arrested. Across Canada, trade union sympathy was stirred, resulting in resolutions and protest demonstrations. Following this show of support, the Estevan strike was soon settled. The terms included recognition of the union district committee, an 8-hour day for contract work, and the miners' right to appoint their own checkmen — in sum, a partial victory for the union.

Another major strike was that of the Stratford Furniture Workers in 1933. The authorities sent in troops, tanks, and machine guns. The strikers countered with mass picketing. The outcome was a partial victory for the strikers; wage increases ranging from 10 to 25%, a 45-hour week, and recognition of the shop committee. The strike was led by the WUL but it won assistance from locals of other unions and received express support from the Trades and Labour Congress.

The U.S. Experience

In the United States, 1932 was a presidential election year. Franklin D. Roosevelt, who campaigned on the program of a "New Deal", was elected president. In his campaign, he gave clear evidence of his sympathy for the labourers and pledged assistance for the "forgotten men at the bottom of the economic pyramid".

In March 1932, labour had received some encouragement from the passage of the Norris-LaGuardia Act (The Federal Anti-injunction Act). It held no solution for the troublesome unemployment of the day but did mark a significant advance for collective bargaining. The full freedom of collective association without the interference of employers was declared as public policy.

At the time of Roosevelt's election, the American and in effect the whole North American economy could be described as being in a deflationary spiral. In order for the manufacturer to sell its goods, it often had to cut its prices. After it cut its prices and sold its goods, it went back and cut wages in order to get its costs in line.

Immediately after the Presidential inauguration in 1933, a great deal of legislation was quickly passed. Much of it was intended to get the economy moving again. Some of this legislation, with the purpose of ending the downward spiral of prices, allowed employers to form associations which were allowed to exchange information on pricing. Some of the legislation was designed to create public works projects such as the Tennessee Valley Authority to create job opportunities for the unemployed. One of the more important pieces of legislation was the National Industrial Recovery Act (NIRA) of 1933.

Section 7A of this Act guaranteed the right of employees to organize into unions of their own choosing and to bargain collectively with employers. Although the basic purpose of the NIRA was, in the President's words, to put people back to work, it meant far more than that to American labour. Confident in the protection of the law, labour commenced organizing and recruiting campaigns everywhere. However, in May 1935, the NIRA was declared invalid. This was a severe blow to union aspirations.

A new deal for labour made its appearance with the passage of the National Labour Relations Act (the Wagner Act) in 1935. Incorporated into this Act were the provisions of Section 7A of the NIRA. However, the incentive for union growth provided by the Act was subject to delay. Many employers doubting the validity of the new legislation refused either in spirit or in practice to carry out its provisions. But in April 1937 the U.S. Supreme Court validated the Act and labour got legal sanctions for further advances.

5.5 CRAFT UNIONS VERSUS INDUSTRIAL UNIONS

All the early trade unions in Canada and elsewhere were associations of persons performing a certain type of skill or trade — for example, carpenters or bricklayers. However, other unions came to be formed, the membership of which was open to all persons working in a certain company or industry. This new type of union came to be known as an ''industrial union''. The most important early example of such a union in North America was the Knights of Labor established in the 1880s, with many locals in Ontario and Quebec as well as in the United States, particularly Chicago. The craft unions were opposed to industrial unions in large part because they feared that craft workers in a particular company or industry might join the industrial union rather than the craft one. However, the growth of the manufacturing industry, with an increasing number of relatively unskilled jobs, meant that the industrial unions had more and more potential members. The craft unions, on the other hand, had a more gradual increase in the number of potential members. The Knights of Labor, one of the strongest of the early industrial unions, became gradually weaker, giving way to other industrial unions.

American Federation of Labour

The conflict between craft and industrial unions became the subject of bitter debate at the annual convention of the American Federation of Labour, or AFL, in San Francisco in 1934.

The national unions composing the AFL were of the craft or horizontal type. They were constituted of a rather homogeneous level of skilled labour stretching laterally over many different types of industries. The United Brotherhood of Carpenters and Joiners, for example, included carpenters who were employed in building a house, in a cabinet shop, or on shipboard. The important thing was skill, knowledge, and training of the carpenter, no matter where he was found.

The non-AFL unions were of the industrial or vertical type. The mere fact that a person was employed in a certain industry made him eligible for membership. No particular skill was necessary. Only because of this could the great mass of workers carry their collective bargaining ambitions to fruition.

At the AFL's San Francisco convention, it was finally agreed that union charters would be issued in the automotive, cement, and aluminum industries and in ''such other mass production and miscellaneous industries that in the judgement of the executive council may be necessary to meet the situation''. It also authorized the council to ''inaugurate, manage, promote, and conduct'' an organizing campaign in the steel industry as soon as practical. During the next months, the AFL granted charters to unions in the automobile and rubber industries. In defining the jurisdiction of these unions, the executive council specifically excluded certain skilled craftsmen and maintenance employees who already came under the jurisdiction of existing craft unions. This was a source of much irritation to the industrial unions. However, the crowning blow occurred when the steel organizing drive failed to materialize. The executive council reported that "we did not deem it advisable to launch an organizing drive for the steel industry". As far as the industrial union element within its ranks was concerned, the AFL had added insult to injury.

Congress of Industrial Organizations

In November 1935, the industrial union crusaders completed plans to set up their own Committee for Industrial Organization (CIO) with John L. Lewis as chairman. The ten unions participating in the CIO were then suspended from the AFL. In May 1937, Lewis and his associates transformed the Committee into the Congress of Industrial Organizations.

The organizing efforts of the CIO in the late 1930s were helped by the provisions of the Wagner Act but ran into very strong resistance in the major industrial mass production units such as the steel, packing house, and automotive industries in the United States. Gradually over that period the CIO was successful, in spite of very considerable violence, in organizing large numbers of employees in these industries and in negotiating contracts with their employers.

The leaders of the CIO recognized that part of the reason for their success in the United States was the Wagner Act. They also realized that there was no equivalent to the Wagner Act in Canada. They believed the CIO was making a significant contribution toward improving the welfare of industrial workers in the United States and believed that Canadian workers should also have improved conditions and that the CIO was the organization that could bring this about. In addition to that, they recognized that many of the employers that had strongly resisted the CIO in the United States had branch plants in Canada. One of the methods available to these employers to resist the CIO in the United States was to expand their operations in Canada, thereby exporting American jobs to Canadian workers. For both of these reasons, the CIO unions moved into Canada to conduct strong organizing campaigns.

Along with the CIO unions, other industrial unions became more active in Canada. As a result of the general economic conditions of Canadian workers, the rise of Canadian industrial unions, and the activity of the CIO, a strike movement began in Canada in 1937. In the winter of 1937, 850 workers at Empire Cottons struck against conditions branded by Ontario Minister David Croll as brutal underpayment and shameless exploitation.

However, the largest textile strike was in Quebec at Dominion Textiles. Hours were 60 per week on the night shift and sixty-four per week on the day shift. Wages were as low as $3.50 per week for women. The workers who were members of the National Federation of Textile Workers, an affiliate of the Canadian Catholic Confederation of Labour, or CCCL, demanded a 40-hour week, a wage increase, and union recognition. The company refused to negotiate. Strike fever mounted and, in August 1937, employees went on strike at Montreal, Valleyfield, Drummondville, Magog, Sherbrooke, St. Gregoire, and Montmorency. Maurice Duplessis, just elected for his first term as premier of Quebec, proposed that Cardinal Villeneuve mediate. The union accepted and recommended a return to work. An agreement concluded later between the company and the union granted wages increases and a 50-hour week.

The automotive industry was another storm centre. Oshawa 1937 its eye. On April 8, 4 000 General Motors workers went on strike for a forty-hour week, pay at time-and-half for overtime, recognition of shop stewards, seniority, and recognition of the union, the United Automobile Workers.

Ontario Premier Mitchell Hepburn said he would break the strike. He branded the CIO communist and sent in a special squad of Provincial Police which was assisted in turn by a contingent of the RCMP. He said he would, if necessary, raise an army too. The strikers continued to picket in numbers reaching 600 and set up their own strike police. Across Canada, many labour councils called for solidarity with the strikers. Two members of Hepburn's cabinet submitted their resignations. The strike ended with a settlement for a forty-four hour week, wage increases, recognition for the stewards, and no discrimination against the striking employees.

5.6 THE SECOND WORLD WAR AND ITS AFTERMATH

In 1939, Canada went to war. During the war-time years, the union movement made great advances. Production expanded enormously. Between 1939 and 1944 the value of manufactured goods annually produced increased from 3 billion dollars to 9 billion dollars. Over a million men and women were engaged directly in the "war effort". Union membership more than doubled between 1940 and 1945.

However, during the war, the Federal government introduced wage and price controls. And the unions, to support the war effort, generally followed a no-strike policy.

During the war, labour relations, which is largely a matter of provincial jurisdiction, was taken over by the Federal government under the war emergency provisions. Orders-in-council were passed dealing with labour relations and some of these gave labour certain rights, some of which resembled rights provided in the United States under the Wagner Act. After the war, provincial labour relations jurisdiction was returned to the provinces and provincial Labour Relations Acts were passed. While these Acts vary they have certain similarities and some of their provisions were somewhat similar to provisions of the Wagner Act.

In 1945, with the war at an end, there was considerable economic uncertainty. Whereas the 1930s were typified by economic depression and mass unemployment, the years 1940 to 1945 were typified by full employment caused by the war effort. When the war ended, some people expected full employment to continue, while others expected the economy to revert to the conditions of the 1930s.

Unions had made a great deal of progress in organization during the war years. However, the objectives of both union leaders and the union membership had been severely restricted by war-time wage and price controls. Consequently, in 1946, strikes broke out right across Canada from Cape Breton to Vancouver Island, affecting one major industry after another, mostly in manufacturing but also in mining, logging, and transportation. The strike movement began in May when the British Columbia loggers, members of the International Woodworkers of America, walked out. Then came strikes of seamen, textile workers, and rubber workers. Later, electrical and steel workers in Hamilton went on strike. Then in the Fall, lumber workers in Northern Ontario left their jobs. Generally, these strikes had one common characteristic — they were won by the unions.

Union Rivalry

During the 1940s, there was constant rivalry in recruiting union members, both craft and industrial, between the AFL and TLC on the one side and the CIO and CCL on the other. In the 1950s, however, it became apparent that it was becoming more and more difficult to obtain new members. Consequently, in June 1954, the presidents of the AFL and the CIO, George Meany and Walter Reuther, agreed to a two-year no-raiding pact. Then in February 1955, a merger of the AFL and CIO was decided upon, with George Meany as president and over 15 million members. This was followed in April 1956 by the merger in Canada of the TLC and the CCL, the main rival union federations, to form the Canadian Labour Congress (CLC), with over one million members.

The dominance of U.S.-controlled, "international unions" continued in Canada for many years. However, over the last twenty-five years, Canadian nationalism has begun to be felt more and more strongly in the union movement. One dramatic example was the formation in 1974 of the Canadian Paperworkers Union by breakaway members of the United Paperworkers International Union. And many other national unions have been formed in Canada over recent decades — for example, the Canadian

Autoworkers Union. The international unions themselves, in recognition of Canadian nationalism, have gradually reduced control over their Canadian sections so as to discourage any further breakaways.

5.7 LABOUR UNIONS IN QUEBEC

The growth of labour unions in Quebec was greatly influenced by the Roman Catholic church which desired that French-Canadian workers remain French in language and Catholic in religion. To the Roman Catholic clergy, as well as to many other French Canadians, the activities of the English-speaking American and Canadian labour unions could only mean a further loss of Quebec's cultural identity. Consequently, following a lockout in the boot and shoe industry in Quebec City in 1900, that was arbitrated by the Archbishop of Quebec, new and solely French-speaking unions were formed with the assistance of the Roman Catholic clergy, in various industries in the province.

Later, following the establishment of various central councils, a permanent province-wide federation of these French- Canadian unions came into being in 1921, called the Confederation des Travailleurs Catholiques du Canada (CTCC). However, the CTCC and its affiliated unions, although French-Canadian, were not militant enough in the nineteen-twenties and thirties to attract the majority of French-Canadian unionists. In fact, well under half of such workers belonged to the French-Canadian unions.

During and after World War II, the situation changed rapidly. First, Quebec became much more industrialized, with a consequent influx of workers to the towns and cities. Second, the Catholic unionists, led by new and more aggressive non-clerical officials, became more and more dissatisfied with the large wage gap between themselves and English-speaking workers in certain industries and trades.

In 1949, this dissatisfaction erupted in a bitter and violent strike by the asbestos workers in Quebec. On the one side were the striking workers, supported by the Roman Catholic Church; and on the other, the employer, the subsidiary of a large American company, supported by the provincial Duplessis government. The latter, a supporter of the *status quo*, even went so far as to declare the strike illegal, decertify the union, and send in several hundred heavily armed police to keep order.

The QFL and the CTCC

Although the workers' gains were minimal, the CTCC acquired considerable prestige among Quebec workers for its firm stand. It also helped convince the CTCC that it should seek allies among other labour organizations rather than trying to operate independently. However, although the rival provincial federations of the Trades and Labour Congress of Canada (TLC) and the Canadian Congress of Labour (CCL) merged in 1956 into a new CLC-sponsored Quebec Federation of Labour, the QFL remained suspicious of the CTCC and unresponsive to its overtures. Nevertheless, the two main labour organizations did co-operate on certain issues such as the strike by copper mining and smelting workers in Murdochville, Quebec. However, in 1959, the lack of support by English-speaking Canadians for the CBC producers strike in Montreal, together with a hostile attitude by the executives of the CLC parent union towards their French-speaking locals, persuaded the latter to switch their allegiance to the CTCC. This event marked the end of any further cooperation between the two central labour federations in Quebec, the QFL and the CTCC.

Confederation of National Trade Unions

At its 1960 convention, the CTCC, changed its name to the Confederation des Syndicats Nationaux (CSN), thereby dropping its identification with the Catholic Church. During the nineteen sixties, the Confederation of National Trade Unions, or CNTU, as the CSN was called in English, more than doubled its membership. This was due in part to a new more liberal Quebec labour code. Membership by the end of the decade was over two hundred thousand, including six former CLC unions.

During the nineteen seventies and the nineteen eighties, the leadership of both the CNTU and the QFL in Quebec became more radical in character, with a more aggressive stance in support of labour negotiations by member unions. Today, politically, the Quebec labour movement is sympathetic to the Parti Quebecois.

KEY CONCEPTS

Conspiracy to restrict trade

Membership eligibility

Nationalism

External influences

Trade councils

National unions

International unions

General strike

Great Depression

New Deal

Craft unions

Industrial unions

American Federation of Labour

Committee for Industrial Organization

War effort

Union rivalry

Quebec Federation of Labour

Confederation of National Trade Unions

REVIEW QUESTIONS

1. What factors delayed the growth of trade unions in Canada during the nineteenth century?

2. Compare the British and American influence in the development of trade unions in Canada.

3. Explain the nature and role of trades councils in the trade union movement in the late nineteenth century.

4. Explain the reasons for the early popularity of international unions in Canada.

5. Describe and assess the significance of the Winnipeg general strike of 1919.

6. What was the effect of the "Depression" on the Canadian trade union movement in the nineteen thirties?

7. Compare and discuss the handling of the Estevan and Stratford strikes in the 1930s with the way that strikes are handled today.

8. How did Franklin D. Roosevelt and his "New Deal" affect the trade union movement in the United States and Canada?

9. Explain and discuss the reasons for the conflict between the craft and industrial unions in both the United States and Canada.

10. Why did the CIO unions move into Canada to conduct strong organizing campaigns?

11. Why did the AFL and CIO eventually decide to merge?

12. "Canadian nationalism is slowly beginning to make itself felt in the trade union movement." Explain and discuss.

13. Why did the Church become involved in the union movement in Quebec? How long did this involvement last? How and why was its influence eventually reduced?

14. What were the effects on the Quebec labour movement of the asbestos workers' strike in 1949?

15. What were the two rival labour federations in Quebec? Why were they rivals?

16. "Through its support for the Parti Quebecois, organized labour in Quebec won many goals that would otherwise have had to be fought for on the factory floor." Explain and discuss.

CHAPTER 6: EMPLOYERS: ORGANIZATIONS, ATTITUDES AND PRACTICES

Chapter Objectives

- *To distinguish between the different types of employer associations*
- *To explain why employer associations have come to exist*
- *To clarify the legal status of employer associations*
- *To spell out employer attitudes towards labour unions*
- *To list and explain the various methods some employers use to oppose unions*

Chapter Outline

6.1 Types of Employers Associations

6.2 Employer Associations and Collective Bargaining

6.3 Legal Status of Employer Associations

6.4 Employer Attitudes

6.5 Anti-union Practices

6.1 TYPES OF EMPLOYERS' ASSOCIATIONS

There are many different types of employers' associations in Canada that are involved in industrial relations. As the great diversity suggests, lack of employer unity is a key characteristic, compared with other countries such as Germany and Sweden.

Bargaining Associations. Some employers' associations — in, for example, clothing, printing, construction and trucking — act as the formal bargaining agent for their members. They are in effect, therefore, ''bar-

91

gaining associations''. The reason for their establishment is that in these industries there are many small firms representing employers on the one hand but only one common trade union or group of unions representing the employees on the the other. Such associations, acting on behalf of their member employers, undertake the bargaining with the union, sign the collective agreement, and may even administer the agreement. Sometimes an employer association may carry out the bargaining with the union but the member firms will each sign a separate collective agreement and administer it themselves. In this case, the organization may be known as a ''consultative association''.

Co-ordinating Associations. Other associations such as the Railway Association of Canada act only as a ''co-ordinating association'' — co-ordinating the collective bargaining activities of their members.

Educational Associations. Other associations such as the Canada Construction Association and the Canada Pulp and Paper Association serve mainly as an ''educational association'' — educating members in all aspects of industrial relations and acting as a central depository for all information useful for collective bargaining purposes.

Lobbying Associations. Some employer organizations such as the Canadian Chamber of Commerce and the Canadian Manufacturers' Association do not participate at all, either directly or indirectly, in the collective bargaining process. Instead, they act as a spokesperson for employers in Ottawa and the provincial capitals. They are what may be called ''lobbying associations''.

6.2 EMPLOYERS' ASSOCIATIONS AND COLLECTIVE BARGAINING

The practice by some employers of joining together in associations to negotiate with unions is an attempt by employers to strengthen their bargaining position. It is considered a logical move designed to counteract, to some extent, the increasing strength of labour unions in modern times.

By joining together, employers can agree beforehand on a desirable and realistic level of wages, fringe benefits and other conditions of employment and negotiate more effectively, using specialized, full-time negotiators, to achieve a settlement with the union as close to these goals as possible. Also, after a settlement has been reached, the members of the employers' association have the satisfaction of knowing that everyone is in the same boat — no employer has a competitive advantage over another as all wage and benefit increases and non-monetary concessions are the same for all members.

Another advantage for employers of a common front is that, if there is a strike, public and government attention and, hopefully, support will be forthcoming more quickly than if an individual firm is shut down.

In some industries, such as construction, where many different types of workers are employed, it is much more convenient for employers to negotiate as an association with the various unions. Each type of worker — for example, carpenters — can be covered by a master agreement that is effective for all employers in the association. If there is no employer association, a union or group of unions may be tempted to strike one company so as to secure a generous settlement that can be used as a standard in negotiations with the other employers.

6.3 LEGAL STATUS OF EMPLOYERS' ASSOCIATIONS

There is no restriction in law on the right of employers to join together for collective bargaining purposes. In fact, certain Labour Relations Acts (or Labour Codes, depending on the province) have an accreditation procedure for employers' organizations. In British Columbia, this applies to all industries. In other provinces, only to the construction industry.

According to the Ontario Labour Relations Act, an employers' organization is:

> "an organization of employers formed for purposes that include the regulation of relations between employers and employees and includes an accredited employers' organization and a designated or accredited employer bargaining agency".

The procedure for accreditation requires an employers' association to apply to the Labour Relations Board for accreditation as the bargaining agent for all employers in a particular sector of an industry and in a certain geographic area. The Board then has to determine that the employers' unit is appropriate for collective bargaining purposes, that it is properly constituted and that it has appropriate authority vested in it by the employer members to act as an accredited bargaining agent. Upon accreditation, the association becomes the exclusive bargaining agent for all employers in the bargaining unit. The Board, as one of its responsibilities, will try to ensure that there has been no union interference in the establishment of the employers' organization.

Duty of Fair Representation

An important responsibility for an accredited employers' association is the "duty of fair representation" of its members. Thus, according to Section 132 of the Ontario Labour Relations Act:

> "An accredited employers' organization, so long as it continues to be entitled to represent employees in a unit of employers, shall not act in a manner that is arbitrary, discriminatory or in bad faith in the representation of any of the employers in the unit, whether members of the accredited employers' organization or not."

6.4 EMPLOYER ATTITUDES

In the nineteenth century, when trade unions were first established, most employers were quite hostile to them. Nowadays, with the various Labour Relations Acts or Codes that require an employer to bargain in good faith with a certified trade union, most employers accept unions as part of the industrial relations system and the collective bargaining process as a normal part of doing business. Some employers continue, however, to resist strongly any union activity. Others try to prevent unionization by offering relatively high rates of pay and generous fringe benefits. Others try to resist unionization of their employees by less acceptable means such as the dismissal of employees engaged in union activity or suggesting that employees will be worse off economically and otherwise by joining a union.

6.5 ANTI-UNION PRACTICES

In the past, employers have used several different methods of opposing unions. These include blacklists, "yellow-dog" contracts, labour spies, and intimidation.

Blacklists. These were lists of persons who were known to be union members or union sympathizers. Employers have been known to circulate these lists among themselves and refuse to employ anyone shown on them.

Yellow-Dog Contracts. This was a contract that a job applicant was required to sign, stating that he was not, and would not become, a member of a union. Such contracts were first used by the railroad companies but gradually spread to other industries.

Labour Spies. Persons were often hired by employers to work in a plant and inform on any pro-union employees — who would then be dismissed. Sometimes a worker might even be blackmailed to report on his colleagues.

Intimidation. Often an employer, faced with the possibility that its employees might join a union, would try to intimidate them. The usual method was to threaten that they would be worse off if the plant became unionized — by the reduction or elimination of benefits now being received, and by a reduction in the number of jobs. An extreme way was by locking out the employees.

Today, still, there are reports of employers trying to intimidate their employees. This can occur at any one of the four main stages of the collective bargaining process—when the union is recruiting members in order to gain certification; while the union application for certification is being processed; during negotiations for a collective agreement; and during the life of the agreement itself. Also, an employer will sometimes lock out its employees. However, the use of blacklists and labour spies has greatly declined and the so-called "yellow-dog" contracts are illegal.

Infiltration. One modern anti-union practice that has been reported in the press has been the infiltration of the work force by undercover operatives hired by the employer or by a related company such as a security service. The undercover operatives then try to dissuade other employees from joining a union and themselves vote against the union when a certification vote is held.

Staged Incidents. Another modern anti-union practice also reported in the press has been the staging of incidents that provide the employer with plausible grounds for dismissing employees actively involved in union activities or known or suspected to be highly sympathetic towards unionization of the company work force. Such incidents may be staged by management — for example, by provoking an employee into an emotional outburst against a supervisor or into an act of disobedience. Alternatively, incidents can be staged by the undercover operatives mentioned previously. For example, they may start a fight with the union sympathizers that gives management grounds for dismissing all the persons involved and thus creating an appearance of fairness.

Unfair practices by management are discussed further in Chapter 8.

KEY CONCEPTS

Employers' association	*Co-ordinating association*
Employer unity	*Education association*
Bargaining association	*Lobbying association*
Consultative association	*Collective bargaining*

Legal status

Duty of fair representation

Employer attitude

Anti-union practices

Blacklist

Yellow-dog contract

Labour spy

Intimidation

Infiltration

REVIEW QUESTIONS

1. What are the various types of employer associations involved in industrial relations?

2. What advantages do employers obtain by joining together for collective bargaining purposes?

3. What is the legal status of employer associations?

4. Outline the procedure for accreditation to be followed by an employers' organization under your provincial Labour Relations Act or Code.

5. Explain the "duty of fair representation".

6. One modern anti-union practice is "infiltration". Explain.

7. Another practice is "staged incidents". Explain.

8. In what other ways have some firms tried to prevent unionization of their employees?

9. What labour relations policy would you recommend a firm to follow? Why?

10. How do employers' labour relations policies vary in practice? Give examples.

CHAPTER 7: THIRD PARTIES — THE GOVERNMENT AND THE PUBLIC

Chapter Objectives

- *To emphasize that the public interest is harmed by strikes and lockouts*

- *To explain what government does to protect the public*

- *To indicate how conflict can arise between the public and private sectors because of overly generous wage settlements*

- *To point out that organized labour, in trying to protect workers' interests, often finds itself in conflict with government*

Chapter Outline

7.1 The Public Interest

7.2 Government Involvement

7.3 Public versus Private Employees

7.4 Organized Labour versus Government

7.1 THE PUBLIC INTEREST

The two parties most directly involved in the collective bargaining process are employers and labour unions. However, their interaction can have serious repercussions on the public — whether it be the hardship caused by a strike in an essential service such as public transportation, education, or hospital care; by the effect on prices of substantial wage increases; or by loss of worker income as a result of a union strike or an employer lockout. Consequently, the collective bargaining process is not something that the public, or its elected representatives, provincial, federal, and municipal, can afford to ignore.

7.2 GOVERNMENT INVOLVEMENT

In fact, our federal and provincial governments do have an important say in the industrial relations process. As we saw in Chapter 3 (the Constitutional and Legal Environment), the federal parliament and provincial legislatures have all enacted statutes that set out the rules covering all aspects of the collective bargaining process in the private sector. They have also passed statutes governing collective bargaining by certain types of public employees. These are described later in Chapter 20 (Public Employees).

At one time, governments usually sided with the employer, making it very difficult for workers to form trade unions or otherwise improve their conditions of work. Gradually, however, hostility changed to recognition and co-operation. Nowadays, union leaders are consulted in Ottawa and the provincial capitals and many public employees have been given not only the right to join trade unions but also the right to strike. However, certain types of public employees — for example, police officers — are still forbidden to strike in many jurisdictions and others may be threatened with government intervention should they decide to exercise their right.

Safeguarding the Public Interest

As a custodian of the public interest, our governments cannot play a merely passive role — setting up the legal framework for collective bargaining and then leaving the employers and trade unions to get on with it. If a strike goes on too long and the public suffers hardship thereby, a government may well decide to intervene. However, there are no hard-and-fast rules for such intervention. Very often the government's decision will be influenced by the political implications of such intervention. Will it help or reduce a government's chances of re-election? Also, a government must keep up with the times. Thus the legal framework of industrial relations in Canada has been amended in recent years to extend the right to strike to public employees. However, since then, our governments have for budgetary and other economic reasons imposed occasional wage controls and even ordered public service strikers back to work.

Ensuring Fair Shares

Our modern economy has been characterized by inflation — a steady rise in prices mainly as a result of an increase in the country's money supply. This means, as the purchasing power of the dollar declines, that a person's wages gradually buy fewer goods and services. Thus a person's real income may fall even though an increase in pay has been obtained — for example, a wage increase of 6 per cent when the annual rate of inflation is 10 per cent. In inflationary times, all workers are inevitably involved in a mad scramble to at least keep up with the rise in prices. However, the workers best equipped to do this, other than politicians, are the ones that have a union to represent them. As a result, unionized workers tend gradually to increase their share of the national economic pie, whereas non-union workers, workers denied the right to strike, and pensioners and other fixed-income receivers, gradually find themselves with a smaller share. The indexing of pensions is one attempt by government to address this problem. Generally speaking, however fixed-income receivers have been left to fend for themselves.

Keeping the Economy Competitive

An important responsibility of our governments is to keep the country economically prosperous. If excessive union power causes wages to increase too rapidly, this may jeopardize the competitiveness of Canadian products at home and abroad. However, in the late nineteen seventies, the imposition of wage and price controls by the federal government caused the increase in wages to fall behind the rate of inflation, thereby bringing about a reduction in workers' real incomes. This led in turn to accusations by labour spokespersons that the federal government had abused its power in favour of employees. In 1982, the introduction by the federal government of the ''6 and 5'' wage restraint program in the public sector, followed suit by many provincial governments, was also greeted with labour outrage. Since that time, there has been no further recourse to mandatory wage and price controls in Canada. Instead the government has used monetary policy to try to control inflation. However, in 1991, the federal government did endeavour to restrict pay increases for federal civil servants for three years.

7.3 PUBLIC VERSUS PRIVATE EMPLOYEES

One of the most perplexing aspects of modern industrial relations in Canada is the growing importance of government as an employer. Unlike the private business firm that will go bankrupt if it grants wage and benefit increases beyond its capacity to pay, the government is often regarded as having a bottomless purse. If a government department or a Crown corporation spends more than it earns, it can look to the government to provide the necessary funds to cover the deficit. Also, suppose that a Crown corporation (such as the Post Office) or any other government body that provides a service to the public, has a monopoly or semi-monopoly position. Then it can raise its charges to the public to cover the cost of perhaps above-average salaries or benefits (such as inflation-indexed pensions) received by the public employees involved. Private firms by contrast face the discipline of the market-place. If their expenses are too high, their efficiency too low, or their products no longer in demand, they can soon be put out of business. In many eyes, most public servants now enjoy a privileged position — their pay is equal to or better than that of their private sector counterparts, their fringe benefits (vacations, pensions, etc.) are often better, and their job security outstanding. The question arises: should public sector employees lead the way in better pay and fringe benefits, or should they exercise a moderating influence on the private sector employees?

7.4 ORGANIZED LABOUR VERSUS GOVERNMENT

In the early 1980s, as the federal government attempted to control inflation by wage and price controls and then by a tight-money, high-interest rate policy, unemployment substantially increased in Canada. This was particularly so in the manufacturing sector where, according to the president of the Canadian Manufacturers Association, 300,000 jobs were lost in one year alone. Part of the blame could be assigned to slow demand in the U.S., Canada's principal export market. However, labour leaders believe that the federal government could have done more, by investment and other incentives, and by stricter control on imports and on the actions of foreign multinationals operating in Canada, to reduce the number of jobless Canadians. As a result, fruitless meetings between government and labour leaders were followed by public demonstrations by union members and their families in Ottawa and elsewhere. Now, in the early 1990s, similar hostility exists as the unemployment rate approaches 10% of the civilian labour force.

At the provincial level, governments attempting to curb budget deficits ran up against militant public sector unions. In Quebec, for example, an attempt by the PQ government in 1982 to persuade unions representing Quebec's 300,000 public and para-public employees to accept a 60 per cent rollback in salary increases scheduled for that year met with an outright no by the leaders of the Quebec Federation of Labour, the Confederation of National Trade Unions, and the Centrale de l'enseignement du Quebec (the teacher's union) which represents about 182,000 public employees. The union leaders were angered even more by a government ultimatum that the alternative would be the layoff of 17,400 civil servants, teachers, hospital and social service workers in 1983 and a freeze on public sector salaries for 1983 and part of 1984.

In the early 1990s, Canada is again faced with an economic recession, triggered in part by high interest rates and a strong Canadian dollar. Despite a tight-money policy, unions continue to succeed, often after long strikes, in obtaining satisfactory settlements. Both federal and provincial governments continue to have enormous debt, thereby reducing their willingness to accede to the wage demands of public-sector labour unions. And public sector strikes by, for example, nurses have become more frequent.

KEY CONCEPTS

Public interest	*Economic competitiveness*
Government involvement	*Wage leadership*
Fair shares	*Labour-government conflict*

REVIEW QUESTIONS

1. How do our governments have an important say in the industrial relations process?

2. How does a government decide when to intervene in a labour dispute to protect the public interest?

3. "In times of inflation, unionized employees have an unfair advantage over other members of the community." Discuss.

4. "Government control of union activity is essential to maintain the international competitiveness of Canadian industry." Discuss.

5. "Public employees are the most privileged members of the trade union movement." Discuss.

6. The interests of organized labour now usually conflict with those of government. Discuss.

PART C

Union Organization and Certification

CHAPTER 8: UNION ORGANIZATION

Chapter Objectives

- *To indicate why some employees may decide to have a labour union represent them*
- *To explain how contact is made between the employees and a union*
- *To explain the role of a union organizer*
- *To explain the composition and role of an organizing committee*
- *To examine the various steps in an organizing campaign*

Chapter Outline

8.1 Interest in Joining a Labour Union

8.2 Contact with a Labour Union

8.3 The Union Organizer

8.4 The Organizing Committee

8.5 The Organizing Campaign

8.1 INTEREST IN JOINING A LABOUR UNION

At any time, some of the employees in a non-unionized firm may come to believe that they would be better off as members of a labour union. This may be because of a newspaper article, because of conversations with friends or relatives who are themselves union members, or because of a real or imagined grievance or complaint at work, or because they have been approached and and persuaded by members of an existing union. This interest in a union may be based on the fact that unionized employees in other firms, perhaps in the same industry or geographical area, seem to be doing much better than the non-union employees are. Certainly the hope that, by joining a trade union, employees can obtain higher rates of pay, more generous fringe benefits, improved job security, and more respect from management is an important motivating factor.

8.2 CONTACT WITH A LABOUR UNION

Once interest in joining a labour union has been aroused, whatever the reason, one or two disgruntled employees within that firm might then get in touch with an existing labour union, perhaps by telephoning or visiting the union's local office. They would probably select a union that represents employees in other companies doing the same kind of work or making the same kind of product. The officials of the union they contact would very likely agree to discuss their problems with them or alternatively refer them to another union with more appropriate jurisdiction. Very often, however, a union does not restrict its organizing activities to only certain types of employees. Thus there are many examples of employees being represented by what would appear to be at first sight an unlikely union. A union might want to organize these employees in the hope that it would, through the larger number of employees and firms covered, improve the bargaining position of its existing members. Obviously, the larger the percentage of an industry's employees the union represents, the greater is its bargaining power. Also, the larger this percentage, the less chance there is of non-union employees hurting the union membership by taking work away from unionized employees.

8.3 THE UNION ORGANIZER

The term *union organizer* is used to describe the person employed on a full-time, permanent basis by many large labour unions to plan, organize, and carry out membership recruitment campaigns at plants that are not yet unionized. Such persons usually specialize in the *organizing* of certain types of employees — for example, women, ethnic groups, white-collar workers (such as bank employees) or employees in certain types of industries such as steel, fisheries, and lumbering. Because of their personality, intelligence, and specialized experience, the full-time organizers provide the spearhead for union organizing activities.

8.4 THE ORGANIZING COMMITTEE

Once the decision has been made to go ahead with an organizing campaign, the union organizer or other union official in charge will try to assemble a group of employees dedicated to the goal of unionization. This group, or *organizing committee*, would consist of people willing to devote the time and effort necessary to contact other employees, present the union's case for unionization, and ask the persons contacted to join the union by signing a union membership card and paying the required fee

(usually one dollar). The group, or committee, consists of union representatives, including the "organizer", and may also include the employees
who first made contact with the union, and who are sympathetic to union
organization. These persons must be prepared not only for a lot of hard
work but also, in the case of the employees, for considerable job risk.
Although the provincial Labour Relations Acts prohibit an employer from
discriminating against an employee for participating in union organizing
activity, this does not always prevent employers from doing so — even
though they may later be required to reinstate the dismissed workers and
make up lost pay. Consequently, it is the usual practice, based on common
sense, to keep any union organizing campaign as low-key as possible, at
least initially. One way to help achieve this to keep the organizing
committee fairly small.

8.5 THE ORGANIZING CAMPAIGN

The committee would make a careful assessment of the probable success
of an organizing campaign. Then, if there is agreement to proceed, it
would provide the necessary assistance, leadership and expertise.

Gathering Information

The first step in the organizing campaign is to gather together as much
information about the company as possible — for example, its products,
customers, finances, production methods, employees, management,
ownership and attitude towards employees. Information should also be
collected about other firms in the neighbourhood who employ the same
types of workers. Once this data has been collected, analyzed, and
discussed, the committee can start to plot its campaign — particularly the
type of appeal to be made to the employees to join the union — showing,
for example, how the company can afford to pay better wages or how the
employee needs greater job security in the face of impending technological
change.

In trying to organize a small firm, representatives of the organizing
committee might contact individual employees on a personal basis, usually after work, just outside the plant or at home. In a larger firm, initial
contact might be made through other means such as union bulletins,
mailings to the employees' homes, through newspapers, etc. The overall
objective of the contact would be to persuade the employees to join the
union, have them sign a membership card, pay a membership fee, and be
given a receipt for payment.

List of Eligible Employees

The second step in the organizing campaign is to obtain an accurate, up-to-date list of all the employees eligible to join the union in the particular plant or company that is the object of the organizing campaign. If this cannot be obtained from within the firm (and the employer is under no obligation to provide such a list), resort must be made to other means. Using the list, the committee can record the responses received when a committee member later makes personal contact with each employee to solicit membership.

Personal Contact

The next step is for the committee members to start making personal contact with the various employees. The aim is to secure their agreement to join the union and acknowledge this agreement by signing a union membership card and paying the required initiation fee.

Usually, to get the campaign off to a good start, the employees who are believed to favour unionization are approached first. They are also the ones most likely to keep quiet about what is taking place. To avoid any suggestion of intimidation, the personal contact with the employee is often made on a one-to-one basis. For maximum confidentiality, it may take the form of a visit to the employee's home where the purpose of unionization, the potential benefits to the employee, and the possible disadvantages, can be openly discussed, often with the participation of the employee's spouse as well as the employee.

If lucky, the union organizer will get the employee to "sign-up" on the first visit. In many cases, however, a second or third visit may be required. On each visit, the union organizer will try to determine such matters as: the attitude of the employee and family to the union; possible "beefs" that the employee may have about pay, working conditions, immediate supervision, and the way the firm is run generally; and the employee's fears about joining the union and other possible arguments against membership. The organizer will also ask the employee to keep as quiet as possible about the contact until the union has a majority of the eligible employees signed up and is ready to make its application for certification to the Labour Relations Board.

The fact that the committee members making the personal calls are fellow-employees is usually helpful to the recruitment process. They are acquaintances, even personal friends, rather than strangers. They have shown by their own action that they are in favour of the union and they are asking the person approached to follow their example, not just to "do what we say''. As a fellow-employee, the committee member shares a common lot with the prospective union member and tends to be trusted in a way that no outsider would. He or she can chat about the plant, the people, and their problems from first-hand experience and thereby quickly put the person approached at ease. However, the union organizer must ensure that the committee members are carefully briefed on what to say (including the fact that the union intends to push ahead whatever management says or does) and on how to deal with objections. Basically, what the committee members are doing, as union canvassers, is a selling job. Obviously, not everyone is suited for it.

Because house-calls are a time-consuming process, many labour unions prefer to restrict them to employees who are considered essential to the recruitment drive. The other employees are often contacted on their way to or from work, perhaps outside the company gate or at a nearby gathering place.

All-Out Public Campaign

Once management has become aware of the union's organizing activities, the union may switch from a policy of discreet recruitment to an all-out public campaign. It may then advertise its intentions in the media and in handbills for distribution outside the plant, inviting eligible employees to sign up, or perhaps to attend an open meeting to obtain further information. At the meeting, the organizer, other union officials and committee members would explain the reasons why the employees should join the union, answer questions, and invite the persons present to sign up for membership. Union membership recruitment meetings are not used as much today as they used to be. This is mainly because of the relatively poor turnouts. An exception might be a plant in which the employees have a long history of grievances, or one in which a labour issue has just arisen, such as automation, that may critically affect the well-being of a large number of the employees.

Signed Membership Cards

After the employee's signature has been obtained, the union canvasser turns the membership card over to the union office or to the organizer. The union will try to ensure that no cards are handed in with forged signatures. This is because such an occurrence might lead, under the Labour Relations Act, to the union being disqualified from certification as the bargaining agent for the employees of the company being organized. The Labour

Relations Board will check the validity of the signatures and will accept only validly signed membership cards. The number of employees that have signed up for union membership is kept a closely-guarded secret by the union office until a substantial majority of the eligible employees have done so.

KEY CONCEPTS

Union organizer	*Personal contact*
Organizing committee	*Signing up*
Organizing campaign	*Public campaign*
Eligible employees	*Membership card*

REVIEW QUESTIONS

1. What reasons can motivate some of a non-union firm's employees to get in touch with a labour union? How is this contact usually made? What type of union would they approach?

2. Why would a union be interested in representing the employees of a firm not normally considered to fall within its jurisdiction?

3. Explain the composition and role of the union organizing committee.

4. What is the background and role of the organizer?

5. Do members of the organizing committee and other active canvassers for the union undergo any risk of losing their jobs or other retaliation by the employer? How can any risk be reduced?

6. What information can be usefully gathered by the organizing committee? What purpose does it serve?

7. How can the union obtain a list of employees eligible to join the union?

8. How do the organizing committee members approach eligible employees with a view to persuading them to join the union?

9. When might a union decide to use an all-out public campaign to recruit members? How would it go about it?

10. What can happen if membership cards are submitted with forged signatures?

CHAPTER 9: UNION CERTIFICATION

Chapter Objectives

- *To define certification*
- *To explain how a labour union becomes certified as the bargaining agent for a group of employees*
- *To specify the persons excluded from union membership*
- *To explain which labour relations statutes apply to different groups of employees*
- *To indicate when a labour union may apply for certification*
- *To point out the Labour Relations Board's responsibility for determining whether a unit of employees is appropriate for collective bargaining*
- *To explain how the Labour Relations Board determines whether the eligible employees want the labour union to be their bargaining agent*
- *To point out the employer's duty to permit union access to employees residing on company property*
- *To indicate that a union may be denied certification if an employer has taken part in its formation or administration or if the union discriminated against anyone because of race, creed, colour, etc.*

Chapter Outline

9.1   Certification Defined

9.2   Persons Excluded

9.3   Jurisdiction

9.4   Appropriateness of Bargaining Unit

9.5   Certification Procedure

9.6   Timing of Application

9.7   Determination of Union Members in Bargaining Unit

9.8   Board Response to the Application

9.9   Representation Vote

9.10 Voluntary Recognition

9.11 Right of Access

9.12 Unions Not to be Certified

Appendix 9A: Termination of Bargaining Rights

9.1 CERTIFICATION DEFINED

It is considered to be in the public interest for government to encourage harmonious relations between employers and employees by facilitating a process of orderly collective bargaining. Therefore, each province, in its labour relations statute, sets out a method by which a union may acquire the right to represent a group of employees for collective bargaining purposes. *Certification* is the procedure whereby a union obtains a certificate from the Labour Relations Board declaring that the union is the exclusive bargaining agent for a defined group of employees in a bargaining unit that the Board considers appropriate for collective bargaining.

9.2 PERSONS EXCLUDED

Depending on the province, not all employed persons have the right to be represented by a labour union.

Specific Exceptions

Exceptions, in Ontario, include domestic workers employed in private homes; persons employed in agriculture, hunting or trapping; persons employed in horticulture; and members of the architectural, dental, land surveying, legal and medical professions employed in a professional capacity.

Management

Managers, and persons considered by the Labour Relations Board to exercise managerial functions or to be employed in a confidential capacity in matters relating to Labour Relations are excluded from the bargaining unit. Usually, all levels of management, including supervisory staff are considered to be exercising managerial functions. Therefore, most bargaining units tend to be defined as non-supervisory production employees or non-supervisory office employees.

Groups Covered by Their Own Legislation

Some groups of employees are covered, for collective bargaining purposes, by their own special legislation and are therefore excluded from the Labour Relations Act. In Ontario, these are as follows: members of a police force; full-time firefighters; teachers; provincial employees; hospital employees; and community college employees.

Security Guards

In Ontario, the Labour Relations Act prohibits persons employed as guards to protect the property of an employer from being included in the same bargaining unit as other employees for that plant. Furthermore, the Board will refuse to certify another trade union as the bargaining agent for such guards if persons other than guards are included in it. Nor is an employer required to bargain with a trade union that attempts to act for such a mixed group.

9.3 JURISDICTION

In Canada, there exists both provincial and federal labour relations legislation — so one of the first questions, when employees wish to become unionized, is under which labour jurisdiction they would fall.

Province of Employment

If the plant or office workers of an employer located in a particular province choose to become unionized, they would fall under the jurisdiction of that province's Labour Relations Act. Similarly, workers employed by a person located in another province would come under the jurisdiction of that province's Act. However, suppose that an employer located in one province chooses to open a second plant or office in another province. Then the employees in the new location, should they choose to become unionized, would come under the jurisdiction of the province in which they are employed.

Suppose a firm sets up its head office in one province and eventually sets up operations in all the other provinces. Then, if its employees in the ten different provinces are unionized, the firm would be dealing with ten different provincial Labour Relations Acts.

Federal Jurisdiction

Persons employed by certain firms, because of the nature of their operations, come under federal jurisdiction. Examples of these would be employees of the national railways, banks, airlines, shipping companies, and ports.

Summary

In summary, the Labour Relations Act for each province deals with union representation for employees in that province unless they happen to be covered by federal legislation or by some other special provincial legislation.

9.4 APPROPRIATENESS OF THE BARGAINING UNIT

A labour union, when it thinks it has sufficient membership support, will apply to the provincial Labour Relations Board to be certified as the bargaining agent for the employees in the group it considers to be appropriate for bargaining.

The union will give consideration, in its application, to the common interest among members of the group, geographical location, and the likelihood that the group will be acceptable to the Labour Relations Board for certification. Consideration will also be given to the question of whether the application should be made as a single-plant, multi-plant, single-employer, or multi-employer group.

The Labour Relations Board

Although the union, in its application for certification, will claim the unit of employees is appropriate for bargaining, it is the Labour Relations Board that makes the decision. The employer is also given the opportunity to express its view to the Board as to the appropriateness of the unit.

Standard units recognized by the Board include production units, office units, technical and professional units. The Board will also recognize *craft units* — groups of skilled workers engaged in some trade who commonly bargain together, separate from other employees. In every case, the unit must consist of more than one employee. Normally, if a manufacturing company has both a plant work force and an office work force, the Labour Relations Board will consider the non-supervisory plant employees as one unit appropriate for bargaining, and the non-supervisory office employees as another. As mentioned previously, certain employees would automatically be excluded. The Board may also certify a trade union as bargaining agent even before the final composition of the bargaining unit is determined so long as it is satisfied that any dispute as to the composition of the unit cannot affect the trade union's right to certification.

The criteria used by the Labour Relations Board in deciding appropriate industrial units include the following: (a) the wishes of the employer and the trade union; (b) the community of interest among employees, taking into account the nature of the work performed, and the skills of the employees; and (c) the Board's general policy of not putting office staff and production workers in the same bargaining unit.

9.5 CERTIFICATION PROCEDURE

Once the labour union has applied to the Labour Relations Board to become the bargaining agent, the Board will send a copy of the application to the employer. The employer must then post the application where it can be seen by all the workers concerned. The employer and/or the employees may then ask the Board to add or delete certain categories of employees and the Board will decide whether such action is appropriate.

If the Board is satisfied that the union has the support of 55% or more of eligible employees, based on signed membership cards, the union may be certified without a vote. If it has between 45% and 55%, a secret ballot will be held.

To determine whether the union has sufficient support among employees in the bargaining unit, the Labour Relations Board looks at the percentage of employees in the bargaining unit who have become union members.

9.6 TIMING OF APPLICATION

A labour union may apply at any time to the provincial Labour Relations Board for certification as bargaining agent. However, this assumes that no other labour union has already been certified as the bargaining agent, that the employees in the unit are not already bound by a collective agreement, or that the procedure available to the parties to assist in the negotiation of a collective agreement has not yet been exhausted.

No Other Labour Union Certified

In this case, there is no restriction on the right of a union to apply for certification.

No Collective Agreement

Suppose that another labour union has already been certified as the bargaining agent but has not entered into a collective agreement with the employer. Also that no declaration has been made by the Board that the labour union no longer represents the employees in that bargaining unit. Then a second labour union may apply to the Board for certification as bargaining agent — but only after one year has elapsed from the date the certificate was issued to the first labour union.

Union Recognized by Employer but no Collective Agreement Entered Into

Suppose that an employer has recognized in writing that a union is the exclusive bargaining agent of its employees but the employer and the union have not entered into a collective agreement. Then another trade union may, unless conciliation proceedings are under way, apply to the Labour Relations Board for certification as bargaining agent — but only after one year has elapsed from the date the certificate was issued to the first trade union.

Collective Agreement for up to Three Years

Suppose that another labour union has already been certified and has signed a collective agreement with the employer, but for a term of not more than three years. Then a second labour union may apply to the Board for certification as bargaining agent of any of the employees in that bargaining unit after the commencement of the last two months of operation of such an agreement.

Collective Agreement for over Three Years

Suppose, however, a collective agreement is in force for a term of more than three years. Here, a second labour union may apply to the Board for certification only (a) after the commencement of the thirty-fifth month of the agreement's operation and before the commencement of the thirty-seventh month of its operation and (b) during the two-month period immediately preceding the end of each year that the agreement continues to operate thereafter or (c) after the last two months of its operation, as the case may be.

A collective agreement continues to operate if either the the union or the employer fails to give the other party notice of termination or of its desire to bargain for a renewal of the agreement or for the making of a new one. In this situation, a second trade union may apply to the Board for certification during the last two months of each year that the agreement continues to operate, or after the commencement of the last two months of its operation, as the case may be.

Lawful Strike or Lockout

If a union has been certified but no collective agreement has been reached, an application for certification or termination by another union may not be made during a lawful strike or lockout until (a) six months have elapsed since the strike or lockout commenced or (b) seven months have elapsed since the Minister released to the parties the report of the conciliation board or mediator or a notice that the Minister does not consider it advisable to appoint a conciliation board.

9.7 DETERMINATION OF UNION MEMBERS IN BARGAINING UNIT

Once an application for certification is made, the Labour Relations Board is required to determine the number of employees in the bargaining unit at the time the application was made and the number of employees in the unit who were members of the trade union at that time. The Board has the power to determine how and when evidence of membership in a trade union is to be presented to the Board.

9.8 BOARD RESPONSE TO THE APPLICATION

The Board will normally dismiss the union application for certification if less than 45 per cent of the employees in the unit are members of the union. Only if the Board believes that the employer has contravened the Labour Relations Act so that employees are reluctant to join or vote in favour of the union, will it certify the union as bargaining agent even though it has less than 45 per cent of the employees signed up.

Usually, the Board will certify the union, if more than 55 per cent of the employees are union members. However, it may instead order that a representation vote be taken.

Table 9.1 — *Membership Support Required forUnion Application Certification*

	Percentage support among total number of persons in bargaining unit	Board response to application
Normal Certification Procedure	— less than 45%	— dismissal of application
	— 45% to 55%	— holding of representation vote
	— over 55%	— certification without a representation vote, unless advisable to have one
Request for Pre-hearing Vote	— less than 35%	— dismissal of application
	— 35% or more	— holding of a representation vote

9.9 REPRESENTATION VOTE

If the Labour Relations Board is satisfied that not less than 45 per cent and not more than 55 per cent of the employees in the bargaining unit are members of the trade union, it *must* order a representation vote to be taken.

This is a vote conducted by the Labour Relations Board in which the employees in a bargaining unit indicate by secret ballot whether or not they wish to be represented by the union.

If, on the taking of a representation vote, more than 50 per cent of the secret ballots cast are in favour of the trade union, then the Board must certify the trade union as the bargaining agent.

Pre-hearing Representation Vote

A labour union has the right, when applying for certification, to request that a *pre-hearing representation vote* be taken.

If the Board concludes, from an examination of the records of the trade union and of the employer, that not less than 35 per cent of the eligible employees in the bargaining unit were members of the trade union at the time the application was made, it may direct that a representation vote be taken. The Board may also order that the ballot box containing the ballots cast be sealed.

If the Board is satisfied that not less than 35 per cent of the employees in such bargaining unit were members of the trade union at the time the application was made and more than 50 per cent of the ballots are cast in favour of the union, it will certify the trade union as bargaining agent.

9.10 VOLUNTARY RECOGNITION

An employer may voluntarily recognize a union as the bargaining agent for its employees, if it considers the bargaining unit to be appropriate and believes that the majority of employees, without having been subject to undue pressure, have indicated their desire to be represented by that union. In this case, the employer agrees in writing to recognize the union as the exclusive bargaining agent for a group of its employees as defined in the agreement with the union. Voluntary recognition is an alternative to certification and is usually done privately between the employer and the union, without any government supervision.

9.11 RIGHT OF ACCESS

Sometimes employees reside on property owned by the employer, or on property to which the employer has the right to control access. Then, if necessary, the Labour Relations Board may order the employer to allow the representative of a trade union access to the property — so that he or she may attempt to persuade the employees to join the trade union.

9.12 UNIONS NOT TO BE CERTIFIED

The Board may not certify a trade union if any employer or any employers' organization has participated in its formation or administration or has contributed financial or other support to it. Nor if the trade union discriminates against any person because of race, creed, colour, nationality, ancestry, age, sex or place of origin.

KEY CONCEPTS

Certification

Persons excluded

Provincial jurisdiction

Federal jurisdiction

Bargaining unit

Representation vote

Right of access

Voluntary recognition

REVIEW QUESTIONS

1. Do all employees have the right to join a union under the terms of the provincial Labour Relations Act? Who, if at all, is excluded?

2. Certain persons are deemed not to be "employees". Who are they? Is this logical?

3. The ABC Co. has its headquarters in Calgary and manufacturing and sales branches in Alberta, Manitoba, Saskatchewan and Ontario. Do its branch employees fall under the jurisdiction of the Alberta Labour Relations Act?

4. Under the jurisdiction of which Labour Relations Act do the following employees fall: (a) letter carriers, (b) firefighters, (c) teachers, and (d) hospital workers?

5. The United Assemblers Union has signed up, as members, a large number of employees from the Ace Electronics plant. How long must it wait before applying for certification?

6. Suppose another union was certified six months ago but, as far as the employees were concerned, "never did anything for us". Can the United Assemblers Union still be certified? Would it make any difference if the employer had already recognized in writing the first union as the certified bargaining agent for its employees?

7. Suppose there is a collective agreement already in force between the employer and the first union. When, if at all, can the second union apply for certification?

8. Do the following have any effect on the second union's application for certification: (a) conciliation proceedings between the employer and the union already certified, and (b) the existence of a lawful strike or lockout?

9. Who decides what group of employees is appropriate for collective bargaining? What factors would be taken into account? Are there any minimum or maximum numbers?

10. What is a "representation vote"? When is it necessary? What is its purpose?

11. Are trade union members legally entitled to enter an employer's premises to explain to the employees the benefits of joining the union and to solicit membership?

12. Are security guards allowed to join a union? What is their legal position under the Ontario Labour Relations Act?

13. Under what circumstances is a union not permitted to be certified as a bargaining agent?

14. What is "voluntary recognition"? Why is certification more usual?

APPENDIX 9A: TERMINATION OF BARGAINING RIGHTS

Just as it is possible for a labour union to become legally certified as the bargaining agent for a group of employees, so also is it possible for a union to become *decertified*. In fact, most Labour Relations statutes provide for both certification and decertification. There are in fact many different reasons that may cause a union to have its bargaining rights terminated.

Failure to Make a Collective Agreement

First, if a labour union does not make a collective agreement with the employer within one year after its certification, any one or more of the employees in the bargaining unit may apply to the Labour Relations Board for a declaration that the labour union no longer represents the employees in the bargaining unit.

Employee Request

Second, if there is a collective agreement in force, any one or more of the employees in the bargaining unit may apply to the Board for declaration that the labour union no longer represents the employees in the bargaining unit. However, in the case of an agreement for a term of not more than three years, such an application may be made only after the commencement of the last two months of its operation. In the case of an agreement for a term of more than three years, the application may be made only during the two-month period prior to the third anniversary or in the two-month period prior to each subsequent third anniversary. Then, if 45 per cent of the employees in the bargaining unit voluntarily signified in writing that they no longer wish to be represented by the labour union, the Labour Relations Board is required to satisfy itself that the majority of the employees desire that the right of the trade union to bargain on their behalf be terminated. It does this by holding a representation vote. Then, if more than 50 per cent of the ballots are cast in opposition to the labour union, the Board will declare that the union no longer represents the employees in the bargaining unit.

Certification of Another Union

Third, if another labour union obtains certification to represent a group of employees already represented by a union, then the first union automatically loses its bargaining rights.

Union Request

A fourth reason for terminating a union's bargaining rights is the Labour Relations Board being informed by the labour union that it no longer wishes to continue to represent the employees in the bargaining unit. This is called ''termination on abandonment''.

Union Fraud

A fifth reason is the discovery that the union obtained a certificate by fraud. In such a case, once the Labour Relations Board has declared the union no longer represents the employees in the bargaining unit, any collective agreement is void.

Failure to Give Notice of Desire to Bargain

A sixth reason is the failure of the union to give notice, within sixty days following certification, of its desire to bargain with a view to making a collective agreement. In such a case, the Labour Relations Board may, upon application of the employer or any of the employees in the bargaining unit, declare that the union no longer represents the employees in the bargaining unit. This decision may be made with or without first holding a representation vote.

Failure to Bargain

Seventh, bargaining rights may be terminated because of the union's failure to bargain within sixty days of giving notice to the employer of its desire to bargain with a view to making a collective agreement. Or because of failure to bargain within sixty days from the collapse of negotiations but before the appointment by the Minister of Labour of a conciliation officer or mediator. The Board may terminate the union's bargaining rights following application by the employer or any of the employees in the bargaining unit and with or without a representation vote.

Voluntary Recognition

Eighth and last, the bargaining rights of a union may be terminated, upon application by any employee in the bargaining unit, or by a labour union representing any employee in the bargaining unit, where there has been *voluntary recognition*. This is a situation in which an employer and a union that has not been certified as the bargaining agent enter into a collective agreement or a recognition agreement (whereby the employer recognizes the labour union as the exclusive bargaining agent of its employees and the agreement is in writing signed by both parties). In such a case, the application for termination of the bargaining rights of such a voluntarily recognized union must be made during the first year of the collective agreement. If no collective agreement has been entered into, the application for termination must be made within one year from the signing of such a recognition agreement.

Conclusion

In conclusion, we should stress that, despite the many different grounds on which bargaining rights may be terminated, such an event is unusual. Certainly, an employee hoping to decertify a union would first need to talk with a good labour lawyer or labour consultant.

REVIEW QUESTIONS

1. The United Assemblers Union fails to make a collective agreement with Ace Electronics despite months of negotiations. Some of the employees complain to the Labour Relations Board that the union has been "bought" by management and they want to get rid of it. What can the Board do?

2. Suppose that the union did sign an agreement but the employees feel that they have been "sold out". What can they do, if anything?

3. Explain the meaning of the term "termination on abandonment".

4. The United Assemblers Union, through incredibly poor management, failed to give notice to Ace Electronics, within two months of the date of certification, of its desire to bargain. The Board was asked to declare that the union no longer represented its employees. What might the Board do?

5. What is meant by the term "voluntary recognition"? If this occurs, what is the union's legal position?

CHAPTER 10: UNFAIR PRACTICES

Chapter Objectives

- *To explain what is meant by "unfair practices"*

- *To indicate what unfair practices were used in the past and how they have been gradually outlawed*

- *To list the unfair practices committed by some employers while a labour union is being organized, while it is applying for certification, while it is negotiating a collective agreement, and while a collective agreement is in operation*

- *To summarize the unfair practices that a labour union may commit*

Chapter Outline

10.1 Unfair Practices Defined

10.2 History of Unfair Practices

10.3 Unfair Practices by Employers

10.4 Unfair Practices by Labour Unions

Over the years, one of the less attractive aspects of collective bargaining has been the attempt by some employers and by some trade unions to thwart each other's aspirations by means of a variety of "unfair practices".

10.1 UNFAIR PRACTICES DEFINED

These are actions taken by employers or unions that contravene the principle of bargaining "in good faith". One example would be an employer dismissing a person, perhaps on some false pretext, for attempting to form or join a union. Another would be union organizers physically or mentally intimidating an employee into joining a union against that person's real wishes. Unfair practices vary somewhat in definition from one labour relations statute to another. Nevertheless, they can be defined

125

generally as: actions by employers and employees, or their representatives which are prohibited by statute because they interfere with the proper operation of the collective bargaining process.

10.2 HISTORY OF UNFAIR PRACTICES

For many years, while unions were in their infancy, unfair practices were associated mainly with management. Thus, as we saw in Chapter 3 (The Constitutional and Legal Environment), the Wagner Act passed in the U.S. in 1935, specifically named and outlawed five such management practices:

a) interfering with an employee's right to join a union;

b) dominating a labour union;

c) discriminating against an employee for engaging in union activities;

d) dismissing or otherwise penalizing an employee for filing charges under the Act; and

e) refusing to bargain with the union representing the employees.

The Wagner Act also provided for a National Labour Relations Board to investigate any complaints of unfair labour practices by management; to prosecute the companies and persons involved; and to hold and supervise elections to determine which union it should certify as the official bargaining unit.

As trade unions became stronger, management began to complain bitterly that employers were also the victims of unfair practices — this time by the unions. Eventually, in 1947, the Wagner Act was amended to permit unions also to be prosecuted for unfair labour practices.

In Canada, the history of unfair practices is also a long and stormy one. Employers have, on occasion, had the assistance of special police, the R.C.M.P., and government back-to-work orders in order to break strikes. They have also used such measures as threats, bribes, dismissals, black-listings, physical beatings, factory spies, and employer-run unions to prevent the unionization of their workers. But gradually, as in the U.S., the various labour relations statutes, both provincial and federal, have outlawed many of these practices and the provincial and federal Labour Relations Boards, together with the courts, have tried to make their elimination a reality. Labour unions have also been accused of unfair practices.

10.3 UNFAIR PRACTICES BY EMPLOYERS

For purposes of analysis, we can identify four main stages in the collective bargaining process during which employers may engage in various types of unfair practices. First, while a union is being organized; second, while its application for certification is being processed; third, while it is negotiating a collective agreement with the employer; and, fourth, while a collective agreement is in operation.

While a Union is Being Organized

In Canada today, under the various labour relations statutes, an agreement between an employer and a trade union is held not be be a collective agreement if an employer or employer's organization helped to establish, or administer the trade union involved.

However, an employer still has the freedom to express its views so long as it does not use coercion, intimidation, threats, promises or undue influence. Obviously, the distinction between an employer expressing its views on the one hand and attempting to dissuade its employees from joining a labour union on the other is not always clear. Consequently, there are many cases that come before the Labour Boards that revolve around this point. Normally, an employer is free to explain its labour policy, including a presentation of the advantages and disadvantages of unions. However, such an exposition should not contain threats of reprisal or promises of benefit if employees join a union or not.

An employer is also forbidden from interfering with an employee's rights to join a trade union or become an officer in one or to exercise any other rights under the applicable labour relations statute. Specifically, the employer is prohibited from using intimidation or coercion — for example, the threat of dismissal or of a reduction in wages, or even of closing down the plant — to discourage a person from becoming a union member. However, an employer still retains the right to dismiss an employee for "just cause" — for example, because of persistent lateness, drinking, etc. Another example of interference with an employee's rights would be questioning him or her about union activities.

Sometimes there may be more than one union trying to "organize" a firm's employees. Whatever the employer's preference for one union rather than the other, it would be considered an unfair practice to attempt to persuade the employees to join the union that the employer prefers. Nor must the employer assist one or other of the unions in its campaign to recruit new members.

While a Union is Applying for Certification

During this period, it would also be illegal for the employer to engage in the conduct mentioned in the previous section. It would also be illegal for the employer to alter the working conditions of the employees without the consent of the trade union that has applied for certification.

If the trade union is considered to have been influenced by the employer, its application for certification will be disqualified by the Labour Relations Board. A union which receives financial help from the employer is known as a *company union* and would be ineligible for certification.

While a Union is Negotiating a Collective Agreement

A collective agreement would be disallowed under the various Labour Relations Statutes if it discriminated against anyone because of his or her race, creed, colour, nationality, ancestry, age, sex, or place of origin.

An employer is also prohibited from including in a contract of employment any conditions that would prevent a person from joining a trade union or exercising any other rights under the applicable labour relations statute.

Failure to recognize or bargain with the certified union is another unfair practice specifically prohibited by the labour relations statutes. Should negotiations break down, the union may legally call a strike once the required period of conciliation has been exhausted. In this case, a possible unfair practice by the employer would be the dismissal of employees sympathetic to the union.

While a Collective Agreement is in Operation

An employer is expected to observe the terms of the collective agreement that has been negotiated with the trade union acting on behalf of the employees. Any disputes that arise are to be handled according to the grievance procedure set out in the agreement, with any outstanding issues being referred to arbitration. While the agreement is in force, the employer may not therefore lock out its employees. Also, an employer must reinstate any employee who has previously been engaged in a legal strike so long as the employee makes a written application to return to work within six months from the beginning of the strike. And there must be no discrimination in the terms of employment offered. The only exception to reinstatement is if the employer no longer has persons performing the same or similar work. An employer is also forbidden to discriminate against anyone who has acted as a witness or filed a complaint under the applicable labour relations statute.

While a Union is on Strike

Nowadays, in Ontario, British Columbia, and Manitoba, the hiring of professional strikebreakers by employers is considered to be an unfair practice and is specifically prohibited by law (see Chapter 15: Strikes and Lockouts).

10.4 UNFAIR PRACTICES BY LABOUR UNIONS

Under the various labour relations statutes, a trade union, or persons acting on its behalf, is also prohibited from engaging in various types of conduct. Many of these parallel the actions forbidden the employer — for example, discriminating against anyone (in this case, for trade union membership) on grounds of race, creed, colour, nationality, ancestry, sex, or place of origin.

The following is a list of unfair practices that a union, or persons acting on its behalf, may commit:

1. Participating in or interfering with the formation or administration of an employer's organization or contributing financial or other support to such an organization.

2. Bargaining with or entering into a collective agreement with an employer while another trade union continues to be entitled to represent the employees in the bargaining unit.

3. Not representing fairly the employees in the bargaining unit.

4. Attempting to persuade an employee at his or her place of work, during working hours, to become or continue to be a member of a union.

5. Not making secret a strike vote or a vote to ratify a proposed collective agreement.

6. Not giving those employees entitled to vote, ample opportunity to cast their ballots.

7. Calling or authorizing an unlawful strike, or threatening to do so.

8. Suspending, expelling, or otherwise penalizing a member who refused to participate in an unlawful strike.

9. Discriminating against a person in regard to employment.

10. Intimidating, coercing, fining or otherwise penalizing a person because of a belief that he or she has made, or is about to make, a

disclosure in a proceeding under the Labour Relations Act or because he or she has made an application or filed a complaint under the Act, or because he or she has participated, or is about to participate in, a proceeding under the Act.

KEY CONCEPTS

Unfair practice	*Discrimination*
Bargaining in good faith	*Dismissal*
Threats	*Refusal to bargain*
Interference	*Just cause*
Domination	*Undue persuasion*

REVIEW QUESTIONS

1. Explain how an employer might be involved in the establishment of a trade union. Why is this considered undesirable?

2. A collective agreement is not recognized as such by law if it discriminates against any person on one of the various specified grounds. What are they? Should any others be included?

3. What employee rights is an employer forbidden to interfere with under the terms of your province's Labour Relations Act or Labour Code?

4. Give some examples of intimidation and coercion used by employers and trade unions that the Act or Code aims to prevent.

5. May a trade union or employer attempt, during working hours, to persuade an employee to join or refrain from joining a union? Discuss.

6. Are strikes and lockouts permitted while a collective agreement is in force? Explain the situation.

7. Does an employer have the right to insist that a vote be taken by the employees whether to accept or reject the employer's last offer? Who is permitted to vote?

8. The ABC Co. refused to take back several employees who have been on strike, claiming that they are trouble-makers. What is the employees' legal position?

9. During negotiations for a new collective agreement, but before the old one expired, the ABC Co. locked out its workers, claiming that the union demands, at the time of falling company sales, were excessive. What is the union's legal position?

10. Terry Moore, although a union member, refuses to participate in a strike called by his union, claiming that "we're just asking for trouble". What is his legal position vis-a-vis the union: (a) if the strike were called before the existing agreement expired and (b) after the agreement expired?

11. The XYZ Co., which had been steadfastly opposed to the unionization of its employees, announced after certification of a union as its bargaining agent, that it was no longer going to pay medical treatment, group insurance and other employee benefits. Can the employees do anything about this?

12. Frank Woods, a senior employee, complained to management about the non-payment of the benefits and announced that he was going to tell the Labour Relations Board about it. A few days later, he was fired because, according to management, he could no longer do his work properly. What is his legal position?

PART D

Negotiation of a Collective Agreement

CHAPTER 11: THE NEGOTIATING PROCESS

Chapter Objectives

- To indicate how collective bargaining is initiated
- To review the composition, attitude, etc. of the company negotiating committee
- To examine the composition, attitude, etc. of the union negotiating committee
- To understand how company and union demands are drawn up
- To indicate the types of information required for collective bargaining
- To consider where and when the negotiating teams will meet
- To review the negotiating procedure
- To consider the basic negotiating tactics that are used in company-union meetings
- To explain how and when a first agreement may be imposed on the employer and the union
- To explain why multi-employer bargaining is sometimes preferred by unions
- To discuss the rationale behind the way in which contract negotiations are conducted
- To emphasize the critical role in contract negotiations played by the threat of a strike

Chapter Outline

11.7   Company-Union Meetings

11.8   Negotiating Procedure

11.9   Negotiating Tactics

11.10 Imposition of a First Agreement

11.11 Single versus Multi-Employer Bargaining

11.12 Rationale Behind Contract Negotiations

11.13 Critical Role of the Strike

11.1 INTENTION TO BARGAIN

Under the terms of the Labour Relations Act, either party to a collective agreement may give notice in writing to the other party of its desire to bargain with a view to renewing, with or without modifications, the agreement then in operation or to making a new agreement. The time period for giving such notice is also usually specified in the existing collective agreement. Thus, for example:

> This Agreement shall remain in force for a period of one year, from the date hereof, and shall continue in force from year to year thereafter unless in any year not more than 90 days before the date of its termination either party shall furnish the other in writing with notice of termination or of proposed revision of this Agreement.

During this open period, it is normal for the union to notify the company of its intention to bargain.

However, before negotiations for a new collective agreement can begin, the company and the union will need to establish negotiating committees.

11.2 THE COMPANY NEGOTIATING COMMITTEE

Composition

In a medium-sized manufacturing firm of several hundred employees, the company negotiating committee would probably consist of three to five people. It would commonly include the Industrial Relations Manager, or representative, because of his (or her) knowledge of the collective bargaining process and labour relations in general; the plant manager, or representative, because of his or her responsibility for the operation and also for knowledge of practical operating problems; perhaps another manufacturing representative for knowledge of particular problem areas to be discussed; perhaps a specialist in wage administration, depending on the anticipated subject matter; and perhaps a specialist in work measurement. The company negotiating committee might also include an outside consultant.

The composition of the committee and the background of each of its members should be such as to demonstrate to the union that the members of the company team have a good knowledge of the relevant facts and of the various pressures influencing both management and the union. It is important, in the eyes of the union, that the company team has integrity and accepts the bargaining process; also that the committee members have the ability to listen patiently, think creatively, and to speak and write clearly, precisely, and effectively.

Attitude

The attitude of the company negotiating team is very important. In this regard, we assume that the employer's objective in the negotiations is to seek a settlement based on a reasonable and realistic assessment of the bargaining circumstances. These would include such factors as the company's financial situation, the demand for its products, wage settlements in this and other industries, and the general economic situation. Therefore the committee, both as a whole and as individuals, should adopt in the negotiations with the union, a constructive, realistic, problem-solving approach. The personalities of the persons comprising the company negotiating team should generally be agreeable and acceptable to the union and the persons themselves should demonstrate a conciliatory rather than antagonistic attitude in their discussion of the issues involved.

Organization

The organization of the committee should be clearly understood by all its members. Normally, the Industrial Relations representative on the committee acts as its chairperson. However, it is conceivable that the chairperson of the committee might be the person responsible for the operation — for example, the manufacturing manager — who would then use the Industrial Relations representative as a staff advisor.

Initial Preparation

It is essential that committee members discuss the various issues amongst themselves and reach agreement as to the company's initial bargaining position before meeting with the union. The chairperson, who is normally the chief spokesperson, can then speak on behalf of the committee to the union, knowing that there is agreement within the group. Normally, the chairperson does all the talking for the company except in regard to certain matters which, by pre-arrangement, are handled by other persons on the committee.

Also, from time to time, the chairperson may request, during a meeting with the union, that one or more of the other persons on the committee speak in regard to certain points being raised by either side in the negotiations.

The responsibility for the successful completion of negotiations belongs to the committee as a whole. However, it should be established beforehand that in the event of disagreement amongst the members, someone must have the authority to make decisions and have the responsibility for them. Normally this is the chairperson.

Authority

The members of the company negotiating committee should possess sufficient authority and status in the company organization to convince the union that they have the authority to reach an agreement on the company's behalf. However, the company team should not have unlimited authority to make a settlement and should not give the appearance of having such unlimited authority. The company president should refrain from becoming a member of the negotiating committee — thereby making it clear to the union that there is still somebody who can put limits on what the negotiating committee may agree to.

If the company negotiating committee is unable to reach a settlement with the union, the normal result is a strike which can be very damaging to the firm. It is vital therefore for the committee to know exactly what authority it has and how it can report quickly to top management on the progress of the negotiations, on the problems that may have arisen, and on any concessions or other measures that may be required to avert a breakdown of the talks. Consequently, the chairperson of the negotiating committee should have ready access to the president of the company. The committee head must also know exactly how far the company is willing to go in meeting union demands and whether it is willing or not to put up with a strike and the financial and other loss involved.

11.3 THE UNION NEGOTIATING COMMITTEE

Composition

In some situations, the union negotiating committee would consist, on a predetermined basis, of a select group of union representatives, such as the president of the local, the vice-president, the chief steward, etc. Each of these persons is elected by the membership. Alternatively, since the purpose of the union negotiating committee is to represent the views of the union membership, the rank and file membership might be asked to select the negotiating committee by means of a special election.

If the union has a business agent, he or she would almost certainly also be a part of the negotiating committee. If there is no business agent, and sometimes even if there is a business agent, the central union organization, the ''national'', will most likely supply a national representative to assist the local group in the negotiation of their collective agreement.

Whatever the manner of selection, the union negotiating committee should have a good, detailed knowledge of the firm's general operating situation and of the particular problems to be discussed. It should also have a sound understanding of collective bargaining procedure and labour relations in general.

Many of the comments in regard to the company negotiating committee are also applicable to the union negotiating committee. It is certainly important that they have a good knowledge of the relevant facts and pressures influencing both sides and that their integrity be recognized by the company negotiating committee.

Attitude

It follows almost without question that the union representatives accept the bargaining process. Certainly they should be able to speak and write precisely and effectively, and think creatively with regard to the problems that will inevitably arise. Also they should have experience in the collective bargaining process. Most unions would feel it desirable that they bring a constructive approach to the negotiations with a realistic approach to problem-solving. Also most unions would think it important that the union representatives appear to be agreeable and conciliatory in their approach to the various issues.

11.4 COMPANY DEMANDS

Important company demands, based partly on experience from operating under the previous agreement, will have been discussed many times between the Industrial Relations people and the line management who are responsible for the company's operations. However, it is considered judicious to review also any arbitration decisions made during the life of the agreement. These would suggest other possible changes to the benefit of the company. The consequences of any adverse arbitration decisions that have been made will underline just how important it is for the company to get the new agreement changed.

Furthermore, a review of the grievances that have been filed may indicate areas in which the company has been having difficulty in operating under the terms of the agreement. It may also pinpoint areas of continuing and unnecessary conflict because of the provisions of the agreement. It is also judicious to give supervisors who operate under the agreement an opportunity to suggest changes.

11.5 UNION DEMANDS

As part of the process of drawing up union demands, many unions hold meetings for all union members at which individual members have the opportunity to suggest items for inclusion among such demands. Also, many unions provide special opportunities for stewards and chief stewards to make their suggestions. In addition, officers and various experts of the union would normally review the grievance and arbitration procedures. Perhaps there have been arbitration decisions which adversely affected the union and which, from the union's point of view, require changes in the agreement. The union would undoubtedly consider the advice of the union's national representative and of the local business agent in regard to the demands that should be made to solve existing problems or to avoid anticipated future problems. Furthermore, union national policy objectives might result in the placing of additional demands. The national representative and the business agent should have a good knowledge of collective bargaining trends and of settlements elsewhere and this knowledge could also influence the demands to be made by the union.

11.6 INFORMATION REQUIRED

For negotiating purposes, it is essential for both the company negotiating committee and the union one to have adequate information. To start with, both committees are probably fully conversant with the terms of previous collective agreements and recognize their importance as a reference point in the upcoming negotiations. Such terms may be above average, thereby causing a problem for the company, or below average causing a problem for the union.

Wages and Benefits

Both negotiating committees need information on the company's wage benefit package compared to that of other firms in the industry and other firms in the area. There is an abundance of this type of information available to each of the parties. Government information such as that from Statistics Canada, government wage surveys, and Ministry of Labour settlement reports are available to both sides. Information is also available from private publications. In addition, the company normally has access to information provided by various employer associations such as the Canadian Manufacturers Association, personnel associations, Chambers of Commerce, and so on, and often can obtain information on request from other employers. The union can obtain additional information from the various collective agreements from other unions and also by making contact with unions representing other employees in comparable firms or industries. From all this information, each party can draw conclusions about wage, employment, and other trends in the economy and in labour relations in general which are going to affect the negotiations for a new collective agreement.

Work Force

Both sides will have access to information about the work force which makes up the bargaining unit. The union members may be relatively old, perhaps making them more concerned with security and pensions; or they may be relatively young, perhaps making them more concerned with the hourly wage rates rather than benefits and job security.

Ability to Pay

The employer's ability to pay is an important factor for both sides. The employer may well look at its present relative position as an employer in the labour market, and at the overall trends and patterns in wages, fringe benefits, and so on and recognize there are many arguments for improving working conditions in his company. But looking at its overall profitability picture, it may well conclude that it is impossible to do these things at least for the present.

The union may decide, on the basis of these trends, what it thinks the company should pay and take the position that the company's ability to pay is the company's problem rather than the union's. However, the union must recognize, at least eventually, that there is a definite limit on a company's ability to pay and that, if it insists on obtaining a settlement beyond that which the company can afford, it may provide the company with no alternative other than to close the plant or endure a long strike. And conceivably, if such a strike goes on long enough, it may cause the company to go out of business, taking the employees' jobs with it.

It is possible for a company to agree to an excessive settlement to avoid a strike and to give time for the company to decide on an appropriate course of action. After the union has obtained an excessive settlement, the company may decide that there is no alternative other than to close the operation. The union can then be in a situation of having been successful in obtaining its objectives in the short run but having completely lost out in the long run. On the other hand, the company may well be able to afford better wages and improved benefits.

11.7 COMPANY-UNION MEETINGS

Location

Meetings between the two negotiating teams might be held on company premises, in a conference room or business office, or in the union hall or a similar type location, or in some neutral area such as a local hotel. The company negotiating committee is usually reluctant to meet in the union hall as it would feel itself at a psychological disadvantage going to the union in order to negotiate with it. While it is cheaper to negotiate on company premises rather than to go elsewhere, there are also some significant handicaps in this location. The people on the company negotiating committee are normally taking time away from their regular duties. If they are on the company premises, they run the risk of being interrupted by these duties or being distracted by them — with the result that less attention is paid to negotiations than is required. Also, it is important that events that arise in the course of negotiations not be misinterpreted either by company non-union employees or by employees represented by the union. Negotiations can become emotional or appear to become emotional. Therefore, when people leave a negotiation meeting, it is quite possible that their personal appearance or some off-hand remark may be misinterpreted by those not involved in the negotiations. Problems may be relatively minor in the context of the negotiations but can be easily misinterpreted by those not involved. Once put into the rumour mill, such problems may cause unfavourable reactions that are completely out of proportion, thereby unnecessarily complicating the negotiations. Therefore most companies and most unions feel that is is advantageous to negotiate in some neutral location away from the day-to-day responsibilities of both parties. Usually, negotiations are held in a hotel where, in addition to a room for the negotiations, each group has the opportunity to obtain a separate room for themselves for preparation and discussion purposes.

Frequency and Duration of Meetings

There are various opinions as to how often the meetings should be held and how long they should last. However, many people believe that meetings should be held as often as either or both parties consider it desirable — so long as they help the parties move closer to a settlement, even one issue at a time. Most companies and most unions also believe that meetings should start at a sensible time in the morning, such as 9:30 or 10:00 o'clock, giving both sides some time for preparation prior to the meeting. They also believe that they should last as long as they are serving their purpose. Either side has the privilege of suggesting, when it feels it is appropriate, that a meeting be adjourned.

However, other companies and unions believe that negotiations should fit into the overall operation of the business. In one situation the union representative and the plant manager agreed that they would set aside one day per week — Wednesday — for the purpose of negotiations. Also that, in the interest of the overall efficient use of time, the meetings would start at 8:00 a.m., adjourn for lunch at 12:00 noon, reconvene at 1:30 p.m. and end for the day at 4:30 p.m. In practice, it seemed as though these meetings were held every Wednesday and went on for the full seven hours whether they served any purpose or not. Also, it would not have mattered whether more meetings were necessary — Wednesday, between 8:00 and 4:30, was the only time available for this purpose, whatever the need.

11.8 NEGOTIATING PROCEDURE

At the same time, that the union gives notice to the company of its intention to bargain, it may also submit to the company its proposals for a new or modified agreement. Alternatively, it may reveal these proposals in subsequent correspondence or at the first or second meeting arranged for the purposes of negotiating the agreement. The company may also have proposals to modify the agreement. If the union submits its proposals by mail prior to the first meeting, the company might respond similarly or it might notify the union only of its intent and wait for the first or second meeting before presenting its own proposals. Alternatively, the union might submit its demands at the first meeting and the company may submit its proposals also at that first meeting or perhaps at the second meeting. In any event, proposals to amend the agreement are sooner or later exchanged between the parties.

Written Proposals

The proposals submitted are normally in writing and may either propose precise changes in the agreement or may express the intention to change the meaning or content of the agreement without specifying the wording to be used in the revised agreement. Very often, after the proposals are exchanged, each party is expected to explain to the other the intent of its proposed changes so as to ensure proper understanding. Next, the other party is usually asked to justify its demands. This involves giving the origin of the problem, the reasons for the proposed change, and an explanation as to why the proposed change is considered to be the most satisfactory solution to the problem. After all this has taken place, serious discussion of each item will begin. Also, each party can then consider other possible solutions to each problem not just the solution proposed by the other party.

Private Assessment

At this stage, the company and the union will probably make a private assessment of each other's demands. Each party will then probably conclude that it can agree to certain proposals made by the other party and can see areas of possible compromise on certain items. Each party may also tentatively conclude that the other side will not push certain items beyond reasonable limits, whereas certain other items are strike or lockout issues.

Monetary versus Non-Monetary Issues

Very often the parties will separate the demands into so-called monetary issues and so-called non-monetary issues. *Non-monetary issues* include such items as contract language, procedural matters, and administration matters which do not result in direct cents-per-hour labour cost increases.

Very often, the parties will decide to discuss the so-called non-monetary items first — usually because of the assumption that such items are easier to resolve and that by resolving them first, the overall area of disagreement will be reduced. Also, quick resolution of such items tends to give a positive impetus to the talks, acting as an early signal of progress.

Normally, the two parties will meet with each other a number of times to resolve the various issues, non-monetary and monetary, before a new or amended collective agreement is accepted by both sides.

Each party usually considers, at an early stage, the concessions that it will be willing to make to the other party — knowing that negotiations will proceed for some time with continuing pressure to make concessions. It will also give consideration as to when any concessions should be made.

Conciliation Services

Both parties will be aware of the government conciliation services available and the statutory requirement to use them before a legal strike or lockout can take place. Both parties will also be aware that a government conciliator will exert strong pressure on them to make further concessions. If, after conciliation, there is still no settlement, there will probably be further negotiating sessions before the strike deadline arrives.

11.9 NEGOTIATING TACTICS

In all the meetings between the company and the union, from the very start of negotiations, each party will be arguing for its demands and resisting those of the other party. At the same time, each party will be looking for compromise alternatives that may enable an agreement to be reached. Ideally, both parties will come away from the negotiations feeling that they have secured many of their basic bargaining goals, even though in modified form; and confident that the agreement will be acceptable to both top management and the union membership.

Bargaining Positions

The union cannot allow the company to announce a settlement without first going through the bargaining process. The employees might believe that the company has just ''sold out'' to the union or the union members that the union has ''sold out'' to the company. One of the basic reasons for employees joining a union and agreeing to pay union dues is the assumption that the union can obtain for its members benefits that they would not otherwise have received from the employer. In other words, the union must constantly justify to the membership its role as bargaining agent.

When the company makes its first offer, it is almost axiomatic that the union reject it. Therefore if the company's first offer is the maximum that it can afford, or the maximum that it can justify, the company is in effect forcing the union to call a strike or lose in the eyes of its members, the justification for its existence. Therefore, to be practical, the company should initially offer considerably less than it can really afford or justify. The union can then reject the offer, thereby justifying its existence to its membership, and paving the way for a further series of offers and counter-offers. Eventually a settlement will be reached which the union can recommend to its members either as a fair settlement or the best it can get without calling a strike and certainly one that is a lot better than that originally offered by the company. Sometimes, of course, a proposed settlement is unacceptable to top management or the union membership and a lockout or strike becomes inevitable.

Some negotiators dislike the use of a bargaining position. However, most negotiators consider it an indispensable means for achieving their bargaining objectives.

Maximum and Minimum Objectives

The bargaining goal in, for example, a wage negotiation usually has a range. From the company point of view, the lower end of the range is the maximum objective and the higher part of the range is the minimum objective. The union goal likewise normally has a range and a maximum company offer below the union's minimum expectation would result in a strike.

In the hands of a skilled negotiator, the bargaining position has a dual role: it reveals and conceals. It is used first to reveal, move by move, the maximum expectation of the negotiating team, and second to conceal, for as long as is considered desirable, the negotiator's minimum expectation.

The negotiator tries to convince his (or her) opposite number that the maximum of his target range is really the minimum. He does this mainly by the manner and timing of changes in his bargaining position. Since he has taken a much more demanding bargaining position at the beginning of the negotiations, each concession brings him closer to his maximum expectation. Each concession should also be designed to encourage or pressure the other negotiator to respond with similar concessions of his (or her) own and to provide at least as much information about his expectations as the party making the first concession has revealed about his.

Three Main Activities

The company and the union are combining three main activities in negotiations:

1. Attempting to influence each other and the employees by advocating the merits of their respective positions.

2. Indicating their strength to each other.

3. Exploring the possibilities, in terms of the other party's minimum expectations, of a settlement without an economic contest or, failing that, an economic contest of minimum duration.

These three activities are inter-related and may be treated separately only for purposes of analysis.

The need to assert strength and to explore the possibility of a settlement is at the very heart of negotiations. A negotiator must have the ability to combine the two in such a way that one does not undermine the other. The basic purpose of each party in the negotiations is to convey strength and at the same time explore possibilities for a peaceful settlement to avoid a strike.

Advocacy of a Position

Even highly experienced and sophisticated negotiators sometimes under-estimate the importance of adequate preparation and effective presentation of their position. This is because there is a tendency to consider the preparation and presentation as only the preliminaries to actual hard bargaining based on relative economic strength — a feeling that logical or persuasive discussion has little or nothing to do with the actual settlement of the issues in dispute. However, although relative economic strength is vital, logic and reason have in many instances significantly affected a final settlement. A good negotiator may give the impression that he is not influenced by a carefully presented, logical argument. However, in consultation with his own committee, when perhaps subsequently considering different courses of action, he may well give it the consideration it deserves.

Indication of Strength

The need for the parties to indicate their strength to each other is constantly present in the negotiations. The union, in arguing its own position or probing the company's position, is constantly saying or implying we can strike you, the membership will support a strike, and we will strike you if certain minimum conditions are not met. Similarly, the employer is constantly conveying the impression to the union that the amount of money for pay and other benefits is limited, the union and its members cannot afford to strike, and if the union does, the company can take it better than the union and its members can. Both sides are subtly and indirectly suggesting that there is a possibility of a lockout or strike if acceptable minimum conditions are not met.

Although both parties are endeavouring to convey an impression of strength and the possibility of a lockout or strike, both parties are usually careful to avoid outright threats. Threats are probably the most dangerous and least effective methods of indicating strength. Negotiators are not inclined to believe something just because it is expressed as a threat. Often people who make threats find it necessary to do so because they are bluffing. If a negotiator has bargaining strength, he does not need to make threats. If he makes threats then, when the showdown comes, he may have to eat his words. In delivering an ultimatum, he is asking the other side to openly surrender. Obviously, that makes it more difficult for the other side to agree. As a result, the two parties are in a position where neither can back down gracefully without weakening their bargaining effectiveness.

One way of conveying strength is by the timing of changes in bargaining positions. In retreating from a bargaining position to the area in which the final objective is to be found, it is important for the negotiator to avoid giving the other side the impression of weakness. Perhaps therefore he can proceed to his objective under conditions which require the other side to match this step for step.

Exploration of Possible Areas of Settlement

The character of the negotiations is strongly influenced by the need to work towards a deadline. Both sides know that if there is no agreement, a strike will result. And this possibility is in the background right from the beginning of negotiations. There must be a successful effort to reach an agreement or the negotiations will be followed by a strike — usually with very serious economic consequences for both sides. So the two sides will, as the deadline approaches, carefully review each area of negotiation to determine how much each can yield to reach agreement and, through a series of proposals and counterproposals, gradually settle their differences — hopefully, before the deadline arrives.

11.10 IMPOSITION OF A FIRST AGREEMENT

If no settlement is negotiated for a first agreement, some provinces provide for the imposition of an agreement on the parties. These provisions were designed to help establish a workable relationship in cases where the employer and the union failed, through bargaining, to establish a relationship, perhaps because of unrealistic union demands or the uncompromising nature of the employer's response.

In Ontario, after conciliation, either party may apply to the Labour Relations Board to direct the settlement of a first collective agreement by arbitration. The Board will do this, if it appears to the Board that bargaining has been unsuccessful because of one or more of the following circumstances:

a) the refusal of the employer to recognize the bargaining authority of the trade union,

b) the uncompromising nature of any bargaining position adopted by the respondent without reasonable justification,

c) the failure of a respondent to make reasonable or expeditious efforts to conclude a collective agreement, or

d) any other reason the Board considers relevant.

The settlement will be imposed by a Board of Arbitration unless the parties notify the Labour Relations Board that they have reached an agreement on their own.

The B.C. Act provides that the Commissioner of the Industrial Relations Council (B.C.'s equivalent of a Labour Relations Board) may at the request of either party direct a panel of the Industrial Relations Council to enquire into a dispute of a first agreement. If the Commissioner deems it advisable, the panel can settle the terms and conditions of the first agreement. But the panel must give the parties an opportunity to present evidence and make representations beforehand.

In Quebec, the dispute is handled by a Council of Arbitration, which may consist of a single arbitrator.

In Manitoba, the parties may apply to the Board 90 days after the union is certified. However, the Board will not impose an agreement for at least 60 days after that, at which time the Board may suggest that the parties continue to try to reach an agreement alone or with the help of a conciliation officer or go ahead and impose a first agreement.

11.11 SINGLE VERSUS MULTI-EMPLOYER BARGAINING

Usually, labour unions organize and become certified to bargain on behalf of the employees in one particular plant of a corporation. However, when negotiating with multi-plant corporations, unions normally prefer a company-wide agreement, supplemented by individual plant agreements that cover local issues. Some employers have long accepted such agreements as, for example, in the automotive industry. However, there appears to be no desire among labour unions to go any further than this — by including not just all the plants in a multi-plant corporation, but all the corporations in a particular industry. In other words, most unions prefer the single-employer negotiation which is in fact the most typical form of bargaining relationship. This union preference is not difficult to understand. By being free to concentrate its attention on the major corporation in an industry that is most likely to agree to the most favourable terms for the employees, the union can obtain a settlement that can be held up as a pattern for the industry. In other words, the union will be able to put pressure on the other firms in the industry to grant similar terms, or to show why they are unable to do so. If a firm can demonstrate that it cannot afford to accept the pattern, the terms might eventually, after some hard bargaining, be altered somewhat.

With this approach, the union chooses the company from which it expects to secure the most favourable terms and then tries to bring all the other firms in the industry up to that level or as near to it as possible.

In general, most large employers prefer to bargain individually. They dislike having other firms decide what wages, etc. they are to pay. They prefer to maintain their own freedom, and rely on their own bargaining power, to arrive at a settlement that reflects their own needs.

Multi-employer bargaining is considered by many unions to be the approach most likely to yield good results in industries in which there are many small firms and a high degree of competition. This is because no individual firm, faced with fierce competition, can afford to make significant wage improvements. Otherwise its costs will be out of line and its vulnerability increased. Only by getting all the small firms in the industry to agree simultaneously to improve wages and other benefits, can the union hope to make progress. In this scenario, no individual firm would be at a competitive disadvantage as a result. In addition, employers in such industries often prefer to negotiate with a union through an employers' association rather than by themselves. The small individual firm feels weak against the union. The employer knows that a strike can soon put it out of business, particularly if its competitors continue to operate. On the other hand, to grant a wage increase that is out of line with other firms in the industry can be equally disastrous. The answer to this problem is for all the firms in the industry to negotiate together so that all grant the same wage increase and, if necessary, all take a strike together.

11.12 RATIONALE BEHIND CONTRACT NEGOTIATIONS

Why do labour negotiations so often appear to be irrational with table thumping and threats, absurd demands, and frantic all-night meetings as the strike deadline approaches? Why do not the parties rely more on facts and less on propaganda and power? And why does society permit bargaining disagreements to be settled, if conciliation fails, by the brute force of a strike?

One of the most perceptive analyses of the bargaining process has been made by Professors Richard E. Walton and Robert B. McKersie who point out, in their McGraw-Hill book, *A Behavioral Theory of Labour Negotiations*, that labour negotiations actually consist of four different systems of activity: distributive bargaining, integrative bargaining, attitudinal structuring, and intra-organizational bargaining. Each of these processes deserves examination, for each makes different demands upon negotiators and each also sheds light on the above questions.

Distributive Bargaining

By distributive bargaining, the authors mean that type of negotiation with which most people are familiar — namely, haggling over how to divide up the pie. Nearly everyone has engaged in this type of bargaining in buying a used car or a house. In labour negotiations, wages are the classic example of a distributive issue.

Hard facts have only limited value in determining a wage settlement. The union will admit that wages of, say, $30.00 per hour would bankrupt the average employer who, in turn, will admit that wages of $3.00 per hour would leave it without enough good workers. But such outer limits do not greatly help in deciding whether workers who are receiving $12.00 per hour should receive an increase of 40, 50, or 60 cents per hour. With this situation, each negotiator has an incentive to bluff. If the union representative really would settle for a 50 cents per hour increase, rather than call a strike, why not open with a demand for $1.00 per hour and plead and threaten and bluff with the employer in the hope of persuading it to grant at least 60 cents an hour to avoid a strike?

If the bluff succeeds, the union negotiator has done his (or her) job well. If it fails, he can still fall back to his true position of 50 cents. Also, for all the union representative knows, perhaps the employer has privately determined that it will go as high as 60 cents to avoid a strike and the union negotiator would consider it foolish to risk opening for less than the employer might eventually be willing to give. But the employer is also thinking in the same terms, so each party often opens with a transparently unrealistic position; each knows what the other is doing and the art of distributive bargaining is to probe for (and possibly alter) the true position of the opponent while concealing its own as long as appropriate.

Integrative Bargaining

At the same time, however, the parties may also be engaged in "integrative bargaining" — meaning the negotiation of an issue on which both parties may gain or at least neither one loses. Suppose, for example, the parties have decided in principle on a job evaluation system or a dental plan. Once the contentious issues of money and principle are out of the way, both parties may well gain from a co-operative search for the best job evaluation plan or the best dental plan. For this purpose, a different approach is needed — an open discussion of alternatives with perhaps joint efforts to obtain the necessary facts.

Attitudinal Structuring

Third, collective bargaining differs from many other types of negotiations by its strong involvement in *attitudinal structuring*. This means the shaping of such attitudes as trust or distrust, friendliness or hostility between the parties. Management and union representatives must live with each other and with their agreements, day after day, on a continuing basis. This factor can promote restraint between negotiators but if it has the opposite effect, the friction developed in their daily dealings under the old agreement can erupt and make a shambles of the negotiations for a new agreement.

Intra-organizational Bargaining

The aspect of bargaining which perhaps receives the least consideration is the aspect of intra-organizational bargaining. This is the manoeuvering to achieve consensus within (rather than between) the labour and management organizations. Perhaps most people view collective bargaining as a clash between two monoliths, because each party tries to present a solid front to the other and to the public. In fact, internal bargaining is very widespread and has a strong effect on bargaining between the employer and the union.

First consider the union. There are always groups within the union that believe their interests are not being given adequate consideration. The skilled workers may believe the union pays too much attention to the unskilled. Women workers may think that their interests are inadequately considered by the men who may run the union. In a company with two plants, the union local at one may feel that its interests are subordinated to those of the other, and so on. Perhaps the younger workers think too much money is being spent on pensions whereas the older workers may think the opposite. In the election of union officers, these interest groups are in the same kind of bargaining relationship as the voter and the politician in the broader political society. Candidates for union office will try to appeal to factional interests to win votes, and the factions or special interest groups within the union will seek to use their votes to place in office the persons most favourably disposed towards their concerns.

Sometimes differences arise between the local union and the national organization (or central office). Perhaps, by way of illustration, the local leadership is convinced that management will not grant more than a 50 cents an hour increase but the national pattern is 70. To permit a settlement at the lower figure may jeopardize what the national union can obtain in other organizations; to insist on the higher figure may involve the local union in a long and fruitless strike. The competing interests in the union must be resolved and this resolution comes about through an informal bargaining process. Bargaining with the employer cannot even begin until this internal bargaining has taken place.

The bigger or more complex the bargaining group, the more likely it is that aspirations will be divergent and competitive rather than common. Individual groups that believe their interests are being sacrificed and their aspirations being ignored may threaten to disassociate themselves from the group as a whole. They may then try to obtain greater bargaining power for themselves in the inter-union bargaining process.

In bargaining with the employer, the union negotiator must still be sensitive to these internal pressures. A union often submits a very large number of initial demands not only for purposes of distributive bargaining — to provide itself with a stock of trading materials but also to demonstrate to each group in the union that its demands have been voiced to the employer. They can never win everything the members want, but at least they can appear to be tough and aggressive in hammering out a settlement.

On the employer's side, there may also be conflicting points of view which have to be resolved — for example between the sales manager and the treasurer. The sales manager may urge that a settlement under almost any conditions is necessary in order to satifisfy the customers while the treasurer may argue that a settlement beyond a certain cost is unacceptable.

The company too must harmonize the objectives of the local plant and the company as a whole. Plant management may be directed to take a stand which is either contrary to its own best judgement or not suited to its own needs for fear that a precedent may be set which the union will seek to use in bargaining with other plants of the same company.

For the management negotiator, all of this means that he (or she) too must please the constituents on whom his job depends. He too can never win everything in bargaining that he would like to have, so a show of militancy may also help him to show he is not selling out to the other party when he ultimately makes concessions.

In summary, Walton and McKersie's analysis shows that the negotiation process is far more complex than it may appear to be to the casual observer. It is not just a poker game for high stakes or another buyer/seller relationship, although it contains elements of these and other types of economic and political (and theatrical) activities — nor does it impugn the integrity of labour and mangement negotiators to point out the ritualistic nature of the bargaining process. The players usually know the rules of the game and that serious issues are at stake.

Because there is seldom a single "right" answer to the economic issues in dispute and because the union-management relationship also involves a clash of political, psychological and organizational interests, the negotiation process inevitably bears little resemblance to a dispassionate search for the truth.

11.13 CRITICAL ROLE OF THE STRIKE

How is this complicated negotiation manoeuvering ever resolved? The answer lies in the fact that a collective agreement has an expiration date. Upon expiration of the agreement and completion of conciliation services, the union is free to strike.

Negotiations for a new agreement begin before the current agreement expires, often drag on for a few weeks and then quicken in pace and movement as the expiration date approaches, for that is the deadline where all the bluffs are called and all the speeches must end. Either the parties agree on a new agreement or both will incur the costs of a strike.

It is important to understand the critical role of a strike in the bargaining process. When labour and management disagree, how might the disagreement be resolved? One way of course is for the employees to quit and look for work else where. However, if this free market alternative worked satisfactorily, there would be no need for unions.

Second, the workers could marshall all the facts at their disposal and plead their case before management. However, in effect, management wins every dispute as long as the workers can only talk and management maintains the right to determine wages and working conditions.

Third, society could require both parties to submit their dispute to some authority for a binding decision. But such binding arbitration is opposed by most management and union officials. Among the reasons for this opposition is the opinion by both labour and management that better decisions are reached between the parties than if decisions were imposed by an outside arbitrator or a government agency. Furthermore, company and union officials would ask, if the government is to fix wages, why should it not also fix prices and profits and make all the other economic decisions now left in private hands, and how capable is it of making all of these decisions?

That appears to leave only the alternative of permitting workers to cut off their employer's income by means of a strike. No one can claim the right to strike has not been abused. But neither has anyone uncovered an alternative generally acceptable to both parties which permits workers an effective voice in establishing their terms of employment. A union can only call an effective strike when the issues are important enough to the membership to cause them to be willing to give up weeks or months of lost earnings to convince the employer to give further consideration to their views.

KEY CONCEPTS

Intention to bargain	Maximum objectives
Company negotiating committee	Minimum objectives
Union negotiating committee	Advocacy of a position
Company demands	Indication of strength
Union demands	Areas of settlement
Company-union meetings	Imposition of a first settlement
Negotiating procedure	Multi-employer bargaining
Non-monetary issues	Distributive bargaining
Monetary issues	Integrative bargaining
Negotiating tactics	Attitudinal structuring
Bargaining position	Intra-organizational bargaining

REVIEW QUESTIONS

1. What factors influence the composition of a typical company negotiating committee? Who is usually included? Why is the company president normally excluded?

2. What should be the attitude of the company negotiating committee?

3. How much authority should the company negotiating committee have?

4. How should the committee be organized? Who should act as the spokesperson?

5. What preparations should the committee undertake before negotiations begin?

6. What is the usual composition of a union negotiating committee? How are the members selected?

7. Should the members of the union committee be "agreeable and conciliatory in their approach to the various issues"?

8. How are company "demands" prepared?

9. How does the union draw up its own demands?

10. What types of information are necessary for negotiating purposes?

11. When and where are negotiating sessions usually held?

12. What is the procedure for re-negotiating an existing collective agreement that is about to expire?

13. What is the purpose of separating company and union demands into monetary and non-monetary issues?

14. "The union cannot allow the company to announce a settlement without first going through the bargaining process." Discuss.

15. "To be practical, a company should initially offer considerably less than it can really afford or justify." Discuss.

16. "In the hands of a skilled negotiator, the bargaining position has a dual role. It reveals and conceals." Explain and discuss.

17. What three main activities are the company and union combining in negotiations?

18. Why is multi-employer bargaining sometimes preferred by a union?

19. Explain the concept of distributive bargaining.

20. What is "integrative bargaining"?

21. How do attitudes affect the process and outcome of contract negotiations?

22. How and to what extent do internal pressure groups affect contract negotiations?

CHAPTER 12: CONTENTS OF A COLLECTIVE AGREEMENT

Chapter Objective

- *To list and comment on the topics usually covered in a collective agreement*

Chapter Outline

12.22 Sick Pay and Welfare Plan

12.23 Union Notices

12.24 Strikes and Lockouts

12.25 Duration of Agreement

Collective agreements vary considerably. This is because they must take into account the peculiar circumstances of each firm and industry and the relative bargaining strengths of management and labour. Nevertheless, there are many similarities in the topics covered. This is because each agreement represents a serious effort to cover all aspects of the employer-employee relationship. Also, agreements achieved in one firm and industry come under the careful scrutiny of union and management elsewhere. An example of an actual agreement is contained in Chapter 24 of this book.

12.1 Preamble

Here the two parties usually recognize the need to maintain orderly collective bargaining and to provide for satisfactory working conditions and prompt settlement of grievances.

12.2 Recognition and Coverage

In this article of the Agreement, the Company officially recognizes the union as the exclusive bargaining agent for the employees covered by the agreement. Also, the bargaining unit is defined. Thus, it may include all employees of the Company, with certain exceptions.

Example:

> All employees of the Company at the designated location below the rank of sub-foreman except employees certified in other bargaining units, security staff, plant clerical staff, scientific workers, and employees in confidential positions as listed in Appendix A.

The article may also state that foremen and higher levels of management and sub-foremen will not perform the work usually performed by members of the Bargaining Unit except as specified elsewhere in the Agreement.

Next, the article may set out the status of part-time and casual employees. Then perhaps state what has been agreed upon with regard to the *contracting out* of work by management — that is, the right of management to have outside firms rather than its own employees do work such as office cleaning.

12.3 Rights of Management

This article provides that all rights of management belong to the Company except for those that are specifically given up under the provisions of the agreement with the Union.

Example:

> Subject only to the provisions of this Agreement, the management and operation of the business and the employment, direction, promotion, transfer, lay-off, and suspension, discharge, or other discipline of employees for just cause shall be vested solely in the Management of the Company.

12.4 Wages

This article sets out the rate of pay for each job covered by the agreement for each year of the agreement. It may also specify an additional cost-of-living increase tied to the Consumer Price Index. The article may also specify the starting rate for a new employee — perhaps 10 cents per hour below the base rate, with an automatic increase after so many weeks of service, followed by another increase in the base rate after so many more.

12.5 Union Security

In this article, management usually agrees to collect union dues and union initiation fees from employees and to pay them to the union.

The Company may also agree as a condition of employment that all employees who were members of the Union at the time of the signing of the Agreement must continue to be members and that any persons hired later must become members.

It may also be agreed in this article that no coercion or intimidation shall be used to compel or influence an employee to join the union and that no discrimination may be made against present or prospective union members. Also, both the Company and the union usually explicitly agree not to discriminate against any employee because of race, creed, colour, age, sex, marital status, nationality, ancestry, or place of origin.

This whole topic of Union Security, a vital one for the union, is discussed in some detail in the next chapter of this book (Chapter 13: Union Security).

12.6 Officers and Stewards of the Union

The union agrees to appoint or elect stewards to deal with matters affecting employees in the Company's plants and to supply a list of these stewards and officers to the Company. The Company agrees to recognize the stewards and officers and to treat them the same as other employees, except as set out in the Agreement.

Example:

> A Union Steward, and any other representative of the Union shall continue to perform his regular duties on behalf of the Company and shall not leave his regular duties without obtaining permission from his supervisor who shall be given a reasonable explanation for such absence, and shall report back to his supervisor after engaging in Union duties which are permitted by this Agreement. Such a Union representative shall also report to the Supervisor of a section in which he is not employed when entering such section.
>
> A Union representative shall record all the time that he is absent from his regular duties, pursuant to this Article, in accordance with the plant time-keeping procedures.

12.7 Grievance Procedure

In this article, the Company and the union first emphasize the desirability of a satisfactory grievance procedure which will have the purpose of settling grievances promptly. The union may then be given the right to appoint or elect a Grievance Committee to deal with matters not settled in the first, second or third steps of the grievance procedure and to supply the Company with a list of the committee members. Third, the grievance procedure is agreed upon and explicitly described.

In Chapter 16, we explain and discuss grievance procedures.

12.8 Dismissal or Suspension

Such an article may provide that an employee who believes that he has been unjustly dismissed (permanently lost his job) or suspended (temporarily lost his job) may have his case handled as a grievance.

12.9 Arbitration

In this article, the Company and the Union agree to settle any alleged violation of the agreement by arbitration — that is, by referral to a neutral third person or persons who will study the dispute and make a decision about it that is legally binding on both the Company and the Union. A possible decision of the Arbitration Board may be, however, that the matter in question is not arbitrable. The inclusion of such an Arbitration article is required by the provincial Labour Relations Act. In this way, all disputes arising during the life of the Agreement must be resolved peacefully, without resort to strikes or lockouts.

In Chapter 17, we look at Arbitration more closely.

12.10 Hours of Work and Overtime

Such an article may specify the standard hours of work as not more than 8 hours daily and 40 hours weekly, on five days per week. It may also specify the payment to hourly-rated employees of one and one-half the regular rate of pay for overtime work.

12.11 Holiday Pay

This article usually provides for the payment by the Company of regular pay on specified holidays, and double time for work on these holidays. It might also deal with employees on sick pay or receiving Workers' Compensation; employees who are absent immediately before or after a public holiday; and employees who are on vacation during a public holiday.

12.12 Seniority

Seniority is usually defined in terms of accumulated service in the bargaining unit, with credit for certain other types of service.

The article may state that seniority begins when a new employee has completed his three-month probationary period and is retroactive to the commencement of his employment. It is lost if he voluntarily quits, fails to return on recall, or has been on lay-off in excess of the allowable time to which he is entitled.

12.13 Notice of Lay-Off

Here the Company may agree to provide employees with a specified number of days of prior notice of lay-off.

12.14 Lay-Offs and Recalls

This article stipulates the order of lay-off should it become necessary to reduce the working force. Usually this is on a seniority basis, with the more junior members being laid off first. The order of recall is also usually set out in this article, again on a seniority basis, with the more senior employees recalled first, but usually with a requirement that the senior employee be qualified to perform the work being done by the junior employee. Shift preference based on seniority and recognition of seniority despite transfers between different company plants might also be covered in this article.

12.15 Transfers and Promotions

In this article, the basis for the permanent and temporary transfer of employees from one department to another is agreed upon. Employees may be given the right to request a return to their regular department or to request a transfer from their present department.

Vacancies and promotions are often handled on the basis of seniority, provided an employee possesses suitable qualifications for the job or can qualify reasonably quickly. The application of seniority in transfers and promotions, as well as in lay-offs and recalls, is discussed in detail in Chapter 17 of this book.

12.16 Authorized Absence from Work

In this article, the Company may agree to grant or consider granting an employee a leave of absence without pay if a written application is made providing sufficient reasons. The Company may also agree to permit absence from work for reasons of pregnancy; appearance in court; full-time appointment with the union; attendance at union schools, conventions or conferences (by a limited number of employees for a limited time); election to public office; or attendance at the funeral of an immediate relative.

12.17 Off-Shift Premiums

The Company usually agrees to pay a premium of so many cents an hour, in addition to the basic rates of pay, to employees working at certain times during the day and on regularly scheduled Saturdays and Sundays.

12.18 Rest Periods

This article specifies the number of rest periods that an employee may take:

Example:

> The Company agrees to grant rest periods of 10 minutes each during the morning and afternoon shifts, provided the working time of shift exceeds 2 1/2 hours. A rest period of ten minutes shall be granted in overtime, provided the overtime shift exceeds 2 1/2 hours after the return from the second meal period. The union agrees that, except in cases of personal necessity, employees shall not ask for additional time off during the working day. The union agrees that rest periods must not be abused.

12.19 Vacations

In this article, the amount of vacation with pay to which an employee is entitled is set out. Usually, the number of weeks increases according to the number of years of service — ranging, for example, from two weeks after one year's service to five weeks after twenty years' service. The method of calculating vacation pay is also specified — for example, the normal weekly hours at the regular hourly rate. The article may also specify the time at which the vacation pay may be taken and the preference, if any, given to vacation requests.

Example:

> Vacations may be granted at any time subject to the demands of the business, but the Company will make a sincere effort to grant vacations at times requested by employees. Senior employees in each department will be given preference. No vacations shall be granted between October 1st and December 31st unless by special arrangement with the Plant Superintendent.

The article may also deal with vacation credit owing on termination of employment. Also, it may stipulate that there is to be no carry-over of vacations from one year to another.

12.20 Safety and Health

In this article, the Company may agree to be responsible for the safety and health of its employees.

Example:

> The Company shall make reasonable provision for the safety and health of employees during the hours of their employment. Protective devices on machinery and other devices deemed necessary properly to protect employees from injury shall be provided by the Company.

This, however, shall not be construed to include such personal necessities as safety boots or any article which becomes the personal property of the employee. Should such reasonable provisions not be made or such protective devices not be provided, the matter may be subject to the grievance and arbitration procedures.

12.21 Tools, Licences and Clothing

This article may cover the provision by the Company of tools, clothing, and necessary licences.

12.22 Sick Pay and Welfare Plan

This article may provide for income during absences due to illness; specify the amount of life insurance to be provided each employee by a Group Life Insurance Plan fully paid for by the Company; and specify the continuation of existing Hospitalization, Medical-Surgical, and Major Medical Plans.

12.23 Union Notices

This article may be as follows:

> The Company agrees to extend to the Union the use of plant Bulletin Boards provided that the use of such Bulletin Boards shall be restricted to the posting of notices of Union Meetings, recreational, and social affairs. Such notices shall have received the prior approval of the Supervisor, Industrial Relations, or his nominee.
>
> The Union agrees that it will not distribute or post or cause or permit to be distributed or posted on the property of the Company, for or on its behalf, any pamphlets, advertising or political matter, cards, notices or other kinds of literature except with prior written permission of the Supervisor, Industrial Relations, or his nominee.

12.24 Strikes and Lockouts

In this article, the union agrees not to undertake strikes or slowdowns and the Company not to lock out its employees during the life of the Agreement.

Example:

> The Union agrees that there shall be no slowdown, strike or other work stoppage or interference with work. The Company agrees that there shall be no lockout.

12.25 Duration of Agreement

This article stipulates how long the Agreement is to be in force. One, two, and three-year agreements are the most common.

KEY CONCEPTS

Collective agreement	Recall
Recognition	Transfer
Coverage	Promotion
Management rights	Authorized absence
Union security	Off-shift premium
Union steward	Rest period
Grievance procedure	Vacation with pay
Dismissal	Safety and health
Suspension	Sick pay
Arbitration	Union notices
Overtime	Strikes
Holiday pay	Lockouts
Seniority	Duration of agreement
Lay-off	

REVIEW QUESTIONS

1. What is usually contained in the preamble to a collective agreement?

2. Which employees are usually excluded from coverage?

3. What is meant by "contracting out"? Why would reference be made to this in a collective agreement?

4. What "rights" may be specifically reserved for management in a collective agreement?

5. What is the Consumer Price Index? Why does it appear more and more frequently in collective agreements?

6. What are union dues? Why does management agree to collect them on behalf of the union? Does every employee in the bargaining unit have to pay them?

7. Does management have to agree, in the collective agreement, that union membership be a condition of employment?

8. What privileges are usually included in an agreement for union officers and stewards?

9. Should a person who believes that he has been unjustly dismissed or suspended have the right to have his or her case treated as a grievance? Or is this an infringement of the employer's management rights?

10. What is meant by "arbitration"? Why is such a clause always included in a collective agreement?

11. How is "seniority" usually defined? When does it normally begin? When it it lost?

12. What is the purpose of a seniority clause? What are the advantages and disadvantages of employee seniority (a) for the employee and (b) the employer?

13. What principle is usually followed in lay-offs and recalls? How satisfactory is this procedure?

14. A supervisor in a large electrical products manufacturing firm complained to a friend that the three workers that he had just finished training had been "bumped" out of the plant and he now had to start all over again. Explain and discuss.

15. Explain the need for off-shift premiums.

16. Do the employer and the union have a completely free hand in deciding what vacations employees will receive? Should employees be free to choose when to take their vacation, with reasonable notice to management? Discuss.

17. "An employee's safety and health, even at work, is basically his or her own responsibility." Discuss.

18. Why does management so strictly control the posting of union notices?

19. What are the various types of strikes and slowdowns that would be forbidden by the collective agreement? What is meant by a lockout?

CHAPTER 13: UNION SECURITY

Chapter Objectives

- *To explain what is meant by "union security"*

- *To stress the importance of union dues for the financial well-being of the union*

- *To indicate how hiring practices and collection of union dues vary in five basic types of situations: compulsory checkoff, voluntary checkoff, union shop, dues shop, and closed shop*

- *To explain how religious grounds may exempt a person from union membership or financial contribution to the union*

- *To explain and discuss the employer practice of contracting out work previously performed by company employees*

Chapter Outline

13.1 UNION SECURITY DEFINED

The fact that a labour union is certified as the bargaining agent for the workers in a particular plant does not automatically mean that all eligible employees must become union members. This will depend on the terms of the collective agreement.

A labour union, in its written agreement with the employer, will often therefore negotiate the inclusion of what is known as a *union security clause*. This is a clause that requires management to assist in the collection of monthly payments to the union from its members. These payments are called *union dues* and their automatic deduction from an employee's pay cheque is called a *checkoff* of union dues.

The situation in each firm, as regards these two matters, will depend on the agreement that has been negotiated between management and the union. However, there are five basic types of union security clause: compulsory checkoff, voluntary checkoff, union shop, dues shop, and closed shop. Each of these is explained later.

13.2 COLLECTION OF UNION DUES

As in many other organizations, the members of a labour union are required to pay a regular monthly fee, known as ''union dues'', to the union local. If a person has chosen not to join the union, he or she may or may not have to pay these union dues. By trying to get as many employees as possible to become union members, the union not only helps ensure that it is certified as the bargaining agent, but also obtains a solid financial base for its activities.

13.3 COMPULSORY CHECKOFF OF UNION DUES

Some provinces, including Ontario, Quebec, Manitoba and Saskatchewan, have statutory provisions which require that collective agreements contain compulsory checkoff clauses.

In Ontario, legislation provides that, where a union so requests, there shall be included in the collective agreement a compulsory checkoff provision. This provision requires the employer to deduct from the pay of all members of the bargaining unit, whether they are union members or not, the amount of regular union dues. Such dues are to be remitted to the union forthwith.

13.4 VOLUNTARY CHECKOFF OF UNION DUES

In practice, it has not always been easy for unions to collect dues from their members. And without the dues, the unions have found difficulty in covering their expenses. Consequently, pressure was exerted on employers in labour agreement negotiations to undertake to deduct from an employee's pay an amount of money equal to union dues and to forward it to the union. However, employers have agreed to do this only if they first received a written authorization and direction from the employee to do so. This is known as the "voluntary check-off" of union dues.

13.5 UNION SHOP

In the early days, the unions felt that the voluntary deduction of union dues, although a step in the right direction, did not go far enough. This was because only a portion of a firm's employees would agree to have union dues deducted from their pay. As a result, the cost of union representation, although for the benefit of all, was being borne only by some. The unions considered it unjust that workers who were not union members should be "free riders"— that is, obtain the benefits of union activity without sharing the cost. Therefore, the unions battled hard to make union membership and the compulsory deduction of union dues from each employee's pay a requirement of employment. Where in fact an employer agreed to these conditions, the situation is known in the labour movement as a "union shop".

Many firms now have this arrangement — one in which all present and future employees are required to join the union and stay paid-up union members.

13.6 DUES SHOP

Some employees felt strongly that they should not be forced to join a union if they did not wish to do so. And many employers agreed that union membership should be a matter of individual conscience and decision. As a compromise, Ivan C. Rand, former Chief Justice of the Supreme Court of Canada, suggested that collective agreements might require all employees to pay normal union dues but give them the choice of becoming union members or not. This is known as the *modified Rand Formula* and has gained considerable acceptance among employers and labour unions. A firm which operates in this way is known in the labour movement as a "dues shop" (also "agency shop" in the U.S.). With this arrangement, there is no obligation for an employee to become a member of the union. However, there is an obligation for the employer to deduct from the employee's pay an amount equal to union dues and to forward this money to the union. In this arrangement, the dues are considered to be a charge for services performed by the union as bargaining agent for all the employees.

The dues shop is quite widespread. Some unions prefer this arrangement because no union member can justifiably claim that he or she was forced to join the union.

13.7 CLOSED SHOP

In a union shop, explained previously, a person has to become a member of the union in order to be employed there. However, this requirement normally applies only after he or she has become an employee. It is the employer, therefore, who decides who is eligible to be employed.

In a "closed shop", on the other hand, a person must already be a union member before he or she can be hired. Thus a person who wishes to work for the employer must first obtain union membership and must remain a member in good standing. Since a closed shop virtually transfers control of hiring from management to the union, this type of arrangement has been strongly opposed by employers.

A closed shop is common in the construction industry and in the longshoring industry. Workers are supplied to employers by the union by means of *hiring halls* where persons are assigned work by the unions. A closed shop is uncommon in manufacturing or office union situations.

13.8 RELIGIOUS GROUNDS FOR EXEMPTION

In Ontario, an employee in a bargaining unit who, because of religious beliefs, objects to belonging to a union or making a financial contribution to a union may be exempted from doing so. Instead, that person must agree to pay an amount equal to the union dues to a charity which is selected by the employee and the union or, failing agreement, by the Labour Relations Board.

This is also true of Saskatchewan and Manitoba except that in Manitoba the union ceases to be required to represent the employee.

British Columbia, in its legislation, recognizes religious objections to belonging to a union but, where union dues are compulsory, the employee must make an assignment of wages, equal to union dues, to the union.

13.9 CONTRACTING OUT

The term *contracting out* refers to the practice by some employers of having certain activities in the manufacturing process, plant maintenance, delivery, etc. performed by outside firms, with their own employees, on a contract basis. Obviously, such a practice takes work away from members of the employer's own unionized work force and gives it to outside workers who are usually lower paid.

Many collective agreements do not make any reference to contracting out since employers consider this to be one of their management rights. However, unions have sometimes challenged this position, as illustrated by the case, Lake Shore Mills Inc., included in Part I of this book.

KEY CONCEPTS

Union dues	*Rand Formula*
Checkoff	*Dues shop*
Compulsory checkoff	*Closed shop*
Voluntary checkoff	*Contracting out*
Union shop	*Religious grounds*

REVIEW QUESTIONS

1. What are regular "union dues"? What are they used for? Where do they go?

2. Is compulsory checkoff of union dues required by statute in your province? Which employees in the bargaining unit, if any, are exempted from this requirement? Outline the pros and cons of a compulsory checkoff.

3. Distinguish between the dues paid by an employee who is a member of the bargaining unit, but not a member of the union, and the dues paid by one who is a union member.

4. Why does the union consider it only fair that non-union members who are members of the bargaining unit pay the same regular union dues as union members?

5. What is meant by the term "union shop"?

6. What is the Rand Formula? How does this satisfy both the union and the employees who do not want to join the union?

7. Distinguish between a union shop and a closed shop. A closed shop can sometimes give rise to abuse. Explain and discuss.

8. Can an employee be exempt from union membership because of religious reasons?

9. What is meant by the term "contracting out"? Should employers have a free hand in this matter? Discuss.

CHAPTER 14: CONCILIATION

Chapter Objectives

- *To explain what is meant by conciliation*
- *To point out that conciliation is required by law before a strike or lockout can take place*
- *To distinguish between conciliation and mediation*
- *To distinguish between conciliation and arbitration*
- *To outline the conciliation process*
- *To review the role of the conciliator*
- *To indicate the need for contract ratification by the union membership*
- *To consider the situation of federal employees*

Chapter Outline

14.1 CONCILIATION DEFINED

The term *conciliation* refers to the use of an outside third party called a *conciliator* to assist a company and the union representing its employees to arrive at a mutually satisfactory collective agreement. Such conciliation occurs after direct negotiations between the company and the union have broken down. It is required by statute in many jurisdictions some weeks prior to the date upon which the company is legally entitled to lock out its employees or the union to call its members out on strike because of failure to reach a new collective agreement. Its purpose is to help the company and the union to reach a new collective agreement without the hardship involved in a lockout or strike. With conciliation, the only means available to the conciliator to bring the parties to agreement is persuasion. Therefore, there is never any guarantee that the parties will in fact reach an agreement before the lockout and strike deadline arrives. Much will depend on the skills of the conciliator and the desire of the company and the union to settle their differences without a lockout or strike.

14.2 CONCILIATION REQUIREMENT

Under the Labour Relations Act, a union does not have the right to strike, and an employer does not have the right to lock out its employees, without having exhausted the conciliation procedure specified by the Act. In Ontario, for example, the general practice is that, on the request of either party for conciliation services, the Minister of Labour will appoint a *conciliation officer*. There is also provision in the Act for appointment of a three-person *conciliation board* should the conciliation officer fail to obtain a settlement. In practice, conciliation boards are not usually appointed and the conciliation process is that of the conciliation officer alone. Under the Ontario Labour Relations Act, a union has the right to strike and an employer has the right to lock out its employees fourteen days after the Ministry of Labour has released the report of the conciliation officer to the parties involved. There are similar conciliation-type provisions in the Labour Relations statutes of other provinces.

14.3 MEDIATION

The term *mediation* is often used instead of conciliation as it also means the use of an outside third party (called a *mediator*) to bring the two parties to an agreement by peaceful persuasion. However, the term is most commonly used to describe such negotiations when undertaken either on the eve of a strike or lockout or during the existence of one. Such mediation is undertaken at the request of one of the parties involved or at the suggestion of the government. Whereas conciliation is required by provincial statute prior to a strike or lockout, mediation is usually a voluntary process. However, both processes are similar in that they involve the services of a third person, usually a professional, to bring the parties to agreement by persuasion. Unlike arbitration, discussed later, there is no compulsory or imposed settlement. With conciliation or mediation, the parties directly involved always have the right to reject the conciliator's or mediator's suggestion.

In Ontario, the Ministry of Labour has designated a select group of people as mediators. Usually, they are former senior conciliation officers. Although there is no provision in the Act covering this situation, the Ministry of Labour will often appoint one of these people as a mediator during the fourteen-day waiting period before the union has the right to strike. This is sometimes at the request of one or both of the parties. The mediator will meet with the parties and endeavour to get a settlement without a strike. If his (or her) efforts fail and there is a strike or lockout, he may well meet with the parties again from time to time to attempt to resolve their differences. Both conciliation officers and mediators in this context are full-time employees of the Ministry of Labour.

Sometimes the company and the union will appoint a mediator agreed upon by themselves rather than one appointed by the government. Mediators may also be drawn from the ranks of lawyers, retired judges, university professors, and consultants who have developed, usually through past experience, expertise in industrial relations matters and acceptability to people in the industrial relations area. Such persons are available for employment on an *ad hoc* basis, as the need arises.

14.4 CONCILIATION VERSUS ARBITRATION

A clear distinction must be made between conciliation (or mediation) on the one hand and arbitration on the other. The conciliator (or mediator) has no power to impose a settlement on the disputing parties. He or she can only make suggestions. The purpose is to bring the parties to an agreement by persuasion. An arbitrator by contrast has the right, after investigating the matter or matters in dispute, to impose a legally binding settlement. This power may be conferred by statute, as it is in the case of many public sector employees, for whom compulsory arbitration rather than the strike weapon is the only permitted way of resolving outstanding labour-management disputes in negotiations for a new agreement. On occasion, in order to avoid or settle strikes, the federal parliament or provincial legislatures have passed special legislation requiring employees to end a strike and return to work with a settlement to be imposed by arbitration.

14.5 THE CONCILIATION PROCESS

Let us assume that a conciliation officer has been appointed to help resolve a dispute. The first step in the process is for him or her to get in touch with the company and the union and arrange a combined meeting at a place and time in the near future.

Prior Research

Next, the conciliation officer may undertake some research into the dispute, the parties involved, and the nature and problems of the industry concerned. In this way, the conciliator has some basic knowledge upon which to draw at the first meeting. He does not need to waste valuable time, the others' as well as his own, learning the essentials. However, some conciliators believe that it is better to attend the first meeting with a completely open mind and that prior reading about the matter prevents this. Thus, there are two schools of thought as to the preparations that should be made.

First Meeting

At the first meeting, often a relatively short one, the conciliator will try to determine, first of all, whether the two parties are serious about the conciliation process or whether they merely wish to go through the motions of conciliation so as to fulfil the requirements of the law. The conciliator will then try to determine the issues that have been resolved, those that are still outstanding, and the present attitudes of each party towards the outstanding issues. He or she may also try to assess, to some extent, the personalities of the negotiators for the opposing sides.

Separate Meetings

Often, the next step is for the conciliator to arrange separate meetings with the company and the union negotiating teams. At such meetings, he or she will attempt to determine the concessions that each party is willing to make in order to reach a settlement and the extent of each party's desire for a settlement. With this knowledge, the conciliator is in a position to start making suggestions for the solution of problems, involving give and take on both sides. In reality, the parties are usually quite secretive about their bargaining positions and stubborn and reluctant to make concessions. Apart from what they may feel about the righteousness of their cause, the negotiators must also keep in mind the way that any settlement may be received by the company directors and shareholders and the union membership. However, in the back of everyone's mind, is the fact that until the conciliator hands in his report to the Minister, the countdown to a strike deadline cannot commence. Hopefully, as conciliation continues, the two parties will draw closer together and, finally, as the threat of a strike or lockout approaches, reach an agreement. But, of course, conciliation does not always work out this way. And sometimes, even when the conciliator believes that he has brought about a settlement, the unexpected can occur — for example, that the agreement is rejected by higher management or the union membership.

14.6 ROLE OF THE CONCILIATOR

In practice, some parties to an industrial dispute merely observe the letter of the law with respect to conciliation. They hold meetings with the government-appointed conciliation officer at an early stage of the negotiations but do not make serious use of the services offered. Others make use of the conciliator's services only after negotiations have been carried on for some time, hoping that he or she may be able to break a negotiating impasse.

Impartial Go-between

Very often, the existence of an impartial ''go between'' has proven of inestimable value. Because of personality, intelligence, and past experience of the conciliation process, the conciliator may be able to make suggestions for solutions that enable both parties to move closer towards an agreement without abandoning their major goals. Perhaps both parties are fearful of modifying their formal negotiating positions. However, they may be willing instead to confide in the conciliator. With such additional information, the conciliator may be able to suggest an acceptable area of settlement to both parties and help bring the two parties together. Perhaps on his own initiative, with diligent probing and questioning, the conciliator can guide, coax, cajole, educate and even pressure both parties into making or accepting proposals which will in the end bring about a settlement.

Willingness to Listen

A good conciliator or mediator is one who is always willing to listen. During direct negotiations the employer is trying to convince the union and the union is trying to convince the employer. At conciliation, their function is to try to convince the conciliator and they will often try to do this with perhaps long and detailed presentations.

Waiting Period

One common frustration for conciliation officers is that, no matter what they do or say, there is a waiting period of fourteen days after the release of their report to the parties before there can be a strike. As a result, no matter what recommendation the conciliator may make, or what logic he may present, the union's real answer may be that the employer has another fourteen days in which to improve its offer. Alternatively, the employer may say that, no matter what it offers, the union can turn it down and spend the next fourteen days trying to get some more.

How Mediator's Job Differs

The mediator, on the eve of a strike, is in a much better position to get the parties to agree. Immediately before the strike deadline, the union knows that the alternative is for the union to accept the offer now or perhaps be on strike tomorrow. The company also knows immediately before the strike deadline that either a settlement will be made now or perhaps no goods will be produced tomorrow. The mediator also knows this and it makes his job very different to that of the conciliation officer.

Early Settlement

If a settlement is reached before the deadline, some managements would believe their negotiators had not bargained hard enough. Similarly, the union membership might not be convinced that their representatives had secured the best settlement possible. As a result, there is a tendency for top management and the union not to approve a settlement unless negotiations have continued right up to the deadline. In such a situation, the mediator has to recognize the importance of the timing of any settlement.

Sometimes an early settlement can spell trouble. In one company, the company and union teams would normally negotiate right up to the settlement deadline, reaching a settlement only at the last minute. The conciliator in the most recent contract negotiations thought this practice unwise and by his competence and persistence caused the company and the union negotiators to reach a settlement somewhat prior to the deadline. However, when the union took the settlement to their membership, it was voted down — the only apparent logic for this being that the membership did not believe the union had obtained the best settlement it could without going right to the deadline. Similarly, when the company negotiator reported to his principals, they also reacted that, since he had settled so soon, he had not secured the best deal possible. The conciliator failed to recognize that both negotiators needed to give their principals the impression that they bargained as hard as possible.

Judicious Pressure

One of the functions of the conciliator is to apply pressure to the parties to get them to make concessions which will bring about a settlement. However, this pressure has to be applied very judiciously. The conciliator must recognize that there is an appropriate time to apply pressure, also an appropriate time at which maximum pressure can be applied. He or she must also recognize that the negotiating parties, whatever the pressure applied, need to be given time to modify their positions.

Assessment of Positions

Another part of the conciliator's job is to assess the negotiating positions of the parties, the target settlements, and the ultimate settlements that both parties are prepared to make. The conciliator cannot go in and ask those questions directly and expect to have them answered, so he or she will probably go slowly — perhaps listening hard to find out what the company and union will and will not do — and then asking indirect questions. Perhaps the parties will do things they have said they will not do. However, unless the company makes it clear that it intends to have a lockout or the union a strike, it is only logical to assume that both want a settlement. If they do, there must be some flexibility in their respective demands. If they are reasonably close in their demands, then not a great amount of flexibility is required. If the conciliator can eliminate the strike and lockout issues from both sides, presumably what is left is negotiable. Perhaps the conciliator can coax both parties into making slightly more concessions in the negotiable area. If the conciliator can establish that the only problem left is to see who makes the final move, perhaps he can go to the company and say in confidence that if the union would do this, would you do that? If he gets some encouragement, he can go to the union with a similar proposition. If he gets some encouragement, perhaps he can recommend to the committees jointly, or perhaps more safely separately, that a settlement can be reached on that basis and have both parties agree.

In many situations, the employer's negotiating team starts off by looking for the ideal settlement desired by the employer, and the union, the ideal settlement desired by the membership. Over a period of time, one or both parties may come to recognize that their original objective is impractical. As a result, in order to avoid or end a strike or lockout, the union may settle for what is merely acceptable to its members, or the company for what will barely satisfy its top management.

14.7 CHANGING CIRCUMSTANCES

Negotiations often proceed for a considerable period of time during which circumstances may change. The company may then be faced with the choice of paying somewhat higher wages than it had planned or, for example, losing a large order or a significant share of a market. As another example, the employees and the union may have previously concluded that certain demands must be met. However, during the period of negotiations, they may find that other unions are settling for less and that a pattern of settlement has developed which they are compelled to accept without accomplishing their original objectives. Also, general economic conditions may have changed. Thus when the company and union started negotiations, the economy may have been prospering and personal prospects seemed encouraging. However, if a general economic downturn or an industry downturn develops during the course of negotiations, this will reduce the union's optimism as to the possible settlement. These changes can occur during the life of a strike as well as during the life of negotiations.

14.8 CONTRACT RATIFICATION

Before a newly negotiated contract can be signed by union officials, it must be approved or "ratified" by the union members. Such a ratification takes the form of a vote at a meeting, usually at the local union hall, which members are invited to attend. If the members reject the proposed new contract, the union negotiators must go back to the bargaining table to try to resolve the problem.

14.9 FEDERAL EMPLOYEES

A conciliation board or conciliation commissioner may be appointed to investigate an industrial dispute involving federal employees or other federal employees under federal jurisdiction and to make recommendations for a settlement. However, unlike an arbitration report, such recommendations are not binding on the employer or employees. They represent what the conciliation board or commissioner feels is an acceptable settlement, taking into account all the facts involved.

Since such recommendations are not binding, the question arises: what good do they achieve? In fact it has been argued that they do more harm than good — encouraging the party whose bargaining goals are most favoured in the recommendations from softening its bargaining position. Such a softening may be essential if a negotiated settlement is to be reached. For this very reason, a federal task force on Canadian industrial relations recommended some years ago that conciliation boards be cut back in favour of conciliation officers (or mediators). In other words, that more positive steps can be achieved by having a conciliator act as an intermediary, helping the parties to reach a negotiated settlement, rather than by having a board to pass judgment and produce a set of recommendations binding on no one. In practice such conciliation board reports may have helped bring about and prolong strikes rather than hasten a settlement. Because of this, Ontario some years ago effectively gave up the practice of appointing conciliation boards.

KEY CONCEPTS

Conciliation	Mediator
Conciliator	Arbitration
Conciliation Board	Conciliation process
Mediation	Ratification

REVIEW QUESTIONS

1. What is meant by the term "conciliation"?

2. When is conciliation required?

3. Distinguish between conciliation and mediation. What do they have in common?

4. What types of persons act as conciliators and mediators? By whom are they appointed?

5. Distinguish between conciliation and mediation on the one hand and arbitration on the other.

6. What preparation should a conciliator undertake before starting his or her conciliation efforts. Explain.

7. What might the conciliator attempt to do at the first meeting with the union and employer negotiating teams?

8. Why can the conciliator's role be so valuable in negotiations?

9. What problems does the conciliator face? Why is the conciliator's task more difficult than the mediator's one?

10. Why is the timing of a settlement so important? Why is an early settlement usually undesirable?

11. How can a conciliator exert pressure on the negotiating parties? Why is such pressure necessary?

12. What assessments does the conciliator have to make? How does he go about making them?

13. How can changing circumstances affect negotiations? Give examples.

14. What is a "ratification vote"? Who is allowed to participate?

15. Sometimes a union may reject an employer's final offer and call a strike even though a majority of the employees may be willing to accept the offer. Is this situation (a) desirable? and (b) inevitable?

CHAPTER 15: STRIKES AND LOCKOUTS

Chapter Objectives

- *To define the terms: strike, lockout, and work stoppage*

- *To indicate the various types of strikes in which workers may take part*

- *To explain the purpose of a strike and how it can be most effective*

- *To explain why a firm would lock out its employees and consider how effective this can be*

- *To point out that workers occasionally engage in wildcat strikes — ones that are not approved by their union*

- *To explain the use of picketing by union members to hamper production in a strike-bound plant*

- *To explain how a boycott can be used as a means of industrial action*

- *To indicate the nature and purpose of court injunctions*

- *To point out that in all provinces of Canada, except Quebec, employers are permitted to hire replacement workers during a strike*

- *To stress that the use of professional strike breakers by employers is now considered to be an unfair labour practice*

Chapter Outline

15.1   Types of Strikes

15.2   Purpose and Effectiveness of a Strike

15.3   Locking Out the Employees

15.4   Unlawful Strikes and Lockouts

15.5   Unauthorized Strikes

15.6   Picketing

15.7   Boycotts

15.8   Injunctions

15.9   Replacement of Strikers During a Legal Strike

15.10 Professional Strike Breakers

Failing a settlement through negotiations and conciliation, a union has the legal right to call its members out on strike and an employer the legal right to lock out its employees. A *strike* is the temporary refusal of the employees to continue working for the employer. A *lockout* is the temporary refusal of the employer to continue providing work for its employees and may involve the temporary closing of the employer's establishment. The term *work stoppage* is now also used, particularly in statistical documents, to describe such events — thereby avoiding the need to assign responsibility for the breakdown in labour-management relations. The number of person-days lost in Canada in recent years through work stoppages is shown in Table 15.1. The total includes all industries, not just those shown separately.

15.1 TYPES OF STRIKES

When a union declares a strike, its members usually leave the employer's premises and go home, perhaps stopping by the union hall or other meeting place. In other words, there is *walkout*. Sometimes, however, the union members stay on the job but slow down the pace of their activity. This is known as a *slowdown*. Often it serves as a prelude to a full strike, giving warning to the employer of the employees' dissatisfaction. Although causing aggravation to the employer and its customers, union members are still employed and continue to receive their pay. This state of affairs may continue until a settlement is reached, or the employer loses patience and sends the workers home, or attempts other disciplinary measures. Similarly, union members may remain at work but observe many of the detailed rules governing their jobs which may have previously been ignored in order to maintain a reasonable rate of production. As a result, fewer goods are produced or poorer service is given to customers. Such a form of industrial action is termed *work-to-rule*.

Another form of strike in which union members withdraw their services but stay on the work premises is a *sit-down strike*. As a matter of interest, this type of industrial action was successfully used by the United Automobile Workers' Union in 1937 to secure recognition by General Motors Corporation. In more recent times, union members, when faced with plant closings and loss of jobs and even pensions, have resorted to similar types of action. One important advantage of a sit-down strike from the union's point of view, is that it makes it more difficult for the employer to bring in replacement labour. Another advantage is that the forcible removal of the striking workers can become a highly publicized event, likely to arouse public sympathy and to focus public attention on the labour-management dispute.

Table 15.1 — *Time Lost in Work Stoppages, in thousands of person days*

Year	Mines, quarries oil wells	Manufacturing	Construction	Transportation
1976	580	4 493	2 857	623
1977	91	1 693	405	527
1978	1 700	2 528	1 233	946
1979	1 586	3 129	88	1 182
1980	418	3 137	1 107	729
1981	581	4 638	43	1 514
1982	257	1 691	2 200	566
1983	178	1 385	244	275
1984	37	2 356	213	550
1985	90	1 578	11	479
1986	352	1 387	1 963	305
1987	229	1 758	54	699
1988	162	1 395	633	2 012
1989	190	1 220	137	365

Year	Trade	Community, business and personal service	TOTAL
1976	209	2 822	11 610
1977	129	436	3 308
1978	246	672	7 393
1979	247	1 490	7 834
1980	219	2 632	8 976
1981	149	1 603	8 879
1982	171	903	5 795
1983	252	2 093	4 444
1984	188	518	3 872
1985	468	547	3 181
1986	239	863	7 134
1987	326	916	3 984
1988	190	636	5 046
1989	211	1 452	3 663

Source: Labour Canada, *Research Bulletin*

Note: (1) Statistics on work stoppages include all strikes and lock-outs, whether legal or illegal, which last for one-half day or more and amount to 10 or more person-days of time lost. Time lost by workers indirectly affected, such as those laid off because of a work stoppage by other employees, is not included.

(2) The *total* includes all work stoppages, including agriculture, forestry, fishing, trapping, finance, insurance and real estate, and public administration and defence industries — not shown separately.

Occasionally, other unions may call their members out on strike to support the strikers. This is called a *sympathy strike*. However, such an action is considered to be illegal.

Sometimes, the workers on a job may, according to their different skills, be represented by several different unions rather than by just one. In such circumstances, there can occasionally be disputes as to which workers (for example, labourers or bricklayers) are entitled to perform a particular type of work. Inevitably the employer will tend to favour the workers with the lower rate of pay so long as they can perform the work competently. The union representing the higher-paid workers may then call its members out on strike to protest the awarding of the work to the members of the other union — work that should, by custom, belong to its own members. Such a strike is known as a *jurisdictional strike*. Somewhat similar in origin is the calling of a strike by a union to protest the "contracting out" of work formerly performed by its members — for example, maintenance, cleaning or security services. Instead of having its own employees do the work and having to pay them wages and benefits, the employer may find it cheaper and more convenient to engage the services of an outside firm.

15.2 PURPOSE AND EFFECTIVENESS OF A STRIKE

A labour union, by means of a strike, is trying to exert financial and, to some extent, public pressure on the employer to accept the union's demands as to the terms for a new collective agreement. However, to be successful, the union and its striking members, must be able to stop or at least substantially reduce the firm's production or other operations. Otherwise, the employer sustains no immediate financial loss, no loss of customer goodwill, and no permanent loss of customers to competitors.

When a strike takes place, the employer is sometimes able to continue production by using other non-union employees such as supervisory personnel and by hiring new workers (known to the strikers as "scabs") to perform the tasks formerly done by the striking workers. Usually, however, the firm cannot continue to operate during a strike, except in a crippled fashion. And the strike is a highly effective means of persuading the employer to modify its bargaining position.

Sometimes, however, the union may fail to halt production. As a result, the union may continue to weaken itself financially by paying strike pay to its members and by paying advertising and other expenses, without moving any closer to a favourable settlement of the dispute. The individual union members may suffer even more severely, receiving only strike pay, if anything, instead of their regular wages.

The longer a strike goes on, the better the settlement that the union must obtain in order to make all the financial and other hardships worthwhile. Otherwise, the extra pay, etc. will not be sufficient to offset the financial losses taken during the strike. The worst of all worlds is to have a long strike and a meagre settlement. The best is a short strike and a generous settlement. Consequently the decision to strike, irrespective of any social or political implications, should not be taken lightly but must be based on a careful appraisal of all the factors involved: rates of pay elsewhere; the economic climate; the ability of the employer to pay; the public demand for the employer's product; possible public reaction; and so on. Some strikes have in fact been followed by the permanent closing of the employer's establishment and the permanent loss of jobs, a highly undesirable and unforeseen outcome. On a less drastic scale, strikes have sometimes been followed by the contracting out of some types of work such as maintenance unless expressly forbidden as one of the terms of a new settlement.

15.3 LOCKING OUT THE EMPLOYEES

In order to cover ongoing expenses and make a profit, an employer must continue to produce and market its goods or services. Obviously, therefore, the employer will not lightly decide to lock out its workers. The only factors that will make such a decision a logical one include: the belief that it is a necessary measure to place economic pressure on the union to come to a settlement; the belief that such a lockout will only need to be of short duration; perhaps the previous declaration of a strike by the union; the existence already of a slow-down or work-to-rule movement among its employees; or the belief that the union and its members are in no financial position to withstand a continued loss of wages and benefits.

If the employer is to be successful in its lockout, the loss of wages and benefits by the union members must create financial hardship. If, however, the union has a large strike fund, it may, at least for some time, be able to negate or at least mitigate the economic effects of the lockout. Also, if other unions provide financial assistance, this will reduce the impact of the lockout. The longer the lockout continues, the greater the hardship on the employees and the greater the pressure on the union to come to a settlement.

15.4 UNLAWFUL STRIKES AND LOCKOUTS

The calling of a strike, or the declaration of a lockout, must conform with the provisions of the Labour Relations Act or other similar provincial or federal statute. An *unlawful strike* is a strike that contravenes one or more provisions of the labour relations statute and lays the union and its members open to charges and possible fines and/or periods of imprisonment, if found guilty. Similarly, an *unlawful lockout* is a lockout that also contravenes one or more provisions of the statute and which lays the employer open to similar charges and possible penalties. It would be unlawful, for example, for a union to call a strike during the term of an existing collective agreement. It would also be unlawful for a union to call a strike prior to the expiration of the waiting period after conciliation and after the termination of the collective agreement. Also, of course, it would be unlawful for the union to call a strike in an industry whose workers, because of the essential nature of their services, are not by statute, permitted to strike. Similarly, it would be unlawful for an employer to lock out its employees in any of these circumstances.

15.5 UNAUTHORIZED STRIKES

So far, we have assumed that all strikes are called by the union. In practice, this may not always be so. Those that are not, are termed *unauthorized, unofficial or wildcat strikes*. Sometimes a union leadership will lose touch with the mood of its membership and work too slowly to correct injustices that the membership may feel strongly about. Unofficial leaders, perhaps younger and more dynamic, may capture support of the union members and persuade them to down tools. This may occur just before the union's declaration of a strike or perhaps in direct defiance of union orders to stay on the job. An unofficial strike may be lawful or unlawful, depending on when it takes place. Thus, if a wildcat strike takes place during the life of a collective agreement, it is unlawful. If it take place, once the union is in a legal strike position after negotiations and conciliation, it is lawful.

15.6 PICKETING

To hamper the employer in its efforts to maintain production and sales during a strike, the union will arrange for its members to picket the employer's premises. *Picketing* is the stationing of union members at the entrances and exits of the struck plant to discourage the movement of materials, parts, and non-striking and replacement workers (the so-called ''scabs'') into the premises and the shipping of finished goods out of them. Union members are required to take turns on the picket line and help prepare placards and other signs. Payment of strike pay is often conditional on picket duty. Picketing workers are sometimes joined ι .nembers of their families and by other supporters including, occasionally, politicians.

Picketing is supposed to be non-violent, involving only the physical presence of the striking workers in modest numbers and the use of signs and verbal communications: to explain their point of view and to solicit support from non-striking workers of the employer or employees of other firms who need to visit the premises in the course of their work — for example, to deliver materials or collect products. In practice, tempers may occasionally become frayed and the presence of the police may be required to keep order at the factory gates. If violence breaks out or police orders are ignored, the offenders may be arrested and charged with one or more criminal offences such as obstructing a police officer in the course of his duty or committing assault.

Although unusual in Canada, *secondary picketing* occurred extensively in the United Kingdom some years ago, notably in the various coal miners' strikes. Such picketing involves the placing of pickets comprised of striking union members and their supporters outside the premises of firms which supply materials, parts, fuel, transportation and other services to the firm that is being struck.

15.7 BOYCOTTS

Another method that a union can adopt to increase pressure on the employer is a *boycott* of the employer's products. This means that union members and their supporters refuse to buy the firm's products so long as the strike or lockout continues. However, to have any great impact on the employer, the boycott must be wide-spread. It must involve a large segment of the buying public rather than just the strikers and their immediate supporters. Thus there must be a great deal of public sympathy for the striking workers if a boycott is to succeed.

15.8 INJUNCTIONS

Another weapon that management may use is the *injunction*. This is a court order forbidding the persons to whom it is directed from carrying on a certain activity. Formerly, court orders were used to forbid a wide variety of union activities. Nowadays their use appears to be restricted to persons damaging the employer's property, committing acts of violence, trespassing, and engaging in acts of intimidation — for example, mass picketing. An injunction may be granted if the court is convinced that damage will otherwise be done to the employer's property and that this damage could not be compensated for by a monetary award. An injunction can also be used against any conspiracy to commit personal injury, to induce breach of contract, or to interfere with contractual relations. The injunction carries the weight of the law behind it.

There are several types of injunctions. A *restrictive injunction* orders a person to stop doing something — for example, to stop intimidating workers. A *mandatory injunction* orders a person to do something — for example, to remove barriers. Because of the time it takes for a dispute to be tried in court, a judge may grant a temporary injunction. This may be for a fixed period of time, in which case it is called an *interim injunction*; or it may be for an indefinite period until the matter is finally judged in court, in which case it is called an *interlocutory injunction*. An *interim injunction* is one made for a short period and without notice to the other party. When a case is tried in court, the judge may grant a *permanent injunction* if he or she finds in favour of the plaintiff and considers an injunction a necessary remedy.

The use of the injunction has been strongly criticized by labour unions on the grounds that by limiting pickets, for example, a strike is made ineffective. In other words, they consider that the use of the injunction confers an unfair bargaining advantage on the employer.

15.9 REPLACEMENT OF STRIKERS DURING A LEGAL STRIKE

In all jurisdictions in Canada, except Quebec, employers are permitted to hire employees during a strike and assign to them work previously done by strikers. Therefore a small employer, particularly of relatively unskilled employees, may be able to hire enough replacement employees to continue normal operations during a strike.

For a very large employer, such as General Motors in Oshawa, it is relatively impractical to be able to hire and train enough new employees to maintain a high level of production during a strike. Similarly, it is usually impractical for an employer of large numbers of highly-trained technical employees to find sufficient appropriately qualified replacement people to carry on normal production during a strike. However, many other firms do hire replacement workers.

In the latter case, some argue that strikers should be able to return to their jobs after a strike is over and that the replacement workers should be dismissed. Others argue that employees hired during a strike are entitled to some form of job security. Some argue that employees who went on strike have the right to employment status but not necessarily the jobs they had before the strike.

According to Section 73(1) of Ontario's Labour Relations Act:

> "Where an employee engaging in a lawful strike makes an unconditional application in writing to his employer within six months from the commencement of the lawful strike to return to work, the employer shall . . . reinstate the employee in his former employment on such terms as the employer and the employee may agree upon, and the employer in offering terms of employment shall not discriminate against the employee by reason of his exercising or having exercised any rights under this act."

In Alberta, subsequent to a lengthy strike at the Gainers Meat Packing Plant in which the employer did hire employees in its efforts to maintain production, a new section was introduced in the Labour Relations Code as follows:

> "When a strike or lockout ends . . . as a result of a settlement . . . any employee affected by the dispute whose employment relationship with the employer has not been otherwise lawfully terminated is entitled, on request, to resume his employment with the employer in preference to an employee hired by the employer as a replacement employee for the employee making the request during the strike or lockout."

The Manitoba Labour Relations Act prohibits employers from hiring permanent workers during a strike. Workers may be recalled to their previous jobs according to seniority and as such work becomes available.

By contrast with the other provinces, Quebec alone prohibits the hiring of replacement workers during a strike — thereby avoiding the need to consider what happens to them after the strike is over.

Quebec's no-replacement provision reads as follows:

> "Every employer is prohibited from:
>
> 1. The direct replacement of workers legally on strike;
>
> 2. The hiring of additional workers prior to the commencement of a strike or lockout, on the understanding they will work during the strike or lockout period;
>
> 3. The use of workers who are in the bargaining unit on strike but who are prepared to work in another of the employer's establishments;
>
> 4. The importation of workers from other establishments operated by the employer for the purpose of keeping a strike-bound establishment functioning."

15.10 PROFESSIONAL STRIKE BREAKERS

It is now considered to be an unfair labour practice for employers to use professional strike breakers during a strike in Ontario, Manitoba and British Columbia.

According to the Ontario Labour Relations Act:

> "No person, employer, employers' organization or person acting on behalf of an employer or employers organization shall engage in strike-related misconduct or retain the services of a professional strike breaker and no person shall act as a professional strike breaker."

The Act further states:

> " 'Professional strike breaker' means a person who is not involved in a dispute whose primary object, in the Board's opinion, is to interfere with, obstruct, prevent, restrain or disrupt the exercise of any right under this act in anticipation of, or during, a lawful strike or lockout.
>
> 'Strike-related misconduct' means a course of conduct of incitement, intimidation, coercion, undue influence, provocation, infiltration, surveillance or any other like course of conduct intended to interfere with, obstruct, prevent, restrain or disrupt the exercise of any right under this Act in anticipation of, or during, a lawful strike or lockout."

KEY CONCEPTS

Strike	*Scabs*
Lockout	*Unlawful strike*
Work stoppage	*Unlawful lockout*
Walkout	*Wildcat strike*
Slow down	*Picketing*
Work-to-rule	*Boycott*
Sit-down strike	*Injunction*
Sympathy strike	*Replacement workers*
Jurisdictional strike	*Strikebreakers*
Contracting out	

REVIEW QUESTIONS

1. Explain the terms: (a) strike, (b) lockout, and (c) work stoppage.

2. Why would union members go on a slow-down or engage in a work-to-rule action rather than leave their jobs?

3. Why would union members choose to engage in a sit-down strike rather than go home?

4. What is a sympathy strike? What other actions might be taken?

5. What is a jurisdictional strike?

6. What is the immediate purpose of a strike?

7. What determines the effectiveness of a strike?

8. How can an employer overcome the effects of a strike?

9. What factors should be taken into account by a union before it calls a strike?

10. Why would a firm lock out its employees? What would determine the success of such a lockout?

11. When would a strike or lockout be unlawful? What are the possible legal implications for the union or employer?

12. What is an unofficial or wildcat strike? Why would it occur? Would it be legal or illegal?

13. Explain the nature and purpose of picketing. Why are police sometimes required?

14. What is secondary picketing?

15. A boycott has been used more as a political weapon than as an industrial one. Discuss.

16. What is necessary, if a boycott is to be effective?

17. Explain the use of injunctions by employers.

18. Should employers be allowed to hire replacement workers during a strike? If so, what should be the right of such workers after the strike is over? Discuss.

19. What are "professional strike breakers"? Are they legally permissible? Explain and discuss.

PART E

Administering the
Collective Agreement

CHAPTER 16: GRIEVANCE PROCEDURE

Chapter Objectives

- *To explain what is meant by a grievance, as distinct from a complaint*
- *To point out that a time limit exists for filing a grievance*
- *To outline the basic steps involved in a typical grievance procedure*
- *To review an example of an actual grievance procedure*
- *To discuss the "complaint stage" of this procedure*
- *To examine each of the steps involved in the actual grievance procedure*
- *To discuss the matter of retroactive payment where appropriate for employees whose grievance has been successful*
- *To indicate that under most collective agreements the company and the union, as well as the employees, have the right to file grievances*
- *To explain the term "grievance rate" and consider why a grievance rate may be high or low*
- *To discuss the value of grievance procedures from the viewpoints of the employees, the employer and the public*
- *To explain whether an employee has the right to proceed with a grievance against the wishes of the union*

Chapter Outline

16.1 Grievance Defined

16.2 Time Limit for Filing a Grievance

16.3 Steps in a Grievance Procedure

16.4 Example of an Actual Grievance Procedure Clause

16.5 Retroactive Payment

16.6 Right of Company and Union to File Grievances

16.7 The Grievance Rate

16.8 Value of a Grievance Procedure

16.9 Duty of Fair Representation

16.1 GRIEVANCE DEFINED

Every collective agreement contains a *grievance procedure* — the steps by which a dispute between management and labour during the life of the agreement may be amicably settled. A *grievance* is usually considered to be an alleged violation of the collective agreement. A complaint (for example, "it's too hot in here") may not constitute a grievance. The person who files a grievance is called the *grievor*.

The grievance procedure shown in Exhibit 16A provides no definition of a grievance and this is true of many grievance procedures. Many people consider it desirable to have a definition but in practice there is a problem as to how to define, in a manner acceptable to both union and management, the concept of a grievance. One approach is to define a grievance as "an alleged violation of a collective agreement". When the company proposes such a definition to the union, one of the likely responses of the union is to say: What about the employee complaint that is not an alleged violation of the agreement? Should he or she not also have the right to process such a complaint? There is also some advantage to the employer in having such complaints processed. In this way the company finds out what problems are bothering its employees. Certainly, in the interest of good employee relations, the employer should be interested in resolving such problems.

One very practical approach to resolving this dilemma is to allow any matter bothering an employee to be processed through the grievance procedure. However, when such matters are processed, a distinction is made between those that allege violations of the collective agreement and are therefore subject to arbitration, and those that do not allege any violations. The latter will be handled as complaints that are not subject to arbitration. Hopefully, the employer is interested in resolving both kinds of problems in a proper manner.

16.2 TIME LIMIT FOR FILING A GRIEVANCE

Nearly all collective agreements have a time limit for filing a grievance. These time limits range from say 24 hours up to 6 months or a year, with the occasional one having no time limit at all. Perhaps the most common types of time limit are in the range of 30 to 60 days after the event which gave rise to the grievance.

16.3 STEPS IN A GRIEVANCE PROCEDURE

A grievance procedure specifies the steps which must be followed in settling an alleged violation of the collective agreement. These steps vary according to the particular collective agreement, but may be as follows:

1. The employee first asks the foreman's help in settling the complaint — for example, why the employee did not receive the proper overtime pay.

2. If no satisfactory solution is found, the employee will report the grievance to the shop steward, who is the unpaid union representative in each shop, or section, of the plant. Very often, the employee will go directly to the shop steward rather than first talking to the foreman or supervisor. The shop steward, who is normally permitted time off from his or her job in the shop to process grievances, will normally put the matter in writing and then attempt to settle the grievance with the shop foreman.

3. If the foreman's decision is not acceptable to the employee, the chief steward for the plant may take the matter up with the department superintendent.

4. If the grievance is still not resolved to the employee's satisfaction, the union may ask for a meeting of the firm's Industrial Relations Manager and the Union's Grievance Committee.

5. If this meeting fails to achieve a decision acceptable to both sides, arrangements are made for an arbitrator or an arbitration board to settle the matter. This arbitrator is an outside person (such as a university professor), acceptable to both labour and management, who will listen to the two viewpoints, ask questions, and finally make an award. Arbitration is the making of a decision, or award, which is legally binding on both the employer and the union. The provincial Labour Relations Acts make compulsory the inclusion of an arbitration provision in all labour agreements. The cost of the arbitrator is usually shared equally by management and the union. In the next chapter, we look in some detail at arbitration.

16.4 EXAMPLE OF AN ACTUAL GRIEVANCE PROCEDURE CLAUSE

Exhibit 16A (below) contains an example of an actual grievance procedure:

EXHIBIT 16A: *Example of a Grievance Procedure Clause in a Collective Agreement*

Article 6

GRIEVANCE PROCEDURE

6.01   It is the mutual desire of the parties hereto that complaints from the employees shall be adjusted as quickly as possible, and it is generally understood that an employee shall not file a grievance until he has first given his supervisor an opportunity of adjusting his complaint.

6.02   The complaint shall be taken up as a grievance only within six months of the event giving rise to the complaint.

6.03   *Step No. 1* — Between the Employee, his Steward, and his Supervisor.
An employee with a grievance may discuss the matter with his steward who may present the grievance in writing, signed by the employee, to the supervisor indicating the time and the date of receipt by him. The supervisor shall give an answer in writing to the steward within two working days.

6.04   *Step No. 2* — Between the Employee, the Chief Steward, and the Manufacturing Manager or his nominee.
If settlement of the grievance has not been reached under Step No. 1, then this step shall commence within four working days following receipt by the steward of the answer in Step No. 1. The Manufacturing Manager or his nominee shall give an answer in writing to the Chief Steward within three working days of receiving the grievance.

6.05   *Step No. 3* — Between the Employee, the Union, and the Supervisor, Industrial Relations or his nominee.
If a settlement of the grievance has not been reached under Step. No. 2, then this step shall commence within ten calendar days following receipt by the Chief Steward of the answer in Step No. 2. The Supervisor, Industrial Relations, or his nominee shall arrange a meeting within one week of receiving the grievance and shall give an answer in writing to the Union within not more than five working days following such meeting. The union will be given a minimum of forty-eight hours' notice prior to such meeting. Union representatives at the third step of the grievance procedure may consist of the President of the Local, the Chief Steward, and the Steward representing the grievor, and one Union representative who is not an employee of the Company, and any employee possessing factual knowledge bearing on the mat-

ter in dispute. The Union may appoint an alternate to act in place of any of the foregoing employes, when such employee is unavailable at the time of a third step grievance hearing.

6.06   A grievance which is not processed within the time limits set out in this article, or which is not posted to arbitration within thirty calendar days after the answer has been given under Step No. 3 hereof, shall be deemed to have been settled or abandoned.

6.07   If the Company fails to comply with the time limits set out in this Article, the grievance may be entered at the next step.

6.08   The Company shall have the right to have present at the third step of the grievance procedure any officers, officials, or agents of the Company.

6.09   It is recognized that the Company shall have the right to take up a grievance with the Union relating to the conduct of the Union, its officers, or any other Union representatives, or the conduct of the employees, or concerning the application or interpretation of any provision of this Agreement. The grievance shall first be presented in writing to the Union and a meeting will be held within one week between the Company and the Union. The Union shall answer the grievance within one week of such meeting.

6.10   It is recognized that the Union shall have the right to take up a grievance with the Company relative to the violation, misinterpretation, or non-application of any provision of this Agreement. The grievance shall be first presented in writing to the Company and a meeting will be held within one week between the Union and the Company. The Company shall answer the grievance within one week of such meeting.

6.11   Any adjustment arising out of the settlement of a grievance relating to a claim for retroactive payment shall be limited to a period of six months prior to the date on which the grievance was first presented hereunder.

Complaint Stage

At the beginning of this procedure, there is a provision for a complaint stage prior to filing a grievance. This step, designed to help resolve problems, exists in some grievance procedures but not in all. It provides an opportunity for employees with a complaint to discuss with their supervisor the nature of the problem. Perhaps the supervisor was not aware of the problem. Perhaps he or she did not realize the effect it had on the employee. Sometimes, in this way, the problem can be quickly resolved. The complaint procedure tends to be informal; there is nothing in writing. Often, a discussion of the complaint enables the supervisor to take some action that will resolve the matter.

Unions are reluctant to agree to a compulsory complaint procedure that requires employees to discuss any problem with their foreperson without the presence of their union representative. Such a procedure tends to inhibit employees from raising complaints and perhaps, because of lack of knowledge of the collective agreement, encourages employees to agree to things that they would not have agreed to if there had been proper union representation. Also from the union point of view, it does not give the union the opportunity to bring to bear its experience in other parts of the company or to express its concern as to how the action might affect other employees.

Handling Grievances

In this particular example, the first step in the grievance procedure is between the employee, the steward and the supervisor. The second step is between the employee, the chief steward and the manufacturing manager or nominee, and the third step between the employee, the union and the supervisor of industrial relations or nominee.

Logic Behind the Grievance Procedure

Perhaps the logic behind this arrangement is that the first step gives an opportunity for the employee to tell his or her story, for the union steward to point out the alleged violations of the agreement, and for the supervisor to be able to quickly correct the matter if the grievance is deemed justifiable.

If the problem is not resolved at the first step, then the logic is to allow the employee, the chief steward — hopefully with more experience than the shop steward — and the manufacturing manager, again hopefully with more experience and authority than the supervisor, to deal with the problem. Sometimes, the more senior manager can look at the problem with less emotion and perhaps bring more experience to bear on it. He or she will then overrule or uphold the supervisor's decision.

Similarly, the chief steward, again hopefully with more experience than the steward, may perhaps see weaknesses in the union position or alternatively, argue the union position more effectively and thereby bring about its resolution. In Step 3, the union representation would normally include an outside union representative who probably has much more experience and much more training, and perhaps better judgment than the inside union representatives. As a result, the outside representative may bring more to bear on the decision-making process, and also may argue the union case more effectively than the others.

On the company side, the Supervisor Industrial Relations should have a good knowledge of what the employee can or cannot win in arbitration. Being removed from line management, he or she may perhaps make a judgment somewhat different to that which the line management would make.

Therefore, since the same problem is being looked at in each of three different steps, it is in effect being looked at by three different groups of people who should consider all the various aspects of the problem. Hopefully, this procedure should result in the employee and the union being accorded their legitimate rights. Where the employee and the union do not have the rights they claim, this should hopefully become apparent to them and the problem be resolved without recourse to arbitration.

In order to expedite the problem solving and to prevent procrastination or uncertainty on either side, there is, at each step, a time limit on both the union and the company. Failure to meet any of these time limits can result in the grievance being automatically processed to the next stage, or automatically considered to have been withdrawn or resolved.

16.5 RETROACTIVE PAYMENT

One of the items that has to be resolved sooner or later is the amount of retroactive payment that can result from a grievance about rates of pay. Some agreements provide no time limit to retroactive pay; others provide that there will be no retroactive payment prior to the date of filing of a grievance. In practice, a company may argue that, even if there has been a violation of the collective agreement, there should be no payment for the period prior to the date of filing of the grievance. This is because no one has called attention to the alleged violation of the agreement. Surely, the company may argue, it should not be held responsible for retroactive payment for the period prior to its being made aware of such a problem.

The counter-argument could be that the employee is entitled to the payment, because it is required by the collective agreement. It is the company's fault that it was in violation of the agreement. The only redress available to the employee for the violation is compensation. The employer's requirement to pay what is required under the collective agreement should not be limited by the fact that the employee did not immediately file a grievance. From these and other conflicting arguments, agreement should eventually be reached on the amount of retroactive payment.

In many collective agreements, a maximum period for retroactive payment is set out. In our example, the period is six months prior to the date on which the grievance was first presented. Many other agreements provide maximum time limits, such as 30 days, 60 days, 90 days or perhaps a year prior to the date of filing the grievance.

16.6 RIGHT OF COMPANY AND UNION TO FILE GRIEVANCES

It is fairly common in a collective agreement for the company and the union to set out specifically the right of each to file grievances (as distinct from an employee's right). However, it is unusual for a company to file a grievance. An example of a *company grievance* would be in regard to a work stoppage or in regard to the conduct of the union, its officers or any other union representatives, or it might want simply to file a grievance in order to deal with the interpretation of a certain provision in the collective agreement.

A *union grievance* filed under this provision of the collective agreement relates to something that no individual employee would be able to deal with effectively. It might, for example, be the violation, misinterpretation or non-application of a provision of the agreement that affects a large number of the employees. Thus the union might file a grievance questioning the method of calculating statutory holiday pay, or the requirements for employee entitlement to it. As another example, it might file a policy grievance with regard to the conditions under which employees are entitled to receive overtime payment. Both of these grievances differ from the claim of any individual employee with regard to statutory holiday payment or overtime payment.

16.7 THE GRIEVANCE RATE

The *grievance rate* is the number of grievances filed in relation to the number of union members in the company. Some firms enjoy a low grievance rate while others suffer from a high one. In the latter case, something is obviously wrong — either on the management side or on the union side.

Factors that help determine the rate of grievances in a firm include the following:

1. Union-employee relations

2. Past history of union-employer dealings

3. Personalities of key union and company officials

4. Pay and seniority

5. Technological changes

6. Union policies

7. Grievance procedure

8. Management policies

1. Union-Employer Relations

The better the relations, the lower is likely to be the grievance rate, and vice-versa. Good relations help reduce the number of grievances because employees are less likely to be militant, raising technicalities and bringing cases just for the purpose of harassing management; also employees are more likely to settle their complaints orally with the foreperson. If bad relations exist, a trade union will tend to stir up grievances just to strengthen the solidarity of the union and to provoke and upset management. In such a situation, a larger proportion of disputes turn into written formal grievances rather than being settled quickly at the foreperson level.

A low grievance rate does not always mean that relations are good. Nor does a high rate necessarily mean they are bad. Sometimes a low grievance rate accompanies bad union-management relations — for example, if the employer has recently defeated the union in a long strike. Grievances in the company are few, mainly because management is tough and the defeat of the union in a strike has left the union too weak to challenge the employer. A low grievance rate may also indicate that many disputes are settled outside the formal grievance procedure.

A high grievance rate may sometimes exist, despite good management-labour relations, because the union does not screen complaints properly or because the particular work situation produces a great many problems or disputes.

2. Past History of Union-Employer Dealings

The amount of experience that union and management have previously had in dealing with each other has a decisive influence on a firm's grievance rate. Unreasonable positions may be taken by one side or another or even by both, just because they do not know what is reasonable. As a consequence, the grievance rate is a lot higher than it should be. Also, when a union is newly certified, it may lack leaders who are willing and able to distinguish between complaints that are violations of the labour agreement and ones that are not. Often the union stewards, trying to win approval from the rank and file employees, accept too easily as grievances the complaints brought to their attention.

3. Personalities of Key Union and Company Officials

Sometimes an individual with a strong personality will tend to impose his or her view as to the way that the union or management should be treated. The other officials are relegated to a back seat. There have often been drastic changes in the labour relations climate and hence in grievance activity following changes in either management or union representations or both.

4. Pay and Seniority

The pay system used in a plant can greatly affect the rate of grievances. Even with an hourly system there are disputes about job grades, overtime rates, and so on. However, the use of incentive pay standards can result in many more disputes. Every piece rate or every production standard used to determine bonus payments may be challenged. Piece work and bonus plans inevitably result in different earnings by different employees and groups of employees. This can give rise to jealousy, suspicion and claims of unfair treatment which eventually bubble to the surface in the form of grievances.

Another source of friction is the application of seniority in transfers and layoffs. If the firm is thriving, there is little or no need for transfers or layoffs. Consequently, few grievances will result. However, if production has to be curtailed and the labour force reduced, the opposite will be the case. This is especially so if the seniority system includes some room for management judgement, such as the relative skills and ability of the persons involved.

5. Technological Changes

Many workers view with suspicion any change in production technology because of the belief, often based on past experience, that the main purpose of such change is to reduce the number of workers required, to place greater demands upon them with no additional pay, or to replace many of the present employees with lower paid, less skilled workers. Changes in production technology and work methods can be a major source of grievances.

Changes in managerial methods and policies, particularly ones that require transfers, promotions or layoffs, are also likely to raise issues that produce grievances. If a firm is losing money, or finding that its production costs are becoming too high relative to those of its competitors, it will probably undertake drastic changes in its organization and work methods. This often brings about a rash of grievances.

6. Union Policies

Some unions deliberately encourage their members to bring forward grievances. Others discourage them from doing so, trying to settle the matter without filing grievances. Some unions are fairly neutral. Whatever the case, union policy can greatly influence the rate of grievances in a firm.

At the shop floor level, the fact that a steward is elected rather than appointed may greatly affect the number of grievances filed. The elected steward, in order to maintain or promote personal popularity with the union members, might encourage them to make claims even though many of such claims stand little chance of success. Position in the union hierarchy, rivalry for presidency or for places on the union grievance committee, can also affect the militancy of attitude of the union leaders in their relations with management — that is, their willingness to confront rather than co-operate with management.

7. Grievance Procedure

The way in which grievances are handled has a lot to do with grievance rates. If, for example, the collective agreement provides for a large number of shop stewards compared with the number of employees, for payment to shop stewards and committee members for time spent on union business, and no time limit or other checks on the activities of union representatives, then the number of grievances might be higher.

8. Management Policies

Both the number of grievances and the manner of their settlement can be affected by the policies pursued by management. If management wishes to keep the number of grievances small, it should try to ensure a management-labour contract that is generally regarded by union members as a fair one. Also, before making any changes in work methods, output quotas, methods of remuneration, and so on, it should consult with the union to gain its understanding and, if possible, support. Certainly, management should not try to operate outside the collective agreement.

16.8 VALUE OF A GRIEVANCE PROCEDURE

In conclusion, we should ask ourselves: just how useful is the grievance procedure?

Employees' Point of View

From the employees' point of view, there is no doubt that a grievance procedure provides a straight-forward, clearly-defined way in which to have a grievance reviewed and resolved. In the "old days", employees would most likely just have had to grin and bear any perceived injustice. With a grievance procedure, by contrast, they can have their "day in court", assisted if necessary, at the appropriate time, by competent, articulate union officials and even a labour lawyer in presenting their case. No longer can their complaints be ignored by the forepersons or supervisors or their employment terminated at will by the company because of their "beefs". Also, since a grievance procedure sets out certain time limits for each of its steps, employees know that their grievances will be heard and answered within the time limits provided. Then, perhaps most of important of all, the employees know that should the employer and the union fail to agree on a remedy for their grievances, or even to agree on whether the "grievance" is in fact a grievance, there is provision for an outside, third party, to arbitrate the matter.

Employer's Point of View

From the employer's point of view, a grievance procedure may or may not be welcome. On the positive side, it does provide an orderly procedure for handling employee complaints. It also acts as a communications device, letting the employer know fairly quickly just what matters — for example, unfair treatment by a supervisor or dangerous working conditions — are sources of discontent on the factory floor. That is why many employers are willing to accept a wide variety of complaints for handling under the grievance procedure. Furthermore, a grievance procedure plays an important role as a "safety valve", letting an employee blow off steam before a grievance committee rather than turning to sabotage, or to low productivity, as a silent revenge for the company's failure to recognize his or her complaints. The absence of a grievance procedure could even mean, should a dispute arise, that the labour force as a whole may end up putting down their tools and going on an official or unofficial strike or making other interference with work. On the positive side, therefore, the grievance procedure can be an important means of boosting employee morale. In line with modern managerial thinking, this can only mean better labour productivity. On the negative side, some employers feel that employees and the union abuse the grievance procedure, filing unnecessary complaints and grievances, wasting valuable management and labour time, undermining the authority of first-line, or shop-floor management, and incurring unnecessary arbitration expenses.

Public's Point of View

From the public's point of view, it is undoubtedly better for management and labour to talk rather than fight about their differences. In a strike or lockout, the public often suffers as well as the parties directly involved. Also, in a society that prides itself on being civilized, a grievance procedure can undoubtedly be the most rational way to settle such differences. But, of course, like every procedure, it is open to abuse. It is the responsibility of both the company and the union to ensure that the grievance procedure is used in the way intended — not as a means or irritating or confounding the other party.

16.9 DUTY OF FAIR REPRESENTATION

Commonly, under a collective agreement, an employee has the right to file a grievance and have the grievance processed through the grievance procedure and perhaps on to arbitration. However, the processing of the grievance is controlled by the union.

Normally, if the grievance is without merit, the union and the grievor will agree that the grievance be withdrawn.

However, cases do occasionally arise where the grievor insists on having the grievance processed to arbitration even though the union, for whatever reason, may not wish to proceed. From the grievor's point of view, failure to proceed would prevent a third party resolution of the matter. So there arises the question of the union's duty of fair representation on the employee's behalf.

Ontario, British Columbia, Quebec, and the Federal jurisdiction have included this duty of fair representation in their labour relations legislation.

The Ontario Labour Relations Act, for example, states:

> "A trade union or council of trade unions so long as it continues to be entitled to represent employees in a bargaining unit, shall not act in a manner that is arbitrary, discriminatory or in bad faith in the representation of any of the employees in the unit, whether or not members of the trade union or of any constituent union of the council of trade unions, as the case may be."

The Canada Labour Code states:

> "Where a trade union is the bargaining agent for a bargaining unit, the trade union and every representative of the trade union shall represent fairly and without discrimination all employees in the bargaining unit."

In general, the Ontario Labour Relations Board has accepted the principle that the individual employee does not have an absolute right to have his claim arbitrated. Instead, the Board places the burden of proof on the complainant who is expected to exhaust all other available internal remedies before proceeding to the Board.

KEY CONCEPTS

Grievance	Retroactive payment
Grievor	Company grievance
Grievance procedure	Union grievance
Time limit	Grievance rate
Complaint	Fair representation
Complaint stage	

REVIEW QUESTIONS

1. What is a "grievance"? How might the definition vary depending on the firm and union involved? What time limit, if any, is involved in filing a grievance?

2. Outline the steps usually involved in a grievance procedure. Explain the logic behind such a system. How is unnecessary procrastination avoided?

3. Why is a formal grievance procedure considered a necessary part of a collective agreement?

4. How should any claim to retroactive pay, as the result of a grievance, be handled?

5. Contrast, with examples, grievances that might be filed by the union and ones filed by the company.

6. What is the "grievance rate"? What does a low grievance rate imply? A high grievance rate?

7. The main factor that determines whether a firm has a high or low grievance rate is its level of pay and fringe benefits. Discuss.

8. Technological change has always been a fertile source of labour unrest. Discuss, with reference to current examples.

9. Discuss, from the employee's point of view, the advantages and disadvantages of a grievance procedure.

10. How desirable is a grievance procedure, from the employer's point of view?

11. Should a person who believes that he has been unjustly dismissed or suspended, have the right to have his case treated as a grievance? Or is this an infringement of the employer's management rights?

12. Can a union refuse to support an employee's request to file a grievance or to process it to arbitration?

CHAPTER 17: ARBITRATION

Chapter Objectives

- To explain what is meant by "arbitration" and the role of an arbitrator or arbitration board

- To distinguish between two basic types of labour disputes: "interests disputes" and "rights disputes"

- To point out that arbitration is required by law to settle any disputes as to an alleged violation of a collective agreement

- To explain that an arbitrator may first have to decide whether a dispute may be taken to arbitration

- To distinguish between an arbitrator and an arbitration board

- To distinguish between an "ad hoc" arbitrator and a permanently appointed one

- To explain the procedure for choosing an arbitrator

- To specify the powers of an arbitrator or arbitration board

- To explain how an arbitration hearing proceeds

- To explain how an arbitrator's decision is enforced

- To indicate who pays the costs of arbitration

- To explain the role of a specially-appointed "single arbitrator"

- To explain what is meant by "final offer selection" as a means of resolving differences

- To explain the term "mediation-arbitration"

- To explain why the use of arbitration has increased greatly since the 1930s

Chapter Outline

17.1 ARBITRATION DEFINED

Arbitration is the use by two parties to a dispute of a third, impartial person (called an *arbitrator*) or group of three persons (called an *arbitration board*) to settle the outstanding issue. The decision of the arbitrator or arbitration board is binding on both parties to the dispute either by voluntary prior agreement or by law. In practice, the parties involved in a dispute resort more often to an arbitration board than to a single-person arbitrator. This provides assurance that each side, through its representative on the board, will have its point of view forcefully expressed.

17.2 PURPOSE OF ARBITRATION

Arbitration has been used throughout history as a sensible, civilized way of resolving disputes between kings and countries, without use of military force, and between businesspeople engaged in international trade. It has also been used since the nineteenth century in Canada and elsewhere in resolving labour-management disputes without recourse to strikes or lockouts.

In normal contract negotiations, the function of each party is to convince, coerce, or pressure the other side to agree to its position or to reach an acceptable compromise.

In arbitration, the function of the parties becomes one of trying to convince the arbitrator to decide in their favour or to impose an acceptable compromise.

17.3 INTERESTS DISPUTE

There are two main kinds of labour disputes that are often the subject of arbitration. The first is what is known as an "interests dispute"; the second, what is called a "rights dispute".

An *interests dispute* is one that arises between an employer and a union in the course of negotiations for a new collective agreement. In such negotiations, the employer and the union can agree to replace the employees' right to strike and the employer's right to lock out with final and binding arbitration. However, this is done very exceptionally.

Union Reluctance

Unions generally are reluctant to agree to outside arbitration because of their traditional conviction that they get their demands satisfied only through strike action or through the threat to strike. History convinces them that outside parties have been unsympathetic and opposed to them and they associate arbitration with these outside parties.

Right to Manage

The employer is concerned with its right to manage the company. Some employers feel that this right includes determining wages, benefits, and other conditions of employment, as well as work arrangements, and that they should not give up these rights to an arbitrator. Some managers feel that they are being paid for carrying out certain responsibilities for operating the business which include the foregoing. They would be giving up their responsibilities to the shareholders if they delegated these functions to an arbitrator. In addition, they fear the kind of decision that might be made by an arbitrator. This fear reflects their concern with the arbitrator's possible lack of knowledge or lack of understanding of the economic and other consequences of the arbitration decision.

17.4 RIGHTS DISPUTE

A *rights dispute* is one that occurs between an employer and a union with regard to the interpretation of the collective agreement that governs their relationship. Thus, for example, an employer may argue that it should not reimburse shop stewards for time spent on company-union meetings during their non-working hours whereas the union might argue that it should. The matter officially filed by the union, known as a grievance, may defy settlement within the company whatever the amount of discussion that takes place between union and company representatives. Only an impartial third party, the arbitrator or arbitration board, can resolve the matter. In all provinces, every collective agreement must now contain a provision for compulsory arbitration of alleged violations of the agreement that are not otherwise settled.

17.5 ARBITRATION REQUIREMENT

The use of arbitration may be voluntary. However, most labour- management arbitration is of a compulsory nature. This is because the Canada Labour Code and all the provincial Labour Relations Acts require the inclusion in every collective agreement of a clause that provides for compulsory arbitration of any alleged violation of the agreement that cannot be settled at any one of the stages of the grievance procedure.

> *For example:*
> Every collective agreement shall provide for the final and binding settlement by arbitration, without stoppage of work, of all differences between the parties arising from the interpretation, application, administration or alleged violation of the agreement, including any question as to whether a matter is arbitrable.

If no arbitration clause is included, then the collective agreement is deemed to contain the one set out in the Labour Relations Act.

> *For example:*
> Where a difference arises between the parties relating to the interpretation, application or administration of this agreement, including any question as to whether a matter is arbitrable, or where an allegation is made that this agreement has been violated, either of the parties may, after exhausting any grievance procedure established by this agreement, notify the other party in writing of its desire to submit the difference or allegation to arbitration and the notice shall contain the name of the first party's appointee to an arbitration board. The recipient of the notice shall within five days inform the other party of the name of its appointee to the arbitration board. The two appointees so selected shall, within five days of the appointment of the second of them, appoint a third person who shall be the chairman. If the recipient of the notice fails to appoint an arbitrator, or if the two

appointees fail to agree upon a chairman within the time limited, the appointment shall be made by the Minister of Labour upon the request of either party. The arbitration board shall hear and determine the difference or allegation and shall issue a decision and the decision is final and binding upon the parties and upon any employee or employer affected by it. The decision of a majority is the decision of the arbitration board, but if there is no majority, the decision of the chairman governs.

Compulsory arbitration occurs after the last step in the grievance procedure set out in the collective agreement. However, only a small percentage of grievances actually go this far.

New Agreements

Compulsory arbitration does not apply to the negotiation of a new collective agreement. No outside party has the authority to impose a settlement on an employer or labour union covered by a Labour Relations Act. Special legislation would be necessary.

17.6 ARBITRABILITY

Not all disputes during the life of a collective agreement may be taken to arbitration. Usually, a collective agreement will specify that only disputes involving an alleged violation of the agreement are arbitrable. If necessary, the arbitrator will decide whether a dispute is arbitrable. Thus a Labour Relations Act may stipulate:

> "Every collective agreement shall provide for the final and binding settlement by arbitration, without stoppage of work, of all differences between the parties arising from the interpretation, application, administration or alleged violation of the agreement, including any question as to whether a matter is arbitrable".

Therefore, even if one party, employer or union, argues that a particular issue is not arbitrable, the other party can submit it to arbitration. Each party would present its arguments as to why it thinks the matter is arbitrable or not and the arbitrator or arbitration board would make the final decision. If the arbitrator's ruling is that the matter is arbitrable, the arbitrator would go on to hear and decide the case. Otherwise, he (or she) would not.

17.7 ARBITRATOR OR ARBITRATION BOARD

Although the various Labour Relations Acts provide for arbitration by either an arbitrator or an arbitration board, in practice the vast majority of collective agreements in Canada specify the latter. Also, if an agreement fails to include an arbitration clause, it is deemed to contain the one set out in the Act which in fact provides for an arbitration board rather than an arbitrator.

The advantage of a single arbitrator is that the hearing is faster and cheaper. However, some people think that a three-man board of arbitration reduces the chances of poor decisions or arbitration awards that have unfortunate or unanticipated ramifications.

Arbitration boards usually consist of three persons: an impartial chairperson and a person nominated by each of the parties to the dispute. The company nominee would probably be a lawyer or consultant experienced in labour relations from the management viewpoint or perhaps an employee of another company. The union nominee would probably be a lawyer or a consultant experienced in labour relations from the union point of view or a representative of some other union. The procedure is for the parties to appoint, first of all, their nominees to the Board and then for the nominees to endeavour to agree on the choice of an impartial chairperson. Arbitration board chairpersons are most usually law professors, other university professors, or other persons experienced in labour arbitration.

An arbitration board, as well as being able to render a decision, provides an opportunity for the company and the union to mediate, or negotiate, a last-minute settlement rather than rely on the arbitrator's decision, for better or for worse. The disadvantages are, first, the longer time involved in choosing the board and in hearing and resolving the dispute. Second, being partisan in nature, each party's nominee may indulge in long, time-consuming reviews of the proceedings in an effort to persuade the chairperson to look more favourably on that party's point of view.

17.8 AD HOC ARBITRATORS OR PERMANENT UMPIRES

Usually an arbitrator or arbitration board is chosen by the company and the union for each specific dispute. Because of this, the term "ad hoc" ("for the purpose") is sometimes applied to them, as compared with a permanently appointed arbitrator, sometimes known as an "umpire".

Choosing an arbitrator or arbitration board can be a slow and complicated process. To do this for each dispute might seem to be an unnecessary expense. However, the company and the union, by choosing this route, avoid being saddled with a person in whom they may not have confidence. Also, such a person may not have the range of technical knowledge required to deal satisfactorily with a variety of industrial problems.

An ad hoc arbitrator, by contrast, provides flexibility — being chosen for his or her particular knowledge and experience as demanded by the nature of the dispute. Also such a person need be paid only for services rendered. Furthermore, if an ad hoc arbitrator enjoys the respect of both parties, he or she can continue to be used. In this way, full use can be made of this person's increasing knowledge of the company and the union, the employees, the technology, work methods, and so on.

17.9 CHOOSING AN ARBITRATOR

The procedure for choosing an arbitrator or a chairperson of an arbitration board, to settle a dispute, is usually set out in the arbitration clause of the collective agreement. The following is an example:

> Within seven days of the notice of desire to arbitrate, each of the parties shall notify the other of the name of its appointee to an Arbitration Board. The two appointees so selected shall, within seven days of the appointment of the second of them, appoint a third person who shall be the chairperson. If the two appointees fail to agree upon a chairperson within this time, the appointment shall be made by the Minister of Labour upon the request of either party.

If the procedure has not been set out in the collective agreement, then the standard arbitration clause set out in the Labour Relations Act is deemed to be included in the agreement. This clause might, for example, state in part that the notice by one party to the other of its desire to submit their dispute to arbitration must

> . . . contain the name of the first party's appointee to an arbitration board. The recipient of the notice shall within five days inform the other party of the name of its appointee to the arbitration board. The two appointees so selected shall, within five days of the appointment of the second of them, appoint a third person who shall be the chairperson. If the recipient of the notice fails to appoint an arbitrator, or of the two appointees fail to agree upon a chairman within the time limit, the appointment shall be made by the Minister of Labour upon the request of either party. . . .

It is common practice, after the company and union nominees have been appointed, for one nominee to contact the other with regard to the appointment of a chairperson. One or both nominees may have candidates to suggest. Usually agreement is reached fairly readily between them, and the agreed upon person is asked to be chairperson of the arbitration board.

However, as indicated above, if agreement is not reached, the appointment shall be made by the respective Minister of Labour upon the request of either party.

17.10 POWERS OF THE ARBITRATOR

These powers are set out in the particular Labour Relations Act or Code.

> *For example*:
> An arbitrator or the chairman of the arbitration board, as the case may be, has power,
>
> (a) to summon and enforce the attendance of witnesses and to compel them to give oral or written evidence on oath in the same manner as a court of record in civil cases; and
>
> (b) to administer oaths,
>
> and an arbitrator or an arbitration board, as the case may be, has power,
>
> (c) to accept such oral or written evidence as the arbitrator or the arbitration board, as the case may be, in its discretion considers proper, whether admissible in a court of law or not;
>
> (d) to enter any premises where work is being done or has been done by the employees or in which the employer carries on business or where anything is taking place or has taken place concerning any of the differences submitted to him or it, and inspect and view any work, material, machinery, appliance or article therein, and interrogate any person respecting any such thing or any of such differences;
>
> (e) to authorize any person to do anything that the arbitrator or arbitration board may do under clause (d) and to report to the arbitrator or the arbitration board thereon.

If an employee believes that he or she has been unjustly dismissed or otherwise punished and the matter goes to arbitration, the arbitrator may, if he deems it appropriate, substitute another penalty, even ordering reinstatement of the former employee. However, this right exists only if the collective agreement has not specified the penalty for the breach of discipline that is alleged to have occurred.

> *For example*:
> Where an arbitrator or arbitration board determines that an employee has been discharged or otherwise disciplined by an employer for cause and the collective agreement does not contain a specific penalty for the infraction that is the subject matter of the arbitration, the arbitrator or arbitration board may substitute such other penalty for the discharge or discipline as to the arbitrator or arbitration board seems just and reasonable in all the circumstances.

17.11 THE ARBITRATION HEARING

The next step, after the employer and the union have chosen an arbitration board, is the hearing of the dispute.

The dispute may be a difference between the parties relating to the interpretation, application or administration of the collective agreement, including any question as to whether a matter is arbitrable, or an allegation by one party that the agreement has been violated in some way by the other party.

Normally the arbitration hearing is held in a conference room in a hotel or similar place. The tables are usually arranged in a T-shape. At the head of the T sits the arbitration board with the chairperson in the middle and a union nominee and a company nominee on either side.

Down the length of the T sit the parties to the dispute — the persons appearing on behalf of the company on one side of the table and the persons representing the union on the other. The arbitration case is presented for each side by a person normally known as *counsel*. In the case of the company, the counsel might be a lawyer, it might also be a consultant, or perhaps an employee specialized in labour relations, or conceivably a person such as a plant manager. On the union side, the counsel might perhaps be a lawyer, but is more likely to be the union's business agent or a representative from the union's head office. The counsel on either side is in charge of and responsible for the presentation. Normally, the hearing, although of a judicial character, is conducted in an informal, and even friendly way.

Most grievances are filed by an employee or by the union and allege that the employer is in violation of the collective agreement. At the hearing, the union usually begins and tries to establish that there has been such a violation.

17.12 METHOD OF PROCEDURE

The method of procedure depends on the circumstances. However, it is quite common for the union to start off by submitting to the arbitration board a copy of the collective agreement and also a copy of the grievance which is subject to arbitration. The company and the union, either before the hearing or at the hearing, might agree upon a "statement of fact" to be submitted to the arbitrator. The union then proceeds to submit its evidence. This is most commonly done by the union counsel, who would call on witnesses to testify on the union's behalf, much as in a court of law. The union counsel would call its first witness and ask appropriate questions, designed to have the witness state the evidence necessary to uphold the union's position. After this evidence has been presented, the company counsel has the opportunity to cross-examine the witness. When the examination and cross-examination has finished, the witness normally returns to his or her place and plays no further part in the proceedings, unless recalled to the witness stand. Using the same procedure, the union then calls further witnesses, as it considers judicious. The union may also want to submit certain other kinds of evidence, such as documents and other exhibits.

As soon as the union has completed submitting its evidence, the counsel for the employer has the opportunity to submit his or her evidence. He or she proceeds in the same manner, calling witnesses, examining them and then having them subject to cross-examination by the union counsel. The employer also has the opportunity to submit documentary evidence, exhibits, etc. to uphold its position. The chairperson, or the company or union nominee, may ask additional questions of the witnesses or with regard to other evidence.

After all the evidence has been submitted by both sides, the union counsel has the opportunity to argue his or her case based on the evidence submitted. When the union counsel has finished, the company counsel then has the opportunity to do the same and will attempt to refute the union's arguments. After that, the union counsel gets an opportunity to refute the arguments presented by the company's counsel. This completes the arbitration hearing.

The remaining task for the arbitration board is to make its decision, based on the grievance submitted, the applicable collective agreement or sections of the collective agreement, and the evidence submitted at the hearing. The arbitration decision becomes one of deciding, based on the evidence submitted, whether there has or has not been a violation of the agreement. If there has been, the grievance will be upheld. If there has not been a violation, the grievance will be dismissed.

Normally, the company nominee on the arbitration board is convinced that the company's position is correct, and the union representative that the union's position is correct. As a result, each endeavours to convince the chairperson of the arbitration board that only its position is valid. The chairperson then reviews the evidence and makes a decision. Normally, if the chairperson upholds the grievance, the union nominee signs it, making it a majority award. If the chairperson dismisses the grievance, the company nominee signs it, also making it a majority award. In the former case, the company may well write a dissenting opinion. In the latter case, the union nominee may do so. Occasionally, the arbitrator may make a decision which suits neither the company nor the union nominee. In that case, the chairperson's award becomes the board's award with perhaps two dissenting opinions.

17.13 ENFORCEMENT OF THE ARBITRATOR'S DECISION

In most cases, whatever the award, the parties involved in the dispute are willing to implement it. However, should one party fail to do so, the other party has the right to apply to the provincial Supreme Court for the decision to be entered and enforced in the same way as a Judgment or Order of Court.

Thus a Labour Relations Act might state, for example:

> The decision of an arbitrator or of an arbitration board is binding,
>
> (a) upon the parties; and
>
> (b) in the case of a collective agreement between a trade union and an employers' organization, upon the employers covered by the agreement who are affected by the decision; and
>
> (c) in the case of a collective agreement between a council of trade unions and an employer or an employers' organization, upon the members or affiliates of the council and the employer or the employers covered by the agreement, as the case may be, who are affected by the decision; and
>
> (d) upon the employees covered by the agreement who are affected by the decision.
>
> and such parties, employers, trade unions and employees shall do or abstain from doing anything required of them by the decision.

Furthermore, if an employer, trade union, or employee fails to comply with an arbitration decision within a given period to time, the decision may be enforced by means of a court order. Thus, with regard to the enforcement of arbitration decisions, the provincial Labour Relations Act might state:

> Where a party, employer, trade union or employee has failed to comply with any of the terms of the decision of an arbitrator or arbitration board, any party, employer, trade union or employee affected by the decision may, after the expiration of fourteen days from the date of the release of the decision or the date provided in the decision for compliance, whichever is later, file in the office of the Registrar of the Supreme Court a copy of the decision, exclusive of the reasons therefore, in the prescribed form, whereupon the decision shall be entered in the same way as a judgment or order of that court and is enforceable as such.

17.14 COSTS OF ARBITRATION

The company and the union share equally the costs of the chairperson of the arbitration board. These costs include the arbitrator's fee for time involved in hearing and deciding the case and writing the decision, and his or her travel and accommodation expenses. Normally, the company and the union each pays for its own additional expenses.

17.15 MINISTER-APPOINTED SINGLE ARBITRATOR

In some provinces (e.g. Ontario), a party to a collective agreement, union or employer, may request the Minister of Labour to appoint a *single arbitrator* who would be empowered to arbitrate any difference between the parties to the collective agreement with regard to the interpretation, application, administration, or alleged violation of the agreement, including any question as to whether a matter is arbitrable. This right to request the appointment of a single arbitrator exists regardless of what is stated in the arbitration clause of the collective agreement, or deemed to be stated under the Labour Relations Act.

Such a request may be made in writing by a party to the collective agreement after the grievance procedure under the collective agreement has been exhausted, or after 30 days have elapsed from the date the grievance was first brought to the attention of the other party, whichever occurs first. However, no such request shall be made beyond the time, if any, stipulated in or permitted under the agreement, for referring the grievance to arbitration.

Where such a difference between the parties is discharge or other termination of employment, such a request may be made in writing after the grievance procedure under the agreement has been exhausted or after 14 days have elapsed from the date the grievance was first brought to the attention of the other party, whichever occurs first. However, no such request shall be made beyond the time, if any, stipulated in or permitted under the collective agreement for referring the grievance to arbitration.

Where such a request is received, the Minister shall appoint a single arbitrator who shall have exclusive jurisdiction to hear and determine the matter referred to him, including any question as to whether the matter is arbitrable and any question as to whether the matter was timely.

Where a request, or more than one request, concerns several differences arising under the collective agreement, the Minister may, at his discretion, appoint an arbitrator to deal with all the differences raised in the request or requests.

The Minister may appoint a settlement officer to confer with the parties to endeavour to effect a settlement prior to the hearing by an arbitrator so appointed.

An arbitrator appointed under this section shall commence to hear the matter referred to him within 21 days after the receipt of the request by the Minister.

Upon the request of the parties, such an arbitrator shall deliver an oral decision forthwith or as soon as practicable, without giving his or her reasons in writing.

Where the Minister has appointed such an arbitrator, each of the parties shall pay one half of the remuneration and expenses of the person appointed.

The Minister may establish a list of approved arbitrators. For the purpose of advising him or her with respect to persons qualified to act as arbitrators and to matters relating to arbitration, the Minister may constitute a labour-management committee. This would consist of a chairperson to be designated by the Minister and six members. Three of these members would represent employers and three would represent unions and their remuneration and expenses would be determined by the Lieutenant-Governor in Council.

17.16 FINAL OFFER SELECTION

This is a form of arbitration in which, unlike the normal type of arbitration, the arbitrator must choose, without modification, either the final offer of the union or the final offer of the company. However, this method of resolving industrial disputes has been received with little enthusiasm by labour and management. This is because a negotiated settlement, or even a normal-type arbitration award (in which the arbitrator has taken into account both the union's and the company's points of view) is more likely to satisfy both parties.

Some of the persons who favour final offer selection would prefer an "issue by issue" approach. Under such a system, the arbitrator would have the right to choose, on a item-by-item basis, either the union or the company proposal. Thus the final settlement would embody both union and company proposals rather than consist of one complete final offer or the other.

Advocates of final offer selection, whatever its form, say that it encourages the union and the employer to put forward more reasonable proposals than they otherwise would, each side hoping that the arbitrator will choose the more reasonable proposed settlement.

In Ontario, for example, the provincial government once used the threat of final offer selection as a means of encouraging high school teachers and a school board, involved in a prolonged strike, to come up with a voluntary settlement of their differences.

17.17 MEDIATION-ARBITRATION

In this form of compulsory arbitration, a third party is appointed to mediate the differences between the union and the employer. Any issues still outstanding after the mediation efforts have been made, are then settled by the mediator who makes his award after having studied the rival submissions.

17.18 PUBLIC EMPLOYEES

Private versus Public Sectors

In the private sector, a union can call a strike and the strike can go on until the union, employer, or both, are hurt enough that one or both decide to modify their positions and agree to a settlement. In the meantime, the customers obtain the product or service from another supplier, and the only ones hurt are the employees, the union, and the employer.

In the private sector, one of the factors that brings about the settlement is the pressure on the employer's profit and the recognition by the employees that there is a limit on what the employer can pay, because there is a limit on what the customer will pay.

However, in the public sector, where the employer's revenue comes from the government, the pressure is not the same as in the private sector. The employer can go to the government and ask for more money which the government can get by increasing taxes. The customers are also the taxpayers and the voters who can complain to the government if they are not getting the service they are paying for in their taxes. It is not the same as a dispute between the employees, the union, and an employer in the private sector.

In addition, there are certain services which the government is not prepared to see refused because of a labour dispute. One illustration, in some jurisdictions, is the hospital service.

The Public Interest

Our society, through legislation, has decided that strikes are not acceptable in certain relationships where collective bargaining is practised but which involve the public interest. In such cases, the right to strike has been replaced with the requirement of binding arbitration.

In some jurisdictions, legislation has been passed relating to certain types of public employees (for example, police and firefighters) which does not prevent collective bargaining but makes strike action illegal and final and binding arbitration a legal requirement.

In Ontario, for example, nurses and other hospital employees are not excluded from the Ontario Labour Relations Act. However, the Hospital Labour Disputes Act provides that once negotiations for a collective agreement have gone through conciliation without any settlement being reached, the matters in dispute shall be decided by arbitration. In other words, nurses and other hospital employees, although having the right to bargain collectively, do not also have the right to go on strike because of the essential nature of their work. Similarly, the employer may not lock out the employees. The following are excerpts from Ontario's *Hospital Labour Disputes Arbitration Act.*

1. (1) — In this Act,

    (a) "hospital" means any hospital, sanitarium, sanatorium, nursing home or other institution operated for the observation, care or treatment of persons afflicted with or suffering from any physical or mental illness, diesease or injury or for the observation, care or treatment of convalescent or chronically ill persons, whether or not it is granted aid out of moneys appropriated by the Legislature and whether or not it is operated for private gain, and includes a home for the aged; ("hopital")

2. (1) This Act applies to any hospital employees to whom the *Labour Relations Act* applies, to the trade unions and councils of trade unions that act or purport to act for or on behalf of any such employees, and to the employers of such employees.

    (2) Except as modified by this Act, the *Labour Relations Act* applies to any hospital employees to whom this Act applies, to the trade unions and councils of trade unions that act or purport to act for or on behalf of any such employees, and to the employers of such emplo- yees. R.S.O. 1980, c. 205, s. 2.

3. Where a conciliation officer appointed under section 16 of the *Labour Relations Act* is unable to effect a collective agreement within the time allowed under section 18 of that Act, the Minister shall forthwith by notice in writing inform each of the parties that the conciliation officer has been unable to effect a collective agreement, and sections 17 and 19 of the *Labour Relations Act* shall not apply. R.S.O. 1980, c. 205, s. 3.

4. Where the Minister has informed the parties that the conciliation officer has been unable to effect a collective agreement, the matters in dispute between the parties shall be decided by arbitration in accordance with this Act. R.S.O. 1980, c. 205, s. 4.

11. (1) Notwithstanding anything in the *Labour Relations Act*, no hospital employees to whom this Act applies shall strike and no employer of such employees shall lock them out.

17.19 INCREASED USE OF ARBITRATION

Labour arbitration in Canada has mushroomed since the 1930s because of two factors: first, the enactment of labour relations legislation providing for compulsory arbitration and, second, the growth in the number of workers represented by labour unions and covered by collective agreements.

KEY CONCEPTS

Arbitration	Ad hoc arbitrator
Arbitrator	Umpire
Arbitration board	Arbitration hearing
Interests dispute	Statement of fact
Rights dispute	Arbitrator's decision
Voluntary arbitration	Costs of arbitration
Compulsory arbitration	Single arbitrator
Arbitrability	Final offer selection
Arbitration powers	Mediation-arbitration

REVIEW QUESTIONS

1. What is "arbitration"? How does it differ from conciliation? Why is it now used so much?

2. Explain, with an example, an "interests" labour dispute.

3. What is a "rights" dispute? Explain with examples.

4. Is it necessary to include an arbitration clause in a collective agreement? If so, why?

5. Does compulsory arbitration apply to the negotiation of a new collective agreement? If not, why not?

6. "Not all disputes are arbitrable." Explain, with examples.

7. Compare the merits of an arbitration board with those of a single arbitrator. Why is the former the most usual?

8. Why do most firms used ad hoc arbitrators rather than permanent ones?

9. What is the procedure for choosing an arbitrator?

10. What are the main powers conferred on an arbitrator by the Labour Relations Act?

11. How is the arbitration hearing organized? Who takes part?

12. Explain the way in which the arbitration hearing is normally conducted.

13. Suppose the company or the union refused to accept the arbitration board's decision. How can it be enforced?

14. What costs are involved in an arbitration hearing?

15. How are arbitrators selected by the Ministry of Labour in your province?

16. What is "final offer selection"? Why are employers and unions unenthusiastic about it? In what form might it be more acceptable?

17. What is "mediation-arbitration"? What are its merits?

18. Why is arbitration now used so frequently in labour-management disputes?

CHAPTER 18: DISCIPLINE

Chapter Objectives

- *To indicate the rights of an employer with regard to employee conduct*

- *To emphasize the need for employee discipline to maintain an efficient work climate*

- *To examine the different type of disciplinary action available to employers*

- *To distinguish between discretionary and automatic systems of disciplinary action*

Chapter Outline

18.1 Conduct of Employees

18.2 Types of Disciplinary Action

18.3 Discretionary versus Automatic Systems of Discipline

18.1 CONDUCT OF EMPLOYEES

Most collective agreements give the employer the right to make reasonable rules and regulations governing the conduct of its employees and the right to take *disciplinary action* (i.e., impose some form of sanction or punishment) if they are broken. Also, most collective agreements give an employee and the union the right to file a grievance if they consider that a disciplinary action was taken by the employer without just cause. In fact, many of the grievances that are filed by a union during the life of a collective agreement relate to problems of employee discipline.

If such disputes are not settled by union and management negotiation during the early stages of the grievance procedure, they are then subject to arbitration. In arbitration, the union will attempt to show that the employer did not have just cause for its action, while the employer will attempt to show that it did. The arbitrator's decision will be binding upon both parties.

Need for Discipline

In every organization, *discipline* (i.e. a system of punishments for breaches of rules and regulations) is necessary to maintain a working climate in which subordinates willingly and promptly carry out the instructions of superiors, abide by the accepted standards of business and personal conduct, and use common sense in performing their duties on the organization's behalf.

Most company employees act in a disciplined, responsible manner and are only irritated if forepersons, supervisors and other management personnel constantly make disciplinary threats — "do this or else". However, there are some employees who, for one or more reasons, are unwilling to work properly and to abide by the established rules and standards of conduct, even after these have repeatedly been brought to their attention. In such cases, disciplinary action by management may well be necessary.

Many companies have concluded from experience that it is very difficult to anticipate all the possible kinds of violations that may take place and all the unusual circumstances that may surround them. Consequently, the amount of disciplinary action called for in any given situation must depend partly on the nature of the circumstances involved, as judged by company management.

18.2 TYPES OF DISCIPLINARY ACTION

The usual types of disciplinary action that may be taken by management are the following:

1. verbal warning

2. written warning

3. suspension

4. discharge

Verbal Warning

This type of action is normally taken to deal with all offences of a relatively minor nature — for example, being late for work — particularly if it is a first offence. The verbal warning gives the supervisor an opportunity to discuss the breach of discipline with the offender and to try to discover the causes of it, with a view to their possible future elimination. An interview between the supervisor and the employee also presents the employee with an opportunity to "get something off his chest", perhaps an explanation or a complaint, to see his own errors, and in some cases to suggest the means of self-improvement.

When a supervisor gives a verbal warning to an employee, he should state clearly to the employee that it is in fact a verbal warning and that it will go on the employee's record. The supervisor should then record the fact that this warning has been given so that the employee's history file can be amended to include the date, nature of, and reasons for such a warning.

Written Warning

This is normally given to an employee who has already received a verbal warning for the same or a similar offence. However, such a warning is sometimes given without any previous verbal warning if the offence is sufficiently serious. It is desirable that the written warning be given to an employee only after the supervisor has given him or her an opportunity to explain the misconduct. Written warnings are normally issued on a special form with one copy to the employee, probably another one to the union, and a third one for the employee's file in the personnel department. In issuing a written warning, the supervisor should stress to the employee that it is a serious matter and that further breaches of discipline may lead to more serious disciplinary action, perhaps even discharge.

Suspension

This action is normally taken after an employee has already received one or more written warnings. However, it may also be taken in the case of an employee who has not previously received a warning but who commits a very serious type of misconduct. Most commonly, the period of suspension is from one to fourteen days, although in some instances much longer periods of suspension may be considered necessary.

Discharge

This is the most serious disciplinary action of all and is normally taken only after an employee has been given every opportunity to improve his or her performance, following the issuance of warnings and/or suspensions. Occasionally, a very serious and flagrant breach of discipline may result in discharge even when no previous warning or suspension has been given.

However, even in such serious cases, it is considered wise first of all to provide the employee with an opportunity to present the employee's version of the incident. Following such an interview, it may still be necessary to order the employee to stay away from work until notified otherwise. In some circumstances, it is considered desirable to remove an employee immediately from the company premises pending final decision as to discharge.

If it is subsequently decided to discharge the employee, he or she should be notified by the supervisor, usually in the presence of another member of management, and depending on the collective agreement or the relationship that exists with the union, also in the presence of a union representative. It is usually advisable, because of possible emotional outbursts, to inform the employee of his or her dismissal in a room or other place away from the work area.

18.3 DISCRETIONARY VERSUS AUTOMATIC SYSTEMS OF DISCIPLINE

The comments above refer to a system in which the amount of disciplinary action taken varies according to management's judgment of the offence and the particular circumstances of the case. However, some organizations have a more automatic system of discipline. In effect, they have a predetermined and stated punishment for each offence. Suppose, for example, that a person is late so many times during a week or other given period. The first time, the employee will receive a warning, the second time a suspension, and the third time a discharge. For certain offences, the first time may result in a suspension and the second time in a discharge. Perhaps for a third group of offences, the first time may mean discharge.

This system has the advantages, first, of making it clear to each employee exactly what the penalty will be; second, of ensuring that the company's action is always consistent; and third, of saving the time required to make a more careful judgment. However, one of the problems that arises is management's difficulty in anticipating each possible offence and to make a judgment that is both fair and seen to be fair by the employees concerned. For example, if the rule is for an employee to receive a warning after being late three times, no room is allowed for exceptions based on peculiar circumstances. Again, if exceptions are allowed for peculiar circumstances, a decision must presumably be made in advance as to the peculiar circumstances which would be considered exceptions and which would not. And, as stated before, it is extremely difficult to anticipate all of these unusual circumstances.

KEY CONCEPTS

Employee conduct   Written warning

Disciplinary action   Suspension

Discipline   Discharge

Verbal warning

REVIEW QUESTIONS

1. What disciplinary powers does management usually retain under the terms of a collective agreement?

2. How does the union ensure that its members are not unjustly treated?

3. What exactly is discipline? Why is it necessary in a business firm?

4. When should a verbal warning be issued to an employee?

5. How and when should a written warning be issued?

6. What is the purpose of a suspension? How effective is it?

7. How and when should an employee be discharged?

8. Is it better to have a pre-determined and stated punishment for each possible offence rather than a discretionary system?

CHAPTER 19: SENIORITY

Chapter Objectives

- *To explain what is meant by a seniority clause in a collective agreement*
- *To explain the conflict that arises between seniority and ability in promotions, job assignments, layoffs, etc.*
- *To point out the different basic types of seniority/ability provisions found in collective agreements*
- *To indicate the problems that can occur in applying seniority/ability provisions*
- *To explain "job bumping" and how seniority is involved*
- *To explain the basic types of seniority systems that exist*
- *To provide an example of seniority clauses from an actual collective agreement*

Chapter Outline

The term *seniority* means a person's status in a company based on the number of years and months of service relative to other employees.

19.1 SENIORITY CLAUSE

Nearly every collective agreement has a *seniority clause*, in which the employer and the labour union affirm the principle of job preference for one employee over another, according to length of service with the company. This seniority clause also usually defines how the principle of seniority is to be applied in layoffs, recalls, promotions and transfers. Thus, for example, employees with the longest continuous service are usually the last to be laid off and the first to be recalled. They are also given priorities in promotions and transfers. But this is usually subject to their *ability* to perform the available work. Many collective agreements also provide for the application of seniority in work assignments, shift preference, allocation of days off, and vacation times. These latter applications may be spelled out in the seniority clause or may be scattered throughout the collective agreement in appropriate places.

19.2 SENIORITY VERSUS ABILITY (OR MERIT)

The principle of seniority has been accepted in many areas as an equitable and objective decision-making criterion. In union-management relationships, the concept has existed ever since the earliest collective agreements. However, it has been the source of considerable controversy, especially as related to promotions, job assignments and layoffs. Even though labour unions and managements often agree that length of service is an important factor in determining these matters, they often start to disagree when seniority versus ability (or *merit*) arguments arise. Many managements seek to place greater weight on ability or merit while many unions place more emphasis on seniority.

19.3 DIFFERENT TYPES OF SENIORITY/ABILITY CLAUSES

In practice, there are many different types of seniority/ability clauses in collective agreements. The four types listed below serve to illustrate the range of such provisions:

1. Promotions, demotions and layoffs due to lack of work will be solely on the basis of seniority.

2. The most senior applicant shall be promoted, and the most junior shall be demoted or laid off due to lack of work, provided the senior has sufficient ability to do the job.

3. Where skill, ability and physical fitness are relatively equal, seniority shall govern which employee is promoted, demoted, or laid off due to lack of work.

4. Promotion, demotion or layoff due to lack of work shall be made on the basis of skill, ability and physical fitness to be determined solely by the employer.

Clauses like 1 and 4 are very rare. Employers are generally unwilling to accept seniority as the sole criterion for the promotion of employees, or for their demotion or layoff due to lack of work. Conversely, employees, as represented by their unions, are generally unwilling to give the employer unilateral control over promotions, demotions or layoffs due to lack of work. The result is usually therefore a contract clause like 2 or 3. Clause 2 provides that as long as the senior person can perform the job satisfactorily, that person is entitled to it, even if other applicants have greater ability. Under clause 3, the applicant with the greatest seniority would get the job even if that person had no more ability than the other applicants.

19.4 PROBLEMS IN APPLYING SENIORITY/ABILITY PROVISIONS

Regardless of the type of clause found in the collective agreement, certain administrative problems are likely to arise in promotion situations. How is "ability to do the job" to be defined? When does an employee have the ability to do the job, and when not? What does "relatively equal" mean? Hence the large number of seniority disputes that eventually go to arbitration.

Some of the criteria for judging ability are the following: work experience on the job; work experience related to the job; results of a proficiency test; education; and previous training.

Where the seniority clause is of the sufficient ability type (no. 2 on our list), arbitrators have generally held that when a junior employee is promoted or held on the job despite lesser seniority, management has the burden of proof to show clearly that the senior employee was not competent to perform the job.

Where relative ability clauses are present (no. 3 on our list), most arbitrators will place the burden on management to prove that the senior employee was not qualified. However, the requirements are less stringent. In either type of clause, minor differences in ability will not be sufficient to allow the promotion of a junior employee over a senior one, or the retention of a junior employee despite lesser seniority. As a result, a junior employee may be promoted ahead of a more senior employee, or held in a position despite lesser seniority, only when he or she has clearly superior ability.

19.5 JOB DISPLACEMENT OR "BUMPING" RIGHTS

In the absence of clear differences in ability, it is generally accepted that the most senior employees should have the greatest job security. In most situations, this means they are the last to be laid off and the first to be recalled.

In order for this to happen, it is often necessary for a senior employee to displace, or "bump" a more junior employee. However, the right of a senior employee to replace a junior employee is often restricted by the requirement that he or she be able to do the work satisfactorily. Usually the seniority clause specifies the work areas in which workers may exercise their seniority rights when a reduction in the work force becomes necessary.

In situations in which broad displacement or "bumping" rights exist (i.e., where senior employees can displace junior employees in other types of work), there may be a whole chain of displacements or "bumps" triggered by a single layoff. Because of the tremendous administrative problems involved in any chain bumping situation, managements tend to favour seniority systems which permit the exercise of bumping rights on a restricted basis only. Unions, on the other hand, tend to favour plant-wide bumping rights, unrestricted by differences in classifications, even if it means expenditure of time and money by the employer in training replacements and loss of productive efficiency during the changeover of personnel.

19.6 SENIORITY SYSTEMS

Many seniority systems can be grouped under the following headings:

1. *Departmental or Classification Only*
   Under such a system, employees who are no longer needed in their present jobs because of lack of work may displace junior employees in their own department or classification provided that they can do the work. If they are unable to do so, they are laid off.

2. *Departmental or Classification plus Plant-wide Seniority*
   Under such a system, employees who are no longer required, due to lack of work, are able to bump junior employees in their own department or classification. If they fail to do so (because of inability to do the job), they may then exercise their seniority to displace employees junior to them somewhere else in the plant, again provided that they can do these persons' jobs.

3. *Group (or Job Family) Seniority, plus Restricted Plant-wide Seniority*

Under this system, various types of jobs in a firm are grouped together. These groups are called ''job families''. Usually, employees would only have the right to displace other, more junior employees in their own group. Another group of jobs, usually the least skilled ones, are designated as, say, a ''labour pool'' into which any employee with seniority is able to bump. Thus, in this kind of situation, an employee, if no longer required for a job, is able to displace a junior employee in his or her own group or job family and failing this, is able to displace a junior employee in the labour pool.

4. *Lines of Progression*

With this seniority concept, certain jobs are designated as entry jobs. These jobs are the only jobs for which new employees are hired. These entry jobs may be grouped into a labour pool. All jobs within the bargaining unit are then grouped into various lines of progression. An employee is assigned to the bottom job in the line of progression either upon being hired into an entry job or, alternatively, when being promoted from the labour pool. After that, the employee is promoted when there is a vacancy in the designated job immediately above his or hers on the line of progression, and so on up to the top. Therefore, in the event of a work shortage, each employee moves down one notch into the job that he or she had done before. Eventually, the junior in the line of progression is moved down into the labour pool and, if necessary, the junior in the labour pool is laid off.

Conclusion

In some situations, plant-wide seniority is workable; in others, departmental seniority is more practical. Sometimes the group or lines of progression system, combined with a labour pool, works effectively. The possible variations are almost endless.

19.7 LAYOFF AND RECALL SYSTEM

An appropriate layoff and recall system is a major item on the bargaining agenda of most labour unions and managements and is one that is obviously very important to both. Seniority rights are very important to employees and to the union, and a system must be worked out in collective agreement negotiations which is acceptable to both sides.

Usually, the most critical time under a seniority system is when an employee is about to be laid off. It is at this stage that the employee is most likely to claim that he or she has the ability to perform another job held by a person with less seniority. The effect of a layoff on an employee is obviously much more important to that person than the effect of a transfer. From the employer's point of view, great care must be taken to ensure that the right person is laid off. Otherwise, a grievance may be filed on behalf of the person laid off. If the grievance goes to arbitration, as well it may, and the employer loses, it may be required to compensate the employee who was incorrectly laid off, for lost wages. As a result, some collective agreements provide that an employee is entitled to a trial period under certain conditions to establish whether or not he or she can do the job. Some other agreements, instead of permitting a trial period, provide for a training period. Such trial or training periods are normally limited to a specific period of time. In order to obtain such a trial period, an employee must normally provide reasonable evidence that he or she would be successful in it.

Trial or training periods can greatly reduce the number of grievances resulting from the application of seniority clauses. They can also help convince the employee who is unhappy about being laid off that he or she does not in fact have the qualifications required to perform a different, although less senior job.

19.8 EXAMPLE OF SENIORITY CLAUSES IN A COLLECTIVE AGREEMENT

The following is an example of seniority clauses in a collective agreement:

1. With regard to the order of layoff, should it become necessary to reduce the workforce:

   First: Probationary employees provided, however, that employees remaining who have completed the probationary period can perform the required work satisfactorily or can qualify reasonably quickly for the required work. Those who can qualify reasonably quickly will be given an opportunity to do so. Those given such trial must have within one week demonstrated they will be able to perform the required work satisfactorily.

   Second: Employees possessing departmental seniority attached to the department the staff of which is being reduced, on the basis of seniority, provided, however, that employees remaining can perform the required work satisfactorily or can qualify reasonably quickly for the required work in their department. Those who can qualify reasonably quickly will be given an opportunity to do so on the same basis as set out in the previous clause.

   Third: Employees possessing departmental seniority in other departments on the basis of seniority, provided, however, that employees remaining can perform the required work satisfactorily.

2. With regard to the order of recall when the work force is to be increased:

First: Employees possessing plant seniority, in order of seniority, regardless of the departments in which they were previously employed, provided they can perform the required work satisfactorily. Senior employees who have elected to accept layoff rather than transfer will be eligible for recall only to departments elected by them in writing at the time of layoff or at a subsequent time within their allowable breaks.

Second: Employees possessing departmental seniority in the department in which the staff is being increased, in the reverse order to that in which they were laid off, provided they can perform the required work satisfactorily.

Third: Employees possessing departmental seniority in other departments in order of seniority as vacancies occur provided they can perform the required work satisfactorily.

KEY CONCEPTS

Seniority	*Classification system*
Seniority clause	*Plant-wide seniority*
Merit	*Job-family seniority*
Bumping	*Lines of progression*
Departmental system	

REVIEW QUESTIONS

1. What is a "seniority clause"? Why is it necessary in a collective agreement?

2. What problems can arise in applying the principle of employee seniority?

3. What are the four basic types of seniority/ability provisions mentioned in the text? How do they differ? Which are the most commonly used?

4. What is a "relative ability" clause?

5. Why is it that so many seniority disputes go to arbitration?

6. A system of plant-wide bumping rights is a fair and efficient way of handling a temporary or permanent reduction in a firm's work force. Discuss.

7. Explain the following seniority systems:

   (a) departmental or classification only

   (b) departmental or classification plus plant-wide seniority.

8. What is meant by group or job-family seniority, plus restricted plant-wide seniority?

9. Explain "lines of progression" as a seniority system.

10. Which seniority system is the best? Discuss.

11. What type of seniority system is used in the example of actual seniority clauses included in this chapter?

12. What are the advantages and disadvantages of employee seniority for (a) the employee, and (b) the employer?

13. What seniority principle is usually followed in lay-offs and recalls? How satisfactory is this procedure?

14. A supervisor in a large electrical products manufacturing firm complained to a friend that the three workers he had just finished training had been "bumped" out of the plant and he now had to start over again. Explain and discuss.

PART F

The Public Sector

CHAPTER 20: PUBLIC EMPLOYEES

Chapter Objectives

- *To focus on the different types of public employees, their collective bargaining rights, and how they are perceived differently from private sector employees*

- *To trace the unionization of federal public employees*

- *To outline the nature and scope of the Public Service Staff Relations Act*

- *To indicate the certification process for public sector unions*

- *To review the process for arriving at a collective agreement*

- *To indicate how conciliation takes place in the public sector*

- *To explain how grievances are handled in the public sector*

- *To underline the role of the Treasury Board in negotiating, on behalf of the Federal Government, with federal public public service unions*

- *To discuss whether public service unions should have the right to strike*

- *To review the labour relations situation of provincial and municipal employees*

Chapter Outline

20.1 THE PUBLIC SECTOR

Today in Canada about one out of every five employed persons works in the public sector.

Types of Public Employees

Such public employees include: (a) *direct public employees* — that is, persons employed by a government department; (b) *public agency employees* — that is, persons employed by government agencies, commissions, crown corporations, etc.; and (c) *publicly subsidized employees* — that is, persons employed by institutions such as universities and hospitals that receive most of their funds from the government.

Collective Bargaining Rights

For many years, public sector employees were forbidden to join unions and were denied the collective bargaining rights that private sector employees were coming to take for granted. However, in the last two decades, this situation has drastically changed. The vast majority of public employees are now unionized and their leaders have succeeded in obtaining significant improvements in wages and other conditions of work. However, the pattern of unionization varies considerably from one group of employees to another.

Public versus Private Sector Employees

Previously, public sector employees were regarded as persons receiving relatively lower pay than private sector employees, but enjoying substantial job security. Today, the pay and fringe benefits, including indexed pensions, are often more favourable than in the private sector. However, the job security has become less and less assured as governments strive frantically to reduce substantial budget deficits.

20.2 UNIONIZATION OF FEDERAL PUBLIC EMPLOYEES

Unionization of federal public employees in Canada began towards the end of the nineteenth century. In 1891, for example, the Federated Association of Letter Carriers was established as a national organization. Later, in 1907, the Civil Service Association of Ottawa was set up to represent headquarters employees. Then, in 1909, the Civil Service Federation of Canada was established, combining in one loose alliance the Civil Service Association, the postal associations, and a few other groups.

In 1920, the Professional Institute of the Public Service of Canada was set up with the aim of improving the status and conditions of service of professional employees in the Public Service. Also in that year, an association called the Amalgamated Civil Servants of Canada was formed to improve conditions of work for civil servants generally. This was later merged, in 1958, with the Civil Service Association to form the Civil Service Association of Canada. This Association was then merged in the 1960s with another union, the Civil Service Federation, to form a new union, the Public Service Alliance of Canada.

Staff Associations

Over the years, staff associations have been formed in many different government departments. In addition to social functions, they have been instrumental in presenting employee complaints to management, and regular patterns of consultation have often been established. Successive governments have recognized the right of public employees to become members of such associations. These associations have also been active since 1957, following the establishment of the Pay Research Bureau in that year, and of the Advisory Committee on Pay Research in the following year, in the planning of comparative rates of pay and conditions of employment for public employees.

Consultation Process

The process of consultation between management and the staff associations with regard to pay and other working conditions that had gradually been established over the years was formalized by the Civil Service Act of 1961. This Act made provision for consultation between the staff associations on the one hand and the Civil Service Commission and the Minister of Finance on the other. However, in practice, this system of consultation proved cumbersome and inefficient. As a result, the staff associations began to look more and more in the direction of collective bargaining as a means of protecting the interests of their members. This attitude was strengthened by the recommendations of a Royal Commission on Government Organization which suggested greater autonomy for each government department.

Demand for Collective Bargaining Rights

The growing demand by federal civil servants for collective bargaining rights bore fruit in 1965 when a government-appointed Preparatory Committee on Collective Bargaining in the Public Service recommended drastic changes in the existing job classification and pay systems and proposed legislation to permit collective bargaining. This activity resulted in the passing by the Federal Parliament in 1967 of the Public Service Staff Relations Act, or PSSRA.

20.3 PUBLIC SERVICE STAFF RELATIONS ACT

Scope of Collective Bargaining

According to Section 56 of the Act, contract negotiations are restricted to matters not already covered by other legislation. This means that matters of employment such as hiring, merit rating, promotions, demotions, transfers, layoffs, and dismissals, which are already covered by the Public Service Employment Act are excluded from the negotiations. Also, pensions are excluded because the Public Service Superannuation Act already covered them. However, wages, hours of work, seniority, etc., are all legitimate topics for negotiation. Distribution of work, manning of equipment, job descriptions, and job evaluations are not.

Persons Excluded

Certain types of employees are excluded from collective bargaining:

- persons employed in a managerial or confidential capacity,
- persons whose duties include those of a personnel administrator including persons required to deal formally on behalf of the employer with regard to grievances,
- persons paid fees of office,
- part-time employees,
- casual employees with less than six months of service,
- members of the RCMP,
- members of the Armed Forces.

Actions Prohibited

Under the Act, the employer is prohibited from: (a) discriminating against a person because he or she is a member of an employee organization or is exercising rights given under the Act, (b) imposing conditions of employment that interfere with an employee organization, and (c) intimidating an employee to join or not to join an employee organization.

Public Service Staff Relations Board

This Board is responsible for administering the PSSRA. The members of the Board, which can vary from six to ten, including the Chairman and Vice-Chairman, are appointed by the Governor-in-Council, on the advice of the Federal Government. Half the members must represent the employers' interests and half the employees' interests. To carry out its function, the Board has the power to make regulations of general application on a variety of subject matters such as representation issues, complaints, the hearing of questions of law and jurisdiction, and the establishment of rules of procedure for its own hearings. Its investigations of complaints include prohibited acts committed by an employer or by an employee organization, or failure to implement the decision handed down by arbitration. The Board also has the task of defining bargaining units and certifying bargaining agents.

20.4 CERTIFICATION

Before an employee organization can negotiate with an employer for a collective agreement, it must be certified as a bargaining agent by the PSSR Board.

Requirements for Certification

Application for certification may be made either by a single employee organization or by a council of employee organizations (two or more employee organizations that have joined together for collective bargaining purposes). An employee organization can be certified only if (a) the employer does not participate in the administration of the organization in such a way as would impair the fitness of the organization to represent the employee interests in the bargaining process, (b) the employee organization has no monetary affiliation with a political party, (c) it does not discriminate against employees because of sex, race, nationality, colour, or religion, and (d) it is made up only of occupationally-related employees. In this latter respect, the Board has defined 72 different occupational groups in the Public Service. These fall within five basic occupational categories: professional and scientific; technical; administrative and foreign service; administrative support; and operation. However, the 72 bargaining units defined relate only to employees in the "central administration" for whom the Treasury Board acts as the employer.

In order to be certified, an employee organization must, after application, satisfy the Board with documentary evidence that (a) the employees wish that organization to represent them as their bargaining agent, and (b) the representatives of the organization were authorized to make the application for certification.

Certified Bargaining Agent

Upon certification, the employee organization becomes the bargaining agent for the bargaining unit in negotiations with the employer for a collective agreement. Such a collective agreement then becomes binding on all employees in the occupational group until such time as the certification of the organization is revoked. The employee organization, once certified, is also given the exclusive right to represent all employees in that bargaining unit in the presentation and adjudication of grievances relating to the interpretation or application of the collective agreement or arbitral award.

Termination of Bargaining Rights

The Board can revoke certification if it discovers, as the result of a representation vote of the employees, that the employee organization no longer represents a majority of the employees in the unit. Such a representation vote may be held during initial certification as well as during the last two months of the life of an agreement or at any time if no collective agreement is in force. Certification of a bargaining agent can also be revoked if that organization voluntarily gives up its certification, or if it is discovered that the bargaining agent obtained certification by fraud. Also, the certification of a bargaining agent for a council of employee organizations can be revoked if there is a change in the constituent membership of the council, or for any other reason that the Board accepts. If certification is revoked, then any collective bargaining agreement that the bargaining agent has negotiated will immediately cease to be in effect, unless a new bargaining agent specifies otherwise.

20.5 CONTRACT NEGOTIATIONS

Unlike private sector negotiations, the bargaining agent must specify what method it will use to resolve a dispute if one should arise. It can choose either arbitration or a conciliation board (which allows for the occurrence of a strike). To begin negotiations, either party can give written notice to the other party that bargaining should begin. This notice can be given at any time if there is no agreement or award in force. If an agreement or award is in force, then the notice must be given within the two months before the agreement or arbitral award ceases. An *arbitral award* is the decision given by the Arbitration Tribunal about a disputed matter. Previous terms and conditions of employment will continue in force until such time as a new collective agreement is reached and entered into by both parties.

Not more than twenty days after a notice to commence collective bargaining has been issued, the bargaining agent for the employees, and the officers representing the employer, *must* meet and make *every* reasonable effort to conclude a collective agreement. Both parties, in their negotiations, must be aware that no part of a collective agreement can be in conflict with the Government Employees Compensation Act, the Government Vessels Discipline Act, the Public Service Employment Act, or the Public Service Superannuation Act.

20.6 COLLECTIVE AGREEMENT

A collective agreement, once negotiated and signed, must remain in force either for a specified period, or for at least one year, although amendments can be made at any time during the term of the agreement. Unless some other date is specified by either the agreement or the Board, a collective agreement becomes binding on both parties, on the first day of the month after an agreement is reached, and must be implemented within 90 days after the agreement is reached.

20.7 CONCILIATION

Suppose the two parties are unable to reach a collective agreement, even though they may have been negotiating in good faith. Then either party may, by notice in writing to the PSSRB, request the assistance of a conciliator in reaching agreement.

Whether the bargaining agent has specified arbitration or a conciliation Board as the dispute settlement process, it has the right to request a conciliator before invoking either the arbitration or the conciliation board mechanism. The appointment of a conciliator is not, however, compulsory. The parties may, if they wish, bypass the conciliator step and proceed directly to the dispute settlement stage. The chairman of the PSSRB appoints the conciliator, who then confers with the parties and attempts to assist them in reaching an agreement. The conciliator has fourteen days from the date of his or her appointment, or such longer period as may be determined by the Chairman of the Board, to report his success or failure to the Board. The purpose of the conciliator is to bring the parties together and assist them in reaching agreement. His task is to maintain negotiations between the two parties in the hope that such further negotiations will result in the conclusion of a collective agreement. The conciliator cannot make directives, but he can offer suggestions.

The Chairman of the PSSRB may refuse to appoint a conciliator if he decides that a conciliator would be unable to help the parties reach an agreement. In this case, or if a conciliator has been appointed and was unsuccessful, or if no conciliator was requested, either party can request the Chairman of the Board to refer the matter in dispute to the Arbitration Tribunal or to an ad hoc conciliation board. The choice would depend on the process for resolution of a dispute chosen by the bargaining agent prior to commencing negotiations. Arbitration results in a decision that is final and binding on both parties; whereas, in conciliation, the parties are free to accept or reject the report and recommendations of the conciliation board. If arbitration has been chosen, the bargaining agent cannot call a strike, and the employees in the bargaining unit cannot engage in strike action. If, on the other hand, a conciliation board (not to be confused with a conciliator) has been chosen, the employees in the bargaining unit, with the exception of certain designated employees, may ultimately engage in a strike to enforce their "demands".

20.8 HANDLING OF GRIEVANCES

Grievance Defined

Under the PSSRA, a grievance is considered to be any written complaint of an employee for which there is no other administrative procedure for redress under any other act of Parliament, notably the Public Service Employment Act and the Financial Administration Act. The subject matter of a grievance may be: (a) the interpretation or application of a collective agreement or arbitral award; (b) the application of any statement regarding terms and conditions of employment that has been issued by the employer; (c) any other occurrence or matter that affects an employee's terms or conditions of employment — as long as there is no other administrative procedure for redress; and (d) his or her classification. The right to resort to the grievance process is accorded to all employees who are entitled to collective bargaining under the PSSRA, as well as to persons who are "excluded" from the application of the Act because they are employed in a confidential or managerial capacity.

Matters Excluded

Matters that are excluded as grievances from PSSRA because they come under the Public Service Employment Act are appeals arising out of the application of the "merit" system. They include appeals relating to (a) appointment (including promotion); (b) demotion or release because of incompetence or incapability; (c) dismissal for violation of provisions of the Public Service Employment Act, dealing with political activity; and (d) revocation of appointment because of fraudulent practices during an examination held by the Commission. Under the Financial Administration Act, a person can appeal a suspension or dismissal made in the interests of the safety or security of Canada or any allied state.

Representation

On grievances relating to the interpretation or application of a collective agreement or an arbitral award, an employee must, by law, have the approval of, and be represented by, his or her bargaining agent. In all other cases, an employee may submit the grievance personally, or may have an employee organization represent him.

Grievance Procedure

When an employee has a complaint, he is expected to discuss and try to resolve it with his immediate supervisor. However he may, if he wishes, resort immediately to the grievance procedure. This involves, at the first level, submitting his grievance on a special Grievance Presentation Form to his immediate supervisor or local officer-in-charge, who then transmits the information to the appropriate parties. There is a maximum of four levels to which a grievance can go, each level representing a higher level of managerial authority. In some locations, there are less than four levels. Under the PSSRA Regulations, management is required to respond to a grievance received at any level, within 15 days from the time the grievance was received at that level. If a response is not made within the specified time, the employee is entitled to present his grievance at the next level. At the final level, management *must* respond to the grievance. If the employee is not satisfied with the decisions given at any level, except the final level, he can return the grievance to his immediate supervisor or local officer-in-charge for processing to the next level by submission of a Grievance Transmittal Form. The grievance must be presented by the employee at subsequent levels not later than the tenth day after he received a reply to his grievance at the lower level, or not later than fifteen days past the date that the employer was required to reply to the grievance at the previous level. The final level involves a decision taken by or in the name of the Deputy Minister.

Adjudication

Certain types of grievance may be referred to adjudication even though they may have passed through the final level in the grievance process. *Adjudication* is the process established under the PSSRA by which an employee can have a grievance resolved by an independent third party. It may be done by a board of adjudication or by an adjudicator. The adjudication decision is binding for both the employee and the employer. Grievances that may be referred to adjudication are those relating to (a) the interpretation of application of a collective agreement or arbitral award, or (b) disciplinary action resulting in discharge, suspension, or financial penalty. Adjudicators are appointed by the Governor-in-Council on the recommendation of the PSSR Board.

20.9 TREASURY BOARD VERSUS PUBLIC SERVICE UNIONS

The Treasury Board, led by its president, represents the federal government and indirectly the taxpayer in its bargaining for pay and other conditions of work with the thirteen unions (excluding the two postal unions) that represent the federal public service employees. The publicly-stated policy of the Treasury Board is to pay the fair market wage for civil servants. However, the Treasury Board bases its notion of a fair market wage on the results of surveys by the Pay Research Board, a government agency. In arriving at a mean wage, the Treasury Board uses all employers in a comparative group with 200 or more employees, both union and non-union. The public service unions, notably the Public Service Alliance of Canada, state that their goal is to maintain real wages for their members and to make up for losses to inflation in previous rounds of bargaining and that the Pay Research statistics not only tend to be out-of-date but should include only unionized firms. They would also prefer that more attention be paid to the cost-of-living index, something that the Treasury Board refuses to do, even questioning its validity as a real measure of inflation. So far, only one group of public service employees, the postal workers, have been able to negotiate the inclusion of a cost-of-living clause in their collective agreement with the Treasury Board. The unions also question the bargaining philosophy of the federal government which is that it must not, with its wage supplements, be in a position of leading the private sector. As regards the public interest, union officials, although apologetic about the inconvenience to the public of strikes by union members, feel that they are the only way to achieve their goals.

20.10 THE RIGHT TO STRIKE

A key issue in any discussion of public service employees is whether they should have the right to strike to help achieve their goals. Because of the essential nature of the services provided, the general public is often put to great hardship and inconvenience when such strikes take place. This means that the government of the day, wishing to maintain its political popularity, is under great pressure to reach a settlement however generous it may be. This in turn can lead to similarly generous settlements with other public service unions who can use each settlement in a leap-frog approach to obtain ever better terms. Once private sector employees see that their public service counterparts have done so well, they in turn refuse to settle for anything less, and so the inflationary circle continues.

From the union point of view, the extension of the right to strike to the public service unions in the nineteen-seventies was a right long overdue. The right to strike is considered an essential weapon for the achievement of the unions' goals. Without it, public service employees believe that they would be left way behind their private sector counterparts. And the unions argue that, even with it, they are not keeping up with inflation.

The alternative to the right to strike in the public service is compulsory arbitration whereby an independent party makes an award that is binding on both the government as employer and on the union that represents the public service employees concerned.

20.11 PROVINCIAL PUBLIC EMPLOYEES

Each province has its own statutes governing collective bargaining by provincial government employees.

In Ontario, for example, the Ontario Crown Employees Collective Bargaining Act covers direct public employees and public agency employees. An Ontario Public Service Labour Relations Tribunal certifies unions as the bargaining agent for appropriate groups of employees. Certain matters are excluded from collective bargaining. No strikes or lockouts are permitted and any outstanding issues must be submitted to binding arbitration.

In Alberta, a Public Service Act covers direct public employees and a Crown Agencies Employee Relations Act governs public agency employees. In both cases, the Civil Service Association is named as the sole bargaining agent. The Minister of Labour has the final say as to what is negotiable. And any outstanding disputes are resolved by arbitration.

20.12 MUNICIPAL EMPLOYEES

Most municipal employees enjoy the same collective bargaining rights as workers in the private sector. However, some types of essential municipal employees such as the police and firefighters may, depending on the province, have their bargaining rights restricted by provincial statute. Such employees have to belong to separate bargaining units and are forbidden to strike. Any disagreement about a new collective agreement must be settled by binding arbitration.

KEY CONCEPTS

Direct public employees

Public agency employees

Publicly subsidized employees

Staff associations

Consultation process

Public Service Staff Relations Act

Public Service Staff Relations Board

Certification

Contract negotiations

Collective agreement

Conciliation

Grievance

Adjudication

Treasury Board

Right to strike

Provincial public employees

Municipal employees

REVIEW QUESTIONS

1. What are the various types of public employees in Canada? How large is this public sector?

2. The extension to public sector employees of collective bargaining rights, including the right to strike, has been a mixed blessing. Discuss.

3. What was the role of staff associations in the federal public service? What were their limitations from the member's point of view?

4. What was the Civil Service Act of 1961? Why was it considered inadequate?

5. According to the PSSRA, negotiations on behalf of federal public employees are restricted to matters not already covered by other legislation? Explain the significance of this.

6. Which persons are excluded from collective bargaining under the PSSRA?

7. What actions are prohibited under the Act?

8. Explain the composition and the role of the PSSR Board.

9. In order to be certified under the PSSRA, an employee association must fulfil certain criteria. What are they?

10. What documentary evidence must the employee association produce after application for certification?

11. Under what circumstances can certification be revoked?

12. What must the bargaining agent for the employees specify before any negotiations take place?

13. How soon must negotiations begin?

14. What must be the duration of any collective agreement? When does it become binding on the parties? How soon must it be implemented?

15. How and when is a conciliator used?

16. How are grievances defined under the PSSRA?

17. Explain the grievance procedure.

18. What is meant by "adjudication"?

19. What is the Treasury Board's pay policy for federal public employees? Why are the public service unions unhappy with it?

20. What are "essential services"? Should employees performing such work be denied the right to strike? Discuss the pros and cons.

21. What collective bargaining rights do provincial public employees have in your province?

22. All municipal employees enjoy the same collective bargaining rights as workers in the private sector. Discuss.

PART G

The Way Ahead

CHAPTER 21: ATTEMPTS TO IMPROVE CANADA'S INDUSTRIAL RELATIONS SYSTEM

Chapter Objectives

- *To point out that, although Canada's industrial relations system works reasonably well, there are reasons for concern*

- *To describe the various types of profit-sharing plans that some employers provide for their workers*

- *To discuss profit-sharing plans as a means of greater employee involvement and motivation*

- *To explain and review employee stock ownership plans as a means of reducing the adversary nature of traditional labour-management relations*

- *To review the concept of worker involvement in mangement decision-making*

Chapter Outline

21.1 Reasons for Concern

21.2 Profit Sharing

21.3 Employee Stock Ownership Plans (ESOPs)

21.4 Participative Management

It is often pointed out, and statistically confirmed, that the number of hours lost in Canada through strikes and lockouts represents only a very small percentage of the total hours worked either by union or non-union employees. Also that the loss of output is but a small price to pay for the maintenance of a system of industrial democracy under which the employees of a firm are free to bargain collectively with their employer with regard to rates of pay, length of the work week, and other conditions of work. In communist countries, by contrast, industrial output is often low in both quantity and quality, reflecting to a considerable extent the negative attitude of a workforce that is permitted little real say, at least until recently, as to its terms of employment.

21.1 REASONS FOR CONCERN

This point of view may well have been satisfactory some years ago when Canada and other Western industrial countries were experiencing steady economic growth. However, various features are now shaking this complacent attitude; first, the realization that the rate of economic growth in North America may be permanently slowing down; second, the painful competition that Canadian and U.S. manufacturing industries are now experiencing from foreign manufacturers located in relatively low labour-cost countries such as Japan, South Korea, Singapore, Taiwan, Hong Kong, Malaysia and Mexico; third, the drastic effect on production, transportation and energy costs of the multifold increase in the world price of oil since 1972; fourth, the adverse public reaction caused by disruptive strikes in the public sector; and, fifth, the effects of Canada's free trade agreement with the U.S., and the possible inclusion of Mexico in a North American free trade pact.

The question that presents itself is how to move from an adversary system of industrial relations, in which union-management suspicion and confrontation are a way of life, to one in which a much greater degree of harmony prevails.

21.2 PROFIT SHARING

A number of firms already set aside a certain amount of each year's net profit to be shared out among their employees. The amount of the bonus that each employee receives may be (a) the same as that received by everyone else, (b) in proportion to his or her pay, (c) in accordance with years of seniority, or (d) according to some combination of the three previous criteria.

Types of Profit-Sharing Plans

Profit-sharing plans may be of the cash type, deferred distribution type, or a combination of both. With the *cash type*, the whole of the employee's bonus is given to him or her right away at the end of the firm's fiscal year in the form of cash. With the *deferred payment* type, the money is put into a special fund from which the employee can draw his or her share on retirement or, in some cases, for particular purposes such as buying a house.

Growing Popularity

Profit-sharing plans have become increasingly popular in Canada in recent years. This is because they have been reasonably successful in motivating employees to work harder and more responsibly; have reduced labour turnover; and offer significant income tax benefits to an employee when set up in a "deferred" form.

Criticisms of Profit-Sharing Plans

Sometimes the criticism is made that profit-sharing plans, although welcome to the employee as another fringe benefit, do not really cause any improvement in labour productivity. This is because the relationship between company profit and an individual worker's effort is too indirect and remote. Consequently, some managers believe that a much better plan is to link extra money to individual or departmental effort rather than to that of the firm as a whole. For example, prizes can be awarded to individual workers for exceeding output or sales quotas or for coming up with ideas for cost-cutting, improved safety, and so on. Also, bonuses can be awarded to members of a section or department for achieving overall out-put quotas or cost reduction targets. Profit-sharing is considered by most workers to be a step in the right direction, since any profit is due managements feel strongly about the fact that there is no corresponding willingness on the part of the firm's employees to share losses should expenses exceed revenue as can often occur.

21.3 EMPLOYEE STOCK OWNERSHIP PLANS (ESOPS)

More and more interest is now being shown in Canada in employee stock ownership plans, or ESOPs. These enable an employee to become a shareholder, or part owner of the firm in which he or she works. Some firms make stock available to employees, in restricted amounts, according to position held, at specially low prices; others match the employee's monetary investment thereby allowing the employee to buy two shares for the price of one. In many cases, companies in Canada use an ESOP to supplement their pension plan as a means of offsetting the effects of inflation. As well as being entitled to a share of the profits, as with a profit-sharing scheme, employees accumulate capital in the company. As share prices go up, the employees' economic "nest egg" can grow substantially — so that by the time they are ready to retire, they have more than just their company pension to count on. Also, psychologically, being a part owner, employees can have a completely different outlook on their jobs and a boost in morale, particularly if they have some say in how the firm is run.

An ESOP is particularly attractive for younger workers who have not only time in which to build after capital holdings but can also cash it in should they move to another firm.

Unlike the United States, where there is a sharp trend away from pension plans towards ESOPs, Canada has so far given no tax incentives either to business firms or their employees to set up ESOPs.

Effectiveness of an ESOP

As many reports indicate, an ESOP does help to improve labour-management relations in a firm. In fact, the larger the total amount of stock owned by the employees, the less of an adversary position there seems to be. Unlike a profit-sharing scheme, where an employee must wait until year-end for the results, an ESOP means that employees can monitor the progress of their holdings every day. Also, from the company point of view, ESOP contributions can add to the company's inflow of working capital, whereas pension contributions are locked away in a separate fund.

Some firms believe in employee ownership but not employee management. Certainly it is a debatable point as to just how much say employees should have in the running of the firm if it is to maintain its profitability. Some critics argue that participation in an ESOP is still not real ownership and that it has minimal impact on the workplace. Ownership of a few shares, they argue, is not going to deter employees from reporting sick if they feel under the weather or from going on strike if their union so dictates.

21.4 PARTICIPATIVE MANAGEMENT

A more direct way of arousing employees' interest in their work and in the successful operation of the firm is to let them participate in decisions such as work methods, choice of workmates, etc., that were formerly reserved for management. Participative management, as this is known, is already well-established in countries such as West Germany where worker representatives occupy places in many firms' boards of directors and actively participate in managerial decision-making at all levels of management. In Canada, there are some examples of such participative management but usually in non-unionized firms. So far, trade unions in this country have been suspicious of any attempts to change the traditional management-labour relationship.

KEY CONCEPTS

Profit sharing   *ESOP*

Cash type   *Participative management*

Deferred-payment

REVIEW QUESTIONS

1. In communist countries, there is no unemployment, no lock-outs and few strikes. Discuss.

2. The reason why many North American manufacturing industries can no longer compete with Asian manufacturers, even in the North American market, is cheaper labour costs abroad. Discuss.

3. North America can no longer afford its present system of industrial democracy. Discuss.

4. What are the various types of profit-sharing plans? How effective are they in motivating a firm's employees?

5. Profit-sharing is a sensible and effective alternative to the adversary system of industrial relations. Discuss.

6. What is an ESOP? What are its advantages for an employee? For the employer?

7. Some firms believe in employee ownership but not employee management. Discuss.

8. Explain, with examples, how an ESOP can improve labour-management relations?

9. What is "participative management"? How successful has it been in reducing labour-management conflict?

PART H

Collective Bargaining Simulations

CHAPTER 22: WARRINGTON INDUSTRIES LIMITED (Collective Bargaining Simulation #1)

Little Progress in Renegotiating the Collective Agreement

Warrington Industries Limited, a fairly old, but steadily growing Toronto electrical firm, is faced with the task of re-negotiating the two-year collective agreement that it has with the Associated Electrical Workers Union, Local 672. Despite intensive bargaining by the negotiators for both sides, little progress has so far been made. Unfortunately, the present agreement which covers only the Toronto plant, is due to expire soon.

Non-unionized Quebec Plant

The company also owns a plant in Quebec which, so far, is not unionized. The Quebec employees are paid less than their Ontario counterparts. The number of workers in the bargaining unit at the Toronto plant, which has been in operation for about 35 years, is 955. Recently, about 200 Toronto employees were laid off. The Quebec plant, now seven years old, employs 800 persons most of whom have been hired during the last three years.

Financial Situation of Toronto Plant

Last year, the Toronto plant's total sales revenue was just under $63 million, compared with $69 million the previous year. Net income after tax was $3.1 million last year and $3.9 million the year before. Of this amount, two-thirds was distributed in the form of dividends to share-holders, and one-third reinvested. Total assets of the Toronto plant now amount to $21 million as compared with short-term liabilities, mainly to its bank and suppliers, of $6 million and a long-term mortgage loan on the land and buildings of the Toronto plant of $5 million. The loan, which bears a 10% p.a. interest rate, is due for repayment in 12 years' time. The money was used three years ago mainly to expand and modernize the Quebec plant. Despite the unsettled political climate, the company's board of directors see a bright future for the firm's operations in that province. Much of the output of the Quebec plant is now shipped to the U.S., W. Europe, and other foreign markets, as well as to Canadian markets.

Products Manufactured

The products manufactured are the same at both the Toronto and Quebec plants, consisting mainly of commercial and residential heating equipment, including thermostatic controls. Solar heating panels are now being produced in limited quality and company officials are optimistic that this area will experience the biggest growth in the years ahead. Most of the plant's output is sold to building firms and building suppliers. Employees work on a two-shift basis with a 20-cent per hour bonus for those on the second shift.

No Official Strikes

So far there have been no official strikes at either the Toronto or Quebec plants. However, the union came very close to calling one in Toronto, at the time of the previous contract negotiations. It was only averted by management's last-minute agreement to make union membership a condition of employment. Despite strenuous efforts, the union has been unable to obtain sufficient support among the Quebec plant employees to be certified as their official bargaining agent. It seems likely that another Quebec-based union may gradually secure the required worker support.

Wages Paid

In the Toronto plant, the average wage is now about $11.20 per hour whereas in the Quebec plant it is about $10.20. The present agreement includes a COLA provision whereby an increase of 0.5 in the Consumer Price Index entitles an employee to a 1-cent increase in his or her hourly rate of pay. Because of inflation, this is considered an extremely important fringe benefit. The adjustments in wage rates are made on a quarterly basis. Other benefits include: ten paid holidays; a vacation plan under which employees receive 2 weeks' annual paid vacation after one year of employment and 3 weeks after five years; medical premiums paid by the company; and a contributory pension plan in which the company matches the employees' contributions. Altogether, these cost the company about $1.85 per hour worked.

Management-Labour Relations

Management-labour relations have been quite good at both plants. However, an incident at the Toronto plant two months ago resulted in an illegal temporary work stoppage, or "wildcat" strike. One of the shop stewards was dismissed from work after an argument with a foreman. The shop steward was alleged to have used abusive language and to have threatened the foreman with physical violence ("I'll knock your teeth out"). Following his dismissal, employees in the department in which the steward worked put down their tools and went home. They then picketed the plant and managed to stop production for three days until management agreed to reinstate the steward.

Wildcat Strike

Because of the wildcat strike and the resultant loss of production, the company threatened to attempt to collect damages from the union. The company argued that there had been a breach of Article 35 of the Agreement which stated that:

> "There will be no strikes, slowdowns, or other interruption of production because of labour disputes during the contract period. Employees who engage in such prohibited activity are subject to discharge."

The union protested that it had not given its official support to the strike. But the company argued that the union should have prevented its members (a) from going on strike and (b) from picketing the plant. The company also argued that it was the belligerent attitude of the union's official, the shop steward, that had precipitated the crisis. Although the shop steward had been temporarily reinstated in his job, the company feels strongly that any settlement with the union should include disciplinary action against him.

Handling of Grievances

Under the present Agreement, any grievances must be handled according to a standard procedure that culminates, if necessary, in binding arbitration. However, the right to arbitration does not apply to grievances about production standards as management has retained the right, under the management rights clause of the Agreement, to determine them uni- laterally. Nevertheless, there has been quite a large number of grievances about production standards — mainly to the effect that they were "unreasonably high". However, most of these were rejected by management.

Seniority

Another point of contention between labour and management has been the application of seniority in promotions and layoffs. According to the Agreement, the company must take into account both length of service and ability when deciding on promotion. Specifically, the Agreement states that seniority should apply when a senior employee has the same qualifications for the job as a junior employee. Bidding for promotion occurs on a departmental basis. In practice, the company has leaned heavily towards ability, or "merit", and promoted junior employees. This has resulted in a number of grievances, about half of which have been upheld by the arbitrator. With regard to layoffs, the company has generally honoured the seniority clause in the agreement. This has meant therefore that many junior employees have been laid off in Toronto over the last three years. Supervisors in the plant have bitterly complained that the company is losing many of its best employees. This situation has been aggravated by the existence in the Agreement of plant-wide "bumping" rights for employees who are to be laid off, even though the layoff may be only a temporary one. Under the Agreement, shop stewards and other union officials are given "super-seniority". In other words, they are protected from layoff. On average, a steward spends about twelve hours per week of company-paid time on union business. Some foremen complain that stewards often use "union business" as an excuse for "goofing off". However, this is strenuously denied by the union whenever the matter is brought up.

Overtime Work

According to the present Agreement, management can require employees to work overtime. Early this year, however, a large number of employees refused to do so when called upon. Only when threatened with dismissal did they comply and then only unwillingly. Management has the right under the Agreement to choose the persons who are to work overtime. However, this right has led to charges by the union that foremen often exercise favouritism in this respect, permitting some people rather than others to earn extra money.

Skilled Trades

At the Toronto plant, there are five types of maintenance trades: carpenters, electricians, plumbers, mechanics, and tool and die workers. In the past, each type of skilled tradesperson performed only tasks related to his particular trade. Recently, on grounds of efficiency, management has insisted that, if no appropriate skilled work needs to be done, the tradespersons should do other jobs allocated to them.

Ⓑ Subcontracting

This year the company decided to subcontract out several tasks previously performed by the electricians, plumbers, and carpenters. This has aroused the ire of the union as some of these tradespersons were later laid off. However, the union has been unable to do anything about it except to complain. This is because, under the Agreement, the company retains the right to subcontract work when it deems advisable.

write into collective agreement

Ⓐ New Technology

Another issue that has arisen more and more frequently in the Toronto plant is the introduction of new technology. These more automated methods of production have meant a reduction in the workforce. Many of the workers laid off have found great difficulty in finding alternative employment and some are still unemployed. Management has indicated that competitive firms are more highly automated. Also the latest round of tariff cuts is expected to make foreign competition even fiercer.

Women in the Plant

Women comprise 12 per cent of the work force and complain that they are not treated as well as the men.

Age

The average age of employees in the Toronto plant is 45.

Discipline

Management has frequently complained to the union that workers are slow returning from their "coffee breaks" (a 10-minute rest period every four hours). Occasionally, a worker has been reprimanded or even dismissed for being drunk on the job.

ASSIGNMENT

Each management and union team should, by negotiations, try to resolve the differences between them as the basis for a new Labour Agreement.

JACKSON ELECTRICAL ASSEMBLIES
(Collective Bargaining Simulation #2)

Jackson Electrical Assemblies Ltd. is an electrical manufacturer, located in Oakville, Ontario, which has grown steadily in recent years but which is now faced with the task of renegotiating its collective agreement with the Associated Electrical Workers' Union, Local 762.

Waiting for Conciliator's Report

Despite intensive bargaining by representatives of both sides, little progress has so far been made. Conciliation services have been used and the parties are waiting for the report of the conciliation officer to be released by the Minister of Labour recommending that no conciliation board be established. This will mean the Union then has the right to strike within 14 days.

No offer has been made by the company to the union.

Two Plants

The company also owns a plant, located in Brockville, Eastern Ontario, which so far has not been unionized. The employees in Brockville are paid less than those in Oakville.

The number of employees in the bargaining unit in the Oakville plant which has been in operation for about 20 years is 1,100. Last year about 100 of the Oakville employees were laid off. The Brockville plant, now 5 years old, employs 500 persons most of whom have been hired in the last 4 years.

Financial Situation

Last year the Oakville plant's total sales revenue was just under $60 million compared with about $67 million the previous year. Net income after tax was about $2.9 million last year and $3.7 million the year before. Of this amount about 2/3 was distributed in dividends and 1/3 reinvested. Total assets of the Oakville plant amount to $31 million as compared with short term liabilities, mainly to its bank and suppliers, of $6 million. There is also a short-term loan of $4 million owing to the employees' pension plan. Long-term liabilities consist solely of $10 million mortgage loan on the Oakville plant. The loan bears a 12% annual interest rate and is due for repayment in 10 years. The money was used mainly to expand and equip the Brockville plant.

Bright Future

The company's board of directors see a bright future for the Brockville plant because its location on highway 401 and the St. Lawrence Seaway provides ready transportation to the Ontario market and foreign markets and its location, compared to Oakville, offers no significant disadvantage in reaching the Western Canadian market.

The products manufactured in the two plants are largely the same and are related primarily to the commercial and residential construction markets. Management is confident that these markets will develop successfully in the years ahead.

Employees work on a two shift basis, with a 20¢ premium for the second shift.

Union-Company Relations

The Oakville plant was organized by the Union 10 years ago. Management was convinced that employees had been misled by the union to join the union. In the first negotiations, the union rejected the company's "final offer" and threatened to strike. The company's reaction was that our employees will not support a strike. However, the union called a strike, which was 100% effective. Three days later, the company agreed to the union demands in order to settle the strike.

Since then, in each set of negotiations, settlement has been reached on a reasonably amicable basis without a strike. The settlements have related closely to industry patterns.

Brockville Plant

Since the company opened its second plant in Brockville, the union has tried to organize it without success. While wages in Brockville are lower than those paid in Oakville, apparently because of the relatively high unemployment rate in Eastern Ontario and perhaps because of the lower living costs, employees seem to value the opportunity of working for the company. They seem to feel that wages are relatively good for the area which, apparently to them, is a more desirable location.

Other unions have demonstrated their interest in representing the employees in the Brockville plant.

Wages and Benefits

In the Oakville plant, the average wage is $10.80 per hour while in the Brockville plant it is $8.95. There is no provision for a cost-of-living allowance in the Oakville agreement.

Benefits include 10 paid holidays, vacations of 2 weeks after 1 year and 3 weeks after 5 years, medical premiums paid by the company, and a contributory pension plan in which the employer matches the employees' contributions. The cost of these benefits to the company is about $1.65 per hour.

Production Standards

Generally, relations have been reasonable in both plants. However, recently in the Toronto plant, the company had been correcting, or as the union said, tightening production standards. In one department, this resulted in an illegal work stoppage.

The company threatened to try to collect damages from the union through the grievance procedure. The union exerted considerable pressure and the company announced it would not proceed, in the interest of good employee relations.

Management has retained the right to set production standards and as a result they are not subject to arbitration. Many employees think the production standards are unreasonably tight.

The company has increased its activity regarding the introduction of new labour-saving technology. This has resulted in a reduction in the work force, with employee concern for more such changes in the future.

Management has indicated that competitive companies are highly automated and that the latest round of tariff cuts under the Canada-U.S. Free Trade Agreement will make U.S. competition more severe.

Management is also concerned about increased production costs involved in compliance with occupational health and safety regulations and employee equity plans.

Takeover Bid

Lately, there have been rumours that a U.S. firm is planning a takeover bid for the Canadian company. It has been speculated that, if this happens, one of the company's plants may be closed.

Assignment

Each management and union team should, by negotiations, try to resolve the differences between them as the basis for a new Labour Agreement.

APPENDIX 22A: COSTING INCREASES IN WAGES AND BENEFITS

Shaw Enterprises Ltd. operates a plant employing 100 full-time workers each of whom is normally scheduled to work 40 hours per week. The average wage rate is calculated to be $10.00 per hour.

Calculation of a One-cent-per-hour Wage Increase

Assume that each employee works 2,080 hours per year (40 hours × 52 weeks).

For each 1¢/hour wage increase per employee, the extra yearly cost to the company is calculated as follows:

Per employee
(2,080 hours per employee) × ($0.01 increase) = $20.80 per employee

For all employees
$20.80 × 100 employees = $2,080/year increase in total wages

Assume that overtime worked costs the company an extra 10% payment per employee. Then the total annual cost of a 1¢/hour wage increase is:

$2,080 + (10% of $2,080) = $2,288

Proof

Calculation of Total Wages/Year at $10/hour

100 employees × 2,080 hours	208,000 hours
× $10.00	$2,080,000
plus overtime factor of 10%	$ 208,000
Total Wages Paid to 100 Employees Per Year	$2,288,000

Calculation of Total Wages/Year at $10.01/hour

100 employees × 2,080 hours	208,000 hours
× $10.01	$2,082,080
plus overtime factor of 10%	$ 208,208
Total Wages Paid	$2,290,288

Increase in yearly cost:

$2,290,288 minus $2,288,000 = $2,288

Algebraic Equation to Calculate Yearly Increase in Total Cost

Assuming a 40 hour work week, 52 weeks worked per year and a 10% overtime ratio,

let x = # of employees
y = cent/hour increase union is demanding

EQUATION: 2080xy + (10% of 2080xy)
                 or 2080xy + (.1 ×   2080xy)

Plugging in for our first example of a . . . 1¢/hour increase,

            2080 (100) (.01) + [.1 × (2080) (100) (.01)]
        = 2080 + 208
        = 2288

for a 5¢/hour increase

            2080 (100) (.05) + [.1 × (2080) (100) (.05)]
        = 10,400 + 1,040
        = 11,440

Costing One Additional Plant Holiday

The union proposes one additional plant holiday in the first year of the agreement.

The increased cost to Shaw Enterprises would be as follows:

One employee: 40 hours/week × 52 weeks = 2080 hours/year. Therefore 1¢/hour equals $20.80

An employee, earning $10.00/hour for 8 hours, earns $80.00 per day. Therefore one day equals approximately 4¢/hour (80/20.80). Therefore:

Cost for one employee per year: $0.04 × 2,080 = $83.20
Cost for all employees per year: $83.20 × 100 employees = $8,320

Costing Medical Benefits

The union demands that Shaw Enterprises pay for certain medical and dental benefits for the 100 employees, 40% of whom are single, and 60% of whom are married and have families.

Medical Costs: $29.75/month single rate
                $59.50/month family rate

Therefore 40 employees × 12 months × $29.75 = $14,280.00
          60 employees × 12 months × $59.50 = $42,840.00
          Total cost to Shaw Enterprises per year $57,120.00

Costing a Reduction in Vacation Qualifying Period

The union demands a reduction in the qualifying period for 3 weeks vacation to 10 years of service instead of 12 years.

Seniority lists are needed for this costing procedure. In Shaw Enterprises, 20% of the employees have 10 or more years of service but less than 12. Therefore: 20% of 100 = 20 employees who would benefit from the extra one week's vacation.

If these 20 employees were to be replaced by the company for one week at equal cost;

$$20 \text{ employees} \times 40 \text{ hours} \times \$10.00/\text{hour} = \$8,000 \text{ extra cost}$$

The company's annual hours are

$$2,080 \text{ hours per employee} \times 100 \text{ employees} = 208,000 \text{ hours}$$

Therefore, the average annual increase cost equals approximately 4¢/hour ($8,000/208,000) or, on the average, $80 per employee ($8,000/100).

Cautionary Remarks

All the above cost calculations are based on the assumption that employees work 40 hours per week and 52 weeks per year. However, in practice, actual time worked may be less or more because of:

a) sickness, lateness, and absenteeism

b) holidays and vacations

c) layoffs

d) fluctuations in overtime worked

In addition, the labour cost is not just the wage cost. It is also necessary to include the cost of so-called fringe benefits such as group insurance, pensions, bonuses, parking, cafeteria, etc. Also, the cost per hour will vary with the number of hours worked by each employee, since the cost of the employee benefits will be spread over a larger or a smaller number of hours.

Problems

1. The A.M. Company has 500 employees in their Winnipeg plant who are now earning an average of $20.00 per hour. The union is demanding a 15¢/hour wage increase per employee. What will the increase in yearly cost be to the company? (Assume a 40 hour work week, 52 weeks worked and a 10% overtime factor).

2. The union demands a reduction in the qualifying period for 3 weeks vacation, to 5 years of service, instead of 10 years. What will be the increase in yearly cost to the company?

    (Assume that 30% of the employees have 5 or more years of service but less than 10 years).

CHAPTER 23: CONSOLIDATED ELECTRICAL PRODUCTS (Collective Bargaining Simulation #3)

23.1 COMPANY BACKGROUND

Consolidated Electrical Products Inc. is a medium-sized manufacturing firm located on the outskirts of a large Canadian city. In its fairly old plant, it makes light apparatus such as visual landing aids for aircraft pilots; and electric heating units for high-rise apartment buildings and private homes. Last year, it did a substantial amount of export business as well as secure and complete several lucrative government contracts.

Top Management

The president and major stockholder of the company is Albert Walters, who started the firm in a rented garage almost twenty years ago. Assisting him in top management are Jack Morley, Vice-President Manufacturing; Peter Saccomano, Vice-President Marketing; and Jennie Chow, Vice President, Finance. All three vice-presidents have had many years of experience in this and other industries. However, the vice-president marketing has only been with the firm for eleven months. He replaced Graham Cook, the former marketing manager, who left to join another firm. The president has threatened, albeit subtly, that all the vice-presidents' jobs will be on the line if the firm's overall performance in its traditional domestic product lines does not improve.

Plant Environment

So far the firm has been characterized by the fact that it pays above-average wages and rarely lays anyone off. Also, the employees, although unionized, get on quite well with management, particularly at the supervisory levels. However, this situation may well change if management goes ahead with its plan to establish a methods department, raise production quotas, and replace present equipment with new, up-to-date labour-saving machines.

Employee Benefits

The employees have a benefit package providing medical-surgical hospital benefits, a sick benefit plan to provide 60% of earnings during absence due to illness for up to 52 weeks, and life insurance coverage of $10,000 per employee, all of which is paid 75% by the company and 25% by the employee.

The company also contributes an amount equivalent to 5% of each employee's earnings into a pension fund which will be used to buy a pension for each employee at age 65.

Work Force

The work force was substantially increased last year to cope with the extra orders, and now numbers 640.

Contract Negotiations

The firm's present collective agreement with the International Assemblers Union of America is due to expire this year. Negotiations for a new agreement are to be conducted by two teams:

For the firm:

    Director of Industrial Relations
    Vice-President Manufacturing
    Assistant to the Director of Industrial Relations
    Plant Manager

For the union:

    President, Union Local 265
    Business Agent, Union Local 265
    International Representative
    Department Steward, Machine Shop

The existing agreement is shown in Chapter 24 of this book. For purposes of this simulation, N/C alongside an item, means that no change is permitted.

23.2 PARTICIPANT'S ROLE IN THE SIMULATION

In this simulation, you are required to act as a member of one of the teams, as directed by your instructor. So that the whole class can participate, there will be more than one set of negotiations going on at the same time, with the teams labelled A, B, C, etc.

Your task is to help negotiate a new collective agreement that is satisfactory to the persons you represent — either the firm's shareholders or the union members.

Evaluation of Your Performance

Your performance will be judged by your instructor, on the basis of (a) the way in which you and your team conduct negotiations, (b) the written reports submitted by you or your team, and (c) the collective agreement finally made and the extent to which it corresponds with your team's initial objectives.

23.3 STEPS INVOLVED IN THE SIMULATION

1. *Getting Organized*

   • Instructor divides class into negotiating teams:

Company, Team A	Union, Team A
Company, Team B	Union, Team B
Company, Team C	Union, Team C

   • Each team:
     — allocates roles to members,
     — agrees when to meet out of class, if necessary,
     — discusses firm's and employees' situations,
     — examines the existing collective agreement.

2. *Making Plans*

   • Determine bargaining objectives.
     — Make a list of changes required, showing priorities,
     — Estimate the cost of the changes.

   • Decide on an initial negotiating position.

   • Decide on an intermediate negotiating position.

   • Decide on your target final position.

   • Summarize your conclusions in a Planning Report. This is to be given to your instructor before negotiations begin.

3. *Conducting Negotiations*

   • Company and union teams submit their initial proposals to each other, together with supporting arguments. At the request of either team, clarifications should be made.

   • Each team gives its initial reaction to the other team's proposals and comments on the implications of such proposals.

4. *Reviewing Negotiations*

   • Discuss the reaction of the other team to your initial proposal.

   • Discuss the other team's initial proposals.

   • Estimate the other team's priorities.

   • Estimate the other team's acceptable minimum.

   • Determine your acceptable minimum.

5. *Reaching an Agreement*

   • Go over the agreement, article by article.

   • Try to reach an agreement first on non-controversial points.

   • Gradually work through the more controversial points.

6. *Written Report*

   • At the completion of negotiations, submit a written report to your instructor.

   • Show in the report your final settlement (or, if there is no settlement, the position of your team and that of the team with whom you were bargaining).

   • Show the various steps you took in the bargaining process.

   • Show how you deviated from your plan as previously set out in your Planning Report.

NOTE: Your instructor will tell you how many negotiation meetings are to be held. He or she may also decide to bring in a government conciliation officer. If no agreement is reached, the employees will go on strike and the company will lock them out. There is no provision for arbitration.

23.4 ELECTRICAL INDUSTRY DATA

The data shown in Table 23.1 are based on twenty agreements covering almost 7,800 employees. The firms range in size from 16 employees to 1,450.[1] The average of the hourly labour pay rates for the twenty firms is $11.22; and the average of each firm's wage is $12.60. The average length of all agreements is just over 2.7 years.

---

[1] Source of data: CLV Reports published weekly by the Canada Labour Views Co. Limited, 301 - 85 Bloor Street East, Toronto, Ontario M4W 1A9

COLA Wage Adjustments

Of the twenty agreements, seven have cost-of living allowances. Among these, six have limited COLA's which provide for wage increases, excluding any money generated by the COLA, averaging 53 cents or 4.2 per cent in the first year, 38 cents or 2.8 per cent in the second year, and 28 cents or 2.1 per cent in the third year. Only one agreement has an unlimited, or open COLA.

Non-COLA Wage Adjustments

The thirteen non-COLA agreements shown in Table 23.1 provide for an average first-year wage increase of 47 cents or 4.2 per cent.

Excluding the two settlements that contain wage freezes for the first year, the first-year average increase is 56 cents or 5.0 per cent. In the second year, wage increases average 53 cents or 4.4 per cent, and in the third year, 60 cents or 4.6 per cent.

For all the twenty agreements combined, COLA and non-COLA wage increases average 48 cents or 4.1 per cent in the first year, 47 cents or 3.8 per cent in the second year, and 46 cents or 3.5 per cent in the third year.

Working Conditions

The number of annual *paid holidays* ranges from 11 to 15 days. Twelve is the most common (at 10 firms), with an average of 12.5 days (see Table 23.2).

Service requirements for *vacations with pay* are also summarized in Table 23.2. Three week's vacation is provided after an average of 4.6 years, with requirements ranging from three to five years, five years being the most frequent. Four weeks of vacation is provided by all firms after service ranging from nine to 15 years, 10 and 12 years being the most common requirements (seven each), average 11.1 years. Eighteen firms provide five weeks' vacation after service ranging from 18 to 25 years, average 21.1 years. Six weeks' vacation is provided by eight firms, all but one of which provide it after 30 years service.

Shift Premiums

These are paid by 19 of the 20 firms. Two firms provide premiums as a percentage of regular wages, four provide single premiums, and 13 provide two premiums. Afternoon premiums range from 25 cents to 65 cents, average 44 cents. Night-shift premiums range from 30 cents to 75 cents, average 50 cents. The shift premiums are also summarized in Table 23.2.

23.5 COSTING DATA: CONSOLIDATED ELECTRICAL PRODUCTS

Overtime

Assume the average amount of overtime worked by each employee is 4 hours per month.

Call-in Pay

Assume this happens once per year per employee and that extra paid hours return no extra work to the company.

Holiday Qualifications

If you remove this qualification on holiday pay, assume a 2% loss in productivity during the day before and day after the holiday, i.e., a total of 4% of a day's pay per holiday.

Holiday Overtime

Assume this happens once per employee per year.

Vacation Pay

Years of service:	Number of employees
Less than one	58
One but less than three	20
Three but less than five	402
Five but less than ten	81
Ten but less than fifteen	37
Fifteen but less than twenty	42
	640

Wages

In addition to any wage increase, negotiated incentive wages will increase.

Fifty per cent of the employees in the bargaining unit are on an incentive wage payment plan and they average 20% above their base rates.

Employment Benefits

Report added costs in terms of cents-per-hour equivalent. For example, if the negotiated change provides pension benefits at a cost of 3% of payroll, report a cost equal to the cent-per-hour equivalent of 3% of payroll.

You may, however, bargain exact benefits indicating details and cost.

Shift Work

On average, 1/3 of the employees are on the second shift. There is no third shift.

Table 23.1 — *Summary of Wage Adjustments in Twenty Collective Agreements*

No. of Co. No. Emp. Union	Wage Adjustments	Rates of Pay
1. 60 IAM	First Year - 35 cents, average 3.9% Second Year - 30 cents, average 3.2%	Labour - $ 8.45 Maintenance - $12.05 Average - $ 9.35
2. 156 USWA	First Year - 60 cents, plus 1.5 cents increase in increment between job classes, cost 6 cents, total 66 cents or 5.5%, plus $150 lump sum in lieu of retroactivity. Second Year - 60 cents plus 1.5 cents increase in increment, cost 6 cents, total 66 cents or 5.2%. Third Year - 65 cents plus 1.5 cents increase in increment, cost 6 cents, total 71 cents or 5.3%. COLA: Remains inactive	Labour - $11.78 Electronics Technician - $15.92 Average - $12.70
3. 1,500 UE	First Year - 46.4 cents plus 60 cents to skilled trades, cost 2 cents, total 48.4 cents or 3.8%. Second Year - 26 cents, average 2.0% Third Year - 20 cents, average 1.5% COLA: Formula provides 1 cent for each 0.32 change in CPI (1971 = 100) occurring in the previous quarter, with one quarterly adjustment in first year, three in second year, and four in third year, folded in annually.	Assembler - $12.47 Toolmaker - $16.97 Average - $13.25
4. 136 CAW	First Year - No increase in first year, $200 lump sum Second Year - 55 cents, average 4%	Labour - $13.23 Tool & Die Maker - $15.95 Average - $13.61

5. 100 UE

First Year — 27 cents, average 2.1%, plus $75 lump sum in lieu of retroactivity.

Second Year — 27 cents, average 2%

Third Year — 27 cents, average 2%

COLA: Formula continues to provide 1 cent for each 0.34 change in CPI (1971 = 100) in excess of 5 cents a year, adjusted and folded in quarterly.

Labour — $10.65
Toolmaker — $16.34
Average — $13.30

6. 64 UE

First Year — 5%, average 67 cents

Second Year — 5%, average 70 cents

COLA: Folded in 17 cents leaving no float. Formula provides 1 cent for each 0.168 change in CPI (1981 = 100) in excess of 5% in each year, adjusted quarterly, previously 1 cent for each 0.4 change in 1971-based CPI.

Labour — $12.96
Test Man — $14.50
Average — $14.00 (est.)

7. 1,450 CWC

First Year — 43 cents to 61 cents, average 48.2 cents or 3.8%, plus some local adjustments.

Second Year — 22 cents to 40 cents, average 27.2 cents or 2%.

Third Year — 16 cents to 34 cents, average 21.2 cents or 1.5%.

COLA: Folded in 36 cents leaving no float. Formula will provide 1 cent for each 0.32 change in CPI (1971 = 100) during the August to November quarter. In the second year there are three adjustments and four in the third year.

For Oakville plant:
Labour — $12.28
Electrician — $16.38
Average — $13.52

8. 1,350 UE

First Year (Apr.) — 43 cents to 64 cents, average 48.5 cents or 3.7%, plus $750 lump sum, plus some local adjustments.

First Year (Dec.) — 22 cents to 43 cents, average 27.5 cents or 2%.

Second Year — 16 cents to 37 cents, average 21.5 cents or 1.5%.

COLA: Folded in 33 cents leaving no float. Formula will provide 1 cent for each 0.32 change in CPI (1971 = 100) during the June to September first year quarter, plus three adjustments in second year and four in third year.

Labour — $12.30
Electrician — $16.22
Average — $23.69

9. 100 CAW

First Year — 65 cents plus 50 cents to trades, cost 5 cents, total 70 cents or 6.5%.

Second Year — 63 cents plus 50 cents to trades, cost 5 cents, total 68 cents or 5.9%.

Third Year — 49 cents plus 50 cents to trades, cost 5 cents, total 54 cents or 4.4%.

Assembler — $ 8.34
Maintenance Electrician — $18.63
Average — $11.50

Table 23.1 — *Summary of Wage Adjustments in Twenty Collective Agreements—Continued*

Co. No.	No. of Emp. Union	Wage Adjustments	Rates of Pay	
10.	531 CWC	First Year - 60 cents, average 5.7%, plus 20 cents to trades, cost 0.5 cents, total 60.5 cents or 5.7%.	Labour	- $10.10
		Second Year - 50 cents, average 4.5% plus 20 cents to trades	Millwright	- $14.62
			Average	- $11.18
11.	600 CAW	First Year - 5%, average 44 cents	Labour	- $ 7.48
		Second Year - 4%, average 37 cents	Electrician	- $14.02
			Average	- $ 9.17
12.	340 IBEW	First Year - 6%, minimum 60 cents, plus 25 cents to skilled trades, total cost 64 cents or 6.1%.	Labour	- $ 9.65
		Second Year - 5%, average 56 cents	Electrician	- $16.52
			Average	- $11.15
13.	132 IBT	First Year - 50 cents, average 3.2%	Labour	- $15.63
		Second Year - 60 cents, average 3.7%	Millwright	- $18.56
		Third Year - 70 cents, average 4.2%	Average	- $16.15
14.	187 IBEW	First Year - 7%, average 77 cents	Labour	- $10.79
		Second Year - 4%, average 47 cents	Test Technician	
		Third Year - 4%, average 49 cents		- $14.61
			Average	- $11.72

COLA: Folded in $1.53, leaving no float. Formula will provide 1 cent for each full 0.3 change in CPI (1971 = 100) in excess of general wage increase in each year, adjusted quarterly.

Co. No.	No. of Emp. Union	Wage Adjustments	Rates of Pay	
15.	370 CAW	First Year - 1.5% to production employees, 1.8% to aerospace employees, and 2.2% to skilled trades, average 32 cents or 1.9%.	Labour	- $15.11
		Second Year - 1.5% to production, 1.8% to aerospace, 2.2% to trades, average 33 cents or 1.9%.	Top Skilled	- $19.05
		Third Year - 40 cents, average 2.3%	Average	- $17.30

COLA: Folded in $1.02 leaving no float. Formula continues with 1 cent for each 0.3 change in CPI (1971 = 100), adjusted quarterly, no fold-in.

16.	110 IBEW	First Year	- 4.4%, average 38 cents	Assembler	- $ 8.56
		Second Year	- 4.2%, average 38 cents	Maintenance	- $13.51
		Third Year	- 4%, average 38 cents	Average	- $ 9.03
17.	24 CWC	First Year	- 53 cents, average 4.6%, plus 25 cents to Inspector, cost 1 cent, total 54 cents or 4.7%.	Labour	- $11.46
				Inspector	- $12.91
		Second Year	- 55 cents, average 4.6%		
		Third Year	- 60 cents, average 4.8%	Average	- $12.04
18.	125 USWA	First Year	- 55 cents, average 4.3%, plus special increase from 20 cents to 50 cents, cost 15 cents, total 70 cents or 5.4%.	Labour	- $11.56
				Electrician	- $15.93
		Second Year	- 60 cents, average 4.4%		
		Third Year	- 65 cents, average 4.6%	Average	- $13.59
19.	16 IBEW	First Year	- No increase in first year; $250 lump sum to be paid in December.	Labour	- $ 8.17
				Maintenance Mechanic	- $13.03
		Second Year	- 5.8%, average 66 cents		
		Third Year	- 7.1%, average 84 cents	Average	- $11.30
20.	454 UE	First Year (Jan.)	- 40 cents to 60 cents, average 51 cents or 3.8%	Labour	- $12.805
		First Year (May)	- 14 cents to 17 cents, average 15 cents or 1.1%	Maintenance	
		First Year (Sept.)	- 14 cents, average 1%. First year cost equal to 64 cents or 4.7%	Electrician	- $16.298
		Second Year	- 25 cents to 41 cents, average 30 cents or 2.1%. Cost of first year carryover plus second year adjustment is 46 cents or 3.2%.	Average	- $14.39
		Third Year	- 29 cents to 45 cents, average 34 cents or 2.3%.		

Union Code: CAW - Canadian Auto Workers; CWC - Communications and Electrical Workers of Canada; IAM - International Association of Machinists and Aerospace Workers; IBEW - International Brotherhood of Electrical Workers; IBT - International Brotherhood of Teamsters, Chauffeurs, Warehousemen and Helpers of America; UE - United Electrical, Radio and Machine Workers of Canada; USWA - United Steelworkers of America.

Table 23.2 — *Annual Paid Holidays, Vacations with Pay, and Shift Premiums in Twenty Agreements*

Co. No.	Paid Holidays	Vacations with Pay		Shift Premium
1.	11	3 after 5, 4 after 10, 5 after 20		0¢ – 35¢ – 40¢ (0¢ – 32¢ – 36¢)
2.	12	3 after 4, 4 after 10 5 after 20 (NEW)	2nd: 3rd:	0¢ – 25¢ – 30¢ 0¢ – 30¢ – 35¢ 0¢ – 35¢ – 40¢
3.	12	3 after 4, 4 after 10 (12), 5 after 20 (21), 6 after 30		0¢ – 55¢ – 55¢ (0¢ – 50¢ – 50¢)
4.	13	3 after 5, 4 after 12, 5 after 20, 6 after 25		0¢ – 45¢ – 50¢
5.	12	3 after 5, 4 after 11, 5 after 22, 6 after 30 5 after 20	3rd:	0¢ – 34¢ 0¢ – 36¢
6.	14 (13)	3 after 4, 4 after 12, 5 after 23, 6 after 30		0¢ – 40¢ – 45¢ (0¢ – 35¢ – 40¢)
7.	12	3 after 4, 4 after 10 (12), 5 after 20 (21), 6 after 30		0¢ – 54¢ – 75¢ (0¢ – 49¢ – 70¢)
8.	12	3 after 4, 4 after 10 (12), 5 after 20 (21), 6 after 30		0% – 4% – 6%
9.	14	3 after 5, 4 after 10, 5 after 22	2nd:	0¢ – 45¢ – 45¢ (0¢ – 35¢ – 35¢) 0¢ – 50¢ – 50¢
10.	12	3 after 5, 4 after 12 (13), 5 after 21		0¢ – 65¢ – 65¢

#				
11.	11	3 after 5, 4 after 10, 5 after 20	2nd:	0¢ – 40¢ – 40¢ (0¢ – 35¢ – 35¢) 0¢ – 45¢ – 45¢
12.	13	3 after 5, 4 after 12 (13), 5 after 21 (22) 4 after 11	2nd:	0¢ – 51¢ – 56¢ (0¢ – 48¢ – 53¢) 0¢ – 54¢ – 59¢
13.	11	3 after 3, 4 after 9, 5 after 18, 6 after 30		0¢ – 25¢
14.	15	3 after 5, 4 after 15, 5 after 20		0¢ – 40¢ (0¢ – 35¢)
15.	13	3 after 4, 4 after 12, 4 1/2 after 20, 5 after 25		0¢ – 42¢ – 52¢
16.	12	3 after 5, 4 after 12	2nd: 3rd:	0¢ – 35¢ – 39¢ (0¢ – 30¢ – 32¢) 0¢ – 37¢ – 44¢ 0¢ – 40¢ – 44¢
17.	12	3 after 5, 4 after 12, 5 after 22 4 after 11, 5 after 21	2nd:	N/A
18.	14	3 after 4, 4 after 9, 5 after 19		0¢ – 45¢ – 55¢ (0¢ – 40¢ – 50¢)
19.	12	3 after 5, 4 after 13, 5 after 25 4 after 12, 5 after 23 4 after 10, 5 after 21, 6 after 30 (NEW)	2nd: 3rd:	0¢ – 0¢ – 34¢ 0¢ – 0¢ – 40¢ 0¢ – 0¢ – 45¢
20.	12	3 after 5, 4 after 11 (12), 5 after 20, 6 after 30		0% – 4% – 6%

Table 23.3 — *Comparison of Average Hourly Earnings (including Overtime) in Selected Manufacturing Industries (Ontario), August 1990 over August 1989*

Hourly		Average Hourly Earnings		Increase
		08/90	08/89	
1.	Food and Beverages	$13.54	$13.04	3.8
2.	Tobacco products	23.86	23.26	2.6
3.	Rubber & plastic products	11.65	11.48	1.5
4.	Leather industries	8.89	8.90	−0.1
5.	Textile industries	13.25	12.01	10.3
6.	Knitting mills	8.33	8.21	1.5
7.	Clothing	8.94	8.42	6.2
8.	Wood industries	12.19	11.13	9.5
9.	Furniture & fixtures	11.96	11.13	7.5
10.	Paper & allied industries	16.53	15.90	4.0
11.	Printing & publishing	14.03	13.31	5.4
12.	Primary metal	17.95	17.66	1.6
13.	Metal fabricating	14.20	13.90	2.2
14.	Machinery (except electrical)	15.45	13.93	10.9
15.	Transportation equipment	17.42	16.21	7.5
16.	Electrical products	13.78	12.54	9.9
17.	Non-metallic mineral products	15.53	15.10	2.8
18.	Chemicals & chemical products	15.40	14.36	7.2
19.	Miscellaneous manufacturing industries	12.21	11.96	2.1
20.	Durable goods	15.58	14.67	6.2
21.	Non-durable goods	13.33	12.82	4.0

Source: Statistics Canada, *Employment Earnings and Hours*, Cat. 72002.

Table 23.4 — *Consumer Price Index*

ALL CANADA				
	(1971 = 100)		(1981 = 100)	
	1988	1989	1988	1989
January	333.6	347.8	140.8	146.8
February	334.7	350.1	141.3	147.8
March	336.4	351.8	142.0	148.5
April	337.6	353.0	142.5	149.0
May	339.7	356.5	143.4	150.5
June	340.2	358.4	143.6	151.3
July	342.3	360.8	144.5	152.3
August	343.3	361.0	144.9	152.4
September	343.5	361.5	145.0	152.6
October	345.2	362.9	145.7	153.2
November	346.1	364.1	146.1	153.7
December	346.1		146.1	
Annual Average	340.7		143.8	
Average Annual Increase			4.1%	
% Change November 1988 to November 1989				5.2
November 1989 (1961 = 100)				485.7

REGIONAL CITIES		
	November 1989 (1981 = 100)	% Change in last 12 months
St. John's	145.6	3.9
Charlottetown/Summerside	144.5	4.6
Halifax	150.8	4.9
Saint John	149.9	4.5
Quebec City	152.8	4.4
Montreal	154.7	4.5
Ottawa	154.7	5.3
Toronto	161.8	5.9
Thunder Bay	152.3	5.2
Winnipeg	151.8	5.1
Regina	149.0	4.9
Saskatoon	149.9	4.6
Edmonton	145.8	5.6
Calgary	144.4	5.6
Vancouver	147.0	4.9

Source: Statistics Canada

Table 23.5 — *Number of Employees in each Job Level*

1	—	25
	—	80
	—	15
2	—	0
3	—	12
	—	65
	—	17
5	—	160
	—	11
	—	12
6	—	25
	—	32
	—	8
7	—	12
8	—	7
	—	11
	—	24
	—	31
	—	12
9	—	43
10	—	8
11	—	10
12	—	11
	—	9
		640

Table 23.6 — *Consolidated Electrical Products — Consolidated Statement of Income and Retained Earnings*

	Year Just Ended	One Year Ago	Two Years Ago	Three Years Ago
Sales	74,573,012	58,747,936	57,338,733	47,683,300
Cost of Sales	55,581,679	44,459,022	40,936,250	33,751,199
Gross profit	18,991,333	14,228,914	16,402,483	13,932,101
Deduct:				
— Selling, admin. & distribution expense	11,507,692	9,027,412	8,148,173	6,743,533
— Interest on long-term debt	1,474,511	1,160,277	865,568	587,624
— Other interest	1,199,024	419,487	556,425	288,063
	14,181,227	10,607,176	9,570,166	7,619,220
Income before Taxes	4,810,106	3,681,738	6,832,317	6,312,881
Provisions for Income Taxes	1,845,782	1,552,413	2,907,000	2,774,000
Net Income for Year	2,964,324	1,129,325	3,925,317	3,538,881
Retained Earnings at Beginning of Year	17,422,504	16,713,203	14,116,841	11,538,010
	20,386,828	18,892,528	18,042,158	15,076,891
Less: Dividends and related taxes thereon	1,445,878	1,420,024	1,328,955	960,050
Retained Earnings at End of Year	18,940,950	17,422,504	16,713,203	14,116,841
Earnings Per Share	$.58	$.42	$.77	$.70

Table 23.7 — *Consolidated Electrical Products — Financial Highlights for Each of the Last Four Years*

	Year Just Ended	One Year Ago	Two Years Ago	Three Years Ago
Sales	74,573,012	58,747,936	57,338,733	47,683,300
Net Income	2,964,324	1,129,325	3,925,327	3,538,881
— Per Share $	.58	.42	.77	.70
— As a % of Sales	4.0%	3.6%	6.8%	7.4%
— As a % of Capital Employed[1]	9.9%	7.5%	15.7%	15.2%
— As a % of Shareholders Equity[2]	14.4%	10.8%	22.9%	24.5%
— Dividends paid to Shareholders $	.28	.28	.26	.19
Capital Expenditures	6,616,259	2,882,022	3,447,361	4,533,761
Working Capital	18,164,842	15,525,238	19,227,339	11,875,298
— Current Ratio	1.8 to 1	1.7 to 1	2.7 to 1	1.9 to 1
Shares Outstanding:				
— Class A and Class B	3,494,400	3,482,254	3,468,550	3,452,650
— Class C and Class D	1,611,672	1,611,672	1,609,272	1,609,272
— Number of Shareholders	3,185	3,151	3,170	3,206
— Salaries, wages and employee benefits	18,656,729	13,787,239	14,080,418	11,495,166

[1] Net income as related to capital employed represents earnings adjusted for the net cost of interest on long-term debt and is calculated on total assets less current liabilities at the beginning of the year.

[2] Shareholders' equity at beginning of year.

CHAPTER 24: COLLECTIVE AGREEMENT

AGREEMENT entered into this 1st day of November, 19XX

BETWEEN

CONSOLIDATED ELECTRICAL PRODUCTS INC.
(hereinafter called ''The Company'')

AND

INTERNATIONAL ASSEMBLERS UNION OF AMERICA (I.A.U.),
and its Local 265
(hereinafter called ''The Union'')

INDEX

ARTICLE		PAGE NO.

General Purpose

The general purpose of this Agreement between the Company and the Union is to establish and maintain orderly collective bargaining relations, to provide a procedure for dealing with grievances, and to set forth formally, the rates of pay, hours of work and other working conditions that have been agreed upon.

Article 1 — *Recognition and Scope* (N/C)

1.01   The Company recognizes the Union as the collective bargaining agency for all employees of its Plant located at _____, save and except foremen, persons above the rank of foreman, office and sales staff and students hired on a co-operative basis with a school or university programme.

Article 2 — *Relationship* (N/C)

2.01   a) The parties hereto mutually agree that any employee to whom this contract applies, may exercise, or refrain from exercising, his right to become a member of the union.

b) It is agreed that there shall be no discrimination, coercion or intimidation by the Company, the Union or their respective representatives against any employee because of Union activity or lack of activity, Union membership or non-membership, or for reasons of race, sex, colour or religion.

2.02 During the term of this Agreement, the Company agrees that there shall be no lockout and the Union agrees that there shall be no slowdown, strike, or other work stoppage or interference with work.

2.03 The Union agrees that unless duly authorized:

a) Union meetings will not be held on Company premises.

b) No employee or Union official will solicit membership in the Union, collect dues, or engage in any Union activity on Company time, during his working hours, or the working hours of any employee, except as provided for in this Agreement.

Violation by an employee of any of the foregoing provisions shall be cause for discipline up to and including discharge by the Company, but such actions are to be subject to the provisions of the Grievance Procedure.

2.04 The union agrees that, in recognition of the fact that efficient and economic production is in the interest of both parties, it will promote amongst its members good workmanship and regular attendance. It is further agreed by the Union that the employees will at all times protect the property of the Company against damage by themselves or others.

2.05 In the interests of promoting understanding of the Agreement, the Company will supply present and future employees with a copy of this Agreement.

Article 3 — *Management Rights* (N/C)

3.01 It is recognized that management of the plant and direction of the working force are fixed exclusively in the Company, which maintains all rights and responsibilities of management not specifically modified by this Agreement.

The exercise of such rights shall include but not be limited to:

a) The right to hire, assign, increase and/or decrease the working forces, promote, demote, transfer and make temporary lay-offs for lack of business materials.

b) The determination of: the number and location of plants, the products to be manufactured, the methods of manufacturing, schedules of production, kinds and locations of machines and tools to be used, processes of manufacturing and assembling, the engineering and design of its products, and the control of materials and parts to be incorporated in the products produced.

c) The making and enforcement of rules and regulations, not inconsistent with this Agreement, relating to discipline, safety and general conduct of employees, and to suspend and discharge or otherwise discipline employees for just cause.

3.02   To enable the Company to keep its products abreast of scientific advancements the Company may from time to time, without reference to seniority hereinafter set forth, hire, teach, transfer or assign duties to technically trained men and technical students and deal with them as it deems advisable. This practice, however, shall not adversely affect the employees in the bargaining unit.

3.03   The Company agrees that these functions will be exercised in a manner not inconsistent with the terms of this Agreement.

3.04   Claims of discriminatory upgrading, demotion or transfer, or a claim that an employee has been suspended or discharged without just cause may be made the subject of a grievance and dealt with as provided in this Agreement.

Article 4 — *Reporting for Work*

4.01   An employee who reports for work at the normal starting time of his shift shall be given four hours' work and will be paid his regular hourly rate. If work is not available, he will be paid for four hours at his regular hourly rate.

4.02   Section 4.01 will not apply under the following conditions:

a) Where the employee has been informed a minimum of six hours in advance of his regular starting time that he is not to report for work.

b) Where the interruption of work is due to power failure, fire, lightning, flood, tempest, or any other condition of any kind whatsoever beyond the control of the Company.

c) Where the employee is not willing to perform alternate work of a reasonable nature.

d) Where the employee fails to keep the Company informed of his latest address and telephone number.

4.03   An employee is expected to give prior notice when reporting for work following an illness which exceeds one working day. Such notice must be given to the Company by no later than 12:00 noon on his normally scheduled work day immediately prior to the day that he is available to return to work. In the event that such notice is not given, he will not qualify for work or pay pursuant to Section 4.01.

4.04   Employees who are called in outside their regular shift hours will receive a minimum of three (3) hours' work or pay at the appropriate premium rate provided under Section 6.02. This shall not apply if such is immediately prior to or succeeding his regular shift; or if a break is requested by the employee.

Article 5 — *Working Conditions*

5.01   The Company shall continue to make reasonable provisions for the safety and health of its employees at the factory during the hours of their employment. The Union will co-operate with the Company in maintaining good working conditions and will assist in assuring observances of necessary safety rules.

5.02   The Company welcomes from the Union, its members or any employee, suggestions regarding safety and health.

5.03   A Safety and Health Committee is to be appointed with responsibilities as indicated in Appendix D to this Agreement.

Article 6 — *Hours of Work and Overtime*

6.01   The normal hours of work shall be 40 hours per week consisting of five eight-hour shifts Monday to Friday inclusive. This is not to be read or construed as a guarantee to provide work for any period whatsoever.

6.02   Hours of work in excess of 8 hours per day, Monday to Friday, inclusive, and hours of work on Saturday and Sunday, will be treated as overtime hours and will be paid for at a premium rate as provided under Section 6.03(b) below, except that when employees change shifts at their own request, they shall not be entitled to such premium rate by reason of the fact that they have worked two eight-hour shifts in the 24-hour day.

6.03   a) In computing daily overtime hours, a day shall be the twenty-four hour period following the regular starting time of the shift on which the employee is working.

b) Overtime hours worked will be paid for at a premium rate calculated on the basis of one and one-half times an employee's hourly wage rate except in the case of Sunday, when that day is the second day following an employee's normal work week (that is, Monday to Friday, inclusive), in which case the overtime hours worked will be paid for at a premium rate calculated on the basis of two times an employee's hourly wage rate.

6.04   As far as possible, overtime hours worked will be equally distributed amongst the employees. Each employee is expected to co-operate with the Company in the performance of such work and the Company agrees to accept reasonable grounds for the employee declining to perform such work.

6.05   For the purpose of calculating payment for time worked under this Article 6 and under Article 7, time worked on a scheduled shift commencing prior to 10:00 p.m. shall be treated as if worked on the calendar day on which such shift commences. Time worked on a scheduled shift commencing at or after 10:00 p.m. shall be treated as work performed on the immediately following calendar day.

Article 7 — *Specified Holidays*

7.01   During the term of this Collective Agreement, the Company agrees to pay an employee, as provided under Section 7.03 below, for the following specified holidays without requiring an employee to render service:

New Year's Day	Labour Day
Good Friday	Thanksgiving day
Victoria Day	Christmas Day
Dominion Day	

The last half of his regular shift immediately prior to each of Christmas Day and New Year's Day up to a maximum of four (4) hours.

Three additional days to be observed each year in December, as agreed.

7.02   An employee shall qualify for payment of the aforementioned holidays subject to the following conditions:

a) If he works his full scheduled shift on the work day immediately preceding and immediately following a holiday referred to in Section 7.01 and has not reported for work more than one (1) hour after his scheduled starting time.

b) If he has worked one or more full scheduled shifts in the pay period in which a holiday falls and is prevented from complying with the provisions of 7.02(a) above, as a result of a lay-off, leave of absence or illness verified by a doctor(s), when required by the Company.

c) If he has worked one or more full scheduled shifts in the ten (10) normally scheduled working days immediately preceding or immediately following the Christmas Holiday period and is prevented from complying with the provisions of 7.02(a) above, as a result of a lay-off, leave of absence, or illness verified by a doctor(s) when required by the Company.

d) If, in the opinion of the Company, he is prevented from complying with the provisions of Sections 7.02(a), (b) or (c) due to circumstances beyond his reasonable control.

7.03 (N/C) The specified holiday pay as referred to in this Article will be calculated on the basis of the employee's hourly wage rate multiplied by the number of hours in the employee's standard work day.

7.04 An employee required to work on the day on which the specified holiday is observed as referred to in 7.01 will receive overtime pay as shown in Article 6, in addition to the specified holiday pay.

Article 8 — *Vacations With Pay*

8.01 Annual vacations will be paid on the following basis:

i) Three weeks after 5 years' continuous service if completed by December 31st.

ii) Two weeks after 1 years' continuous service if completed by July 31st.

8.02 Vacations will be scheduled by the Company and shall be completed within the calendar year. It is not permissible to postpone the vacation period or any part thereof from one year to another.

8.03 (N/C) The allowance for each week of vacation will be determined by multiplying the employee's hourly wage rate by the number of hours in the employee's regular weekly schedule. This will not include hours for which overtime premium is paid.

a) An employee with less than 12 months' continuous service will be paid a vacation allowance calculated on the basis of four per cent (4%) of the employee's earnings during the period from the employee's date of hiring to July 31.

b) An employee who has been laid off, or an employee who has had leave for a period in excess of 60 working days during the vacation year (August 1st to July 31st) will be paid vacation pay to an amount of 4% or 6%, whichever figure is applicable, of his gross earnings during the year.

8.04   (N/C) a) An employee with less than 12 months' continuous service with the Company, whose service is discontinued, will be paid four per cent (4%) of the employee's earnings.

b) An employee with more than 12 months' continuous service with the Company, whose service is discontinued, will be paid two per cent (2%) for each week of vacation entitlement.

Article 9 — *Wages*

9.01   The regular hourly rates set out in Appendices A-1 and A-2 shall remain in effect for the duration of this Agreement.

9.02   a) The Company shall have the right to establish and implement new job classifications and hourly rates not covered by this Agreement. Such new job classification(s) and hourly rates shall have provisional status for a period of 90 working days.

b) Following the 90 working day provisional period, the Union shall be advised of the finalized regular hourly rate.

c) An employee who receives such regular hourly rate for such job classification, or the Union, may lodge a grievance under Section 13.02(c) of this Agreement within fifteen days of the effective date applicable under Section 9.02(b).

d) In any arbitration of such a grievance, the Arbitrator shall be limited to determining whether or not the new rate is in proper relationship to existing undisputed rates established for job classifications covered by this Agreement.

9.03   An employee alleging that the wrong job classification has been applied to him or that the job content of his finalized job classification has changed to the degree that a new job classification should be implemented may file a grievance. Such a grievance will be filed under Article 13.02(c) of this Agreement.

9.04   a) In any case of a grievance under Section 9.02(c) above, any adjustment shall be made as of the date the rate was first implemented by the Company.

b) In any case of a grievance under Section 9.03 above, any adjustment shall be from the date of the grievance.

Article 10 — *Shift Bonus*

10.01 When employees are engaged on a regularly scheduled shift commencing before 6:00 a.m. or after 12:00 noon, they shall be paid a bonus of twenty (20) cents per hour for all regularly scheduled shift hours worked. There shall be no shift bonus allowed for hours paid at overtime premium rates.

Article 11 — *Seniority* (N/C)

11.01 The seniority of each employee covered by this Agreement shall be established after a period of probation of 60 worked days, and shall then count from the date of employment with the Company.

11.02 a) Plant-wide and Section seniority lists shall be established and compiled by the Company and posted on bulletin boards in the Plant. The lists shall be fully revised by the Company at least once every six months. Copies of the seniority lists shall be supplied to the Union.

b) The plant seniority list shall be made up in the following sections:

1) Feeder Maintenance Section

2) Paint and Assembly Section

c) An employee's name shall be included on both Plant-wide and Sectional seniority lists when he has completed 15 months' service with the Company. Prior to the completion of 15 months' service with the Company, his name shall be included on the Sectional seniority list only.

11.03 a) Seniority will be the major factor governing lay-offs and transfers due to lack of work, subject to the provisions that employees with higher seniority have the necessary skill and ability to perform the normal requirements of the work available.

b) Subject to the provisions of Section 11.03(a) hereof, employees who are laid off shall be recalled in reverse order to that in which they were laid off, subject to their ability to perform the work required. A laid-off employee must advise the Company of his intention to return within 3 working days and must report for work within 7 days from the day such registered letter is mailed, except in the case of verified illness.

c) When a reduction in working force is necessary, all probationary employees will be laid off first provided that the retained employees have the necessary skills and ability to perform the work available.

d) The provisions of this Article will not apply in cases where there is a temporary shortage of work and the Company may then lay off an employee up to a total of 15 working days in each calendar year without regard to the seniority provisions of this Agreement. In calculating the 15 working days above, a lay-off for the second half of a shift or portion thereof will be deemed a half day, and shall be counted against the 15 working days.

Time lost for the following causes will not be subject to the seniority provisions of the Agreement. Neither will it be counted in the 15 day exception referred to herein:

i) Time lost by an employee during the annual vacation shutdown as a result of such employee's vacation entitlement being less than the shutdown period.

ii) Time lost by an employee due expressly to a shutdown caused by fire, lightning, flood, tempest or due to circumstances beyond the Company's reasonable control, causing damage to the Plant, or part of it, or its equipment.

e) An employee who is about to be laid off under under the provisions of the Article will be given at least 5 working days' notice of such layoff. This shall not apply to a layoff under the provisions of Section 11.03(d), but in such case as much notice as possible will be given.

11.04   An employee shall maintain and accumulate his seniority under the following conditions:

a) During a layoff not to exceed twelve months.

b) During absence due to illness not to exceed fifty-two consecutive weeks.

c) During leave of absence granted by the Company in writing.

11.05   Seniority shall be maintained only as follows:

a) During absence due to illness not to exceed fifty-two consecutive weeks for which the Company may require written verification.

b) During a period of layoff in excess of twelve months but not in excess of twenty-four months.

11.06   An employee shall lose his seniority under the following conditions:

a) If an employee leaves the employ of the Company.

b) If an employee is discharged for just cause, and such discharge is not reversed through the grievance procedure provided herein.

c) If a person fails after a lay-off to return to work within seven days after the Company gives such person notice of recall, by registered mail to his latest known address.

d) If a person fails to notify the Company of his intention to return to work within three working days following the date on which he is recalled under Section 11.03(b).

e) If an employee overstays a leave of absence without the written permission of the Company; except where he overstays such leave due to illness verified by a doctor's certificate when required by the Company or other cause, verified in writing, which is in the opinion of the Company beyond the control of the employee.

f) If an employee is laid off for twenty-four consecutive months.

11.07   Notwithstanding his position on the seniority list, a Section Steward who has at least one (1) year's service will be retained in his department provided there is work available for him which he is qualified to perform in accordance with the provisions of Section 11.03(a). Subject to the same conditions, the Local President will be retained within the bargaining unit.

11.08   An employee with seniority who has been absent from work due to illness or accident and, when medically cleared to return to work, is unable in the opinion of the Company to perform the requirements of the job performed by him immediately prior to such illness or accident, may be eligible for an open job provided he has the skill and ability to perform such open job.

Article 12 — *Probationary Employees* (N/C)

12.01   a) An employee shall be considered to be on probation until he has completed 60 worked days with the Company, at which time his name shall be included on the seniority list and dated from commencement of the probationary period. When a probationary employee is transferred to another department he will be required to complete 60 worked days from the date of initial transfer before acquiring security rights. On completion of this 60 worked days, the seniority of the employee will be counted from the hiring date in the original department.

b) The Company has full rights to discharge probationary employees, if in the opinion of the Company, they do not meet the standard required of them by the Company. Such discharge cases will not be subject to the Grievance Procedure. A grievance may be filed by a probationary employee who has been discharged and who alleges that such discharge is an act of discrimination by the Company for reasons of the employee's Union activity.

Article 13 — *Grievances* (N/C)

13.01   A grievance is defined to be any question between the Company and one or more of the employees, as to the application, interpretation or violation of the terms of this Agreement, or any matter involving hours or working conditions covered by this Agreement, or if it is claimed that discriminatory practices are being performed or that an employee is not being paid the proper rate within the rate range of his classification.

13.02   A grievance must be filed within 30 days from the date of the occurrence which gave rise to the grievance except grievances alleging violation of Section 11.03(a) or (b) of Article 11 which must be filed within 7 days of the date of the alleged improper transfer or layoff or thirty (30) calendar days from the date when an employee commences work who has allegedly been improperly hired in place of the grievor. If such a grievance is sustained, liability on the part of the Company will be limited to a maximum of seven (7) calendar days immediately preceding the date on which the grievance is lodged.

The following is the procedure for adjusting grievances:

a) It is recognized that when an employee has a just or reasonable complaint, his immediate supervisor should be informed as quickly as possible and that an employee should not consider that he has a grievance until his immediate supervisor has had an opportunity of adjusting the complaint.

b) If after complying with Section 13.02(a) above, and failing reasonable satisfaction, an employee with a grievance may take the matter to the Union Steward of his Section, and the Union Steward, with the employee, may present the grievance in writing to the foreman. A grievance must be signed by the employee concerned. The foreman shall give a reply within three full working days.

c) If the foreman's disposition of the grievance is unsatisfactory, his section Union Steward may confer with the Chief Steward and if the latter decides to take up the grievance with the Plant Manager or his designated alternate he shall do so in writing, within three working days after the receipt of the foreman's answer.

The Plant Manager or his designated alternate shall give a reply within three full working days.

d) If the disposition of the grievance by the Plant Manager or his designated alternate is unsatisfactory, the grievance may then be referred to the Union Grievance Committee, made up of three members who shall be employees of the Company, and such committee may take the grievance within three working days after the receipt of the Plant Manager's answer or his designated alternate's, and a meeting will then be held within 10 full working days. At this stage, the Union Grievance Committee may be assisted by a duly authorized official of the Union, and any employee possessed of factual knowledge touching on this matter. A reply shall be given within ten full working days.

13.03   Grievances not filed within the time limits of three days as shown in Sections (c) and (d) hereof shall be considered settled or disposed of.

13.04   a) If a grievance has not been settled under the procedure set forth in Section 13.02 and it is alleged that such a grievance involves misinterpretation or violation of this Agreement, such alleged misinterpretation or violation may be referred to arbitration if it is so requested within thirty (30) days after the final answer is given, as in Section 13.02 of this Article.

b) When a grievance is posted for arbitration, it shall state the Article and Section of this Agreement, which have allegedly been breached.

c) Such a grievance should be submitted for final decision to a Board of Arbitration as follows:

Within five working days of the election to arbitrate, each of the parties shall select a representative and the two so selected shall designate a third member of the Board who shall act as Chairman. In the event that the two representatives originally selected shall be unable to agree on the third member within seven working days of their appointment, the Minister of Labour of the Province of Ontario shall have the power on the application of either party, to appoint an impartial Chairman.

d) The unanimous or majority decision of the Board of Arbitration shall, with respect to matters coming within the jurisdiction of such Board pursuant to the provisions of this Agreement, be final and binding on both parties hereto.

e) Such Board of Arbitration shall have no jurisdiction to alter, change, amend or enlarge the terms of this Agreement.

f) Expenses which may be incurred in connection with the Chairman will be borne equally by both parties to this Agreement.

13.05 It is understood that the Company may bring forward and give to the Union at any time any grievance:

a) With respect to the conduct of the Union, its Officers or Committeemen.

b) With respect to the conduct of the employees generally.

c) With respect to the application or interpretation of this Agreement.

The grievance shall first be presented in writing to the officials of the Union and a meeting will be held within seven (7) calendar days with the Union and its representatives. Failure to agree within a period of four (4) calendar days subsequent to the meeting will permit the Company to refer the matter to the Board of Arbitration as herein aforementioned, within thirty (30) calendar days.

13.06   The Union may file a grievance alleging violation, misinterpretation of non-application of any provision of this Agreement. Such a grievance will be entered by the President of the Union Local with the Plant Manager, who, within forty-eight (48) hours, will notify the union at which stage the grievance will be processed.

13.07   The Company shall not, under any circumstances, be subject to any liability for any period more than thirty days prior to the date a grievance was filed in writing.

Article 14 — *Discharge and Suspension Cases* (N/C)

14.01   A claim by an employee, who has completed his probationary period, that he has been unjustly discharged or suspended from his employment shall be treated as a grievance, if a written statement of such grievance is lodged with the Plant Manager within three working days after the employee ceases to work for the company.

14.02   Such special grievance may be settled by confirming the Management's action in dismissing or suspending the employee, or by reinstating the employee with full compensation for time lost, or by any other arrangement which is just and equitable in the opinion of the parties or a Board of Arbitration.

14.03   Except where two (2) or more employees are suspended or discharged, the employee, if he so requests, shall have the right to see his steward prior to leaving the Plant, at a time and place designated by the Company.

Article 15 — *Stewards*

15.01   The Company acknowledges the right of the Union to appoint or elect a Steward to assist employees in presenting their grievances, for each of the following sections of the Shop (one of these Stewards may be designated as ''Chief Steward''):

1) Feeder Maintenance Section.

2) Paint and Assembly Section.

15.02   An employee will not be eligible to serve as a Steward or as a member of any Union Committee until he has established seniority with the Company.

15.03   The Union acknowledges that Stewards, as well as other members of the Union Committees and Union Officers, will continue to perform their regular duties on behalf of the Company and that such persons will not leave their regular duties without first having received permission from their supervisor. Any Union representative who is privileged by the Agreement to take up Union business in a Section other than his own will first report to the foreman of that Section.

15.04   A Steward may assist in the presentation of grievances in the Section which he represents, with the exception that when a steward is absent from the Section, the Chief Steward may assist in presenting grievances for that Section.

15.05   The Company will pay for 50 per cent of time lost on grievance handling with the Company supervision to a maximum of 1 1/2 hours' pay in any one week to the Department Steward and the President of the Union Local (when the latter is acting as a member of the Grievance Committee). In addition, the Chief Steward will be compensated on the same basis as the above to a maximum of 2 1/2 hours' pay in any one week.

Article 16 — *Notices*

16.01   The Company agrees to post in its plant, Union notices on Union activities, subject to the following conditions:

a) Such notice shall first receive the stamped approval of the Management prior to posting.

b) No change shall be made in any such notice, either by the Company or by the Union, after it has received the stamped approval of the Management.

16.02   The Union agrees that it will not distribute or post or cause or permit to be distributed or posted on the property of the Company, for or on its behalf, any pamphlets, advertising, or political matter, notices, or other kinds of literature except with the written permission of the Management having been first obtained.

Article 17 — *Bereavement Pay*

17.01   Subject to the following regulations the Company will make payment of wages to an employee who is absent solely due to a death in his immediate family.

a) Such employee must have completed sixty (60) worked days.

b) Such employee except for the death and funeral would otherwise be at work.

17.02   Members of the employee's immediate family are defined for the purposes of this Agreement as spouse, son, daughter, father, mother, sister, brother, father-in-law and mother-in-law.

17.03   An employee will receive payment for time lost from his regularly scheduled hours on the following basis:

a) Payment will be made on the basis of the employee's hourly wage rate for the employee's regularly scheduled shift up to 8 hours per day, exclusive of overtime and other forms of premium pay, for up to three days' absence.

b) The time to be paid for may be any three consecutive working days from the day of death through the day after the funeral, inclusive.

c) When requested by the Company, the employee will furnish satisfactory proof of death of the member of his immediate family.

17.04   An employee will not be eligible to receive payments under this Agreement for any period in which he is receiving other payments in the form of vacation pay, specified holiday pay, disability benefit, or Workers' Compensation.

Article 18 — *Jury Duty Pay*

18.01   An employee who is called for Jury Duty will receive for each day of absence therefor the difference between pay lost, computed at the employee's hourly wage rate and the amount of jury fee received, provided that the employee furnishes the Company with a certificate of service signed by the Clerk of the Court, showing the amount of jury fee received.

Article 19 — *Information to the Union*

1901. A copy of all general notices which are posted on the Plant bulletin boards, which deal with hours, wages, or working conditions, will be sent to the President of the Local Union.

19.02 A list of employees hired, quit, recalled, laid off, discharged or permanently transferred shall be sent each pay period to the President of the Union.

Article 20 — *Leave of Absence*

20.01 The Company may grant leave of absence without pay for personal reasons, and such leave will not be unreasonably withheld.

20.02 Upon written request by the Union, and if reasonable notice is given, the Company will grant leave of absence without pay of up to two (2) employees for one day per month. The aggregate total of days not to exceed twelve (12) days per year, for the purpose of carrying out business for the Local.

20.03 The Union may appoint or elect an employee(s) to attend a convention or conference and such employee(s) will be granted leave of absence without pay by the Company if reasonable notice is given. The employee will maintain and accumulate seniority during such leave of absence.

The following conditions will apply:

a) each leave must not exceed 7 days.

b) no more than 3 leaves will be granted to an individual employee in any one year.

c) not more than 2 employees will be granted leave at any one time.

d) no more than 25 days total leave of absence will be granted in any one year.

Time spent by an employee on negotiation preparations and processes, or while attending a hearing of a Board of Arbitration in connection with a dispute or grievance involving the parties to this Agreement, shall not be subject to (a), (b) and (d) above.

The Union agrees that, except for leaves for negotiation purposes, the

Company may withhold leaves requested and ask the Union to substitute other employees if the number of leaves requested in respect of any job or section interferes with the operating requirements of the Company.

20.04   Subject to the following conditions the Company will grant leave of absence without pay to a pregnant employee at her request:

i) Such employee must have one year's seniority.

ii) The Company may require medical verification of the employee's conditions.

iii) Leave will normally be granted for a period of three months prior to confinement and two months following confinement.

Nothing in this Section shall restrict the Company from requiring a pregnant employee prior to her confinement to go on such leave of absence or for such longer period as the Company decides on the grounds that her physical condition while at work constitutes a hazard to herself, her fellow employees, or is interfering with her ability to perform her work.

Article 21 — *Transfer and Recall Payment*

21.01   A transfer is defined as a change in an employee's occupational classification, which is entered in the Company's employment records, or a change of more than three continuous weeks in duration.

21.02   On a transfer from a higher to a lower paying job at the request of the Company, the employee will be paid his pre-transfer rate for the duration of the transfer.

21.03   An employee who is transferred to a higher paying job at the request of the Company, when there is work for him on his regular job, for the purpose of utilization of his applicable skills, and not as a result of other causes, shall be paid the job rate for the duration of such transfer.

21.04   An employee who is recalled from layoff to a job in which he has a previous record of employment, and on which he has attained the Job Rate, shall be paid the Job Rate, provided that he has not been off the job for a period in excess of one year.

Article 22 — *Check-off*

22.01   During the term of this Agreement, the Company will recognize dues deduction authorization cards of present employees and will deduct in accordance therewith for each pay period of two weeks an amount equivalent to Union Dues except as otherwise provided in this Article.

22.02   An employee hired or entering the bargaining unit during the term of this Agreement will be required within 30 days after his date of employment or transfer to complete an Employee's Checkoff Card (in the form set out in Appendix B) assigning to the Union, through payroll deductions, an amount equivalent to that provided under 22.01. The same requirement shall apply to any present employee within 30 days after the date of this Agreement for whom no Employee Check-Off Card is on record with the Company.

An employee who has revoked such authorization pursuant to Section 22.03 shall, on the effective date of this Agreement have such authorization reinstated.

22.03   When the dues deduction authorization card has been signed by the employee and deposited with the Company, deduction will be made, in accordance with the provisions of this Article, for the term of this Agreement, and any extension or renewal thereof, subject, however, to the employee having the absolute right to revoke such authorization at any time within the 10 day period immediately preceding the expiration of this Agreement or renewal thereof. During this time an employee may leave with his foreman a notice thereof, which will become effective immediately. Upon receipt of such notice, the company will notify the Union of the employees who have so revoked such dues deduction.

22.04   There will be no coercion or intimidation of any employee by either the Company or the Union in regard to the dues deduction arrangement.

22.05   Union dues are deductible in each pay period for which an employee receives pay, except where such pay is insufficient to cover dues deduction in which cases the omitted deduction will be recovered in the next pay period in which there is sufficient pay.

22.06   The Union agrees to keep the Company harmless from any claims against it by an employee which arise out of deduction under this Article.

22.07   An employee who returns to work from lay-off, sickness, or leave of absence or who re-enters the bargaining unit, shall have current deductions automatically reinstated upon return to work, except as otherwise provided in this Article.

22.08   It is agreed that before an employee enters the bargaining unit, the Chief Steward, or a Departmental Steward deputized by the Chief Steward, shall have the right to interview such employee during a five-minute period at a time and place to be designated by the Company. The expense of such interview will be borne by the Union.

22.09   Upon written authorization from an employee (in the form set out in Appendix B), the company will deduct an initiation fee of $10.00.

Article 23 — *Duration and Termination*

23.01   This Agreement shall remain in effect from the 18th day of September, 19xx to the 17th day of September, 19xx and unless either party gives to the other party written notice of termination or of its desire to modify the Agreement, then it shall continue for such period as the parties agree upon. (Two-year duration).

Notice that modifications are required or that either party intends to terminate the Agreement may only be given within a period of ninety (90) to seventy (70) days prior to the expiration date of this Agreement.

23.02   Negotiations shall begin within fifteen (15) working days following notification as provided in the preceding Section 23.01, or within any extension mutually agreed to by the parties.

SIGNED by the parties hereto on the first day of December, 19XX, at the City of _____ .

CONSOLIDATED ELECTRICAL PRODUCTS INC.:

R.F. Cook _____

J. Morley _____

E.J. McQuillan _____

G.R. Cross _____

INTERNATIONAL ASSEMBLERS UNION OF AMERICA

On behalf of Local 265:

J. Holmes _____

K. Roessler _____

INTERNATIONAL ASSEMBLERS UNION OF AMERICA:

F.K. Swinnerton _____

E. Rohaly _____

APPENDIX A-1

CLASSIFICATION AND WAGE STRUCTURE (YEAR 1)

Effective September 18, 19xx

Job Level	Job Title	Hourly Rate
1	Paint Line Operator	$10.99
	Assembler	
2	Cleaner	11.06
3	Utility Operator	11.13
	Machine Operator — Light	
4	Repair R.M.R.	11.23
5	Assembly Line Attendant	11.34
	Wrapper and Loader	
	Material Handler	
6	Paint System Helper	11.51
	Machine Operator — Heavy	
	Crate Maker	
7	Storekeeper — Trucker	11.66
8	Service — Material	11.79
	Receiver — Shipper	
	Spray Painter	
	Shear and Brake-Set Up & Operate	
	Receiver — Storekeeper	
9	Welder	11.93
10	Paint System Operator	12.12
11	Set Up — Assembly	12.34
12	Set Up and Maintenance	12.49
	Maintenance	

APPENDIX A-2

CLASSIFICATION AND WAGE STRUCTURE (YEAR 2)

Effective September 18, 19xx

Job Level	Job Title	Hourly Rate
1	Paint Line Operator	$11.99
	Assembler	
2	Cleaner	12.06
3	Utility Operator	12.13
	Machine Operator — Light	
4	Repair R.M.R.	12.23
5	Assembly Line Attendant	12.34
	Wrapper and Loader	
	Material Handler	
6	Paint System Helper	12.51
	Machine Operator — Heavy	
	Crate Maker	
7	Storekeeper — Trucker	12.66
8	Service — Material	12.79
	Receiver — Shipper	
	Spray Painter	
	Shear and Brake-Set Up & Operate	
	Receiver — Storekeeper	
9	Welder	12.93
10	Paint System Operator	13.12
11	Set Up — Assembly	13.34
12	Set Up and Maintenance	13.49
	Maintenance	

APPENDIX B

CONSOLIDATED ELECTRICAL PRODUCTS INC.

Employee's Check-Off Card

I authorize the Company to deduct from each pay period of two weeks an amount equivalent to Union dues and to remit the same promptly to the Financial Secretary of Local 265 of the International Assemblers Union of America.

I understand that this authorization is binding on me commencing from the date hereof subject to my right to revoke such authorization within a 10-day period immediately preceding the expiration date of the Agreement or renewal thereof.

DATE ....

SIGNATURE ....

DEPARTMENT ....

BADGE NO. ....

I also authorize the Company to deduct from my next first pay of the month, the sum of $10.00 for my Union initiation fee.

DATE ....

SIGNATURE ....

APPENDIX C

CONSOLIDATED ELECTRICAL PRODUCTS INC.

Dues Deduction Cancellation

I hereby authorize and direct the Company to discontinue immediately the deduction from each pay period of two weeks an amount equivalent to Union dues, authorized by me pursuant to the Agreement between the Company and Local 265 of the International Assemblers Union of America.

DATE ....

SIGNATURE ....

ADDRESS ....

BADGE NO. ....

APPENDIX D

Safety and Health

1. The safety and health of employees is a major concern of the Company and the Union. The Company and the Union both have a responsibility and a desire to eliminate or reduce exposure of employees to accidental injury or to conditions detrimental to their health. It is the objective of the parties to ensure that no condition be allowed to exist in the workplace that is likely to cause injury or illness to its employees.

2. The Company and the Union agree to exert joint efforts to develop and maintain high standards of safety, health, and housekeeping in the workplace in order to prevent industrial injury and illness.

3. The company will provide, without charge, such special protective clothing, equipment and devices as the Company determines are required for the purpose of preventing industrial injury or illness.

4. There will be a Safety and Health Committee consisting of the following members:

   a) One (1) employee appointed by the Company who will act as Chariman, and

   b) One (1) employee appointed by the Company; and

   c) Two (2) hourly-rated employees appointed by the Union. It is understood that the Company may require the Union to temporarily substitute another employee as its appointee on the Safety and Health Committee in the event that the attendance of the regular Union appointee at the meetings of the Committee interferes with the operating requirements of the Company.

   The number of appointees mentioned in (b) and (c) above may be varied through consultation between the Company and the Union.

   The parties agree it is preferable that the timing of appointments be staggered to ensure continuity.

5. The Safety and Health Committee is responsible for:

   a) promoting safety, good housekeeping and accident and industrial illness prevention measures;

   b) seeking the necessary information to properly identify

      i. practices and procedures

    ii. materials and equipment

that may be a source of danger or hazard to employees;

c) recommending to management

    i. accident prevention measures

    ii. health protection measures

    iii. programs promoting safety, health and good housekeeping;

d) maintaining and keeping minutes and records of its proceedings and making them available for examination by an inspector appointed under The Industrial Safety Act or similar legislation; and

e) sending copies of minutes, recommendations, etc., to, among others, the Division Manager, the Manager of the Safety Department, and the Union.

6. The Safety and Health Committee will normally meet monthly except during the month of December or when the Plant has a shutdown for two (2) or more weeks in a month; in these months a meeting need not be held.

7. The Safety and Health Committee will conduct a regular monthly inspection of some portion of the workplace and such inspection shall normally not take more than one (1) hour unless specifically authorized by management. It is agreed that the inspection referred to herein shall not interfere with the regularly scheduled work of any employees or interfere with productivity in any way. In selecting the work location to be inspected, the Committee may have regard to specific suggestions by the Company, the Union or members of the Committee.

8. Members of the Safety and Health Committee are entitled to such time from work as is necessary to attend the scheduled meetings of the Committee and to conduct the inspections outlined in (6) and (7) above without loss of wages for the time so spent.

9. The Company will provide the Safety and Health Committee with a copy of the following documents for each lost time accident:

a) the initial report to the Workers' Compensation Board; and

b) the Foreman's Report of Accident.

10. The Company will post and keep posted in a conspicuous place, the names of the members of the Safety and Health Committee.

11. If an employee has reasonable cause to believe that an unsafe condition exists as a danger to himself or another employee

    a) he shall immediately notify his supervisor.

    b) the supervisor in the presence of the employee shall investigate the matter and if it is agreed that the condition is unsafe, the supervisor will take all necessary steps to correct the condition and attempt to provide alternate work for the affected employee until such condition is corrected. While alternate work is not available the affected employee will be paid his hourly wage rate for the balance of the shift and two additional shifts, following which he will be treated in accordance with the provisions of Article 16.

    c) if the supervisor does not agree that the condition is unsafe, but the employee maintains that it is unsafe, the supervisor will notify the Production Manager, or his representative, who will, without undue delay, notify the Industrial Safety Branch of the Ministry of Labour and request an immediate investigation and decision by an inspector. The supervisor will also advise the Manager of the Safety Department. In the meantime, the supervisor will attempt to provide alternate work for the employee. If alternate work is not available the affected employee will be treated in accordance with the provisions of Article 16. However, if the decision of the inspector is:

        i. the condition is safe, such employee will be returned to the job as soon as possible;

        ii. the condition is unsafe, such employee will be returned to the job as soon as possible after the unsafe condition is corrected and will be compensated for any loss of regular wages for up to the balance of the shift and two additional shifts.

12. The supervisor and the employee concerned are to be present during the investigation conducted by the inspector from the Industrial Safety Branch of the Ministry of Labour as a result of the request outlined in 11(c) above. In addition, and provided they are available, the one (1) Company-apppointed and the one (1) Union-appointed member of the Safety and Health Committee will be present during the investigation. The employee and such members in question are entitled to such time from work as is necessary to be present during the investigation, without loss of wages for the time so spent.

13. While an inspection is being conducted by an inspector from the

Industrial Safety Branch of the Ministry of Labour, he is to be accompanied by the supervisor (or his alternate) for each area that is inspected, as well as the one (1) Company-appointed and the one (1) Union-appointed member of the Safety and Health Committee. These two (2) members of the Safety and Health Committee are entitled to such time from work as is necessary to accompany the inspector without loss of wages for the time so spent.

14. The member of the Safety and Health Committee appointed by the Union designated in 12 and 13 above, shall be considered to be the "employee authorized by a trade union" or the "authorized representative" referred to in the Employees' Health and Safety Act, or similar legislation.

The "Production Manager" means the senior supervisor responsible for production in the Plant, or a part thereof.

15. A copy of any decision or order or direction or report issued by an inspector from the Industrial Safety Branch of the Ministry of Labour will be sent to the appropriate Safety and Health Committee, to the Union, and posted in a conspicuous location in the workplace.

16. The Company will issue a set of Safety Rules to each employee and, depending on the nature of their work, additional manuals such as:

a) Safe Practices for Crane Operations;

b) Safe Practices for Electrical Testing

c) Safe Practices for Fork Lift Truck Operations

A copy of the Safety Rules and each such manual will be provided to the Union.

The Union will actively encourage employees to observe the safety rules, practices and procedures outlined in the documents referenced above, which may be amended, cancelled, and/or added to by the Company. The Company will advise the Union of any changes prior to issuing them to employees.

17. The wearing of Company-approved safety toe protection is mandatory for employees whose regular work assignment is in an area designated as a toe protection area. For employees in such designated areas who have completed one hundred and twenty (120) worked days with the Company, the Company will, effective on and after June 1, 19XX, pay $50.00 once per calendar year toward the cost of safety shoes approved by the

Company. For employees who have not completed one hundred and twenty (120) worked days with the Company, the Company will reimburse employees $50.00 after the completion of one hundred and twenty (120) worked days. (The present subsidy of $30.00 will apply until May 31, 19XX). Payroll deduction will be available to employees requiring approved safety shoes.

18. Company-approved safety glasses will be required to be worn by all employees who work in or enter any area designated as an eye protection area. The Company's responsibility under this program will be to:

a) designate the type and style of safety frames and lenses;

b) designate the opticians authorized to dispense prescription safety frames and lenses;

c) provide at no employee cost (other than prescription and fitting costs), through designated opticians, one (1) pair of safety frames and lenses for employees requiring prescription glasses and who completed one hundred and twenty (120) worked days with the Company;

d) employees who have not completed one hundred and twenty (120) worked days with the Company and who purchase approved prescription safety glasses through designated opticians, will be reimbursed the cost of the glasses following completion of one hundred and twenty (120) worked days;

e) provide "Plano" safety glasses for employees not requiring prescription glasses not more frequently than once (1) every two (2) years;

f) provide visitors' safety glasses for employees and visitors entering an eye protection area who do not normally work in such an area;

g) request the Workers' Compensation Board to replace safety glasses broken or damaged as a result of work-related acitvity;

h) make payroll deduction available to employees requiring approved safety glasses;

The employee's responsibility under this program will be to:

a) provide a prescription from an ophthalmologist or optometrist;

b) pay for any fitting charge levied by the optician;

c) pay for lost, damaged, or replaced prescription safety glasses;

d) pay for ''Plano'' safety glasses that have been lost, broken, or damaged within two (2) years of issue, other than those damaged or broken as a result of work-related activity.

19. At the request of either party a meeting will be held at a mutually convenient time for the purpose of discussing matters related to the safety and health of employees. The party making a request for a meeting will supply to the other, at least three (3) working days in advance of the proposed meeting, a list of topics to be discussed. Each party will send to the meeting not more than four (4) representatives.

20. It is agreed that no matter respecting the safety and health of employees, or this Appendix, nor any differences arising thereunder, shall be subject to grievance or arbitration.

KEY CONCEPTS

Recognition	*Suspension*
Relationship	*Stewards*
Violation	*Notices*
Management rights	*Bereavement pay*
Reporting for work	*Jury duty*
Working conditions	*Information to union*
Hours of work	*Leave of absence*
Overtime	*Transfer*
Holidays	*Recall*
Vacations with pay	*Check-off*
Wages	*Duration*
Shift bonus	*Termination*
Seniority	*Classification*
Probationary employees	*Wage structure*
Grievance	*Safety and health*
Discharge	

REVIEW QUESTIONS

1. What is the general purpose of this Agreement?

2. Which employees are excluded from coverage?

3. What protection are employees given from discrimination by employer and union?

4. What undertakings about lockouts and strikes are contained in the Agreement?

5. What arrangements are agreed with regard to union activity on company premises and during company time?

6. What undertaking does the union give with regard to output and company property?

7. What "rights" are specifically reserved for management in this Agreement?

8. What does the Agreement provide with regard to the employer's provision of work?

9. Explain and discuss the measures contained in Appendix D of the Agreement for the safety and health of employees.

10. What has been agreed with regard to hours of work and overtime?

11. What are the holidays provided? When would an employee not qualify for payment for any of these holidays?

12. How are vacations with pay determined?

13. What wages are to be paid? How can an employee ensure that he or she is in the right job classification?

14. What is the shift bonus? Why is it provided?

15. How is employee seniority determined? What purposes is it used for?

16. When does an employee lose his seniority? What happens during sickness and layoffs?

17. What is a "probationary employee"? What are his rights?

18. How is a grievance defined in this Agreement?

19. What is the grievance procedure?

20. What company grievances are permitted?

21. What can happen if an employee feels that he or she has been unjustly discharged or suspended?

22. What provision is made with regard to union stewards and their work on behalf of the union?

23. Is the union free to post notices in the plant?

24. Explain the provision for bereavement pay.

25. What happens if an employee is called for Jury Duty?

26. What information is to be supplied by the company to the union?

27. When may an employee receive a leave of absence? What conditions apply to such leaves? How is seniority affected?

28. What provision is made with regard to maternity leave?

29. How is a "transfer" defined in the Agreement? What provisions apply with regard to pay?

30. What provision is made for the checkoff of union dues?

PART I

Case Studies

GIBSON PRODUCTS (CANADA) LTD.

Allegation of Employer Interference Prior to a Representation Vote

In a decision dated September 21, the provincial Labour Relations Board found that no less than thirty-five per cent of the employees of Gibson Products (Canada) Ltd. in the voting constituency were members of the union, and accordingly directed the taking of a representation vote which was held on October 5. The union filed a section 79 complaint on September 30, alleging violation of sections 3, 56, 58 and 70(2) of the Labour Relations Act and at the same time asked the Board to certify it without a vote pursuant to section 7a of the Act because, it claimed, the effect of the alleged unfair labour practices committed by the employer was to make it unlikely that the true wishes of the employees would be ascertained by a secret ballot vote. In the face of these charges having been filed by the union on September 30, the Board directed that the boxes be sealed pending a determination in this matter. The vote, therefore, has already been taken but the ballot box has been sealed.

A group of employees who have not heretofore been made a party to the certification application sought to intervene in these proceedings. Their intervention was challenged by the trade union. The Board is of the view that the filing of a request under section 7a of the Act constitutes a new point of departure in the certification process. It is a point at which employees not previously involved in the proceedings are entitled to intervene and be heard. Accordingly, the Board ruled at the hearing that the employees were entitled to intervene, to be made a party for the duration of the process and to make their representations. The Board cautioned the intervening employees, however, that its determination of the Section 79 matter would be based upon an objective assessment of all evidence before it relating to the alleged misconduct of the respondent employer, and not simply upon the claims of individual employees that they had not been unduly influenced. Such claims, following upon the alleged intimidation, coercion or undue influence, are of little probative value. Where there is clear evidence of intimidation or threats, it is of little consequence if one or more employees testify that they were not intimidated. Indeed, the Board must recognize that this testimony itself may be influenced by or be the product of the employer's coercive conduct.

The alleged misconduct in the instant case occurred in the period September 20-September 30, the period following the Board's decision directing the taking of a representation vote. During this period the Vice-President and General Manager of the company wrote four letters to the employees and made two speeches to the employee body during working hours with respect to the upcoming vote. The employees were a "captive audience'' for the two speeches. The initial task which confronts the Board is to decide if the written and verbal comments of Mr. Winters, the Vice-President and General Manager, constitute ''coercion, intimidation, threats, promises or undue influence'' within the meaning of Section 56 of the Act or if his comments are within the bounds of freedom of expression which is protected by Section 56 of the Act.

Section 56 of the Act reads:

> No employer or employers' organization and no person acting on behalf of an employer or an employers' organization shall participate in or interfere with the formation, selection or administration of a trade union or the representation of employees by a trade union or contribute financial or other support to a trade union, but nothing in this section shall be deemed to deprive an employer of his freedom to express his views so long as he does not use coercion, intimidation, threats, promises or undue influence.

The line which separates freedom of expression from undue influence or the other prohibitions found in Section 56 of the Act is a thin one which must be drawn having regard to the facts of the particular case. There are, however, certain broad indicia which have been well set out in the Dylex case (supra) at paragraph 19:

> In seeking to establish where the line lies the Board starts with the presumption that employees recognize that employers generally are not in favour of having to deal with employees through a trade union, and that therefore it ought not to surprise them when their employer indicates that he would prefer if they voted against a trade union. Following from this the Board takes the view that an invitation to employees from their employer to vote against a trade union, in the absence of any surrounding facts or circumstances which would cause the employees to place undue emphasis on such statements, does not constitute undue influence within the meaning of section 56. (See: Playtex Limited, 73 CLLC 16,086, 1972, OLRB Rep. Dec. 1027). On the other hand, however, the Board is also cognizant that an employee may be peculiarly vulnerable to employer influences. This point is clearly brought out in the decision of the Canada Labour Relations Board in the Taggart Service Limited case (1964) CLLR Transfer Binder '64-'66, 16,015, at page 13,055; 64(3) CLLC 16,015, the following excerpt from which was cited with approval by this Board in the leading case of Bell & Howell Ltd., (1968) OLRB Rep. Oct. 695 at p. 706:
>> ''An employer may express his views and give facts in appropriate manner and circumstances on the issues involved in representation proceedings insofar as these directly affect him and has the right to make appropriate reply to propaganda directed against him in relation

thereto. However, he should bear in mind in so doing the force and weight which such expressions of views may have upon the minds of his employees and which derive from the nature and extent of his authority as employer over his employees with respect to their wages, working conditions and continuity of employment. He should take care that such expressions of views do not constitute and may not be reasonably construed by his employees to be an attempt by means of intimidation, threats, or other means of coercion to interfere with their freedom to join a trade union of their choice or to otherwise select a bargaining agent of their own choice.''

The employer established his position of dominance and set the theme for his subsequent comments in the first letter to the employee body, dated September 20, where he stated:

> Your best interests lie with the company. . . . The company pays your wages and provides you with your benefit programs. . . . . .

The underlying thrust of the employer's message is brought home to the employees in the letter of September 28:

> . . . You must always consider the possibility of a financially crippling strike. Strikes are not a pleasant subject to consider, but they are a fact of life in unionized locations. We all know that where there are unions there are strikes and strikes are costly. Costly to the company in terms of loss of business and possibly customers, and costly to you, the employee, in terms of lost wages which can never be regained.
>
> Certainly you have a keen interest in both regards since a loss of customers affects your job security, and a loss of wages would affect your financial security.
>
> Keep working toward job security. Don't place a ''third party'' between yourself and the customer. Avoid this possibility and vote ''no'' on October 5.

The employer's theme can be summarized as follows: Strikes are a ''fact of life''; strikes mean loss of business and possibly customers; ''customers affect your job security''; ''don't place a third party between yourself and the customers''; avoid this possibility and vote ''No''. This theme which was followed by Mr. Winters throughout his remarks was made particularly relevant to the employees of Gibson by the clear message that in order to ''maintain'' their present level of benefits in negotiation with the company, the employees would have to resort to a strike.

> All of these benefits are and have been yours without the necessity of your paying costly dues, for these are benefits provided by your company.

As stated before, your benefits will become negotiable if the union wins the election. The outcome of any negotiations is difficult to predict; however, it is a fact that other locations which are presently represented by unions do not have benefit programs which are as comprehensive as the one which you NOW enjoy.

Consider your alternative carefully. Ensure that you maintain the present level of benefits for yourself and your family. Vote: No Union.

This threat is repeated by Mr. Winters in his "captive audience" speech of September 22 in which he reviewed in minute detail a manual of employee benefits which had been given to the employees on that same day and concluded as follows:

I would like to remind you that the manual is good only so long as there is no union. The minute the union comes in, this book becomes void and each item becomes negotiable. And these are items the company will take a strike on.

The threat was again delivered to the employees in the "captive audience" speech of September 28:

. . . and negotiations often go on for many months and could end up in a strike . . .

We start bargaining as though we had no wage structure and as though the benefits did not exist. There is no law that says that we have to agree to a single particular demand made by the union.

The employer has drawn a direct relationship between strikes, customers and job security and has put his employees on notice that they will have to strike in order to "maintain" the existing level of benefits if they choose the trade union as their bargaining agent. In his speech on September 30, Mr. Winters returned to the theme of job security and implicitly threatened his employees in the following terms:

As matters now stand — you have a job and steady employment here at Gibson. Naturally we hope things get even better. It can be better if you can get this union matter behind us and settle down to the business all of us are supposed to be here for.

The union has asked the Board to apply section 7a of the Act and certify it without regard to the vote which was conducted on October 5. Section 7a of the Act provides:

Where an employer or employers' organization contravenes this Act so that the true wishes of the employees of the employer or of a member of the employers' organization are not likely to be ascertained, and, in the opinion of the Board, a trade union has membership support adequate for the purposes of collective bargaining in a bargaining unit found by the Board pursuant to section 6 to be appropriate for collective bargaining, the Board may, on the application of the trade union, certify the employees in the bargaining unit.

There are three conditions which must exist before the Board may exercise its discretion under Section 7a of the Act. These are:

1) The employer has contravened the Act.

2) The contravention has resulted in a situation where the true wishes of the employees are not likely to be ascertained.

3) The trade union has membership support adequate for the purpose of collective bargaining.

The Board must now turn its attention to the question of whether the trade union has membership support adequate for the purposes of collective bargaining. A remedial authority similar to that now found in Section 7a has been part of the Act for some years. Section 7(4), the immediate predecessor to section 7a, provided:

> If the Board is satisfied that more that 50 per cent of the employees in the bargaining unit are members of the trade union and that the true wishes of the employees are not likely to be disclosed by a representation vote, the Board may certify the trade union as a bargaining agent without taking a representation vote.

Section 7(4) could not be invoked unless the union had filed membership evidence on behalf of at least fifty per cent of the employees in the bargaining unit and the true wishes of the employees were not likely to be ascertained. In introducing Section 7a, the legislature deleted both the requirement for majority support and the reference to the representation vote, and added the requirement that the alleged employer misconduct must amount to a violation of the Act. While in the opinion of the Board there must be membership support adequate for collective bargaining, there need be no specific percentage or majority. Indeed, since the Board must be satisfied that the true wishes of the employees are unlikely to be ascertained, it may be very difficult to find untainted evidence as to the union's support. In such circumstances the Board may have to rely heavily on the membership cards filed with the Board as required by the Act since those cards represent a voluntary and unequivocal expression of support for the union and for collective bargaining.

In this case the Board has before it signed evidence of membership submitted on behalf of more than 50% of the employees in the bargaining unit. This evidence, in the form of combination applications for membership and receipts acknowledging the required $1 payment, was submitted prior to the unlawful interference by the employer. The Board also has before it two statements dated October 13, some eight days after the taking of the vote, which bear signatures of 41 of the 62 bargaining unit employees. The preamble to these statements reads as follows:

> Messrs. Carrie and O'Dea
> Barristers and Solicitors
> 555 Talbot Street
> St. Thomas, Ontario
> N5P 1C5
>
> The undersigned hereby retain you to act as our solicitors and authorize you to appear on our behalf before the Labour Relations Board on October 20th, and there to make the following representations:
>
> a) The results of a vote taken on the premises of Gibson Products (Canada) Ltd. on October 5th, to establish the International Union of Electrical, Radio and Machine Workers as our bargaining agent should stand.
> b) We were not unduly influenced as a result of discussions with and letters received from management of Gibson Products (Canada) Ltd. concerning the application of the Union, nor were we in any way threatened, coerced or intimidated by management or anybody on its behalf.
> c) The interests of the undersigned will not be best represented by the applicant Union.
>
> The undersigned undertake to pay the fees and expenses of our solicitors properly incurred in carrying out the above instructions.

Sixteen of the thirty-three bargaining unit employees who had signed membership cards in support of the union and who had paid the required $1 subsequently signed the above statement in opposition to the union.

DOMINION STORES

Employee Status of Bakery Store Managers Questioned

(Retail, Wholesale and Department Store Union, AFL:CIO:CLC v. Dominion Stores Limited, Ontario Labour Relations Board, July 21, 1976).

Before: Kevin M. Burkett, Vice-Chairman, and N.B. Satterfield and R.H. White, Members.

(Application for certification)

Kevin M. Burkett, Vice-Chairman (for the majority):

1. An Application for certification on behalf of all bakery store managers of the respondent at its retail stores in Sault Ste. Marie was filed by the applicant on March 29, 1976. A dispute arose at the hearing as to the status of the bakery store managers as employees under the Labour Relations Act and accordingly the Board in a decision dated April 15, 1976 appointed a Labour Relations Officer to inquire into the duties and responsibilities of those in the classification of bakery manager. The Board has now reviewed the report of the Labour Relations Officer and the representations of the respondent thereof.

2. Section 1(3)(b) of the Act states:

> 1. (3) Subject to Section 80, for the purposes of this Act, no person shall be deemed to be an employee, (b) who, in the opinion of the Board, exercises managerial functions or is employed in a confidential capacity in matters relating to labour relations.

3. The effective operation of the system of labour relations which presently exists in this jurisdiction is based on an underlying recognition of the inherent difference between employer and employees and a need for an arm's length relationship between the employer, as embodied by those who exercise managerial functions or are employed in a confidential capacity in matters relating to labour relations, and the employees. The purpose of Section 1(3)(b) of the Act is to ensure that persons who in the opinion of the Board exercise managerial functions or are employed in a confidential capacity do not find themselves faced with a conflict of interest because of their inclusion within a bargaining unit of other employees. Persons who exercise such function are deemed not to be employees pursuant to Section 1(3)(b) of the Act and as a result are denied access to the collective bargaining process. In view of this remedial aspect, the onus is placed on the party seeking to exclude a person from the operation of the Act to satisfy the Board of the exercise of managerial functions.

4. The Board has seen fit to exclude as managerial, not only persons who make independent decisions with respect to policy and the running of an organization but also, having regard to the underlying purpose of the section, persons who can materially affect the terms and conditions of employment of other employees. The evidence is clear that Mr. Geddes, the bakery manager examined in the instant case, does not become involved in policy or independent decision-making as it relates to the management of the respondent company or the operation of the bakery. The bakery managers do not become involved in decisions with respect to budgeting, capital outlay or the future development of the respondent company. With respect to the bakery, the products produced, the ingredients and baking formulas and the prices charged are all determined by head office as is the "person-hour structure" which sets out the number of man-hours which the company will permit in a department. The "person-hour structure" relates to the sales volume of the department. The store hours are also determined by head office. The bakery manager does not have a power of independent decision-making with respect to the operation of the baker. All matters of consequence are predetermined by the company head office.

5. There are eight persons assigned to the bakery department "managed" by Mr. Geddes. They include persons in the classification of baker, counter girl, wrapper and decorator. Mr. Geddes testified that he supervises, instructs and assigns work to these persons. The Board accepts this evidence but has taken particular note of the fact that the head office supplies the formulas and the variety book and as a result must conclude that the supervision and instruction are somewhat circumscribed. The Board would point out, however, that it does not exclude a person from the operation of the Act on the basis of supervisory function, circumscribed or otherwise, as borne out by the traditional inclusion within the bargaining unit of the "lead hand" and by the "white collar" cases. The Board must determine if the supervisory duties in combination with other responsibilities enable a person, either directly or by means of "effective recommendation", to affect the terms and conditions of employment of other employees. (See McIntyre Porcupine Mines Limited case (1975) OLRB Rep. Apr. 261 at page 297). The Board has examined the evidence and has concluded that the bakery managers do not exercise managerial functions within the meaning of Section 1(3)(b) of the Act.

Authority of Bakery Managers

6. The persons employed in the bakery department are covered by a subsisting collective agreement which sets out the terms and conditions of

employment including wage, benefits, holidays with pay, vacations, seniority and grievance procedures. The bakery managers do not participate in the negotiations nor are they involved in the grievance procedure. The bakery managers can grant short periods of time off but all leaves of absence are processed through the regional personnel office. The bakery managers set the work schedules but these are subject to the "person-hour structure" which also determines the complement and indirectly occasions the lay-off of employees. Mr. Geddes stated that he makes the lay-off decision but also submitted:

> If the person has the least seniority and doesn't present a problem I may have to deal through the union or the store manager, to find out whether I can do it or not.

Although Mr. Geddes testified that he has the authority to assign overtime, and has done so, he acknowledged that he had been told by the store manager at different times that no one was to authorize overtime. Mr. Geddes does not assign vacation times nor does he make any written assessment of the employees in the bakery department.

7. Although Mr. Geddes testified that he has the authority to hire employees and gave as an example the hiring of Richard Boucher, he admitted that if the store manager had disagreed with the placing of Mr. Boucher on payroll he would not have been hired. Furthermore, Mr. Bruno Temeline, the store manager who was called by the respondent company to give evidence, testified that the store manager makes the decision as to who will or will not be hired. Mr. Geddes admitted that the placement of someone to work behind the bakery counter is determined by the union seniority list. Mr. Geddes testified that he has the authority to discipline other employees. It would appear that the discipline imposed by Mr. Geddes has been primarily restricted to verbal warnings although the evidence establishes that on one occasion he terminated an employee. Mr. Geddes testified that he reported this action to the store manager not to gain final authority but to inform him. This testimony is inconsistent with the circumscribed authority of Mr. Geddes in all other areas as brought out in evidence. It can perhaps be explained, however, by the fact that the store manager has the opportunity to overrule or affirm actions taken by department managers (some of whom are in the bargaining unit) at the first step of the grievance procedure. Step one of the grievance procedure as set out in the collective agreement between the parties provides that:

> The employee concerned and a Union Steward or Union Representative may within five (5) working days of the alleged occurrence said to have caused the grievance, take the matter up with the Store Manager who shall give his answer within three (3) working days. The Store

Manager and a Union Steward will confirm in writing that a Step One meeting had taken place, showing on a form to be supplied by the company, store, date, grievor's name, and indicate that a verbal Step One meeting had been held. This form will be signed by the Store Manager and the Grievor. If the grievance has not been satisfactorily settled, then . . .

No Managerial Function

8. The bakery managers do not exercise duties and responsibilities which enable them to materially affect the terms and conditions of employment of other employees of the respondent so as to create a conflict of interest if they were to be given access to the collective bargaining process. The responsibilities of the bakery managers can be likened to those of the ''lead hand'' in the industrial setting and as such the Board is not prepared to find on the basis of their duties and responsibilities as of the date of this application, that the bakery managers exercise managerial functions within the meaning of Section 1(3)(b) of the Act.

9. The Board finds that all employees of the respondent in its stores at Sault Ste. Marie, Ontario, save and except store managers, assistant managers, persons above the rank of assistant manager, district office staff, persons employed for not more than 24 hours per week, persons employed during the school vacation period and persons covered by a subsisting collective agreement between the applicant and respondent, constitute a tag end unit of employees of the respondent appropriate for collective bargaining.

10. The Board is satisfied on the basis of all the evidence before it that more than 55 per cent of the employees of the respondent in the bargaining unit at the time the application was made, were members of the applicant on April 6, 1976, the terminal date fixed for this application and the date which the Board determines under Section 92(2)(j) of The Labour Relations Act, to be the time for the purpose of ascertaining membership under Section 7(1) of the said Act.

11. A certificate will be issued to the applicant.

Dissent

N.B. SATTERFIELD, Member: I would dismiss the application for certification of bakery store managers of the respondent at its retail stores in Sault Ste. Marie because they exercise managerial functions within the meaning of Section 1(3)(b) of the Act. This conclusion is based on the following facts and arguments derived from examination of the evidence in the report of the Labour Relations Officer.

1. The Bakery Store Managers regularly supervise the bakery employees in the following matters:

a) assigns daily duties;

b) evaluates the quality of employees' performance in these duties;

c) instructs them;

d) hires new employees;

e) assures they follow established time recording procedures and attend at their jobs for the required time each day;

f) grants permission for requested time off up to one day;

g) assigns and authorizes overtime;

i) schedules the days and hours of work of the employees.

The testimony of William Geddes is that he supervises in the above manner eight employees in four classifications. By his own words, he is supervising "All the time I'm there. . .". His performance of work covered by the subsisting collective agreement is limited to filling in for his employees on their jobs. The Bakery Store Managers get much of their authority and supervision from ". . . Bakery Supervision in Head Office" (Toronto), and the balance from their Store Managers. The Bakery in a store is separated from the rest of the store and is a self-contained unit. Therefore, both sources of supervision available to the Bakery Store Managers may be said to be remote and indirect, rather than immediate and direct. Given the nature of the supervision which they exercise and the sources of their own supervision, they can hardly be held to be . . .

> . . . merely a conduit carrying orders or instructions from management to the employees. . .

in the words of the Board in the Falconbridge Nickel Mines Limited case (1966) OLRB Rep. 379. That decision in referring to positions in dispute re their managerial nature states in part as follows:

> . . . if a person is primarily engaged in supervision and direction of other employees and has effective control over their employment relationship, even though the person occasionally performs work similar to the rank and file employees. . . to relieve an employee during occasional periods of absence . . . such occasional work in no way derogates from his prime function as a person employed in a managerial capacity.

The Bakery Store Managers are "primarily engaged in the supervision and direction of other employees". The two stores with bakery units employ 14 full-time and 7 part-time employees. Mr. Geddes' evidence is that he does not spend more than 50% of his time doing work of a non-supervisory nature. If the Managers were not spending the rest of their time supervising, it would not make sense to have them there. The nature of their supervisory responsibilities and the physical and organizational environment in which they must exercise it puts them in a conflict position with their employees in their charge. Therefore the decisions they make do materially affect the conditions of employment of other employees.

2. In addition to managerial responsibilities associated directly with the supervision of other employees, the Managers perform other tasks ordinarily associated with managerial responsibility such as: ordering all supplies for the bakery without having to seek prior approval or direction; assuring that the required mix of product is produced; the correct product formula is used; and the proper manning levels are maintained according to the level of output and the man-hour structure (i.e., budget). Mr. Geddes has a key to the store and is free to enter it at any time, as distinct from having the key so that he can share in the opening and closing of the store as is the case with non-managerial employees.

3. The Bakery Managers are also distinguished from the employees whom they supervise in respect to certain working conditions. They are paid a regular salary; and are not deducted pay for time off; and are not paid overtime; schedule their own hours; and only notify the Store Manager if taking time off.

Responsibility of Bakery Managers

4. I disagree with the conclusions reached in the majority decision at paragraph 4 that "All matters of consequence are predetermined by the company head office", and at paragraph 8 that "the responsibilities of the baker managers can be likened to those of the 'lead hand' in the industrial setting". It is quite clear that these managers have their responsibilities circumscribed by procedures laid down from head office in respect to budgeting, pricing, man-hour structures, store hours, formulas and variety books; from district personnel office in respect to leaves of absence; and by the subsisting collective agreement in respect to wages, overtime, discipline and transfers from part-time to regular employment.

However, as earlier stated in paragraph 1, much of their own supervision is from the remoteness of head office which, coupled with separateness of their units in the stores and the limited form of supervision received from the Store Managers, means someone with more authority than that usually associated with a "lead hand" must be responsible to assure that all of the policies and procedures are properly applied at the local level. In fact, Mr. Geddes supervises a lead hand who is responsible to him for the night shift operation. The Store Managers are clearly not responsible for the bakery units in respect to particular head office procedures such as budgets, man-hour structures, formulas and variety books and they exercise no authority over the ordering of supplies. If the Bakery Store Managers were to be determined as non-managerial within the meaning of Section 1(3)(b) of the Act, it would mean the Store Managers and Assistant Store Managers, in the two stores having bakery units, alone would hold managerial responsibility. These two stores have a total of 191 full-time and 119 part-time employees. By the sheer size of the work force alone, it would impose an unreasonable expectation for a Manager and Assistant Manager in one store and a Manager in the other to provide the only "non-bargaining unit" supervision, notwithstanding the fact that the store Department Managers are included in the existing unit. Furthermore, the Store Managers themselves have their responsibilities circumscribed in an almost identical manner to the Bakery Store Managers. If it is held that such limiting of supervisory function places those jobs within the Act, this conjures the absurd situation of the stores in questions being supervised from district or head office.

I endorse the representations of counsel for the respondent in that ". . . the evidence as a whole demonstrates that the Bakery Managers exercise discretionary powers which exclude them from the Act". On page 4 of counsel's written representations starting in the second paragraph, counsel sums up the totality of the situation as being that, in addition to the specific indicators of managerial status,

> They are responsible to the Company for the operation of an entire enterprise — the Bakery unit. It is an operation which, to a significant extent, operates independently of the main store. There is no interchange of employees between that Department and the rest of the store. The Bakery area is isolated from the store, and the employees enter "through a door which separates it from the main store". All the necessary equipment is in the Bakery area. A separate budget is established for that Department. It is the responsibility of the Bakery Manager to see to it that the budget is adhered to and that the Company's profit margin is maintained. He does this by exercising his own judgment and is not given "any direction in operating the bakery by the Store Manager". Most of the directions he receives from senior management appear to come straight from Head Office

rather than from the Store Manager. This is true of such important matters as the type of product, prices, man-hour structure, and operating hours.

The Bakery Manager is in charge of the operation of the Company's Bakery unit. To the extent that managerial responsibilities are needed, Mr. Loucks and Mr. Geddes exercise them. They make decisions crucial to the successful and profitable operation of the Company's bakery business. Their responsibility to the Company inherently places them in a conflict position with other employees.

The Board, in dealing with the difficult application of the "effective control" test of managerial status, stated in part in the McIntyre Porcupine Mines Limited case (1975) OLRB Rep. April 26 at paragraph 31:

> . . . it is in this area that the Board has most often said it will look at the "totality" of the evidence in making its determination. And in this light one "effective function is unlikely to be sufficient to activate Section 1(3)(b) although this, of course, depends on the nature of the function. On the other hand, the totality approach means that the trappings of managerial status, as opposed to actual functions, are relevant. These trappings (offices, salaries, etc.), may indicate the perspective or intent of the particular parties before the Board and this intent is of assistance when the other indicia of managerial capacity are in balance.

LAKE SHORE MILLS INC.

Contracting Out — Work of Watchmen Assigned to Private Firm — Application of Control and Organization Tests

The grievance was filed by the general chairman of the union and alleges that the company violated the collective agreement by assigning certain watchman's duties to personnel supplied by Allen International Security Services Limited ("Allen"). It is the position of the union that this assignment does not represent a genuine contracting out of the watchman's functions but that the individuals who perform these duties are, in fact, employees of the company.

The collective agreement contains the following provisions:

ARTICLE 1 — BARGAINING UNIT

1.1 The provisions of this Agreement shall apply to all employees in positions listed in Article 4, and to employees who are assigned to positions similar in kind or class to those listed in Article 4 which might be created during the term of this Agreement.

ARTICLE 2 — UNION RECOGNITION

2.1 The Company recognizes the Union as the sole and exclusive bargaining agent of employees in positions listed in Article 4 and employees who are assigned to positions similar in kind or class to those listed in Article 4 which might be created during the term of this Agreement.

Included in art. 4 is the classification of Watchman.

The company operates a grain elevator and is engaged in receiving, storing and transporting grain. Watchman's duties were performed by members of the bargaining unit. One employee was on duty at a time from 5:00 p.m. to 1:00 a.m., Monday to Friday, and from 8:00 a.m. to midnight on Saturdays, Sundays and holidays. The watchman's hours differed from those of the remaining employees who regularly worked from 8:00 a.m. to 5:00 p.m., Monday to Friday. There was, however, some overlap due to the fact that these employees were frequently required to work overtime in order to unload vessels.

The prime function of the watchman was fire detection and prevention, as the dust produced by grain handling creates a substantial risk of fire. The watchman was also required to check for vandalism, trespassers or problems with company equipment and machinery. In addition, the watchman performed certain cleaning functions, as well as a number of miscellaneous duties, such as snow shovelling and answering the telephone in the office.

At the commencement of his shift, an employee occupying the classification of Watchman was required to report to the office of Ross Davidson, the operations manager. At that point, either Mr. Davidson or Joe Hampton, the foreman, provided the watchman with any specific instructions there might have been relating to the shift. When not performing other duties, the watchman returned to Mr. Davidson's office. It was there that the watchman was required to answer the telephone and relay to management any messages in relation to matters such as the docking of a vessel or anything of an emergency nature which arose during the shift. On occasion, the watchman was also required to monitor the use of the telephone by crew members of docked vessels to ensure that all long-distance calls were placed collect.

The watchman was provided with a detex clock and was required to make rounds on the company premises where he would "clock in" at various predetermined stations. The clock produced a tape-recording of the time at which the watchman clocked in and, apart from providing the company with verification that the watchman performed his duties, the tape was required by the company for insurance purposes. At the conclusion of his shift, the watchman left messages for management as to any significant events which had taken place during the shift.

Ross Davidson began to consider the possibility of contracting out the watchman's work and decided to request an estimate from Allen of the cost of providing security services. Allen prepared a confidential security proposal for the company's facility. Mr. Davidson testified that the proposal revealed that there would be substantial cost saving to the company and, on the basis of the proposal, a decision was made to contract out the watchman's work.

By letter dated December 13, 1984, the union was advised of the company's intention to retain the services of a private security firm and to eliminate the position of watchman. This letter provides as follows:

REGISTERED

December 13, 1984.

Mr. D. J. Scott
Union Chairman

Dear Sir:

Please be advised that the position of Watchman is to be eliminated effective December 31, 1984.

Anticipated reduction of available grain business for 1985 makes it more essential that our costs be reduced, wherever possible.

Necessary security functions will be performed by a Private Security firm.

No layoff is anticipated, at this time. The employees now performing watching duties will be employed in the normal operation of the Elevator for the winter shipping season.

Yours truly,

LAKE SHORE MILLS INC.

"W. R. Davidson"

W. R. Davidson
Operations Manager

Mr. Davidson confirmed that no lay-off resulted from the company's decision to contract out the watchman's work. He acknowledged, however, that by retaining the services of Allen, two jobs were lost to the bargaining unit.

With the exception of cleaning duties, the personnel provided by Allen performed essentially the same functions as those previously performed by members of the bargaining unit occupying the classification of Watchman.

The contract provides that Allens shall furnish the company,

> . . . with Security Personnel at location or locations from such starting dates and times and during such hours with special equipment, such as radios, patrol cars, watch clocks, etc. as ALLEN and Client shall mutually agree upon in writing. Uniformed Security Personnel shall be equipped with ALLEN uniforms.

Mr. Davidson testified that, whereas the company was previously obliged to replace a bargaining unit employee occupying the classification of Watchman who became ill and that the company might have incurred overtime costs, Allens now assumes responsibility for assigning personnel. In the event that a security guard is sick, a replacement is provided at no additional cost.

Security guards assigned to the company are paid bi-weekly by Allen and Allen is also responsible for payroll deductions, workers' compensation remittances and for providing comprehensive general liability insurance.

In addition to the items referred to, the contract between the company and Allen also contains the following:

Employees

> The Parties intend that an independent contractor relationship will be created by this contract. ALLEN shall not be considered to be an

agent or an employee of Client for any purpose. Security Personnel of ALLEN are not entitled to any of the benefits that Client provides for Client's employees. Security Personnel are employees of Allen and Allen will pay all wages and other payroll related costs of Security Personnel. Allen will exercise complete control over the conduct, duties and all other matters concerning Security Personnel.

Supervision and Quality Assurance

Allen shall be responsible for the direct supervision of all Security Personnel through designated representatives, who will be available at reasonable times to consult with client.

Service

The services to be rendered under this Agreement by Allen shall be in conformity with operating procedures mutually agreed upon by Client and Allen. If, at the request of Client, Security Personnel are assigned duties other than those agreed to by Allen, Client shall assume complete responsibility for and all liability arising therefrom. Allen will remove from service as soon as a qualified replacement is available any Security Personnel who, in Client's opinion, are not qualified to perform the work assigned.

Mr. Allen testified that he screens and selects the security guards personally. Guards are trained for approximately five hours at the branch office, with the training consisting of a lecture and a film. In this case, the initial orientation to the company premises was provided by Joe Hampton who gave a tour of the operation to the Allen supervisor responsible for the location and to the two security guards who were to begin work at the facility. Mr. Allen testified that replacement personnel have been trained by the Allen security guard on site or the responsible supervisor. In addition, on-the-job training of 8 or 16 hours has been provided by Allen.

When an Allen security guard reports to the company premises, he is required to check in with another member of the Allen staff stationed elsewhere. The security guard reports to Mr. Davidson's office as was previously the case with bargaining unit members and, at this juncture, last minute instructions with respect to the shift may be provided by Mr. Davidson or Mr. Hampton. Although Mr. Davidson suggested that he would relay certain instructions to an Allen supervisor rather than to the security guard directly, Mr. Allen testified that Mr. Davidson is free to give instructions to the guards personally and that if these involve a permanent change in procedure, the post orders would be amended accordingly.

Allen security guards conduct rounds and, again with the exception of cleaning duties, their tasks are virtually identical to those previously performed by bargaining unit watchmen. The security guards, however, do prepare logs and reports with respect to their shifts, as well as incident reports in the event that anything significant occurs on the shift. This procedure was not previously followed by members of the bargaining unit but is apparently standard procedure for Allen personnel and Mr. Davidson acknowledged that he agreed to the preparation of these documents. The originals of the documents are left on Mr. Davidson's desk at the end of each shift. At the conclusion of the shift, the security guard is again required to contact the Allen staff member elsewhere.

Mr. Allen testified that "Allen" assumes responsibility for the supervision of its security guards and that this is accomplished primarily by way of spot checks and the roving supervisor responsible for the company location, endeavours to visit each client's premises once a week.

Allen supplies to its security guards a uniform and safety shoes. Allen also furnishes the report forms and logs which the guards are required to complete. The company provides the detex clocks and keys, a hard hat, flashlight and dust mask, if requested.

The issue then is whether, in the circumstances described, the company has effected a genuine contracting out of the watchman's duties or whether the relationship between the company and the security guards supplied by Allen is truly one of employer and employee. In this case, the collective agreement contains no prohibition against contracting out and, as a consequence, it was not suggested that the company was without authority to contract out the work in issue.

Union Argument

The Union argued this arrangement does not constitute a genuine contracting out of the watchman's functions but that the individuals who perform these duties are in fact employees of the company. With the exception of the cleaning duties, the individuals perform essentially the same functions as those previously performed by members of the bargaining unit occupying the classification of watchman. Further, these individuals are performing these duties under the control of the company.

In support of its position, the Union referred the arbitration board to the following decisions to support its position.

In Norton Co. of Canada Ltd., Hamilton and The United Steelworkers 4 L.A.C., p. 1454, in addressing the factor of control the Board commented as follows:

> In determining whether the contract amounted to one for services, as distinct from a contract of service, some assistance can be derived from the Law of Master and Servant. It is stated in Diamond's "The Law of Master and Servant", Second Edition, at Page 1, that

"The relation of master and servant exists between two persons where, by Agreement between them, express or implied, the one is under the control of the other.

A person is under the control of another as he is bound to obey the orders of that other not only as to the work which he shall execute, but also as to the details of the work and the manner of its execution."

At Page 5 it is stated that

"The question of whether a person is under the control of another is a question of fact. Control may exist between two persons although the one

1. did not appoint the other;

2. does not pay the remuneration;

3. has no power to dismiss; and

4. has not the exclusive control."

Further, the board noted the following:

To weigh the significance of control, arbitrators have assessed the degree of the party-employer's right to direct the person's job performance appropriate to the nature of the particular job and the person's skill. In many awards, the party-employer did not choose the person, did not pay him directly and did not purport to discipline him on the spot. Nevertheless, arbitrators defined the person as an employee if he performed the job with the party-employer's materials on the party-employer's premises with the party-employer exercising to a substantial degree the right to direct the job performance.

The Union argued that the individuals were within the control and direction of the company and that the grievance should, therefore, be upheld.

Company Argument

The Company argued that, under the collective agreement, there was no restriction on its right to subcontract. Mr. Davidson testified that there was substantial cost saving and therefore the decision was made to contract out the work.

Security guards are paid by Allen and Allen is also responsible for payroll deductions, workers' compensation remittances and for providing general liability insurance. Previously, when a watchman became ill, the company had to provide a replacement, which might have involved overtime pay. Allen assumes responsibility for assigning personnel and, in the event of illness, provides a replacement at no additional cost.

Allen screens, selects, trains, and supervises these individuals. They are not employees of the Company and do not have the same relationship to the Company as employees of the Company.

Counsel for the Company, also made reference to the decision of the board in *Re Social Planning Council of Metropolitan Toronto and C.U.P.E., Local 1777* (1980), 28 L.A.C. (2d) 134 (Knopf). The board specified the following criteria to be the most important in determining whether certain project employees were actually employees of the party-employer [p. 150]:

1. Control over the selection of employees.

2. Control over the method and performance of the work.

3. Control over the decision whether money should be paid for wages or other expenditures.

4. Control over the length and duration of the performance of job functions.

5. Whether the work performed was part of or integral to that of the alleged employer.

6. Who benefited from the work performed.

Clearly these individuals are not controlled by the company. For all of these reasons, the grievance should be dismissed.

ADAMS INDUSTRIES LTD.

Language Interpretation — Payment for Time Spent on Union Activities

Background

Adams Industries Ltd. ran its manufacturing operations on a three-shift basis. Shifts were scheduled on a rotating basis — that is, the first week a group of employees would work days, the second week afternoons, and the third week, nights.

From time to time, as required by the collective agreement or for other reasons, the company scheduled meetings with the Union. Under the provisions of the collective agreement, certain Union representatives had the right to attend these meetings. Managers and senior supervisors of the company normally worked days. As a result the company was inclined to schedule meetings with the Union during the day shift when its managers and senior supervisors were at work. Those Union representatives who were scheduled to work during the hours of the meeting and who had the right to attend these meetings would normally leave their assigned work with permission, attend the meeting and, when the meeting was finished, return to work. As provided by the collective agreement, these Union representatives would be paid by the company for the time spent at these meetings.

On occasion, those Union representatives who were scheduled in the second or third shift would come into the plant for the period of time required to attend a meeting which was scheduled in the day shift. When the meeting was finished they would leave the plant and return to whatever they were doing during this period which was outside their working hours.

To some degree the company established a practice of paying such people for the time they had spent at these Union meetings. For example, if a Union representative was scheduled in a given week to work on the 3-11 shift and if he worked the 3-11 shift for eight hours each day, he would receive 40 hours' pay for it. In the event the company called a meeting with the Union at 10:00 a.m., when he was on the 3-11 shift and the meeting lasted for one hour, he would receive one hour's pay for this meeting and therefore at the end of the week he would be paid for 40 hours' work plus one hour for the Union meeting for a total of 41 hours' pay for a 40-hour week.

The pertinent clauses of the collective agreement are as follows:

> "7.01 The Union acknowledges that committee men and Union officers have duties to perform on behalf of the company, and that such persons will not leave their regular duties without arranging the matter with their foreman, or immediate super-

visor, and when resuming their regular duties, they will report to their foreman or supervisor and will give reasonable explanation which may be requested with respect to their absence.''

"7.02 It is clearly understood that committee men will not absent themselves from their regular duties unreasonably in order to deal with grievances of employees or with other Union business and that in accordance with this understanding the company will compensate such employees for the time spent in negotiating with the company, in handling grievances of employees and attending meetings of the Union committee with the management, at their average hourly earnings for piece work employees, and at their hourly rate for day work employees.

It is understood that the time paid by the company to such employees for negotiations shall be limited to an aggregate of two hundred (200) hours.''

In the recent negotiations, the company placed a demand to modify the agreement to provide that Union representatives would be paid under these provisions only for time spent attending such meetings with the company during their assigned working hours. The Union rejected the demand and the agreement was renewed with no changes in these clauses.

Immediately after signing the agreement the company notified the Union that the Company would pay Union representatives for the time spent in meeting with the company only when the Union representative leaves his scheduled work in order to attend the meeting and in proportion to the time spent.

Subsequently the Union filed the following grievance:

"The company have notified us that we will not be paid for time spent in meetings with the company unless time is lost during the shift the meeting is held on. We have previously been paid for time spent in all meetings with the company.''

Union Argument

The Union argued that clauses 7.01 and 7.02 are clear and unambiguous. The clauses state that in accordance with the understanding the company will compensate such employees. The understanding is that committee men will not absent themselves from regular duties unreasonably in order to deal with grievances of employees or with other union business. In return for this understanding the company agreed to certain compensation.

Clause 7.01 further underlines the responsibility of committee men and

Union officers; mainly that they will not leave their regular duties without making prior arrangements with their foreman or immediate supervisor and that they will report on their return to work and will give reasonable explanation which may be requested with respect to their absence.

In clause 7.02 it is clearly stated that the Union has an obligation to the company and the company has an obligation to the Union. What are these obligations?

The Union argued that it is clearly understood that committee men will not absent themselves from their regular duties unreasonably in order to deal with grievances of employees.

First there is not any argument on the first part as the Union clearly upheld their part of the bargain and did not absent themselves unreasonably at any time.

The second part does not spell out any time limits, exceptions or any reasons for not compensating the Union representatives for handling grievances or attending meetings of the Union committee with management. The only exception is made and clearly spelt out when negotiations take over 200 hours. This exception was negotiated into the collective agreement after the original clauses 7.01 and 7.02 were negotiated. This is the only way any change should be made in the collective agreement. This the company tried to do regarding clauses 7.01 and 7.02 during the last negotiations but they were not successful in changing these clauses.

If committee men should only be compensated for time lost during their shift, surely the agreement would have said this, but instead it clearly says for time spent in order to deal with grievances of employees or with other Union business.

It would seem very strange for the company to have compensated Union committee men for so many years in this manner unless it was originally agreed that it was only fair to compensate in this manner for time spent. It would appear that only with many changes in management personnel has there been any change in the company's thinking on this matter.

Article 7.01 states that committee men have many duties to perform on behalf of the company. Surely the company does not wish or expect committee men to perform these duties without compensation.

Company Argument

The company argued that the meaning of the clause was clear and unambiguous. Under the terms of the agreement and the Ontario Labour Relations Act, the arbitrator has the right to interpret the collective agreement. However, he can only consider past practice when the meaning of the language in the agreement is ambiguous. In this case there is no ambiguity in the language. Therefore, the arbitrator does not have the right to consider past practice.

The facts are that a number of years ago the company agreed to put into the collective agreement clauses 7.01 and 7.02, and they were subsequently amended to provide the 200-hour limitation. The company administered the clauses as written and in the same manner as its present practice. There was no objection from the Union. With certain changes in management personnel, in the recent past, an unfortunate practice did develop. The company decided to correct this situation, and return to the proper meaning of the clause with its previous practice. It decided, rather than unilaterally change the practice, to wait for negotiation and discuss the matter with the Union. However, the Union refused to agree to the company's plan. As a result the agreement was renewed with no change in these clauses, and the company advised the Union that it was going to make the change.

Clause 7.01 concedes that Union representatives have duties to perform on behalf of the company and they will not leave their regular duties without arranging the matter with their foreman, and when resuming their regular duties they will report to their foreman and will give reasonable explanation which may be requested with respect to their absence.

Clause 7.02 is dealing with the situation referred to in clause 7.01 and states that Union representatives will not absent themselves from their regular duties unreasonably and in accordance with this understanding, the company will compensate such employees for time spent in negotiating with the company, in handling of grievances and attending meetings with management.

The company is agreeing to compensate such employees. Such employees are those who have not absented themselves unreasonably from their regular duties. One who qualifies therefore is one who absents himself from his regular duties reasonably for these purposes. The only ones who can do this are those who are otherwise scheduled to work at the time. Therefore if a meeting is held on the day shift, an employee on the day shift may qualify for payment. An employee on the afternoon shift does not absent himself from his regular duties either reasonably or unreasonably and therefore does not bring himself within the meaning of clause 7.02 which provides for payment. Therefore he is not entitled to payment.

RONALD FIELDS

Policy Grievance — Seniority

Background

Due to lack of orders at Fairfield Controls Ltd., there was a shortage of work in the light assembly department. As a result, the company found it necessary to reduce the number of employees in the department until the level of orders increased and the amount of work available rose accordingly.

Article 14 — Seniority, included a provision that when it was necessary to reduce the number of employees in a department because of lack of work, the junior employees will be transferred from the department first, provided the remaining employees can do the work available.

A grievance was submitted by one of the persons transferred, Ronald Fields, which stated in effect that he had more seniority than one of the employees retained in the department and claimed that he was capable of performing the work that that employee was doing.

Ronald Fields' grievance was processed to the first step and received a negative answer from the supervisor — namely, that he was not qualified to do the work being done by the employee grieved against. Subsequently Ronald Fields' grievance was processed into the second step and again received a negative answer from the superintendent — namely, that he was not qualified to do the work being done by the person he had grieved against. The company heard nothing more of the grievance which was considered to have been dropped.

If the Union was not satisfied with the company's answer at the second step, it could process the grievance to the third step but only within a period of ten calendar days after the second step answer. However, the Union did not do this.

The Union then submitted a policy grievance under the provisions of clause 6.10 which was worded as follows:

> "Non-application of Article 14 — re departmental seniority. That all people affected because of the company's action be compensated for all monies lost and that they be returned to their old jobs."

The company responded by letter to the Union as follows:

> "The subject matter referred to in the Union's alleged policy grievance is not properly the subject of a Union policy grievance but is the subject of an individual grievance. The subject matter has already been dealt with and as a result is considered to have been settled or

abandoned. As a result the Union's alleged policy grievance under the provisions of the collective agreement is not subject to arbitration.''

The applicable provisions of the collective agreement are as follows:

6.01 It is the mutual desire of the parties hereto that complaints from the employees shall be adjusted as quickly as possible, and it is generally understood that an employee shall not file a grievance until he has first given his supervisor an opportunity of adjusting his complaint.

6.02 The complaint shall be taken up as a grievance only within six months of the event giving rise to the complaint.

6.03 Step No. 1 — Between the Employee, his Steward, and his Supervisor.

An employee with a grievance may discuss the matter with his steward who may present the grievance in writing, signed by the employee, to the supervisor, setting forth the Article of the Agreement which he alleges has been violated. The grievance will be signed by the supervisor indicating the time and the date of receipt by him. The supervisor shall give an answer in writing to the steward within two working days.

6.04 Step No. 2 — Between the Employee, the Chief Steward, and the General Superintendent or his nominee.

If settlement of the grievance has not been reached under Step No. 1, then this step shall commence within four working days following receipt by the steward of the answer in Step No. 1. The General Superintendent or his nominee shall give an answer in writing to the Chief Steward within three working days of receiving the grievance.

6.05 Step No. 3 — Between the Employee, the Union, and the Supervisor, Industrial Relations or his nominee.

If a settlement of the grievance has not been reached under Step No. 2 then this step shall commence within ten calendar days following receipt by the Chief Steward of the answer in Step No. 2. The Supervisor, Industrial Relations or his nominee shall arrange a meeting within one week of receiving the grievance and shall give an answer in writing to the Union within not more than five working days following such meeting. The Union will be given a minimum of forty-eight hours' notice prior to such meeting. Union representatives at the third step of the grievance procedure may consist of the President of the Local, the Chief Steward, and the Steward representing the grievor, and one Union representative who is not an employee of the Company, and any employee possessing factual knowledge bearing on the matter in dispute. The Union may appoint an alternate to act in place of any of the foregoing employees, when such employee is unavailable at the time of a third step grievance hearing.

6.06 A grievance which is not processed within the time limits set out in this Article, or which is not posted to arbitration, within thirty calendar days after the answer has been given under Step 3 hereof, shall be deemed to have been settled or abandoned.

6.10 It is recognized that the Union shall have the right to take up a policy grievance with the Company relative to the violation, misinterpretation, or non-application of any provision of this Agreement. The grievance shall first be presented in writing to the Company and a meeting will be held within one week between the Union and the Company. The Company shall answer the grievance within one week of such meeting.

Article 7 — ARBITRATION

7.01 A grievance which is not disposed of under the provisions of Article 6, which arises from the interpretation, application, administration of alleged violation of any provision of this Agreement, including any question as to whether a matter is arbitrable, may be referred by letter to arbitration within 30 calendar days from the date of the receipt of the third step answer.

7.02 Within seven days of the notice of desire to arbitrate, each of the parties shall notify the other of the name of its appointee to an Arbitration Board. The two appointees so selected shall, within seven days of the appointment of the second of them, appoint a third person who shall be the chairman. If the two appointees fail to agree upon a chairman within this time, the appointment shall be made by the Minister of Labour for the Province of Ontario upon the request of either party.

7.03 The unanimous or majority decision of the Board of Arbitration shall with respect to matters coming within the jurisdiction of such Board pursuant to the provisions of the Agreement, be final and binding on both parties.

Company Argument

In arbitration, the company argued that the matter in question appears to be a policy grievance but it is in fact the individual grievance of Ronald Fields which had already been processed through the first and second steps of the grievance procedure and then dropped.

It was submitted by the company that clause 6.06 applies which says in part: "A grievance which is not processed within the time limits . . . . shall be deemed to have been settled or abandoned."

Clause 6.05 requires that the grievance be processed into the third step within ten calendar days after the answer has been given by the company in the second step. The union failed in this instance to process the grievance within the 10 calendar days and accordingly the grievance of Ronald Fields must be deemed to have been settled or abandoned under the provisions of clause 6.06 referred to above.

The company argued that surely it was not the intention of the parties that when an individual grievance had been settled under the grievance procedure that the Union was not bound by it and at all times had the right to raise the matter again as a policy grievance. In order for any such construction to be put onto clause 6.10 it would be necessary to read into it the words "notwithstanding that the matter had been settled or abandoned under the grievance procedure". To find such meaning in the clause would be manifestly absurd because it was clear that the parties were aware that the settlement and disposal of grievances was a highly desirable objective of their agreement and this was clearly provided in clauses 6.01 and 6.06.

The company argued the case against the policy grievance because the grievor was aware of the rights, did in fact grieve, and his grievance was settled. Whether it was settled by the Union or by the employee himself is immaterial to the decision. The settlement itself is the vital factor in precluding the Union from now bringing the matter forth as a policy grievance.

Union Argument

The Union argued that the grievance submitted by the Union to the Company was in fact a grievance — an alleged violation of the collective agreement. The Union has the right to file a grievance including one that alleges violation of the agreement. The company refuses to process it under the grievance procedure. Therefore, the Union has no alternative but to submit it to arbitration and the arbitrator was bound to make a decision on it.

Under the grievance procedure it is self-evident that an employee has the right to file a grievance. Under clause 6.10 it is clear the Union has the right to file a grievance. There is no restrictions on this right. If it was intended to have restrictions on this right the company would have written such restrictions into the agreement. This the company did not do. The company is asking the arbitration board to imagine that there are restrictions in clause 6.10 which do not in fact exist. The company in effect is asking the arbitration board to amend the agreement but the arbitration board does not have this power. The wording of the clause is clear. The arbitration board must interpret the words of the agreement as written. Clause 6.10 says the Union has the right to file a grievance. It did so. It has been properly processed to arbitration and the arbitration board must deal with it.

The Union grievance deals with the application of seniority in situations such as transfers of employees from one department to another of the firm due to work shortage. Although it includes the transfer of Ronald Fields from the department, it is nevertheless dealing with the question of the overall application of seniority in this kind of situation, and is properly before the arbitration board.

AMALGAMATED BEER DISTRIBUTORS LTD.

Policy Grievance — Management Rights — Drinking and Rules

Background

The Union filed a policy grievance which read as follows:

> The Company has improperly, unreasonably and inconsistent with the current Collective Agreement imposed a company policy in respect to the consumption of alcohol during an employee's work day (lunch break).

> The union requests that the Company immediately withdraw this policy and abide by the Collective Agreement.

Attached to the grievance was a notice to all hourly employees under signature of Mr. R. J. Jalabowski, the president and general manager of the employer.

It declared that as of April 1, 1990, the following policy became effective:

> The consumption of alcoholic beverages by any employee during *any* part of their shift may result in *immediate dismissal.*

By way of explanation the following comment was also made:

> Specifically, no alcoholic beverage may be consumed at any time during your shift including rest periods (coffee breaks), lunch or dinner breaks.

In this place, there were three components to the work-force. Some were involved in bottle sorting, some in the warehouse, and some in the transportation of beer and/or empty bottles to and from breweries, customers and the warehouse. There were also helpers who worked with the drivers and on occasion worked as drivers. The employees working in the bottle-sorting area or in the warehouse were not involved in driving motor vehicles on the public highways but some of them might be involved in the operation of fork-lift trucks, and other similar vehicles within the warehouse.

The lunch or dinner breaks were unpaid.

The total workforce was approximately 200 and there were 50 or 60 drivers in the transport division. The drivers operated tractor/trailers and there were also approximately 30 helpers who could be required to drive.

Within the warehouse, there were approximately 35 employees who used fork-lift vehicles or some similar type of power transportation.

There were approximately 70 employees in various categories who worked in the bottle-sorting area and those employees could be called upon to work on power equipment. As there was moving equipment in that area, all employees had to be extremely alert.

There was an absolute bar to the consumption of any alcoholic beverages within the lands and premises of the employer and this rule had not been contested by the union.

The drivers of the employer generally operated only within the bounds of the perimeter highway and were required, on many occasions, to drive through residential areas.

A group of documents were entered as exhibits. Exhibit 3 was an employee bulletin dated May 28, 1981, and the relevant portion of same read as follows:

> 1. The consumption of *any* alcoholic beverage or non-prescribed mind expanding drugs while on duty is strictly prohibited. "On Duty" is defined to include the entire shift of an employee, from the time he reports for work until he completes his shift as signified by his time card.

Exhibit 4 was another employee bulletin dated November 2, 1982, and the relevant portions read as follows:

> The consumption of *any* alcoholic beverage or non-prescribed mind-expanding drugs while on duty is strictly prohibited. "On Duty" is defined to include the entire shift of an employee, from the time he reports for work until he completes his shift as signified by his time card.

Exhibit 5 was a notice to all employees dated June 8, 1984, and the relevant portions reads as follows:

> The consumption of *any* alcoholic beverage or non-prescribed mind-expanding drugs while on duty is strictly prohibited. "On Duty" is defined to include the time for which an employee receives compensation.

Exhibit 6 was a notice to all drivers and helpers dated October 27, 1986, and reads as follows:

> When you are finished work bring your vehicle back to the warehouse and punch out before you sit in a bar and start drinking.

Exhibit 7 is a notice to all employees dated August 31, 1989, and the relevant portion reads as follows:

> The consumption of alcoholic beverages while on shift is expressly forbidden and any violation of this policy is a dismissable offence.

Union Argument

The Union counsel did not dispute that the employer had the right to promulgate a prohibition against drinking during working hours and/or within the confines of the employer's premises. He stated that the employer did not have any right to direct what the employees did or did not do during their unpaid lunch or dinner breaks if taken away from the premises.

He pointed out that the parties had already mutually agreed that impairment due to the influence of alcohol or non-prescribed drugs was undesirable. Article 8.04 of the collective agreement addressed the issue as follows:

> 8.04 Due to the mutual concern of the parties to this agreement, with respect to the safety and welfare of the employees, it is understood and agreed that employees shall not report for work or work while in an unfit condition due to the influence of alcohol or non-prescribed drugs.
>
> It is understood that any violation of the above understandings will result in disciplinary action.

> 5.03 Seniority shall be considered broken by virtue of the following reasons: . . .
>
> . . . . . .
>
> (b) If an employee is discharged for cause not reversed by the grievance procedure.

The Union counsel defined the issue as follows: "Can the Company unilaterally impose a rule that affects an employee, when that employee leaves the premises during an unpaid lunch break."

He pointed out that there was no objection to the drinking prohibitions during the course of paid labour, nor to the necessity of employees coming to and remaining at work in a fit condition.

He submitted that the reasons given in evidence by the employer for the rule were not reasonable. He summarized the employer's reasons as follows:

1. The employer was concerned that if an employee left the plant he/she would not have just one beer, but might have three or four and that the employer had no control over this.

2. If there was drinking during the lunch hour, then neither the rule nor art. 8.04 could be easily enforced.

3. That the employer had an image problem with respect to employees drinking excessively.

He submitted that the employer could not dictate off-premises behaviour unless it could demonstrate a tangible effect on the employer. He stated that the only issue that the employer could and should be concerned with was conduct while an employee was on duty. If there was an abuse, then the employer had the right to act under the collective agreement.

He argued by analogy that an employer, if this rule stood up, could violate an employee's civil liberties. He pointed out that one or two drinks did not necessarily mean impairment, and that there was no prohibition against driving unless one was impaired. He felt that the employer was going beyond the law which affects all citizens.

With respect to drivers/helpers, he stated that the obligation was on the drivers not to drive while impaired. In his opinion, the employer must demonstrate that there was a problem with drinking drivers, and that the employer had not satisfied that onus. He submitted that similar prohibitions did not apply to bus drivers or people involved in other like work.

In summary he stated that the parties had, in the collective agreement, agreed to a standard as set forth in art. 8.04, *i.e.*, they were not to "report for work or work while in an unfit condition". He stated that in the union's view the employer could not go beyond this provision.

Company Argument

The Company counsel took the view that the employer had a high profile in the community and was subject to extraordinary scrutiny because it was involved in the brewery business. He reviewed the dangers which could ensue if a large trailer load was involved in an accident in any neighbourhood, but especially in a residential area where children might be injured. He stated that the employer would be in an extremely difficult position if, in any hearing, someone was able to come forward and say that the employee was observed drinking prior to the accident and that there was no company rule against drinking. He asked the board to note that the employer, if it relied on the new rule to impose discipline, would still have to prove just cause.

Counsel said that if someone absolutely had to rush out at lunch time to have a drink, then that individual had a problem with alcohol. He asked the board to note three reasons why the rule was reasonable. These were as follows:

1. The enforcement as to the quantity of drinking was practically impos-

sible and it was more realistic to say that there would be no drinking during the working hours.

2. He said that the issue of safety had not been contested by the union and that we also had to consider the effects of a breach of safety on any "non-drinking employees".

3. He submitted that the issue of the image of a purveyor or a supplier of alcoholic beverages was self-evident.

He asked the board to consider that the rule against consuming alcohol had been in force, in one form or another, for 10 years and had never been grieved. He noted that as early as 1981 (ex. 3), the consumption of alcohol while on duty was strictly prohibited. He noted that "on duty" at that time was defined to include the entire shift of an employee, from the time he reports for work until he completed his shift as signified by his time-card. In his view the policy statement of April 1, 1990, simply clarified the rule. He also said that art. 8.04 had been there since the inception of the collective agreement.

He stated that we had to consider the perception of society towards drinking. He disputed that there had to be an incident first before the employer might be involved or that its image could be detrimentally affected.

In conclusion, counsel summarized the employer's position as being: "That the rule was completely reasonable in that it was reasonable, was necessary, was in the best interest of the Employer and the employees, and did not deprive any employee of any substantive right and was clear and unequivocal."

CIVIC GENERAL HOSPITAL

Admissibility of Performance Evaluation in a Discipline Case

Grievance

The grievance, on behalf of Donna Kivachik, alleged that "The letter of termination effective April 16, 1988 is a contravention of the terms and conditions of the Collective Agreement". The relief sought is that the grievor be reinstated without loss of benefits, wages and seniority and the letter of termination be withdrawn.

Articles of Collective Agreement

The pertinent articles of the collective agreement are herein set forth:

ARTICLE 11: SHOP STEWARDS

11.03 The employee or the Local Union shall have the right at time to have the assistance of a C.U.P.E. representative.

ARTICLE 12: GRIEVANCE PROCEDURE

12.02 Settling of Disputes and Grievances

Step 1

a) An employee who believes that she has a problem arising out of the interpretation, application or alleged violation of this Collective Agreement shall first discuss the matter with her immediate supervisor within seven (7) days of the date she first became aware of, or reasonably should have become aware of, the occurrence. "Immediate Supervisor" means that person from whom an employee normally receives her work assignments. The employee shall have the right to be accompanied by a Shop Steward or Local Union Officer while discussing the matter with her immediate supervisor. A sincere attempt shall be made by both parties through discussion to resolve the problem at that level. The immediate supervisor shall advise the employee of her decision within seven (7) days of the date the matter was first discussed.

ARTICLE 35: DISCIPLINE & TERMINATION

35.01 Written disciplinary notice shall be given to employees for poor conduct or unsatisfactory job performance.

a) This does not prevent immediate dismissal for just cause, subject to the grievance procedure.

b) Copies of all disciplinary notices shall be forwarded to the Union. Employees shall be given the opportunity to sign disciplinary notices as having been read.

Admissibility of Evaluations

At the outset of the hearing, having been made aware that the employer proposed to introduce performance evaluations of the grievor in evidence, counsel for the union objected to the introduction of such evidence. It being apparent, from the submissions of counsel, that the issue is complex and of considerable significance, the board decided that it would reserve its ruling on the objection and permit the introduction of the evidence on the understanding that the board's eventual ruling might render the evidence inadmissible.

The Union Argument

The evaluations are not relevant and not admissible because they do not constitute discipline and are therefore not grievable. The evaluations of the grievor's performance could be characterized as negative in comment, but there is nothing in the evaluations suggesting that they are disciplinary or warning that some further action will result if there is not improvement. Furthermore, the evaluations were obviously not considered by the employer to be disciplinary because the employer did not, as required under Article 35.01, and as it did in other disciplinary situations, forward copies to the union.

There was no suggestion in any documentation, relating to the suspension and termination, that the employer had taken into account the performance evaluations. They have done so, at the hearing, simply to "build their case". This board ought not to consider the evaluations other than, perhaps, the most recent evaluation if it can be reasonably construed as giving notice of a particular standard expected of the grievor which she failed to achieve and is therefore being disciplined for. The most recent evaluation was August 15, 1987, which preceded the termination by eight months. The previous evaluations were on August 19 and May 31, 1986 and on November 8, 1985, all of which are stale. Furthermore, the evaluations do not, with very few exceptions, refer to specific situations or examples and would be almost impossible, in a grievance setting, to respond to.

Employer Argument

There is, in the collective agreement, no restricted definition of "record" or what constitutes discipline. A performance evaluation is disciplinary in nature, is communicated to the employee and is therefore relevant and admissible. When an employee is spoken to about her performance, and receives and acknowledges a performance evaluation, that evaluation becomes part of her record. There is nothing in the collective agreement to prevent employees grieving their performance evaluations.

The evaluation serves to present the full picture with respect to an employee's job performance including the standards expected of her and the improvement, or lack thereof, in attaining those standards. The evaluations led, in part, to the discipline of the grievor, and are related to the discipline.

This board should admit the evaluations as being part of the performance record of the grievor and attach such weight as the board deems appropriate.

MUNICIPAL GENERAL HOSPITAL

Call-in — Work assignment — Nurses Required to Perform Only Tasks They Would Normally Perform

The nurses' association brings a policy grievance and group grievance alleging a violation of the collective agreement, arising from the hospital's rule requiring nurses to work four full hours on each occasion they are called in to work outside their regularly scheduled working tours. By way of relief, the association seeks a declaration of such violation and an order requiring the hospital to cease this practice.

The parties filed an agreed statement of fact pertinent to both the grievances which reads as follows:

Agreed Statement of Fact

1. Prior to the implementation of this collective agreement, Operating Room Registered Nurses were placed on standby while outside their regularly scheduled hours, and as required, were called in. They were paid at the appropriate rate (1 1/2 their regular hourly rate) for all such hours worked.

2. Article 14.07 of the collective agreement provides for a standby arrangement and Article 14.06 provides for a call-in arrangement, which includes a minimum guarantee of four hours pay at time and one half the regular hourly rate on a call-in.

3. On or about September 27, 1988, the Employer implemented a new rule regarding Operating Room Nurses and call-in. The rule was articulated as follows:

   "When called back (when on standby) and finished work in O.R., and discharged the patient, notify supervisor of time you arrived. If 4 hours have not elapsed, she will assign other nursing tasks."

4. No discussions were held between the Hospital and the Association prior to the implementation of the rule described in paragraph 3 above.

5. On October 5, 1988, a policy grievance was filed challenging the practice described in paragraph 3 above.

6. On or about October 17, 1988, the grievors, Young and Webber, were called in to the Operating Room outside their regularly scheduled working hours. The grievors attended to duties in the Operating Room from approximately 2120 hours to 2350 hours. From approximately 2350 hours to 0120 hours, the grievors were

assigned work in the Emergency Department. Their assigned duties at that time included, among other duties, scrubbing stretchers in the Emergency Department.

7. Both grievors are experienced and qualified to work in the Emergency Department. However, neither of the grievors regularly works in the Emergency Department.

8. The application of the rule as outlined in paragraph 3 above can and does result in Operating Room Nurses being assigned to nursing duties outside the Operating Room. None of the O.R. Nurses regularly work outside the Operating Room, but may be assigned to other areas when not required in the O.R.

9. Operating Room nursing duties include recovery room nursing duties.

10. Records kept by the Hospital over the period September 10, 1988 to November 3, 1988 indicate the following:

    (a) A nurse will be on standby for a period usually ranging from one to three consecutive days. A nurse may on occasion be on standby for a longer period of consecutive days.

    (b) The incidence of call-in, 2 nurses per call-in, was approximately as follows:

April 1988	—	6 call-ins
May 1988	—	10 call-ins
June 1988	—	7 call-ins
July 1988	—	13 call-ins
August 1988	—	9 call-ins
September 1988	—	10 call-ins

    Total = 55 or approximately 9.16/month

    (c) During the period April to September 1988 there have been approximately 5 instances of more than one call-in on a single day. (Of the total figure of 55 call-ins, on five of the 50 days of call-in, there were two call-ins and in some, both individuals on call-in worked for the entire standby assignment.)

11. The arrangement with respect to call-ins is that a nurse receives time and a half her regular salary or the equivalent in time off.

12. An O.R. nurse who is called-in and works a minimum of 2 hours is given a paid half-hour meal break.

13. The regular duties of an O.R. nurse include cleaning stretchers and the regular duties of an emergency department nurse also include cleaning stretchers (normally on nights for emergency).

A further point was added that overtime is first assigned to operating-room nurses who are on stand-by duty.

Union Argument

The association contended that the hospital's rule is contrary to the provisions of art. 14.06 of the collective agreement and furthermore that the rule is unreasonable and therefore in contravention of art. B of the local appendices. On the first branch of its argument, the association contended that the employer's rule constitutes a unilateral amendment to art. 14.06 to the effect that a nurse on call-in shall be required to perform nursing duties other than those he or she regularly or normally performs and other than those which precipitated the call-in.

Furthermore, the association pointed out that art. 14.06 provides a minimum guarantee of four hours' pay at premium rates irrespective of the number of hours worked on the call-in, whereas the hospital's rule provides a minimum guarantee of four hours' work at premium rates of pay. In this regard, the association claimed that the rule undermined the purpose and effect of the minimum guarantee.

On the other branch of its argument, the association claimed that the employer's rule was unreasonable in that it fails to achieve adequate proportionality between the objective sought of efficient deployment of nursing personnel for dollars spent and the means used to accomplish this objective. The association pointed out that this hospital has a small pool of O.R. nurses to cover considerable stand-by, call-in and overtime requirements in addition to the regularly scheduled shifts. As such, since the number of call-ins during a period of stand-by cannot be ascertained, the association characterized as unreasonable the employer's requirement that the nurses work during the entire four-hour period rather than be allowed to rest until required for O.R. nursing duties on the next call, because it needlessly exhausts the O.R. nursing personnel. Such a rule would thereby threaten safety because the nurses may not be alert or careful in attending to their demanding O.R. duties required subsequently. The association pointed out that from the patient's viewpoint, the nurse who is rested and alert for his or her duties is to be preferred.

While the association concedes that the grievance does not allege violation of art. 18.06 requiring preliminary discussion of a new rule with the association, but the failure of the hospital to so discuss its rule indicates that it failed to consider the interests of the employees as well as its own interest in promulgating the rules.

Employer Argument

The hospital argued that the management rights provisions authorized it to assign nurses to any duties within their classification which they are qualified to perform in any area of the hospital, in the interest of efficient operation and high standards of service. The hospital claimed that the evidence demonstrated that the duties to which the nurses were assigned on October 17, 1988, fell within their classification as graduate or registered nurses and were tasks which the nurses were qualified to perform. It was common ground that the nurses in question although regularly assigned to O.R. duty, could be assigned to other areas when not required in the O.R. The hospital characterized the association's position as an attempt to rewrite the collective agreement so as to prevent transfers to other departments on a call-in. The hospital contended that art. 14.06 did not guarantee that the nurses would not be working for the full four-hour period and in the interest of efficient allocation of nursing personnel and high standards of service to patients it was best to deploy the nurses at nursing tasks which need to be performed, once called in, for the entire four-hour period. Furthermore, the hospital could not understand how the rule could be unreasonable since it was not requiring anything different of the nurses on call-in than during their regular tour when they are no longer required in the O.R. or recovery rooms. The hospital pointed out that it was not requiring the nurses to stay beyond the minimum guaranteed pay period except when their assignments in O.R. extend beyond this period. In summary, the hospital contended that the association had failed to establish any specific limitation on its prerogative to assign nurses to any duties within their classification which they are qualified to perform and had failed to establish that the rule was either unreasonable or inconsistent with the provisions of the collective agreement.

The provisions of the collective agreement pertaining to this dispute are the following:

Article 14 — Premium Payment

14.06   Where a nurse has completed her regularly scheduled tour and left the Hospital and is called in to work outside her regularly scheduled working hours, she shall receive time and one-half her regular straight time hourly rate for all hours worked with a minimum guarantee of four (4) hours' pay at time and one-half her regular straight time hourly rate except to the extent that such four (4) hour period overlaps or extends into her regularly scheduled shift. In such a case, she will receive time and one-half her regular straight time hourly rate for actual hours worked up to the commencement of her regular shift.

Article 18 — Miscellaneous

18.06 Prior to effecting any change in rules or policies which affect nurses covered by this Agreement, the Hospital will discuss the changes with the Association and provide copies to the Association.

. . . . .

LOCAL APPENDIX

Article B — Management Functions

B-1 The Association recognizes that the management of the Hospital and the direction of the working forces are fixed in the Hospital and shall remain solely with the Hospital except as specifically limited by the provisions of this Agreement and, without restricting the generality of the foregoing, the Association acknowledges that it is the exclusive function of the Hospital to:

. . . . .

c) determine, in the interest of efficient operation and high standards of service, job rating and classification, the hours of work, work assignments, methods of doing the work and the working establishment for the service;

. . . . .

e) make and enforce and alter from time to time reasonable rules and regulations to be observed by the nurses provided that such rules and regulations shall not be inconsistent with the provisions of the Agreement.

B-2 These rights shall not be exercised in a manner inconsistent with the provisions of this Agreement.

WILLIAM DANBROOK

Discharge — Previous Disciplinary Record — Significance of Last Incident

Background

The facts leading up to the grievance are as follows: The grievor William Danbrook was first hired by the company on June 7th, 1961. He was employed continuously by the company from that time until the date of his discharge on May 30th, 1986. During the period of his employment, he was elected as Union Steward for the department on February 16th, 1970, and subsequently was elected as Union Chief Steward for the zone of the plant in which he worked in 1974.

On May 29th, 1986, he was absent from work. The next day, May 30th, 1986, he reported for work at 7:45 a.m., without having in the meantime notified the company of his absence the day before. He was subsequently interviewed by two company officials to whom he explained that he was absent the day before because of illness which had prevented him from notifying the company.

Subsequently that day he received notice of discharge which read as follows: "Following review of your recent unreported absence, and your record of continuous violations of company rules, you are hereby advised that you are dismissed from employment effective immediately. Your separation papers and wages will be mailed to you under separate cover."

The grievor then filed this grievance:

> "I contend that I have been discharged without just cause. I am requesting that I be reinstated immediately with full compensation for lost earnings."

Applicable provisions of the collective agreement are as follows:

2. The union acknowledges that it is the exclusive function of the company to

   a) maintain order and efficiency;

   b) suspend or otherwise discipline employees provided that a claim that an employee has been discharged or otherwise disciplined without just cause may be made the subject of a grievance and dealt with in accordance with the grievance procedures;

   c) make and enforce reasonable rules and regulations relating to discipline, safety and general conduct of the employees.

3. The company agrees that these functions will be exercised in a manner consistent with the terms of this agreement.

Rule No. 9 states that an employee should notify by telephone to the Guard's office of inability to report for work as scheduled providing satisfactory reasons before the beginning of the scheduled shift.

Note that the notice of dismissal contains two reasons for the company's action in discharging the grievor:

1. The unreported absence of the grievor on May 29th, 1986, and

2. The grievor's record of continuous violation of company rules.

On June 6th, pursuant to the provisions of the Collective Agreement, a meeting was held between the company and the Union, at which the grievor was present when his grievance was discussed and the union was given a partial listing of the grievor's previous violations of the company rules.

On June 8th, 1986, the Company wrote to the Union Business Agent as follows: ''A claim by Mr. Danbrook that he was discharged without just cause on May 30th, 1986, was heard in accordance with Clause 16.01 of the Collective Agreement, on June 6th, 1986. At the meeting convened to discuss the matter, the union was advised that the grievor had been dismissed from employment because of his unreported absence and because of his record of continuous violations of company rules. Also at this meeting, the Union was given a partial listing of such violations. A more complete listing of Mr. Danbrook's disciplinary record is summarized as follows:

1. November 28th, 1982 — Absent from work station — Warning.

2. March 19th, 1983 — Absent from work station — Further Warning.

3. April 15th, 1983 — Absenteeism — Further Warning.

4. May 29th, 1983 — Absenteeism without proper notification — Warned that 'further infractions of the plant rules will result in further disciplinary action which may include discharge.'

5. September 11th, 1983 — Excessive lateness and absenteeism and failure to notify company when absent — Suspension of three days.

6. July 15th, 1984 — Disregard of Safety Rules — Further Warning.

7. October 3rd, 1984 — Restricting Output — Further Warning.

8. October 6th, 1984 — Absent without prompt notification — Warned that 'any further breach of company rules and regulations could result in a more severe penalty, including discharge.'

9. October 27th, 1984 — Absent from work station — Further Warning.

10. April 29th, 1985 — Washing up before quitting time — Further Warning.

11. April 6th, 1986 — Absent from work station — Further Warning.

12. April 19th, 1986 — Restricting Output — Further Warning.

13. May 3rd, 1986 — Careless workmanship and absent from work station. Suspension of five days, and warned that 'any further breach of company rules and regulations will result in a more severe form of disciplinary action.'

It is noted that the investigation of the grievance has shown that Mr. Danbrook has not denied that he failed to notify the company concerning his absence from work on May 29th, 1986, and it is therefore concluded that Plant Rule No. 9 was in fact violated.

It is further concluded that the penalties imposed as a result of his prior record of continuous violations of company rules and regulations have not had any constructive influence on him. In the light of the facts concerning the company's action, including those facts set out above, the grievance contending that the discharge was without just cause, is denied.''

The company's answer to the grievance was not acceptable to the Union and as a result the grievance was processed to arbitration.

Union Argument

At the arbitration hearing, the Union contended that the company had gone to great lengths to compile and build up a record of the unsatisfactory conduct of the grievor in order to justify its dismissal of the grievor for his failure to notify the company of his absence on May 29th, 1986. The Union suggested that unless the final incident giving rise to the grievor's discharge, being his unexplained absence on May 29th, 1986, could be found to be in itself just cause for the grievor's dismissal, the company then had no right to justify his dismissal on the basis of his previous record of offences.

The grievor testified that on Monday, May 28th, 1986, he worked his regular shift though he was not feeling very well. This being the first day that he was wearing his new prescription bifocals, he attributed his condition to this circumstance and felt that he would shortly adjust to the new optical conditions. When he retired that night, he still did not feel very well, but managed to go to sleep. He awoke between 5 a.m. and 6 a.m., with severe cramps coupled with diarrhea which got progressively worse involving numerous trips to the bathroom. He finally fell asleep between 11 a.m. and 12 noon, and did not wake until between 3:30 p.m. and 4 p.m. He then consumed some hot milk and cheese in an effort to alleviate his dysentery, took a bath, and between the hours of 6:30 and 6:45, left his apartment to see a doctor.

He first called at the offices of a Dr. Cheung, who was his regular medical advisor, found no one in the doctor's office, and inquiring nearby, was advised by a woman that the doctor no longer held office hours at night because he had had a heart attack. He thereupon boarded a bus, and went to the office of a second doctor, Dr. Allen, which was approximately five blocks away from the office of Dr. Cheung, and was the nearest doctor's office to that point. Dr. Allen examined the grievor, and gave him certain tablets to take to correct his condition.

The next morning, while still feeling unwell, he reported for work at the company's premises at approximately 7:45 a.m., and changed into his working clothes. He then found that his blue attendance card was not in the rack provided for that purpose, asked a clerk why this was so, and at this moment, at approximately 8:05, his foreman arrived in the office, and told him not to bother about his card, but to change into his street clothes, and report to the Employment Office for an interview. The grievor did so and then had the interview previously described. In the interview the grievor was asked his reason for not reporting to work on May 29th, 1986 and for not phoning in his reasons for his absence, and the grievor explained that due to his illness, described above, he had not been able to get to a phone, and that no one came to his door that day to whom he could convey a message.

The grievor testified that the lived alone, in an apartment, and that he had no telephone in his apartment, and the nearest telephone was a public telephone approximately a block from his apartment at the intersection of Newington and Rainham Streets. At the interview, above referred to, the grievor was asked: "If you were so sick that you could not get to the telephone, how is it that you are at work today?", to which the grievor replied, "I'm still shaky, but I felt that I should come to work. I am willing to submit myself to an examination by the company doctor, to verify my statements."

Company Argument

The company introduced in evidence as Exhibit 5, a map showing the relative locations of the grievor's residence, the company's premises, the two doctors' offices, and the guards' office of the company. It, and the evidence adduced, indicated that the route taken by the grievor on proceeding at approximately 6:30 p.m., on May 29th, 1986, to Dr. Allen's office, passed right by the public telephone, referred to by the grievor in his evidence and right by the company premises and only a block from the guards' office, where as directed by Company Rule No. 9, he should have notified the company of his absence.

The grievor, in this connection, explained his failure either to telephone the company when passing the public telephone booth or to stop by the company offices by stating that on a previous occasion when he had been absent from work, he did telephone an explanation at about noon on the day of his absence but was subsequently disciplined by receiving a written warning for neglecting to follow Plant Rule No. 9 which warning advised him that a further infraction of the plant rules would result in further disciplinary action which might include discharge. This warning, and others, were filed together as Exhibit No. 2, and this warning referred to an offence listed as No. 9 in the letter to the Union, dated June 8th, 1986, reproduced above.

Evidence was also adduced that the reason for Rule No. 9 was so that the Company could properly schedule the next day's operations. Consequently, the grievor explained, that he did not telephone after 6 p.m. to notify the company of his absence that day because he had been disciplined for not phoning to the company on a previous occasion before noon and also because he did not feel that such notification would be of any use, inasmuch as he hoped to be, and subsequently was, at work the following day.

Two points therefore emerge from this evidence, for the Board's consideration, namely the genuineness and severity of the grievor's illness on May 29th, 1986, and the reasonableness of his explanation for his failure to telephone or otherwise notify the company of his absence.

Concerning the first point the Board was urged in the light of the grievor's past record to consider with suspicion the grievor's allegation that he was ill at all, or the alternative, that he was so ill that he could not, in some way, notify the company of his absence, or induce someone else to do so for him. The Board has before it certain corroborative evidence, namely a copy of a doctor's certificate dated June 7th, 1986, purporting to be signed by R. C. Allen, M.D., at his address, 327 George Street, as follows: "To Whom It May Concern: This is to certify that I attended Mr. William Danbrook, 27 Riley Row, on May 29th, 1986. He had acute entero colitis."

FRED CUMMINGS

Physical Contact — Threatening of Management Personnel

Background

Company and Union representatives agreed on the following:

On March 4, 1987, shortly after 1 p.m., just outside the Crossway's Tavern, four company management employees and four company employees who were members of the bargaining unit represented by the union, were involved in a physical scuffle. This had been preceded by a verbal exchange between some of the parties some 10 to 15 minutes previously while they were all in the tavern. As a result, the four Union represented employees were not allowed to return to work on their next shift. Subsequently the four were advised of their discharge.

They then grieved that they had been discharged without just cause.

The company's answer did not change the discharge and subsequently the Union processed the grievance to arbitration.

At the arbitration hearing, the grievors all testified that there had been trouble at the plant that morning with regard to the matter of raises for certain employees. There had been heated discussion between management and the Union personnel regarding certain management decisions, particularly the policy adopted in giving these raises. Cummings was one of the stewards involved in these discussions. Shortly after these discussions had ended, Cummings requested permission of his supervisor, Walker to leave work that day. He stated that he was upset because of the lack of sleep due to a sick child and the event of the morning had aggravated his condition. Out of concern for the safety of himself and others, permission was granted. He went to the Union Hall where he met the four other grievors. They stated that they played shuffleboard until 11:15 or 11:30 a.m. when they left to have lunch at the tavern as it was one of the places where they could play bank board shuffleboard. They denied they went to the Crossway's Tavern because they were aware that some of the management personnel would also be there for lunch.

At the hotel, the grievors got a table near the shuffleboard, ordered beer and went to the counter to buy a sandwich. Later, according to his statement, Cummings went back to the counter to buy another sandwich. Between his two trips to the counter, four management employees arrived for lunch and seated themselves some distance away from the grievors. Cummings left the lunch counter and went over to the booth where the management people were seated. They were Richards, department manager, scheduling; Miner, department manager, stock cutting; Johnston, time study engineer; and Monroe, safety and security manager. Cummings addressed Richardson as follows: "Hi creep! Where's my f—— telegram?" Cummings stated that he thought Richardson would understand this statement as a private joke. However, Richardson apparently didn't agree. Further discussion between Cummings and the group became an argument between Richardson, Miner and Cummings. Shortly after the argument began, the three other grievors moved from the table where they had been sitting, to a table close to the argument. Nothing was said between them and the management group. However, shortly after they moved, Johnston, the time study engineer, went over to their table and had a conversation with them unrelated to the argument. Eventually the bar manager came and told Cummings to sit down and lower his voice. he apparently sat down but continued to argue. The argument centred around the method of scheduling the work in the plant which Cummings claimed cut his incentive earnings. The argument continued until the bar manager asked Cummings to leave. Cummings requested the bar manager to ask the people in the booth to leave as well, but he refused. Cummings then left.

The management group discussed calling the police for protection because of Cummings' attitude, but decided against it. Both groups got up to leave. The management group moved toward the door. Johnston left the Union group to join them. Johnston said that at that time he did not anticipate any further trouble.

As they walked out, Johnston first, followed by Richardson, Miner, and Monroe, they were followed by three of the grievors. One of the grievors, Dalton, testified that a scuffle ensued when Scott, one of the grievors, apparently tripped over the doorstep and fell forward brushing against Richardson, the department manager scheduling. Immediately afterwards, Miner, the department manager, stock cutting, seized Scott and pushed him up against the outer wall of the building. According to his statement, Cummings, who had been waiting outside for transportation, saw what was happening. Anticipating an assault on Scott's person, he ran over and threw himself between Miner and Scott and in the process attempted to forestall Richardson from attacking Scott.

On the other hand, Richardson and Miner stated that it was Scott who seized Richardson and held him up against the wall as Cummings who had been standing beside a parked car just outside, came towards the group as they were leaving the tavern. Each of them felt Scott was trying to set up Richardson for an assault by Cummings.

The conflicts of evidence became even more pronounced as each of the witnesses gave his version of the events which apparently resulted in each being struck once or twice, not clearly by whom. There was considerable punching and shoving, resulting among other things in Richardson being struck several times, his glasses being knocked off, and a cut opened on his nose.

The bar manager stated that he came out and interpreted the situation as wrestling around in a half-hearted manner between Cummings and Richardson. He said that he told them to stop and take the company's business back to the company. Cummings continued to swear at Richardson and threaten some future action. Monroe stayed behind after Richardson, Miner, and Johnston left and discussed the matter with the grievors without further incident.

Later the grievors were advised not to report for work on their next shift and subsequently were discharged.

Company Argument

The company argued that the actions of the grievors were such that they were directly related to the company, involving altercations between the grievors and the management personnel in regard to company business. Therefore discharge was warranted for protection of other employees, the company and the proper carrying on of its business.

Cummings initiated the action that led to the argument and to the scuffle. If he had had cause for a grievance, he should have used the grievance procedure.

His actions and the actions of the others were a verbal and physical assault on management representatives and, further, in regard to matters relating to management.

There is no need to, and management cannot tolerate such action, and it is essential that the arbitration board uphold the discharge.

Union Argument

The union argued that under all of the circumstances of the case the incident was not sufficiently serious to warrant discharge. The misconduct must be viewed in relation to the nature of the employment, the persons, and the situation involved, all within the context of the material facts. All of the grievors had good work records. Cummings is considered by management to be a skilled competent employee with only a minor reprimand on his record. The others have no disciplinary records. The conduct of the grievors did not harm the reputation of the company. The action of the grievors was not such as to seriously impair employer-employee relationships. None of the grievors was under the direct supervision of the management personnel involved.

The incident could not be considered a serious assault upon the various persons concerned and was quickly and easily broken up. This was an isolated instance with no recurrence of any kind. While the argument was initiated by Cummings, the management people let themselves be drawn into the argument and participated enthusiastically. The incident was in no way premeditated.

EASTERN UTILITY COMPANY

Discharge — Off Duty Conduct — Vandalism and Damage to Public Property

Background

The employer and the union agreed on the following statement of fact.

The grievors were classified as linemen and were sent on a special assignment in April in the Pembroke Sound area approximately 60 miles from their home location. The assignment involved working on a project to upgrade customer service in rural areas. When in Pembroke Sound, the grievors' travelling and living expenses were paid by the employer. During the night of April 26 - 27, the grievors caused damage to a Police cruiser by kicking one of its doors, kicking in the trunk, and twisting and bending signal lights. The cruiser was parked behind other cars on a service station lot on one of the principal streets in Pembroke Sound.

At the time in question, the grievors were off duty and were not wearing any uniform clothing supplied by the employer that would identify them with the employer, nor were they operating any vehicles owned by the company. As a result of the incident, the grievors were arrested, taken into custody by the Pembroke Sound police, and charged with criminal offences. The grievors were scheduled to report for work on the morning of April 27 but did not do so as they were in police custody from the time they were arrested until 1:30 p.m. on April 27.

Later in the afternoon of April 27, the grievors were suspended by a company official pending further investigation of the incident. Following a meeting on May 1 between management and the grievors at which the grievors admitted responsibility for the incident, the grievors were suspended for five working days.

The incident received news coverage by radio, television, and newspaper over about a 100-mile radius. However, the name of the employer was not mentioned. Several charges were laid against the grievors which were subsequently dropped after the grievors paid for the damage to the police cruiser. After the suspensions, the employees were reassigned to the project on which they had been working at the time of the incident.

Employer Argument

The employer acknowledged the general rule of arbitration that an employee's life is his own and that what he or she does away from work is his or her own business and is no affair of the employer.

However, the employer also pointed out that a number of exceptions have developed to this general rule.

There are two cases that set out the questions that determine this type of issue. The first is Huron Steel Products Co. Ltd. and U.A.W. Local 195 (1964) 15 L.A.C. 288 (Reville). The following statement from that case is often cited:

> It has been held in many arbitration cases that under normal circumstances an employer is only properly concerned with an employee's due and faithful observance of his duties on his job. However, no hard and fast rule can be laid down, and in each case the determination of three questions of fact will determine the issue. These are:
>
> 1. Was the employee's conduct sufficiently injurious to the interests of the employer?
>
> 2. Did the employee act in a manner incompatible with the due and faithful discharge of his duty?
>
> 3. Did the employee do anything prejudicial or likely to be prejudicial to the reputation of the employer?
>
> If one or more of the above questions must be answered in the affirmative on all the evidence, then the company is properly concerned with the employee's conduct regardless of whether it occurred on or off the company property or in or out of working hours, and depending on the gravity of that conduct, the company will be justified in taking appropriate disciplinary action.

The second case of relevance is Re Millhaven Fibres Ltd., Millhaven Works, and Oil, Chemical and Atomic Workers Int'l Union, Local 9-670 (1967), IA Union Management Arbitration Cases 328 (Anderson), quoted in the Re Air Canada Int'l Association of Machinists, Lodge 148 (1973), 5 L.A.C. (2d) (Andrews). In the Millhaven Fibres case, the arbitrator said:

> . . . if the discharge is to be sustained on the basis of a justifiable reason arising out of conduct away from the place of work, there is an onus on the Company to show that:
>
> 1. the conduct of the grievor harms the Company's reputation or product
>
> 2. the grievor's behaviour renders the employee unable to perform his duties satisfactorily
>
> 3. the grievor's behaviour leads to refusal, reluctance or inability of the other employees to work with him.
>
> 4. the grievor has been guilty of a serious breach of the Criminal Code and thus rendering his conduct injurious to the general reputation of the Company and its employees.

5. places difficulty in the way of the Company properly carrying out its functions of efficiently managing its Works and efficiently directing its working forces.

In Air Canada, the Arbitrator added that with respect to the factors set out in Millhaven Fibres: "It is my interpretation that it is not necessary for a company to show that all five criteria in the Millhaven Fibres case have followed on the employee's conduct; rather, any one of the consequences named may warrant discipline."

The Counsel for the Eastern Utility Company particularly stressed the first criterion, namely, that the grievor's conduct may harm the company's reputation or product. He stated that this depends very much on the type of company and its place in the commercial world but in this case the company affected is a major public utility with a high public profile. Therefore, its reputation must always be of great concern to it. Accordingly, the employer is entitled to take very seriously any employee conduct that would damage that reputation. While it was true the grievors were not on duty on a company project, their living expenses were being paid by the company, and in a large sense they represented the company.

The employer argued that the fact the employee was not particularly connected with his employer by the news media did not prevent the employer from being associated with the employee as a result of other particular facts of the case, including the serious and flagrant nature of the offence and the widespread publicity surrounding it.

Union Argument

The union argued that none of the criteria set out in the Millhaven Fibres case and outlined above had been met in this case. There was no contention or evidence that the grievors had acted in a manner incompatible with the discharge of their duty to the company; that their behaviour had rendered them unable to perform their duties satisfactorily; that their behaviour would lead to refusal or reluctance or inability of other employees to work with them; or that their conduct had placed any difficulty in the way of the company properly carrying out its functions of efficiently carrying out its works and efficiently directing its working forces. Thus the case comes down to the single question of whether the grievors' behaviour had harmed the company's reputation or was otherwise injurious to the interests of the employer.

CANADIAN AMALGAMATED TRUCK LINES

Criminal Charges Laid Against Grievor — Whether Indefinite Suspension Proper

Background

The Grievance, dated May of last year, reads as follows: ''I grieve that the suspension I received on April 27 was without just cause and that the penalty is too severe. I claim lost pay and benefits from the date of April 27.''

On April 27 of last year, the grievor received a letter notifying him of his suspension. The substance of that letter is as follows:

> You were picked up by the City Police on April 27, and charged with possession of stolen goods from Canadian Amalgamated Truck Lines Limited.
> Therefore, you are suspended (without pay) from Canadian Amalgamated Truck Lines Limited.
> This suspension will remain in effect until your case is heard in court and if found guilty, your employment will be terminated with Canadian Amalgamated Truck Lines Limited.

On June 9, the grievor received another letter, as follows:

> On May 31, you were found guilty as charged on April 27. This became known to me on June 8.
> As per the letter sent to you by registered mail on April 28 (dated April 27), you are terminated from Canadian Amalgamated Truck Lines Limited.

The union and the employer agreed that the subject matter of the arbitration was the suspension not the discharge of the grievor. There was no dispute between the parties with regard to the facts. The grievor had been employed by the company for twelve years. At all material times he worked as a city driver. His duties involved his transporting goods from the company terminal to various customers in the city and from customers in the city to the terminal. City drivers are alone in their trucks and there is no direct supervision by anyone from the Company.

On or about April 27, the grievor was arrested by the City Police and charged with theft of over $200. The items allegedly stolen by the grievor were sets of socket wrenches which were to be delivered to one of the company's customers in the city. Some other employees of the company, all of whom were employed as dockmen, were also arrested and charged with possession of stolen property.

On April 27, the company was informed by City Police that the grievor had been arrested and charged with theft of the goods in question, and had confessed to the theft. The company had not initiated the police investigation.

On May 31, the grievor pleaded guilty to theft over $200 and was convicted. He was sentenced to one day in jail and a fine of $500.

Evidence was also given about other jobs available in the Bargaining Unit which showed that the employees worked with no or very little supervision. All highway and city drivers work with no direct supervision while they drive and employees on the dock are not closely supervised at all. Both drivers and dockmen have access to goods transported in the course of its business as a common carrier. Both drivers and dockmen are directly entrusted with the safe carriage of goods.

Union Argument

The union argued that the company had a duty, under the circumstances, to offer alternate employment to the grievor during the period of his suspension from his regular job as a city driver. And that this duty had been neglected. The union argued furthermore that the company had acknowledged in its evidence that it had not considered alternate employment for the grievor during the period between his arrest and trial.

Company Argument

The company was aware at the time of the suspension that the grievor had been arrested for theft of property carried by the company and had confessed to that theft. It was also aware the grievor's job would place him in constant contact with goods carried by the company and that there would be no effective way of supervising him while he was driving. This knowledge must also be considered in light of the company's concern about thefts and its relation to its customers. The evidence before the Board was that the company's city operations had experienced losses from theft of between $5,000 and $10,000 per year. There was also evidence that the customer who was the intended recipient of the stolen goods had lost about $1,000 worth of goods carried by the company in the past year and that the customer was fed up and was threatening to transfer his business to another carrier.

The company also showed that is operations were such that there were no bargaining unit jobs in which the employee could be closely supervised or in which he would not be in contact with a customer's goods.

For all of these reasons, the company argued that the Arbitration Board should dismiss the grievance.

TOWN PLAZA HOTEL

Discharge — Theft — Minimal Value

The grievor, Mrs. Elisabeth Meyers, was discharged from her employment as a cook on July 10, for alleged theft. She filed a grievance claiming unjust dismissal which was then processed to arbitration.

Facts

The grievor was 54 years old, had six years of service and a good record.

The essential facts are not in dispute. On Friday, July 4, 1990, the grievor was working as a Cook III. At the close of her shift, at approximately 4:00 p.m., she was observed by the food service supervisor, Ms. Karen Schaefer, near the back of the kitchen searching through boxes on a garbage wagon. The grievor approached Ms. Schaefer and told her she needed empty boxes to help a friend who was moving. Shortly after this, Ms. Schaefer noticed the grievor pacing in front of the garbage wagon. The grievor then took a sweater she was carrying under her arm and reached behind a doorway into an adjacent store-room. She appeared to drop her sweater and then extracted a box from the store-room. Ms. Schaefer approached the grievor and removed the sweater from the box. Upon doing so she found in the box three wrapped pairs of muffins and one individually wrapped muffin, two pieces of cheese souffle and a piece of bavarian meat loaf. The items were wrapped in a saran wrap type material.

Ms. Schaefer asked the grievor if she had paid for the food products. The grievor responded by naming specific employees from whom she said she had purchased the muffins and souffle. She told Ms. Schaefer she had not paid for the bavarian meat loaf because it was for her dog and was to be thrown out in any event. Ms. Schaefer said (referring to the bavarian meat loaf) "Elisabeth, this is stealing". The grievor replied "I know". Ms. Schaefer said she would have to investigate the matter and that she would get back to the grievor. Ms. Schaefer confiscated the box and food items and the grievor left the hotel premises.

Ms. Schaefer then contacted the employees from whom the grievor said she had purchased the items. She determined that the grievor had not purchased the muffins or souffle as alleged by the grievor. Ms. Schaefer then contacted the director of dietary services, Mrs. Lydia Greco. Mrs. Greco has direct responsibility for all food production services at the hotel including the supervision and discipline of staff. Mrs. Greco contacted the grievor by telephone at home and told her that the matter was under investigation and the grievor was not to report to work until further notice.

Mrs. Greco testified that during her telephone conversation with the grievor, the grievor reiterated that she had paid for the muffins and souffle but not for the meat loaf because it was going to be thrown out. She again asserted that she was taking the meat loaf home for her dog. Mrs. Greco said that the grievor was very agitated and upset on the telephone. The grievor pleaded with Mrs. Greco to forgive her and said she was very sorry. She asked Mrs. Greco not to take the matter further with administration. Mrs. Greco told the grievor that she would get back to her the following Monday or Tuesday after she had completed her investigation and after she had discussed the matter with hotel administration.

In her own testimony, the grievor quite adamantly denied that she told Mrs. Greco on the telephone that she had paid for the food items. She did, however, acknowledge that she was crying and upset and that she had pleaded for another chance. The grievor said she was under the impression she was probably going to be fired as a result of her conduct.

On Monday, July 7, 1990, the grievor endeavoured to see the assistant executive director, employee relations, Mr. John Kasik. Mr. Kasik was away for that day. She was waiting for him in his office when he arrived at work on July 8, 1990. Mr. Kasik had not yet been briefed by Mrs. Greco concerning the events of the prior week. He agreed to speak with her. He testified that Mrs. Meyers was very upset and that her comments were disjointed and close to incoherent. He testified she told him she was in a lot of trouble. She said "It was the diet that had done it to her — it had driven her crazy". She produced a photocopy of a diet from a tabloid newspaper and explained to Mr. Kasik that she was on a salt-free diet and, as a result, she had a craving for salt. He testified she said she took the food items because they contained an excess amount of salt. Mr. Kasik quickly determined that the matter should more properly be handled by the grievor's department head and referred her to Mrs. Greco.

The grievor's recollection of her conversation with Mr. Kasik differed quite materially. She said she showed him the newspaper diet only to establish that her diet was salt-free. She said her diet only allowed her to eat vegetables and salad. She testified she showed Mr. Kasik the diet in order to establish that she was not taking the food for herself but rather for her dog. The grievor testified that she did not recall telling Mr. Kasik that she had a craving for salt.

When the grievor left Mr. Kasik's office, she went to see Mrs. Greco. Mrs. Greco testified that the grievor showed her a copy of a diet extracted from a newspaper. The grievor told her she was on a low salt diet and, accordingly, it left her with a craving for salt. Mrs. Greco said the grievor told her the reason she took the muffins and meat loaf was because of the salt content. She said the grievor confirmed that the meat loaf was going to be thrown out anyway. Mrs. Greco disagreed and told the grievor that the department would find a use. for it.

The hotel made its decision to dismiss the grievor on approximately July 10, 1990, after reviewing the facts of the case. On July 10, 1990, Mr. Kasik and Mrs. Greco met with the grievor, her husband and union representatives. Mr. Kasik reviewed the facts leading up to the meeting including the various versions of events given by the grievor. According to Mr. Kasik, during the meeting the grievor told him that she had taken all the food products for her dog. She maintained that the food had no value because it was going to be thrown out in any event. She acknowledged that she had not paid for the souffle, meat loaf or six of the muffins. She said that she had paid for one muffin.

In her testimony before this board, the grievor said that her recollection of the meeting on July 10th was unclear. She testified that she had taken valium prior to the meeting to calm her nerves and, as a result, did not recall much of the discussion.

Company Argument

Mr. Kasik outlined the reasons for the termination. Those reasons included the fact that the grievor had committed what the hotel considered a serious offence, *i.e.*, alleged theft; that the grievor had acted in what appeared to be a premeditated manner; that the grievor held a position of trust in that she had access to departmental property and, on occasion, cash; that the grievor had lied to her supervisor on several occasions in endeavouring to cover up her involvement and that the grievor had breached departmental policy on the purchase of food products.

Employee Argument

At this arbitration hearing, the grievor testified she took the food for her dog. She maintained that the food items were of no value because they were to be discarded. She said she had been advised earlier in the day on July 7, 1990, to garburate the souffle. She testified the meat loaf had already been reheated one time and she did not think it was safe for reuse. She testified that during the day of July 7, 1990, she had removed the muffins from a warmer and that, as they appeared "squashed and crumbled" she thought they would be discarded. During the day she removed these food items to the storage room where she placed them in the box. She denied wrapping the muffins in pairs in saran wrap.

She did acknowledge that she told Ms. Schaefer that she had paid for the food product when confronted by Ms. Schaefer in the kitchen. She said she was frightened at the time. She testified she was aware she could not take food home and was also aware of a hotel policy to the effect that employees could not purchase food at the hotel for home consumption. She testified at the time Ms. Schaefer approached her, she ''felt trapped''. The grievor said she did not recall telling either Mr. Kasik or Mrs. Greco in the meetings of July 8th that her diet had created a craving for salt.

UNIVERSITY HOSPITAL

Incompetence — Discharge and Discipline — Long Standing Poor Performance of Employee Tolerated by Employer

Background

The grievor was notified March 17, 1986, that he would be dismissed effective September 19, 1986. The reason for the dismissal can be summarized as poor work performance with no realistic expectation that the employee would improve to a level acceptable to the employer.

The grievor was employed in May, 1979, and has worked continuously as a storekeeper since that time.

While the dismissal, if upheld, would not take place until September 19, 1986, the parties agreed that the grievance was properly before the arbitrator having jurisdiction to rule on the merits of the grievance as though the grievor had actually been terminated on the day of notification, March 17, 1986.

The notification of termination from the grievor's manager follows:

> As you know, the Hospital has been concerned about your poor work performance for some time and I have reaffirmed this concern on numerous occasions. I have stressed the need for improvement in your work performance to the level acceptable for the department.
>
> You have been given numerous opportunities to improve. The last time, you were given a 45 day period in which you were told significant improvement in your performance was required or your employment would be terminated. Although there was some improvement, your work performance is still at a level unacceptable for the department.
>
> As it appears that you are unable to achieve the level of performance required for the department, and there is no indication that further retraining or time on the job would improve your performance, we have no alternative but to terminate your employment.
>
> The Hospital is giving you six (6) months notice of termination. If you are not successful in obtaining alternate employment, you will be terminated effective Friday, September 19, 1986 at 1630 hours.

The grievance dated March 26, 1986 reads:

> The Employer has violated the collective agreement, Article #7 — Grievance and Arbitration Procedure and any other related clauses with a letter of intent to terminate me without just cause to take effect Friday, September 19, 1986 at 1630 hours.
>
> I request that the letter of intent to terminate me be withdrawn and destroyed from my record and that I be fully compensated with full

redress of any loss of wages, benefits and opportunities as of September 19, 1986 at 1630 hours.

Pertinent sections of the collective agreement follow:

ARTICLE 7 — GRIEVANCE AND ARBITRATION PROCEDURE

. . . . .

7.06 A claim by an employee who has completed his probationary period that he has been unjustly discharged or suspended shall be treated as a grievance if a written statement of such grievance is lodged by the employee with the hospital at Step. No. 3 within seven (7) calendar days after the date the discharge or suspension is effected. Such special grievance may be settled under the Grievance or Arbitration Procedure by:

   a) confirming the Hospital's action in dismissing the employee, or

   b) reinstating the employee with or without full compensation for the time lost; or

   c) by any other arrangement which may be deemed just and equitable.

   Wherever the Hospital deems it necessary to suspend or discharge an employee, the Hospital shall notify the Union of such suspension or discharge in writing. The Hospital agrees that it will not suspend, discharge, or otherwise discipline an employee who has completed his probationary period, without just cause.

. . . . .

7.12 The Arbitration Board shall not be authorized to make any decision inconsistent with the provisions of this Agreement, nor to alter, modify, add to or amend any part of this Agreement.

The storekeeper *job description* reads:

Position: STOREKEEPER

Reports to:
Manager — Material Distribution

Qualifications:
Secondary School Graduation Diploma or an equivalent combination of education and experience. Previous distribution experience would be an asset.

Conditions of Employment:
Must be physically able to perform the essential duties of the job.

Job Summary:
Under the direct supervision of the Manager - Material Distribution, performs all duties related to the Materials Distribution function.

Major Duties:

1. Maintains a perpetual inventory control.

2. Performs shipping and receiving functions.

3. Operates printing press, copier, and other related equipment, and performs limited maintenance on them.

4. Processes purchase orders and invoices (Kardex — pricing) and follows up as required.

5. Distributes all supplies as per authorized requisition forms.

6. Maintains work area.

7. Performs I.V. Solution Top Up on a daily basis.

8. Assists in the physical inventories as required.

9. Performs any other related duties as required.

Employer Argument

The employer's case was presented through the evidence of one witness, the grievor's manager. The union did not cross-examine the employer's witness and elected not to call on the grievor.

The uncontested evidence of the employer is that while the grievor had been on substantially the same job for some seven years and though his performance had not deteriorated over that period of time, he had been unsatisfactory over his term of employment and was currently unsatisfactory. Further, there was no reason to think that sufficient improvement would be forthcoming to warrant his continued employment.

The employer counselled the grievor numerous times over the period of his employment but concrete action was not taken until September 4, 1985, when a meeting was held with the grievor, union representatives and management representatives in attendance. This meeting was called by the union. The employer outlined the areas of dissatisfaction which resulted in inadequate service by the department and in concern by the grievor's fellow employees that the workload was not being properly shared. The efficiency of the department was impaired because the grievor could not be trusted to carry out certain assignments on time and with accuracy. The meeting terminated with a three-point programme in place:

1. the grievor would identify those parts of his job where he felt he would benefit from retraining;

2. the grievor's job performance would be evaluated over a period of 45 days with feedback sessions every two weeks; and

3. a formal evaluation would be conducted at the end of the 45 days.

The grievor was given the opportunity to state his retraining needs but did not indicate any requirements. An informal interim performance evaluation was conducted on September 20th and discussed with the grievor. Several areas of concern were expressed by the grievor's manager. Feedback sessions were held with a union representative present. Management expressed continuing dissatisfaction but the grievor appeared to believe that he was doing an effective job.

The formal 45-day evaluation was conducted on November 7, 1985, and was reviewed with the grievor and a union representative on November 12th. The summary of the evaluation showed continuing concern in the areas of work performance, judgment and initiative.

A meeting was held on November 14th including several union representatives, management representatives and the grievor. It was decided to give the grievor another 45 working days to see if he could improve, this time assigning a fellow employee/union representative to act as a working "buddy" for 20 of those days. One reason for this additional trial period and the employment of the "buddy" system was because the union said that there was a personality conflict between the grievor and the manager.

Performance problems continued and the evaluation of January 31, 1986, indicated substantial dissatisfaction and it was noted that, while there was no doubt the grievor was trying, the improvement was not significant enough to meet the standards of the department.

The employer considered other work for the grievor but did not find a suitable opening anywhere in the hospital. The grievor received his notice of termination March 17, 1986.

Union Argument

The union urged that the grievor should be retained on the job because of the several years he had performed the same function without discipline as well as because the employer failed to set out reasonable and clear standards of performance expectations. Further, it was alleged that the employer had released the grievor because he was not as good as other employees rather than because he was not performing the job satisfactorily.

KEITH ROWAN

Seniority — Bumping — Reasonable Evidence — Similarity of Skills

Background

Due to lack of work, Keith Rowan, a sheet metal worker in Department 21, was given notice of layoff on October 1989.

The company had a plant-wide seniority system in its collective agreement with the Union which provided basically that an employee who was otherwise about to be laid off was entitled to take the job of another employee in the company with less seniority whose job he could perform. Rowan, whose seniority date was February 15th, 1987, asked for and was given an up-to-date copy of the plant-wide seniority list and decided to claim the job of Murray Northrup, a welder-fitter in Department 14, whose seniority date was March 10th, 1987. He was interviewed for the job by the foreman, Mr. Irwin, who after the interview informed Rowan he was not qualified for the job. Rowan decided to file a grievance claiming Northrup's job. The grievance was heard and subsequently denied by the company. The Union decided to process it to arbitration.

The grievance read as follows:

> "I contend I am being laid off contrary to the seniority provisions of the collective agreement. I contend I can perform the work of M. Northrup who is being retained by the company and has less seniority than I. I am requesting a five-day trial period as provided for by clause 1205 D(ii) to prove that I can perform this work."

The applicable provisions of the collective agreement are as follows:

1205   Layoffs or transfers due to lack of work will be governed by the following provisions:

> D(ii). Following the application of the procedure under section 1205 D(i) an employee who is about to be laid off (without prejudice to his right of grievance under such section) will be transferred to a job held by an employee with less seniority or an open job on a trial basis where the company has reasonable evidence either that the employee has transferable skills which would enable him to meet the normal requirements of the work of such job within a maximum period of five working days (which may be extended by agreement) or that having previously worked on such job (or on a job requiring similar skills) he could so perform it within such period. The employee so transferred will be acquainted through demonstration and information with the normal duties of the work. Should the

employee upon being so transferred be unable to meet such
requirements during the minimum period of five working days
(or as extended by agreement) or should it become so apparent
in a lesser time than the five-day period, he will be eligible for
one further transfer to a lesser skilled job held by an employee
with less seniority or an open job which he can perform without
trial as otherwise provided in this clause.

Union Argument

For the Union, the grievor testified that he had been instructed to see Mr.
Irwin, Foreman of Department 14, to see if he could bump Northrup, who
was classified as welder-fitter, job code Number 56. It was stated his job
included the following functions:

a) arc welding,

b) gas cut to layout (up to 4'' plate)

c) all position pipe welding

The grievor stated Irwin showed him the welding work and asked him if
he could do the job. He replied yes. Irwin asked if he had any pipe-welding
tests and the grievor produced two certificates — one from the Ministry of
Labour for welding metallic arc in flat positions and secondly, a certificate
from the Canadian Welding Bureau for welding on flat, horizontal and
vertical positions up to three quarters of an inch.

Irwin asked if he had a test of six-inch pipe all-position welding. When
the grievor said he did not, Irwin told him he was not qualified for the job.

The grievor then asked for a test by the Welding Inspector. Irwin replied
the Welding Inspector was out and could not give him a test. The grievor
stated he told Irwin he could do the all-position pipe-welding. He stated for
a period of time he worked in Department 32 where he did gas cutting and
in Department 34 where he did gas cutting on plates of up to one-inch
thickness. In Department 32 he was gas cutting to layout.

He admitted that in October of 1985 he failed a test in gas cutting of two-
inch steel because he was not familiar with the tips and the percentage of
air and oxygen to use, and that he had no further experience in gas cutting.

He also admitted that the had never done all-position pipe welding
although he had read about it.

With respect to the cutting, he said that work was not demonstrated to
him and that if he had a half hour he could do it and certainly could do it
within five days.

Mr. Northrup gave evidence and stated he started to work with the
company as a welder as had the grievor. He stated between then and 1989,

he and the grievor had been transferred to various departments and in each case had done the same work.

He expressed the opinion the grievor could do the work required and was a better than average welder.

He stated that when he was given a gas cutting test, he passed it and that he had been told about the proper mix before he tried the test. Northrup stated he was trained on all-position welding and had failed his first two tests and received training between each test. The training consisted of practices.

Northrup expressed the opinion the grievor would require training on all-position welding.

Mr. Davey gave evidence and stated he bumped into the same department in December 1986. He stated before he took his all-position pipe welding test, he practised on pipe for two or three hours; took a test, and failed it. He again practised for two or three hours, and passed his test.

He expressed the opinion that a good welder could do all-position pipe welding.

Evidence was also given that a number of employees who came into this department passed the test on their first day.

For the grievor, Mr. Rowan, the Union representative, argued the grievor's record showed many transfers and that other employees with similar records had been taken onto this job in this department. He argued that Rowan's experience as a welder entitled him to a test on all-position pipe welding.

He further argued that this section of the agreement provided for demonstration and information with respect to normal duties of the work and if this were given to the grievor he would be able to do the work without training.

Section 1205 D(ii) provides for the transfer of an employee who is about to be laid off "where the company has reasonable evidence of transferable skills which could enable him to meet the normal requirements of the work of such job within a maximum period of five working days."

The Union argues the company did have such reasonable evidence and as a result the grievor is entitled to such a trial.

Company Argument

The Company called no evidence.

For the company, Mr. Nelson argued that the grievor failed to show he had the necessary skills to do the job or that he had worked on the job.

He pointed out that qualification for all-position pipe welding was a requirement of the job and that even Northrup in his evidence stated the grievor would require training for this work.

He also pointed out that the grievor had failed the year before on a gas cutting test and that the grievor admitted he had no further knowledge of or qualification for the work since that test was given.

He argued the section of the agreement relied upon by the grievor does not require the company to train an employee for the job.

GEORGE ROBBINS

Seniority — Bumping — Suitability of Evidence — Concern about Safety Hazards

Background

On November 7th, 1989, George Robbins was advised by his foreman that there was no more work available for him in his present job and as a result he was being declared surplus. The company had a departmental and plant-wide seniority system. Under its provisions an employee like Robbins who was surplus in his job could bump another employee in his department who had less seniority and whose job he could do, and failing that could bump any other employee in the plant who had less seniority and whose job he could do.

Robbins apparently recognized there was no one in his department with less seniority whose job he could do and indicated he wanted to exercise his plant-wide bumping rights. He was therefore sent to the personnel department and after a examination of seniority lists and some discussion, was advised that there was no one in the plant with less seniority whose job he could do and as a result was given written notice as required by the collective agreement that he would be laid off in seven days.

After further examination of the seniority lists, Robbins decided to file the following grievance:

> "I contend I am being laid off out of seniority as I contend I can do the work of John Mills, Maintenance Department, and under the provisions of Clause 1205 D(ii), claim a five-day trial period."

The grievor Robbins had a seniority date of January 14th, 1977 and the person whose job he claimed, John Mills, had a seniority date of November 8th, 1978.

Robbins, immediately prior to his layoff, was classified under Job Code 121-1, Painter Brush and Spray 1st Class. Mills, whose job he claimed, was classified under Job Code 122 — Painter Maintenance. The rate of pay for the job Robbins performed was 6 cents per hour higher than that of the job held by Mills.

The job description of the two jobs are as follows:

Job Code 121-1 Painter — Brush and Spray, 1st Class

Occupational duties:

Experienced brush and spray painter on products requiring a slow finish. Match colours and prepare metal for painting. Sand, fill, mask in, and polish when necessary. Be familiar with the consistency of paints under various conditions. Work from paint specifications. Apply paints such as dulux, duco (baking and air dry) lacquer, enamel, etc., with a smooth even coating to avoid runs and orange peel effect. May do some flowing and dipping of parts. Clean and adjust own equipment. Minimum supervision. Work on products such as metal cabinets, shelving panels, etc.

Job Code 122 — Painter Maintenance

Occupational duties:

Mix up standard paints and varnishes, etc. for all maintenance painting. Paint windows, doors, partitions, walls, pipes, etc., with brushes or spraying equipment. Work from ladders or scaffolding. May be required to perform other duties as per foreman's instructions.

The applicable provisions of the collective agreement are as follows:

1205 Layoffs or transfers due to lack of work will be governed by the following provisions:

> D(ii). Following the application of the procedures under 1205 D(i), an employee who is about to be laid off will be transferred to a job held by an employee with less seniority, or an open job, on a trial basis where the company has reasonable evidence, either that the employee has transferable skills which would enable him to meet the normal requirements of the work of such job within a maximum period of five working days (which may be extended by agreement) or that having previously worked on such job (or on a job requiring similar skills) he could so perform it within such period. The employee so transferred will be acquainted through demonstration and information with the normal duties of the work. Should the employee upon being so transferred be unable to meet such requirements during the maximum period of five working days (or as extended by agreement) or should it become so apparent in a lesser time than the five- day period, he will be eligible for one further transfer to a lesser skilled job held by an employee without trial as otherwise provided in this clause. In laying off an employee because such a lesser skilled job is not available, the provisions with respect to notice of layoff will not apply.

Subject to filing the grievance, Robbins was interviewed by the maintenance foreman who has responsibility for the job claimed, Mr. Dickson, but the decision was made that he was not entitled to a trial period under the provisions of the agreement and as a result he was laid off as scheduled and the grievance was taken to arbitration.

Union Argument

At the arbitration hearing, Mr. Robbins gave evidence and stated that he had worked on a variety of jobs including Bench Hand, Painter-Brush and Spray, for some four months, machine work, as well as Storekeeper and various other jobs in the plant.

He stated that prior to coming to the company he had worked with a painting contractor, painting houses, and had to work off scaffolds and had mixed paint.

He was not interviewed in connection with Mills' job before filing the grievance, but after he did file it, he had an interview with Mr. Dickson, the maintenance foreman.

He said Dickson told him that to qualify for the job he would have to use a pneumatic breaker, chip paint, glaze windows, and various other types of work that were done by Mills.

He said he would be required to work from a bosun's chair (a bosun's chair is a device which is attached to a series of ropes that can be slung across various high bays of the plant; the occupant sits in the chair and is propelled to the appropriate location to do the required work) and showed him some broken windows in one of the buildings some 65 feet up and said if he did get the job, his first assignment would be to replace those broken windows.

He admitted that he had never worked from a swinging scaffold but said that he could. He also admitted he was not an experienced glazier but stated he had done glazing for himself. He told Dickson that he could do the work required of him.

On behalf of the Union, James Morley gave evidence. He stated he had worked in the maintenance department that Mills was now working in from 1977 to 1987. He said he was experienced in the rigging of bosun's chairs and that during the period he was there this work had always been given to the machine movers. He said anyone could learn the job of rigging a bosun's chair in an hour and a half.

On this evidence the Union argued there could be no doubt that Robbins had all of the qualifications required for the painting work involved in the job of painter maintenance. Further, that the other duties according to the occupational duties filed, were to perform other duties as instructed by the foreman and these duties consisted of glazing and general labour work only.

The Union further argued the grievor had had a variety of jobs in the plant, that he undoubtedly had, to the knowledge of the company, transferable skills which would enable him to meet the normal requirements of the work of the job claimed in accordance with the provisions of clause 1205 D(ii) of the collective agreement and he was therefore to have the opportunity of proving he could perform this work during the five-day period provided for in this section.

Company Argument

Mr. Dickson, foreman of the maintenance department, gave evidence.

He said there were thirteen employees in his group including a brick-layer, two machine movers, two painters, a truck driver, a storekeeper, two elevator operators, a group leader and a cement finisher. He said they maintain machines, replace floors, paint, and glaze windows as required, in all the buildings, and on occasion they have to uncover water lines and dig foundation bases. He said some of the work was heavy work such as that of using concrete breakers, and that this could continue for days.

He said that over the last five months prior to December 1989 he went over the company records and a breakdown of Mill's work showed that he spent 21% of his time painting, 16% glazing, 13% machine moving, and 50% general labour. He said at times it was necessary for the painter to work on a bosun's chair and on a swing scaffold and on such occasions two painters worked together.

For the company Mr. Allen, company counsel, agreed the whole question before the Board was whether, on the evidence, Mr. Robbins was entitled to the trial period as provided for in clause 1205 D(ii).

He pointed out the period was a trial period, not a training period, and the question was whether Mr. Robbins had knowledge and experience sufficient to enable him to do the job without training.

He admitted Robbins had the necessary painting qualifications to perform the basic duties of a painter-maintenance.

He argued the company had no evidence the grievor could work from scaffolding or from a bosun's chair, and argued that the foreman had made an assessment of the work to be done and the ability of the grievor to do the heavy tasks involved, and that his assessment was correct.

He agreed Robbins was a capable employee in his own classification.

RUSSELL COLEMAN

Seniority — Bumping — Evidence — Test — Similarity and Difference of Jobs

Background

Russell Coleman was employed as shipper in the assembly department of the switchgear division. He was hired by the company on April 8th, 1985. As a result of the application of the plant-wide seniority provisions of the collective agreement with the Union, he was dispatched from his job by another employee whose job had been eliminated as a result of a work shortage in another department of the company.

His foreman, Mr. Randall, reviewed his own departmental seniority list, and then discussed the matter with the company's personnel department. The conclusion was there was no job held by a person with less seniority that Coleman could perform and as a result he was given notice of layoff.

Subsequently Coleman filed the following grievance:

> "I contend I am being laid off in violation of the collective agreement as H. Schultz has less seniority and is being retained on a job that I can perform. Under the provisions of clause 1205 D(ii), I claim a five-day trial on the job held by H. Schultz, seniority date June 20th, 1985."

Schultz was employed as a storekeeper in the same department in which Coleman was employed.

He was subsequently formally interviewed for the job by his foreman Mr. Randall. The company considered he was not qualified for the job and as a result his grievance was denied and he was laid off.

The Union subsequently decided to process the grievance to arbitration.

Applicable provisions of the collective agreement:

1205 Layoffs or transfers due to lack of work will be governed by the following provisions:

D(ii) Following the application of the procedure under section 1205 D(i) an employee who is about to be laid off (without prejudice to his right of grievance under such section) will be transferred to a job held by an employee with less seniority or an open job on a trial basis where the company has reasonable evidence either that the employee has transferable skills which would enable him to meet the normal requirements of the work of such job within a maximum period of five working days (which may be extended by agreement) or that having previously worked on such job (or on a job requiring similar skills) he could so perform it within such period. The employee so transferred will be acquainted through demonstration and information with the normal duties of the work. Should the employee upon being so transferred be unable to meet such requirements during the maximum period of five working days (or as extended by agreement) or should it become apparent in a lesser time than the five-day period, he will be eligible for one further transfer to a lesser skilled job held by an employee with less seniority or an open job which he can perform without trial as otherwise provided in this clause. In laying off an employee because such a lesser skilled job is not available the provisions of section 1205 C shall not apply.

Union Argument

The evidence in support of the grievance brought by the Union was basically the evidence of the grievor himself. He claimed he was qualified to do Schultz's job because he was familiar with the material handled in that storeroom through his work as a shipper in that department and because he was previously a storekeeper in another department.

He claimed that because he was a storekeeper he was familiar with the duties of a storekeeper and could perform these duties. He said the difference between one storekeeping job and another was primarily the material in the storeroom. Therefore, he was familiar with the storekeeper's job. He stated in his duties as a shipper, he had to go to the storeroom every day for material although he admitted he had been inside the storeroom on only very few occasions. Under cross-examination, he admitted that in his previous job as storekeeper, the stores contained only 400- 500 items and that storeroom was much smaller than the storeroom in the job claimed.

Company Argument

The company called the grievor's foreman, Mr. Stephen Randall to give evidence. Mr. Randall stated the job of storekeeper which the grievor claimed was far more complicated and required far greater knowledge than the job of storekeeper which the grievor had previously held. In addition they were different in that the stores included a different range of material and different forms than required in the previous storekeeper job held by the grievor. He stated there was some 4,500 items kept in the storeroom claimed and there were some 12 forms that had to be used in connection with the storeroom. This was a storeroom from which the manufacturing process in the department was supplied.

It was far different from the storeroom the grievor was accustomed to in the other division. His evidence stated that as shipper he would only become familiar with some 25% of the parts he would be required to know as storekeeper in the department. The storekeeper would also be required to be familiar with the location of the parts in the storeroom and he stated it would take some considerable time for the grievor to familiarize himself with the location of the parts in the storeroom. He stated that in his judgment it would take the grievor at least 4 to 6 weeks to learn the job Schultz was doing.

He stated that, after the grievor filed his grievance, he decided to arrange a formal interview for the job claimed in order to be entirely fair to the grievor and in order to appear to be fair in case the grievance went to arbitration. He stated in the interview he asked the grievor a number of questions and that while he answered some correctly, he was quite hazy in answer to other questions, and there were a number of others where the grievor had no basis for an answer at all. He stated he asked the grievor questions in regard to the job to establish whether or not the grievor was familiar with it. He was completely unfamiliar with quite a number of parts and he acknowledged he was not familiar with quite a number of the forms in the job.

DAVID SHEPHERD

Seniority — Job Posting — Lines of Progression — Language

Background

Labour grades in the company are classified in numerical order. The higher ranking the job, the higher its numerical designation. The labour grades come from a company-wide job evaluation system. The value of each of the jobs in the company is ranked relative to each other. Those that are considered to have the same value are assigned to the same labour grade regardless of the department in which they are located or the type of work being performed. The work in one department with, for example, a labour grade 13 value, might be entirely different from the work in another department which also has a labour grade 13 value. The skills are different but the value of the jobs is considered to be the same.

The lowest labour grade in the company is labour grade 1 and the highest is labour grade 15. There is a differential of 10 cents per hour per labour grade — that is, labour grade 2 is paid 10 cents per hour more than labour grade 1, and so on.

In the metal perforating department the lowest job is labour grade 6 and the highest is labour grade 14. In the clean, heat-treat and coating department, the lowest is labour grade 2 and the highest is labour grade 10. In the shipping department the lowest is labour grade 2 and the highest is labour grade 9.

On October 15th, 1988, the company posted a vacant job of labour grade 6 in the metal perforating department. No employee in the department bid for the job. Mr. Shepherd, with seniority of September 10th, 1983, who was a labour grade 7 in the clean, heat-treat and coating department, and Mr. Weber, with seniority of August 20th, 1985, who was a labour grade 3 in the shipping department, both applied for the job. The company awarded the job to Mr. Weber, whereupon Mr. Shepherd filed the following grievance.

> "I applied for and under the provisions of the seniority article am entitled to the job in labour grade 6 in the metal perforating department posted on October 15th, 1988. I have more plant-wide seniority than Mr. Weber who was awarded the job and I also have the ability to perform the work of the job posted. I request that I be assigned to the above job."

The company refused to grant the grievance. As a result, the Union processed it to arbitration.

The applicable provisions of the collective agreement are as follows:

6.07 Job vacancies shall be posted on plant bulletin boards for 2 working days. Employees may apply for jobs which constitute an opportunity for promotion. The job will be offered to the employee with the most seniority who applies for the job unless a junior employee who applies for the job is more qualified.

Company Argument

In arbitration, the company argued that Weber was assigned to the job because it was a promotion for him. His previous job was in labour grade 3 in the shipping department and the job vacancy was in labour grade 6 in the metal perforating department. It is clearly a promotion to go from labour grade 3 to labour grade 6. The grievor Shepherd was in labour grade 7 in the clean, heat-treat and coating department and applied for a job in labour grade 6 in the metal perforating department. This was clearly not a promotion for him and as a result he was not entitled to the job under the provisions of the collective agreement.

The company stated it was prepared to concede that one employee was as qualified to do the job as the other. The company further argued that Weber was effectively at the bottom of the training progression in the shipping department. While the training he had received in shipping was lost to the company, he had in fact received very little training and therefore there was very little loss. In effect, he would receive training in the perforating instead of shipping, in order to be promoted, and would be promoted in perforating instead of in shipping.

The grievor Shepherd, in the clean, heat-treat and coating department, had received sufficient training to advance to labour grade 7 which was well up the line of promotion in that department.

The company argued to transfer him from labour grade 7 in the clean, heat-treat and coating department to labour grade 6 in the metal perforating department would mean that in future it was wasting all of the training he had received in order to be promoted to labour grade 7 in clean, heat-treat and coating. To reassign him to the other department would require starting the training cycle for him all over again.

The company stated that, in the previous agreement, there had been no job posting provision. The Union placed a demand for such a provision and argued it was necessary in order to give Union employees proper consideration for promotion, which they felt they had not previously been receiving. In the negotiations there has been much discussion back and forth on the problem and many counter-proposals were exchanged between the company and the Union.

Finally, the company made a proposal which the Union accepted, which is the clause in the present agreement. The company stated the intent of the clause was that the company would post job vacancies and those employees for whom the job would be a promotion could apply for it, and the company would make its selection under the provisions of that clause. For Shepherd to go from labour grade 7 to labour grade 6 was clearly not a promotion. As a result, he could not bring himself within the meaning of the clause and was not therefore entitled to the job under the provision.

Union Argument

The Union argued first that, while neither of the employees was qualified for the job because neither of the employees had worked in the area, they were equally qualified. Therefore, the senior employee was entitled to the job. The Union conceded the company would have to train somebody for the job, and therefore the Union argued the company should train the senior employee for the job. The Union argued the grievor was in the clean, heat-treat and coating department on labour grade 7. The department's progression only went to labour grade 10. In the metal perforating department the progression went to labour grade 14. Therefore, the grievor, to go from labour grade 7 in the clean, heat-treat and coating department to labour grade 6 in the metal perforating department, was in fact an opportunity for promotion because he could go to labour grade 14.

In addition, the Union argued that in this particular case the employees in the clean, heat-treat and coating department who held the jobs with the higher labour grades than the job held by the grievor, were only slightly older than the grievor and were in the judgment of the grievor and the Union the kind of people who were healthy and would live for a long time and who would stay with the company until retirement. Therefore probably the grievor would never receive a promotion as long as he stayed in the clean, heat-treat and coating department.

On the other hand, the employees in the metal perforating department were all relatively young and would probably have a fairly high turnover rate. In addition, the metal perforating department was expanding rapidly while the clean, heat-treat and coating department was having no expansion. As a result an employee in metal perforating was much more likely to be promoted than a person in clean, heat-treat and coating. The Union argued therefore that for Shepherd to go from labour grade 7 in clean, heat-treat and coating to labour grade 6 in metal perforating was first of all an opportunity for promotion as provided in the agreement and also on a logical, practical basis was a much greater opportunity for promotion than the opportunity he had in his present department.

COUNTY GENERAL HOSPITAL

Job Posting — Interpersonal Skills — Requirement of Job Posting

Background

This grievance arises out of the filling of a posted job vacancy for "two part-time Registered Nurses for Cat Scan". The grievor had more seniority than one of the successful applicants, Mrs. Jean Grady, and claims she was qualified for the job and that, under the terms of the collective agreement, the job should have been awarded to the grievor. The posting read as follows:

A vacancy exists in the Department of Radiology for:

2 (two) part-time Registered Nurses for Cat Scan

Requirements

5 years nursing experience at R.N. level

Able to perform all general nursing duties as required.

Prior working experience in a Radiology Department (C.T.) an asset.

Will be responsible for the administering of I.V., contrast, etc.

Will liaise with nursing staff from other hospitals concerning transfer of patients.

Job sharing.

Please apply to the Personnel Office *before* December 27, 1985.

The relevant article of the collective agreement is art. 10:05(c) which reads:

> Nurses shall be selected for positions under either 10:05(a) or (b) on the basis of their skills, ability, experience and qualifications. Where these factors are relatively equal amongst the nurses considered, seniority shall govern providing the successful applicant, if any, is qualified to perform the available work within an appropriate familiarization period. Where seniority governs, the most senior applicant from the bargaining unit in which the vacancy arose, if any, shall be selected. Where the applicant has been selected in accordance with this Article and it is subsequently determined that she cannot satisfactorily perform the job to which she was promoted, the Hospital will attempt, during the first thirty (30) days from the date on which the nurse was first assigned to the vacancy, to return her to her former job, and the filling of the subsequent vacancies will likewise be reversed.

Selection Process

Some 26 employees responded to the posting. The format of individual responses varied between a written note or a request for transfer form in accordance with art. 10:05(b) to submission of a personal resume. The grievor, by covering letter of December 22, 1985, forwarded a resume of her qualifications and experience. Dr. Deacon, chairman of the department of radiology and Mr. Ray Travis, chief technologist of the department, concluded that it would be unwieldy to interview all 26 applicants and in order to assess all applicants on a consistent basis then requested the personnel department to contact those applicants who had not submitted resumes and request same. Deacon and Travis then reviewed the applications and resumes, to "weed out those we felt were not suitable candidates".

It was Dr. Deacon's evidence that the "weeding out" process was conducted in accordance with certain criteria. He stated that all criteria had not been spelled out in the job posting in order to avoid having applicants being led to what they might consider a desired response and crafting their response accordingly. Dr. Deacon stated "we wanted to know why they wanted to change jobs. It was a very important point." He enumerated the criteria as:

1. Ability to start I.V. lines.

2. Skills in handling medical emergencies — although he pointed out that the frequency of reaction to intravenous injection was in the order of 1 to 40,000, and so the weighing of this factor was very low.

3. Interpersonal skills were identified as probably the "most important thing we were looking for". He elaborated that the psychological preparation of the patient was very important in explaining the nature of equipment, the process and the necessity for the patient to be very still. He stated that they were looking for someone with "a pleasing, effervescent personality who could work well with the radiologist and technical staff and complement the personality of the chief technologist. It was also pointed out that the acquisition of the CAT Scan equipment had been exclusively the result of community financial support and it was expected that there would be a large number of visitors and therefore an "out-going personality" was desirable in receiving these visitors and explaining the nature of the work.

4. Administrative skills required in organizing the flow of patients and in responsibility for inventory control. It was pointed out that the job had limited supervision and the successful applicant should be a self-starter

and have a genuine interest in the particular job and not merely an interest based on such things as achieving more desirable working conditions.

Employer Argument

The employer argued the job had been posted as required by the collective agreement. It had invited resumes from all applicants and had reviewed the resumes using certain criteria to establish which applicants would be interviewed.

The grievor admittedly had more seniority than the person selected for the job. However, under the provisions of Clause 10:05(c), the grievor is entitled to the job only if she is relatively equal in regard to skill, ability, experience and qualifications.

The initial review of the twenty-six applicants was conducted solely on the applications and resumes submitted by the individual employees, and on this basis the number of applicants under consideration was reduced to eight.

The grievor was not included in this group because Dr. Deacon did not see things in the resume which were as good as others in respect to personal skills and being a self starter. While recognizing the most important of the criteria was nursing skills, that had to be coupled with patient contacts, and while the grievor's resume indicated she had played the church organ, that would not be an activity involving people contact. Grady's resume indicated she had held the position of municipal deputy reeve and had taught nurses indicating a superior people involvement.

In addition, each of the eight was accorded a 15-20 minute interview by Dr. Deacon and Mr. Travis. They were asked questions to which they separately ascribed a numerical score. After a comparison of the numerical rankings, they identified the two present incumbents as the ones to be selected. Later Dr. Deacon talked to people at the hospital and was told the two selected were excellent candidates.

The person selected was clearly properly placed in the job under the terms of the collective agreement and the grievance should be denied.

Union Argument

There is an obligation on the employer to administer the posting and selection process in a fair and reasonable manner. It is self evident that, in order to discharge this obligation, all applicants must have an equal opportunity to put forward their qualifications and to have these judged fairly against the same standards.

The grievor was not made aware in the posting itself that interpersonal skills were "probably the most important thing" and while those interviewed were asked questions to bring out their interpersonal skills, no such opportunity was awarded the grievor.

None of the applicants had previous experience in a radiology department which the posting had indicated would be "an asset".

Both the grievor and the incumbent possess the required nursing qualifications. Both have considerable and varied nursing experience in this hospital.

The evidence establishes them both to meet the qualifications specifically set out in the posting except for prior experience in a radiology department which no applicant had.

In their various assignments, both would have used and demonstrated with patients and their families the type of communications skills required in the job in question. Evidence regarding playing a church organ or acting as a municipal reeve is not relevant to the job in question.

For all of these reasons there is no basis to support the employer's position of placing Mrs. Grady on the job.

Both are qualified for the job and, under the terms of the collective agreement, the grievor, who is the most senior of the two, is entitled to the job and the arbitration board should award the job to the grievor, Mrs. Cusick.

STEEP ROCKS COUNTY SCHOOL BOARD

Seniority — Bumping — Retention of Redundant Teachers

Background

A grievance was filed by a Teachers' Association on behalf of one of its members, Miss Cavendish, claiming improper layoff by the Steep Rocks County School Board in violation of the collective agreement. This was the result of a decision by the Board to terminate the teaching contract of the grievor effective August 31 as a result of staff redundancy.

Certain underlying facts were agreed upon by the parties to the dispute. The grievor was first employed by the Board two years ago and during the current school year she was employed as a primary teacher in Memorial School. Her qualifications under Program 2 of the Qualifications Evaluation Council of the Province was level A1 based on a B.A. degree from McMaster University and a teacher's certificate in Manitoba.

The position of the Teachers' Association is that the Board's decision to terminate the grievor's contract due to redundancy is in violation of the collective agreement between the Board and the Association. In the Association's view, the person whose contract should have been terminated is a Miss Shaw, a primary teacher in Centennial School. Miss Shaw's employment with the Board commenced with the current school year last September. Her qualification is also level A1 based on a Bachelor of Arts Degree and a Bachelor of Education degree, both from Lakehead University.

It was agreed that the question before the Arbitration Board was whether the contract of Miss Shaw or the contract of Miss Cavendish should be terminated.

The evidence established that because of financial pressure and declining student population, a reduction in the number of teaching contracts would be required and that a careful examination had been carried out to determine where the cutbacks should be made. The full teaching complement of Centennial School is four persons. It already has split classes with two grades being taught together and it would not be practical to reduce the teaching complement any further. In addition, there has been a fairly high rate of turnover in the staff of Centennial which has resulted in some dissatisfaction in the community. As the staff is now working well together and achieving community acceptance, it was desired to maintain the stability within that School.

The decision was made that the teaching position to be eliminated would have to come from Memorial School which is the largest school in the system, employing some seventeen teachers. The grievor was the most junior teacher in that school and the Board decided that it was her teaching position that was to be cut. The Teachers' Association did not dispute that, with respect to the staff of Memorial School, the grievor was the member of the staff who should first be declared redundant.

The collective agreement deals with staff redundancy in Article 4:01, as follows:

> "Staff redundancy will be according to Board Policy Statement No. 9." This Policy statement was approved and adopted by the Board on October 26 of last year.

This was the sole contractual reference to staff redundancy and to the rights and obligations of the parties in situations of staff redundancy.

The applicable provisions of Policy Statement No. 9 previously referred to read as follows:

Staff Redundancy

1. In the event that there are not enough teaching positions for the number of teachers presently under contract, teachers wholly or partly redundant to a school are identified by the Board on the basis of the following consideration and criteria:

    (a) Length of teaching experience

    　　i) with the Steep Rocks County School Board and its predecessor Boards

    　　ii) in the province

    (b) Qualifications

    (c) Characteristics of Position(s) with regard to subject and/or level.

2. The Board will make every possible effort to maintain said teacher(s) on staff within the system if there is a position available and if in the opinion of the Board the teacher(s) is suited to that position.

Union Argument

Counsel for the Teachers' Association argued that the language of the policy statement placed on the School Board two basic obligations. First, within a school there are three specific criteria that must be met by the Board in identifying a redundancy. The first paragraph of the policy statement deals specifically with the situation in a particular school, the second paragraph in the policy statement, dealing with the Board's obligation within the entire system applies. He argued that the only rational implication to be drawn from the second paragraph is that the teacher identified in Paragraph 1 has the right to have the Board try to keep him or her in the system. If, in the system, there exists another position for which the teacher would be suitable, he or she is to be placed in that position.

In determining whether or not a position is available under the language of Paragraph 2, consideration must be given to the obvious intent of the paragraph in an industrial relations context. It was argued that the language of Paragraph 2 was very similar to the language found in industrial relations contracts that tended to give rise to bumping situations. It was Counsel's position that the only meaning that could rationally be ascribed to Paragraph 2 is that it puts into the collective agreement the concept of seniority preference, including the whole concept of bumping rights. An available position would then be any position in which the incumbent was junior to the redundant teacher.

Employer Argument

Counsel for the School Board argued that within the policy language, the concept of redundancy is already identified solely with a particular school and a particular teacher becomes redundant in relation to that teacher's school under Paragraph 1. Paragraph 2 then constitutes a very strong best efforts clause imposing on the Board the obligation to employ the teacher elsewhere within the system if there is a position available.

The Counsel for the School Board then argued that the Board is not required to make a position available in the event that teachers with less seniority are employed within the system. And that a redundant teacher has a claim only on teaching positions that become available through natural processes of attrition or through expansion of the overall system.

It was however the Association's position that the Board, rather than terminating the grievor's contract, should have terminated Miss Shaw's contract. Miss Cavendish, the grievor, should then have been moved to Centennial School by reason of the fact that her qualifications were equivalent to those of Miss Shaw, and that she had an additional year's teaching experience.

PART J

Example of an Arbitration Award

COMBUSTION ENGINEERING-SUPERHEATER LIMITED AND INTERNATIONAL BROTHERHOOD OF BOILERMAKERS, IRON SHIP BUILDERS, BLACKSMITHS, FORGERS, AND HELPERS, LOCAL 128

IN THE MATTER OF AN ARBITRATION

Between

COMBUSTION ENGINEERING-SUPERHEATER LIMITED
(hereinafter called the "Company")

and

INTERNATIONAL BROTHERHOOD OF BOILERMAKERS, IRON
SHIP BUILDERS, BLACKSMITHS, FORGERS AND HELPERS
LOCAL 128
(hereinafter called the "Union")

ARBITRATOR: DR. ARJUN P. AGGARWAL

Appearances:
    For the Company:
    Mr. Roy W. Kendall   - Manager, Labour Relations
                                  and Safety

    For the Union:
    Mr. Matt Bakker   - Business Manager
    Mr. Arnie Aylward   - Assistant Business Manager
    Mr. James French   - Grievor

The hearing in this matter was held on March 8, 19__ , in Thunder Bay, Ontario

AWARD

This arbitration concerns with a grievance filed by Mr. James French, a steward, of the International Brotherhood of Boilermakers, Iron Ship Builders, Blacksmiths, Forgers and Helpers, Local 128, alleging that the Company, Combustion Engineering-Superheater Limited, violated the Collective Agreement, particularly article 10:05, by not calling him for work on Sunday, February 28, 19__ . In relief the Union has demanded that the grievor be reimbursed for the loss of wages.

The *facts of this case* are not in dispute and may be stated as follows:

The Company during the period January to March 1982 was engaged in repair and maintenance work for Kimberley Clark in Terrace Bay, Ontario. There were five or more different assignments in operation at the same time during this period. Each assignment was marked and known by the field work number. During this period, the grievor, Mr. James French, was the union steward on the Kimberley Clark - Terrace Bay project.

On February 26, the general foreman, Mr. Taisto Itkonen, asked 5 welders to work on Saturday, February 27, and 3 welders and 2 fitters to work on Sunday, February 28, on the field work project #822502. The work on this project involved the replacing of a portion of the Dome and Body of Number 2 Evaporator.

The two fitters who were called in to work overtime on this project on Sunday, February 28, were Mr. Jung and Mr. Fraleigh. Mr. James French, the steward, was not asked to work overtime on Sunday, February 28. It is the position of the Union that although the grievor, Mr. James French, was not a qualified welder, he was qualified and competent to do the fitting job, and the Company should have included him in the fitters' crew to work overtime on Sunday, February 28. On that basis, the grievor, Mr. James French, filed the following grievance:

> Violation of Article 10:05
>
> On February 26, 19___ , being steward on the Terrace Bay Project, I was discriminated against by not being included in the crew that was asked to work overtime on February 28, 19___ .

The grievance was denied by the Company in its letter of March 16, 19___ , which reads:

> CE Canada feels that the terms and conditions of the collective agreement were followed. Therefore, we reject your grievance.

The Union has contended that the Company discriminated against the grievor by not calling him for overtime on February 28, 19___ , and thus violated article 10:05 of the Collective Agreement.

The relevant provisions of the Collective Agreement read as follows:

ARTICLE 3:00 — MANAGEMENT RIGHTS

3:01 — It is the Employer's right to operate and manage its business in all respects in accordance with its responsibilities and commitments. The location of jobs, the choice of equipment, the schedule of installation, the methods and means of installation, are solely and exclusively the responsibility of the Employer.

3:02 — The Employer has the right to make and alter, from time to time, rules and regulations to be observed by the employees, provided they are not inconsistent with this Agreement.

3:03 — It is the exclusive function of the Employer to hire, promote, demote, transfer, suspend, lay off, discipline or discharge for just cause, employees in the bargaining unit, subject to the provisions of this Agreement.

ARTICLE 10:00 — STEWARDS

10:01 — On all jobs, the Business Manager or Assistant Business Manager of the Union will designate, or otherwise arrange for, the appointment of a Steward from among the qualified working journey-man employees.

10:05 — The Steward shall not be discriminated against and shall receive his fair share of overtime work for which he is qualified. When any part of a crew is required to perform work on overtime or on bad weather days, and the Steward has been performing the type of work involved during the preceding regular shift, he shall be included in such required overtime or bad weather working time.

ARTICLE 16:00 — OVERTIME

16:01 — When an employee is required to work in excess of the regular hours, Monday through Friday inclusive, or to work any hours on Saturdays, Sundays, or Recognized Holidays, he shall be paid overtime at double (2) time rates.

16:02 — Shift premiums as provided for in the appropriate Appendix shall apply for all hours worked on Saturdays, Sundays and Recognized Holidays. The shift premium shall not be compounded for overtime hours worked.

16:03 — It is understood that under no circumstances can it be construed that employees working on a day shift that runs into extended overtime, will earn an entitlement for shift premium pay.

Mr. James French, the grievor, testified that an overtime was scheduled for February 28, 19__ , and he was not asked to work overtime on that day. He further added that prior to that he had always been asked to work overtime. He stated that he was a boilermaker mechanic and had worked as fitter and rigger. However, he admitted that he was not qualified to do welding work. He further testified that on February 28, the overtime work included a fitting job; and two fitters were called in to do that job. He could do that job but he was not called in for overtime work. In cross examination, he admitted that on the whole he got his fair share of overtime.

Mr. Arnie Aylward, Assistant Business Manager of the Union, testified that Mr. James French, the steward, was competent to work on February 28. He added that in his opinion the Company had not treated the steward (the grievor) as has been the practice.

Mr. Taisto Itkonen, general foreman of the Company at the Kimberley Clark, Terrace Bay Project, testified on behalf of the Company and stated that the different work crews work on different field work projects. On Sunday, February 28, the overtime work in question was on the field work project #822502. The grievor, Mr. James French had not worked before on the field work project #822502 prior to that time, whereas the two other fitters, Mr. Jung and Mr. Fraleigh, who were called in to do overtime work on February 28, had both worked previously on the field work project #822502. It would not have been fair not to ask them for overtime, while they had been already working on that project.

Mr. Itkonen further testified that Mr. James French was not working on the field work project #822502 on his scheduled shift prior to February 28. However, he added that the shop steward, James French, had been given most of the overtime, whenever it was available. He also worked overtime on the weekend of March 6.

He further testified that he did not discriminate against Mr. French in distributing overtime. Further that the overtime had been fairly distributed among the employees. He denied any knowledge of the memo written by Mr. Kendall on February 24, to the Union (Exhibit 3). He further added that Mr. Kendall had not discussed the contents of that memo with him at any time.

Thus, the basic issue in this case is whether or not the Company violated the Collective Agreement in failing to offer the grievor, Mr. James French (Union Steward), the overtime opportunity on Sunday, February 28.

It has been contended for the Company that the Collective Agreement did not restrict the management's inherent right to direct the work force, including the right to assign overtime work. It has been generally recognized that where the agreement does not contain any provision guaranteeing overtime to employees, the management has the right to determine whether work shall be performed on an overtime basis. Further, arbitrators have frequently held that unless the agreement provides otherwise, the scheduling of overtime work falls within the exclusive management prerogative. Thus, unless there are specific provisions in the agreement to the contrary, employees do not have any right to have work assigned to them as overtime.

A collective agreement generally specifies some manner or method of distributing overtime amongst those employees who are entitled to it. Frequently such a provision will require that overtime work be equally distributed amongst the group in question or that it be distributed amongst the employees on a seniority basis. However, the "overtime clause" — article 16:00 of the Collective Agreement, in this case, does not provide any basis or criteria for allocation of overtime amongst employees. Thus, in absence of established relative rights to overtime assignment in the Collective Agreement, the Company is relatively free in directing its work force to the overtime assignment. This, however, does not mean that the Employer is not required to exercise its rights fairly and without discrimination. The Ontario Divisional Court in Re *Metropolitan Toronto and Toronto Civic Employees Union, Local 43*, (1977) 79 D.L.R. (3d) 249 at 252 has confirmed that the employer must exercise its rights fairly and without discrimination. The Court observed:

> . . . an employer in the administration of a collective agreement . . . is dealing, not with individual employees employed under separate contracts or service, but with employees whose terms of employment are set out in an agreement negotiated on behalf of them all. Any discretion to be exercised in the knowledge that each employee is only one of many; no one of them should be singled out for special treatment. This obviously implies that the agreement should be administered fairly.

Although the Collective Agreement, in the instant case, has not provided any criteria for the allocation of overtime amongst the employees in article 16:00, it has made a special provision for the allocation of overtime to the steward, in article 10:00, which has been the basis of this grievance. Article 10:05 provides that "The Steward shall not be discriminated against and shall receive his fair share of overtime work for which he is qualified. When any part of the crew is required to perform work on overtime or on bad weather days, and the Steward is performing the type of work involved during the preceding regular shift, he shall be included in such required overtime or bad weather working time."

The expression "discrimination" has been defined in *Black's Law Dictionary* as follows:

> Unfair treatment or denial of normal privileges to persons because of their race, age, nationality or religion.

> A failure to treat all persons equally where no reasonable distinction can be found between those favoured and those not favoured.

The term "fair" according to *Black's Law Dictionary* means:

> Having the qualities of impartiality and honesty, free from prejudice, favouritism, and self interest, just, equitable, even-handed; equal, as between conflicting interests.

Of course, not every discrimination is improper. An employer is regularly called on to ''discriminate'', in the sense of making choices. Re *Metropolitan Toronto Board of Commissioners of Police and Metropolitan Police Association*, (1980) 26 L.A.C. (2d) 117 (Saltman). What must be determined here is whether the discrimination was improper. Arbitrator Arthurs summarized the common bases of an improper discrimination in his decision in re *U.E.W., Local 512, and Standard Coil Products (Canada) Ltd.* (1966), 16 L.A.C. 402 at p. 404.

> . . . (discrimination) should be held to include adverse treatment of an employee for any reasons which are irrelevant or improper. Obviously, race, colour and religion are irrelevant to management's evaluation of an employee, as is his union affiliation or non-affiliation. Equally, management action may be based on irrelevant or inaccurate information, or on the personal animosity of a foreman. In common parlance, such action may be said to be discriminatory.

Was the grievor, Mr. James French, in this case excluded from overtime assignment on Sunday, February 28, 1982, for irrelevant reasons or because of personal animosity?

The Union has contended that the Company discriminated against the grievor because of personal animosity. In support of its contention the Union produced in evidence a memo of the Company (exhibit 3) dated February 24, 19__ . This memo was written to the Union by Mr. Roy Kendall, Manager, Labour Relations and Safety, of the Company from Ottawa, and dealt with various work stoppages and other union-management issues. In that letter, a reference was made to the grievor which reads as follows:

> "Jim French has been the job steward during 4 of the disputes at Red Rock and 1 at Terrace Bay."

The memo reads as follows:

Re: Illegal Work Stoppages

> I am writing this letter to advise of several illegal work stoppages from the Thunder Bay out of Work List jurisdiction at Domtar, Red Rock and Kimberley Clark, Terrace Bay.
>
> The following list outlines the location, dates, trade and reasons for disputes.
>
> . . . .
>
> After several illegal work stoppages at Red Rock and several discussions, and a meeting, a Cease and Desist order was filed with the Ontario Labour Board against the Boilermakers. A management grievance for related damages has also been filed and is still pending

before arbitration. After this action, the job at Red Rock progressed without further work stoppages.

On February 8, 19___ , 12 Boilermakers walked off the Kimberley Clark, Terrace Bay maintenance job. Our crew was working on re-tubing of the evaporator and were upset that Ironworkers with Coastal Steel were doing "their work" on the I.D. Fan.

There were several implications that should be considered in looking at this matter.

1. Financial — The losses at Red Rock for overhead, legal fees, delay of completion and interest loss, amount to approximately $7,500.00/day or $37,500.00. At Terrace Bay we could be liable for the 1 day loss of production of pulp. I don't have a dollar figure, but it would be substantial.

2. It is our understanding that no disciplinary action has been taken against any member of the union, even though we have been advised that the union ordered the men to stay on the job. Our customer at Terrace Bay wants to know what disciplinary action will be taken against your members.

3. Jim French has been the job steward during 4 of the disputes at Red Rock and 1 at Terrace Bay.

4. The Boilermaker image has and is becoming very tarnished in this area.

Your comments, suggestions and actions would be appreciated as CE Canada has a lot of scheduled maintenance work and other contract possibilities in the Thunder Bay area.

We (CE Canada) have had and will continue to have a good working relationship with the Boilermakers, but we must act on this situation.

Yours truly,
R. W. Kendall
Manager
Labour Relations and Safety

On the basis of the above reference to the grievor in the memo of February 24, 19___ , that "Jim French had been the job steward during 4 of the disputes at Red Rock and 1 at Terrace Bay", the Union has argued that the Company had developed a bias against the grievor and that resulted in discrimination against him in allocating overtime.

The Company, on the other hand, has maintained that it did not discriminate against the grievor at all. Rather, the grievor had received more than a fair share of the overtime.

Mr. Itkonen, the general foreman, had testified that he had no knowledge of the memo of February 24, 19___ , or its contents and that Mr. Kendall had not discussed with him the subject matter of the memo.

Further that the exclusion of the grievor from the overtime assignment on February 28, 19___ , was based on fair and reasonable grounds. The grievor had not worked on that project before whereas the other two employees, Mr. Jung and Mr. Fraleigh, had been working on that project for sometime prior to February 28, 19___ . The testimony of Mr. Itkonen had not been denied by the Union.

In my view, an isolated reference to the grievor, in a letter by the Company to the Union, indicating its displeasure over his role as a steward, does not in itself establish a pattern of animosity against the grievor. On the contrary, the evidence overwhelmingly suggests that the grievor had been treated fairly and equitably and had received a fair share of overtime during the time period in question. Even the grievor himself has admitted in his testimony that in the past (except for the day in question, i.e. February 28, 1982) he had always been asked for overtime. He further added, I quote, "I got a fair share of overtime." The Union adduced no other evidence, whatsoever, to establish that the Company had discriminated against the grievor in the allocation of overtime or otherwise.

Whether or not the Company violated the Collective Agreement in failing to offer Mr. James French the overtime opportunity on Sunday, February 28, falls to be determined on the proper construction that is to be placed on article 10:05. That article provides:

> The Steward shall not be discriminated against and shall receive his fair share of overtime work for which he is qualified. When any part of a crew is required to perform work on overtime or on bad weather days, and the Steward has been performing the type of work involved during the preceding regular shift, he shall be included in such required overtime or bad weather working days.

It is evident that article 10:05 deals with overtime for the steward under two distinct situations. The last part of para. 10:05 deals with a situation when a crew, or a part of it, is required to work overtime and the steward has been performing the same type of work during the preceding regular shift. In that case the steward must be included in the crew which is required to work overtime. In other words if, during the preceding regular shift, the steward has been performing the work for which a part of the crew has been called in to work on overtime basis, it is mandatory for the Employer to include the steward in that crew. Thus, it is obligatory for the Employer to offer overtime to the steward *only* if the condition precedent is met, i.e. the steward must have been performing during his preceding regular shift, the type of work for which an overtime crew has been called in. In the instant case, the parties have admitted that the grievor had not been working on the type of work for which an overtime crew was called in on Sunday, February 28, 19__ . Thus, the Union's case does not fall under that category.

The first part of para. 10:05 states that "The Steward shall not be discriminated against and shall receive his fair share of overtime work for which he is qualified." This, however, does not require that the steward shall be offered overtime all of the time. It simply requires that the steward should not be singled out for exclusion from overtime assignment because he might have earned the displeasure of the foreman during the discharge of his duties as a steward. It further states that the steward shall be treated fairly, amongst other qualified employees, in distribution of overtime. In my opinion, article 10:05 does not require that the Company shall always offer overtime opportunity to the steward, whenever overtime crew is required. It was, however, intended to ensure that the overtime work is fairly and equitably distributed amongst the steward and other employees, who are qualified to work. Further it ensured that the steward will not be improperly excluded from the overtime assignments because of his status as steward.

No doubt, some collective agreements, with a view to provide union representation during all working hours, do provide union officers with some "priority rights" to claim overtime work. See Re *Lasalle Machine Tool of Canada Ltd. and United Automobile Workers*, Local 195, (1975), 9 L.A.C. (2d) 227 (Weatherill). However, the parties, in the instant case, in my view, neither intended to create "priority rights" for the steward to claim overtime work nor have they created any such "priority right" for the steward.

The Union has argued that the Company discriminated against the grievor by failing to offer him the overtime opportunity on February 28, 19__ . If the Union's argument is accepted it would amount to read in article 10:05 that "the steward shall receive all the overtime work for which he is qualified". I cannot read that in article 10:05 without modifying or amending the Collective Agreement, for which, I am afraid, I have no jurisdiction. The Supreme Court of Canada in Re *Port Arthur Ship Building Company v. Arthur*, (1969) S.C.R. 85, has said in no uncertain terms that the arbitrator "has no inherent power to amend, modify or ignore the collective agreement". Further the Collective Agreement, in the instant case, has specifically prohibited the arbitrator from modifying or amending the Collective Agreement. Article 13:05 states:

The arbitrator shall not be authorized to make any decision inconsistent with the provisions of this Agreement, nor to alter, modify or amend any part of this Agreement.

Therefore, I am of the view that the failure to call the grievor for overtime on Sunday, February 28, 19___ , in the circumstances of this case does not amount to either discrimination against him or the denial of a fair share of overtime. Further, on the basis of evidence, I am satisfied that the grievor on the whole had received his fair share of overtime.

I wish to thank the representatives of the parties for their able presentations and for the courtesy and assistance they have extended to me.

Dated at Thunder Bay, Ontario, this 28th day of March, 19___ .

Signed: Arjun P. Aggarwal - Arbitrator

ASSIGNMENT

1. *Review the Union's Arguments.*

2. *Review the Company's Arguments.*

3. *Discuss the Arbitrator's Award.*

PART K

Industrial Relations Glossary

Accreditation: the process whereby an employers' organization is certified as the bargaining agent for a unit of employers.

Affiliation: link between two or more labour organizations, whereby each retains a high degree of autonomy, subject to the limits imposed by their affiliation agreement (e.g. between a labour union and the CLC).

American Federation of Labour: the AFL is a U.S. central labour organization, having, as affiliated members, craft or horizontal type labour unions.

Arbitration: use of an outside third party, called an *arbitrator*, to investigate a dispute between the employer and the union and impose a settlement. Sometimes, a three-person arbitration board, rather than a single arbitrator, is used.

Bargaining agent: the union that is recognized as the exclusive representative, for collective bargaining purposes, of a group of workers. In the case of a group of employers, it is the employers' association.

Bargaining unit: the group of employees in a firm, plant, or industry that has been recognized by the employer and certified by a labour relations board as appropriate for collective bargaining purposes.

Blue-collar workers: term used to describe plant workers (production and maintenance) as compared with office workers (white-collar).

Boycott: organized refusal of union employees, families, friends, and others to buy the products of a company whose employees are on strike, in an effort to reduce sales and exert economic pressure on the employer.

Bumping: displacement of employees from their jobs by more senior employees when a firm needs to lay off or dismiss workers.

Business agent: full-time paid employee of a union local whose duties involve handling grievances, helping to enforce the collective agreement, assist with organizing, etc.

Canada Labour Code: federal labour statute that applies to employers and employees in industries falling under federal jurisdiction.

Canada Labour Relations Board: group of persons, consisting of a chairperson, at least one vice chairperson, and not less than four and not more than eight members, appointed under the industrial relations section of the Canada Labour Code. The Board's powers and duties include the determination of appropriate bargaining units, the certification or decertification of trade unions, decisions as to unfair labour policies, failure to bargain in good faith, etc.

Canadian Labour Congress: the CLC is the central labour organization in Canada with the largest number of affiliated union members. It was formed in 1956 from the merger of the Trades and Labour Congress and the Canadian Congress of Labour.

Certification: procedure whereby a labour union obtains a certificate from the Labour Relations Board declaring that the union is the exclusive bargaining agent for a defined group of employees in a bargaining unit that the Board considers appropriate for collective bargaining. This follows proof of majority support for the union among eligible employees in the bargaining unit.

Checkoff: clause in a collective agreement that directs the employer to deduct union dues and remit these funds to the union concerned.

Closed shop: union security clause that requires all persons to be union members in good standing before they may be hired. Usual only in the construction and longshoring industry.

COLA clause: a cost-of-living allowance, included as part of a collective agreement, that provides for the agreed wage to be adjusted upwards to offset increases in the cost of living during the life of the agreement.

Collective agreement: a written agreement between an employer and the union representing its employees, valid for a period of from one to three years, covering rates of pay, hours of work, conditions of employment, etc.

Collective bargaining: term used to describe the negotiations that take place between a labour union, collectively representing the employees of a plant or industry, and the employer or employers' association, in drawing up a mutually acceptable labour-management agreement.

Competition Act: a federal statute that makes illegal various activities, such as price-fixing and bid-rigging, that reduce the amount of competition among business firms in Canada, to the detriment of the public, and establishes an agency to conduct investigations and lay criminal charges.

Conciliation: use of an outside third party, called a *conciliator*, to assist a company and the union representing its employees to come to a mutually satisfactory collective agreement. Unlike arbitration, no settlement can be imposed. The labour dispute is hopefully resolved by compromise or voluntary agreement. Conciliation is required under the Labour Relations Act before a legal strike or lockout may be declared.

Confederation of National Trade Unions: The CNTU is the second largest central labour organization in Canada, with its base in Quebec. Its name, in French, is the Confederation des Syndicats Nationaux, or CSN.

Congress of Industrial Organizations: the CIO is a U.S. central labour organization established in 1937 by a number of industrial-type unions that had broken away from the AFL in 1932 to set up a Committee for Industrial Organization, the CIO's predecessor.

Contracting out: the use by an employer of outside persons, on a contract basis, to do work formerly performed by the employer's own work force.

Cooling-off period: time period required by a Labour Relations Act, following unsuccessful conciliation attempts, before a strike or lockout may be declared.

Cost of living: the amount of money required to pay for food, shelter, transportation and other basic necessities. Usually, attention is paid to changes in the cost of living, as indicated by Statistics Canada's Consumer Price Index (CPI).

Craft: manual occupation, such as plumbing, carpentry, and electrical that requires a high level of skill and prior training, often in the form of an "apprenticeship".

Craft union: a labour organization representing workers practising the same craft or "trade". However, many craft unions now include workers practising skills not closely related to the originally designated craft.

Decertification: process whereby a union is legally deprived of its official bargaining rights for a group of employees.

Equal pay: principle that wage rates should be based upon the job, rather than upon the sex, nationality, race, colour, etc. of the employee that performs it. Also, that workers should receive the same rate of pay for work of equal value.

Directly chartered local union: local labour unions which have been organized by, and received their charter, directly from the Canadian Labour Congress.

Discipline: a system of punishment (including verbal and written warnings, suspension, and discharge) for breaches of company rules and regulations by employees.

Dues shop: also called "agency shop", this type of union security clause gives an employee the option of being a union member or not but requires all eligible employees to pay union dues.

Employee association: association of workers in a particular plant or industry that has not been certified under the Labour Relations Act as the official bargaining agent for these employees. The association may nevertheless be recognized by the employer as the spokesperson for its employees.

Employers' association: an organization representing employers in a particular industry that engages in one or more activities: bargaining with labour unions, co-ordinating the collective bargaining activities of its members, education, and lobbying.

Fair representation: duty of a union or an employers' association to represent fairly the interests of each member of its organization in its dealings with the other party.

Featherbedding: employee practice of restricting output to create the need for more workers than are really required.

Fair employment practice: practice of employers (and unions) of offering workers equal employment (and membership) opportunities regardless of their sex, nationality, race, colour, etc.

Federal jurisdiction: authority of federal government over employers and employees in any enterprise of a national, interprovincial, or international nature such as banking, broadcasting, and air transportation.

Federation of Labour: group of labour unions in one or more industries, within a district, province, or country, allied together. The CLC is an example of a national federation.

Final offer selection: form of arbitration whereby, after a period of unsuccessful union-company negotiations, each side puts forward its final offer and the arbitrator or arbitration board chooses one or other of them, without modification.

Foreperson: supervisory employee, usually considered to be part of management. Also called "supervisor".

Fringe benefits: items such as paid vacations, pensions, health care, and bonuses that are paid to an employee above and beyond the regular rate of pay.

General strike: cessation of work by all workers in a particular geographical area, perhaps as a form of political, as well as economic protest.

General union: a labour organization whose membership is not confined to workers in one type of skilled occupation or to one type of industry.

Grievance: an alleged violation of a collective agreement, or, of traditional work practices, filed usually by an employee, but sometimes by the union or by the company.

Grievance procedure: the steps by which a dispute between an employer and an employee or between an employer and the union during the life of a collective agreement may be amicably settled.

Grievance rate: number of grievances filed in relation to the number of union members in a company.

Grievor: the person (employee, company, or union) filing a grievance.

Hiring hall: hall or office, run by a union or jointly by union and employer, used to direct workers to jobs or to hire them on the spot, subject to prior union membership.

Illegal strike: a strike by the employees in a bargaining unit that contravenes the terms of the Labour Relations Act — for example, a strike called by the union before fulfilment of the conciliation procedure or when certification proceedings are still under way, or even during the life of a collective agreement, because of a dispute over interpretation of the collective agreement in force.

Independent local organization: local labour unions not formally connected or affiliated with any other labour organization.

Industrial democracy: term that refers to the degree in which the rank and file employees, or their elected representatives, are allowed to participate in management decision-making.

Industrial union: a labour organization whose members usually, but not always, include most of the workers eligible for union membership in a particular company or industry, irrespective of the type of work performed.

Industrial relations: a broad term that refers usually to relations between the employer and the union representing its employees.

Injunction: court order forbidding the named persons from carrying on a particular activity.

Interests dispute: a dispute that may arise between a company and a union as to the terms of a new collective agreement that is being negotiated or with regard to the revision of an agreement that has just expired.

International Confederation of Free Trade Unions (ICFTU): an international trade union body, established in 1949, consisting of many national labour organizations such as the Canadian Labour Congress, together representing most union members in the non-communist countries.

International Labour Office: the secretariat of the *International Labour Organization*, responsible for administering and co-ordinating ILO activities.

International Labour Organization (ILO): an international body representing labour, management, and government which, since 1946, has been a specialized agency of the United Nations. It sets minimum international labour standards called "conventions" and invites member countries to ratify them. It also disseminates labour information to workers of all countries.

International union: a labour union with branches and members, in both the United States and Canada, but which has its head office in the U.S.

Job description: a written description of a particular job, including the tasks involved, responsibility, its relation to other jobs, qualifications required, etc.

Job enrichment: attempt to make jobs more interesting and less monotonous for the individual worker by means of job enlargement, etc.

Job security: extent to which a worker has steady employment because of the nature of the good or service produced, special skills, knowledge, employer's attitude, etc.

Jurisdictional dispute: conflict between two or more labour unions as to whose members have the right to perform certain types of work.

Jurisdictional strike: strike by members of a union to protest the performance of work in the same plant by members of another union.

Labour Canada: federal government department with responsibility for administering the Canada Labour Code and providing information on labour-related issues. The goals of the department are (a) to promote stable industrial relations in Canada, (b) to establish appropriate labour standards, and (c) to ensure occupational health and safety in industries within the federal jurisdiction. Also the department tries to promote labour-management co-operation throughout Canada, and to co-ordinate Canada's efforts to help improve labour conditions throughout the world.

Labour College of Canada: bilingual institution of higher education for trade union members, operated jointly by the Canadian Labour Congress,

McGill University, and the Université de Montreal. Its purpose is to provide a training ground for Canada's future trade union leaders.

Labour Council: organization established by a labour federation in a particular town or city, by charter of the CLC, to which the locals of many labour unions in that area are affiliated. It is financed by a per capita tax on affiliated unions.

Labour Federation: organization established in each province, by charter of the CLC, to represent organized labour at the provincial level. Each member union retains its own autonomy yet co-operates to achieve common goals.

Labour force: all persons 15 years of age and over who are either employed, temporarily idle, or unemployed but seeking employment.

Labour law: that area of the law that deals with all matters involving employer-employee relationships and company-union relationships, including collective agreements, employment practices, wrongful dismissal, etc.

Labour organization: a broad term that includes not only various types of labour unions and other employee associations, but also various regional and central labour bodies such as the CLC.

Labour Relations Board: group of persons, provided for under the Labour Relations Act, with responsibility for determining bargaining units, certifying trade unions, ensuring that dispute-settling provisions are included in collective agreements, and investigating allegations of bad faith in collective bargaining.

Labour turnover: rate at which workers change employment — usually calculated by taking the number of employees leaving a plant or industry during a given period of time and dividing this figure by the average number of employees in the plant or industry during the same period, and expressing it as a percentage.

Labour union: an association of workers, practising a similar trade or employed in the same company or industry. Also called a *trade union*.

Lay-off: temporary, prolonged, or final withdrawal by employer of employee's job because of lack of work.

Local: basic unit of a labour union, formed in a particular plant or locality.

Lockout: temporary refusal of a company to continue providing work for its employees which may also involve the temporary closing of the employer's establishment. Its purpose is to put pressure on union members to agree to the employer's offer with regard to wages, working conditions, etc.

Maintenance of membership: union security clause that requires existing union members to maintain their union membership but gives new employees the option of joining the union or not.

Management rights: these are rights traditionally reserved to management that are not subject to collective bargaining — for example, production planning.

Mediation: use of an outside third party to assist a company and the union to reach an agreement by peaceful persuasion. Unlike conciliation (a similar process but one that is required by law before a strike or lockout may be declared), mediation is a voluntary process. Unlike arbitration, no settlement can be imposed.

National union: labour union whose head office, locals, and membership are all within Canada.

Off-shift premium: extra pay for working at unusual times during the day and on weekends.

Organized labour: all labour unions and other employee organizations whose purpose is the protection of worker interests.

Organizer: person employed on a full-time, permanent basis by many large labour unions to plan, organize, and carry out membership recruitment campaigns at plants that are not yet unionized.

Organizing: term used to describe the process of recruiting new union members.

Organizing committee: group of persons consisting of union representatives, including the organizer, if any, and volunteers willing to devote the time and effort necessary to contact employees, present the union's case for unionization, and sign up new union members.

Pattern bargaining: collective bargaining tactic whereby a union first obtains a generous settlement from one employer and then uses it as a bargaining chip to secure a similar settlement from other employers in the industry.

Picket line: groups of striking workers, usually carrying signs, stationed at the entrance and exits of a struck plant.

Picketing: stationing of union members at entrances and exits of a struck plant to publicize union demands, discourage replacement workers from moving in and out, and to hamper the delivery of materials and parts into the plant and the shipment of finished goods from it.

Profit-sharing: arrangement whereby employees receive a set percentage of the employer's net profit, in addition to their regular wages. This may be in cash, in company shares, or as a deferred payment.

Quality circle: a group of production workers who volunteer to meet on a regular basis, usually with management encouragement and assistance, to discuss and suggest improvements in production methods, quality control, job enrichment, etc.

Raiding: a union's attempt to increase its membership by persuading members of another union to leave that union and join it.

Rand Formula: compromise arrangement, suggested by Ivan C. Rand former Chief Justice of the Supreme Court of Canada, that employees be given the choice of joining a union or not but be required, whatever the choice, to pay the normal union dues.

Rank and file: name given to union members with no special status (i.e. not union officers or shop stewards).

Ratification: process of having a proposed new collective agreement approved by the union members, as well as by the employer or employers' association.

Recognition: employer's acceptance of a labour union as the exclusive bargaining agent for its employees.

Representation vote: a vote conducted by the Labour Relations Board in which the employees in a bargaining unit indicate, by secret ballot, whether or not they wish to be represented, or continue to be represented, by a labour union.

Residual rights: all rights belonging to management not specifically mentioned in a collective agreement.

Retroactive payment: in the case of a grievance, payment to an employee who has won a claim about rates of pay for time worked in the past, to compensate for past underpayment.

Rights dispute: a labour disagreement between a union and a company with regard to the interpretation or application of one or more clauses of the collective agreement currently in force.

Right-to-work: right of an employee to work in a company without being forced to join a union.

Scab: derogatory term used by union members to refer to workers currently employed who disregard a strike call and to persons hired as replacements for striking workers.

Scanlon Plan: a plan developed by Joseph Scanlon, one-time research director of the United Steelworkers, to encourage greater worker productivity by sharing the savings achieved, between the company and the employees involved.

Secondary boycott: refusal to buy or handle goods of employers not directly involved in a labour dispute, but who are supplying parts, materials, etc. to the firm subject to a *primary boycott*.

Seniority: an employee's standing in a company, based on length of service. Usually employees with the least seniority are the first to be laid off or dismissed because of lack of work. Those with the greatest amount of seniority usually have greater job security, vacation entitlement, promotion opportunities, etc. Sometimes, depending on the employer, merit may be given equal or greater emphasis.

Severance pay: lump-sum payment made to an employee for whom the company no longer has a job.

Shift: scheduled daily work period for a group of employees (e.g. 9 a.m. to 4 p.m., 4 p.m. to midnight, and midnight to 8 a.m.).

Shift differential: extra pay for working on late shifts (i.e. other than the day shift).

Shop committee: group of workers elected by fellow-employees to act as their representative in grievance and other labour matters.

Shop steward: union member elected by workers in a particular shop or department of a firm to act as their union representative in that area. The shop steward's functions may include receiving, investigating, and attempting to resolve complaints and grievances, disseminating union information, announcing meetings, recruiting new members, and collecting union dues (if not deducted at source by the employer and remitted to the union).

Sit-down strike: a form of industrial action whereby employees stop work and sit down in the plant, thereby bringing production to a halt.

Slowdown: a form of industrial action whereby employees exert pressure on an employer by slowing down the rate of work and therefore productivity.

Speed-up: union term that refers to the employer practice of speeding up production without an offsetting increase in worker pay.

Split-shift: requiring an employee to spread his or her working hours over two different shifts in order to meet peak production needs.

Stretch-out: union term that refers to the employer practice of requiring a worker to assume extra duties, without extra pay.

Strike: temporary refusal of the employees to continue working for the employer, so as to exert pressure in contract negotiations or as a protest against unreasonable working conditions, etc.

Strikebreakers: term variously used to refer to: (a) persons who continue to work during a strike even though their fellow union members are refusing to work, (b) persons hired as replacement workers, and (c) persons hired by an employer to assist in breaking a strike.

Strike benefits: a small regular payment made by the union from its strike fund to striking workers, perhaps conditional on picket duty performance. In some cases, food rather than money is distributed.

Strike fund: funds held by the union to help cover such expenditures during a strike as strike pay, publicity, legal fees, etc. The money for such a fund may be collected from union members while still employed, as a regular monthly assessment, additional to the union dues. The fund may also be augmented during a strike, by donations from other unions.

Strike notice: formal written notice by a group of workers, or their union, to the employer that the employees will cease work on a certain date.

Strike vote: a vote conducted among the workers in a bargaining unit to determine whether the union should call a strike.

Sweat-shop: plant in which the conditions of employment, including pay, health, and safety, are sub-standard.

Sweetheart contract: derogatory term used to describe a contract made between an employer and a union, that grants generous terms and conditions of employment, designed to keep out another labour union.

Sympathy strike: a strike by employees in one plant to express sympathy or "solidarity" with striking workers in another plant.

Technological unemployment: unemployment resulting from the introduction in a plant of more labour-saving equipment.

Trade union: an association of workers, practising a similar trade or employed in the same company or industry. Also called a *labour union*.

Unemployed: persons without work, but who are available and seeking work.

Unemployment insurance: federal program that provides cash benefits for a given period of time to unemployed persons. To be eligible, a person must have contributed to the fund for a specified number of weeks. Also, there is a waiting period before the cash benefits are available immediately.

Unfair labour practice: action by employer or union that contravenes the principle of "bargaining in good faith" — for example, dismissing an employee, perhaps on some false pretext, for attempting to form or join a union.

Union dues: regular monthly payments by union members to help finance the activities of their union.

Union organizer: person hired by the union on a full-time basis to plan and execute a union membership recruitment campaign. Term sometimes also used to refer to volunteer recruiters.

Union security: clause inserted in a collective agreement to protect the interest of the labour union, covering the collection of union dues and requirement of union membership for continued employment. There are several different types of union security clause: union shop, closed shop, dues (or agency) shop, maintenance of membership, and voluntary checkoff.

Union shop: union security clause, used in many collective agreements, that makes union membership and the compulsory collection of union dues a condition of employment.

Union trusteeship: situation in which a union head office suspends the operations of a union local and takes over its administration and assets. Such an action is provided for in the constitution of many national and international unions to counter mismanagement, corruption, etc. at the local level.

Unjust dismissal: dismissal of an employee in a manner that is arbitrary and unfair, and that contravenes the Labour Relations Act or the collective agreement.

Unlawful lockout: lockout of its employees by an employer that contravenes the Labour Relations Act and lays the employer open to charges and possible fines and/or periods of imprisonment.

Unlawful strike: strike by union members that contravenes the Labour Relations Act and lays the union and its members open to charges and possible fines and/or periods of imprisonment.

Voluntary checkoff: a union security clause whereby an employee is not required to join the union but can request that the employer collect union dues from his or her pay and remit them to the union.

Voluntary recognition: an employer agrees in writing to recognize a labour union as the exclusive bargaining agent for a group of its employees, without resorting to the formal certification procedure.

Wage and price controls: controls imposed by the government, through a specially-established review or control body, on increases in wages and prices, as part of an anti-inflation program.

Wage differentials: difference in wage rates between one job and another because of the nature of these jobs, location, skills involved, educational requirements, stress, responsibilities, etc.

Wage parity: the principle of equality of wages for workers in the same occupation but in different geographical areas. Also, for workers in the same sector, but in different occupations.

Walkout: situation when employees spontaneously, but in a co-ordinated fashion, put down their tools, usually at the beginning of a strike, and walk out of the plant.

Wildcat strike: a spontaneous, usually short-lived work stoppage by union members that is not authorized by the union concerned.

Work sharing: plan that involves the sharing of available work among all the employees on a reduced hourly basis, when planned output declines, rather than laying off some employees. Since 1982, under the federal government's Work Sharing Program, employees on reduced time have their pay supplemented by unemployment insurance benefits. Under the same program (which is administered by the Canada Employment and Immigration Commission), appropriate vocational training is provided to workers affected by the work sharing program, to improve their chances of alternative employment.

Work to rule: a form of industrial action whereby the employees slow down production by observing all the rules and regulations relating to the job that are normally ignored.

Work stoppage: general term used, particularly in statistical documents, to refer to strikes and lockouts, without assigning responsibility for the breakdown in labour-management relations.

Worker participation: involvement of employees, either directly or indirectly (through elected representatives), in management decision-making. This can vary, in effect, from mere *communication* of information from management to the workers, to *consultation* before making decisions, or even to *co-determination* where workers share jointly in management decision-making.

Workers' Compensation: provincial system of compensation, funded by employers but administered by a provincially-appointed Board, for injuries sustained by workers during the course of their employment.

Working conditions: factors involved in an employee's job environment, including hours of work, rate of pay, safety, health, paid holidays and vacation, rest periods, shift work and promotion possibilities.

Works Council: a plant level committee of workers, or workers and management, that reviews and makes recommendations to management on employee rights and employee welfare in the organization. A form of industrial democracy found in Britain and other West European countries.

INDEX